Emerald Emperors of the Ring

Emerald Emperors of the Ring

*Irish and Irish American Boxers
in the United States*

Kevin Martin

McFarland & Company, Inc., Publishers
Jefferson, North Carolina

To my brothers Damien and Raymond,
their respective partners Helena and Anna,
my nephew James, my niece Róisín,
and my father Jim for their support
during a time of personal challenges

Library of Congress Cataloging-in-Publication Data

Names: Martin, Kevin, 1969– author
Title: Emerald emperors of the ring : Irish and Irish American boxers in the United States / Kevin Martin.
Other titles: Irish and Irish American boxers in the United States
Description: Jefferson, North Carolina : McFarland & Company, Inc., Publishers, 2025 | Includes bibliographical references and index.
Identifiers: LCCN 2025037124 | ISBN 9781476697048 print ∞ ISBN 9781476655581 ebook
Subjects: LCSH: Irish American boxers—Biography | Boxers (Sports)—Ireland—Biography | Boxing—United States—History | BISAC: SPORTS & RECREATION / Boxing | HISTORY / Europe / Ireland | LCGFT: Biographies
Classification: LCC GV1131 .M27 2025
LC record available at https://lccn.loc.gov/2025037124

ISBN (print) 978-1-4766-9704-8
ISBN (ebook) 978-1-4766-5558-1

© 2025 Kevin Martin. All rights reserved

No part of this book may be reproduced or transmitted in any form or by any means, electronic or mechanical, including photocopying or recording, or by any information storage and retrieval system, without permission in writing from the publisher.

Front cover image: 1883 chromolithograph of John L. Sullivan (Library of Congress)

Printed in the United States of America

McFarland & Company, Inc., Publishers
Box 611, Jefferson, North Carolina 28640
www.mcfarlandpub.com

Table of Contents

Preface	1
Introduction: The Fighting Irish	5

PART 1—The Heavyweights

One. When Two Worlds Go to War: James "Yankee" Sullivan and Tom "The Bowery King" Hyer	12
Two. No Smoke Without Fire: John "Old Smoke" Morrissey	24
Three. "The Benicia Boy": John C. Heenan	35
Four. "The Adopted Son of America": Joe Coburn	43
Five. Jimmy Elliot	50
Six. "The Terror of Mississippi": Mike McCoole	55
Seven. "The Trojan Giant": Paddy Ryan	58
Eight. "The Boston Strong Boy": John L. Sullivan	70
Nine. A Changing of the Guard: James "Gentleman Jim" Corbett	88
Ten. Only Non-Irish Need Apply	106
Eleven. "The Fighting Marine": Gene Tunney	112
Twelve. "The Cinderella Man": James J. Braddock	125
Thirteen. Great White Irish Hopes	133
Fourteen. "The Pittsburgh Kid": Billy Conn	150
Fifteen. "There's no quit in a Quarry": The Tragedy of Jerry Quarry	156
Sixteen. Gerry Cooney: The Last Great Irish White Hope	160

PART 2—Non-Heavyweight Boxers

Seventeen. He Ain't Heavy, He's My Irish Brother	166
Eighteen. "Bold" Mike McTigue	170

NINETEEN.	"The Phantom of Philly": Tommy Loughran	176
TWENTY.	The Other Dempsey: Jack "Nonpareil" Dempsey	179
TWENTY-ONE.	"The Toy Bulldog": Mickey Walker	183
TWENTY-TWO.	"The Baby-Faced Assassin": Jimmy McLarnin	190
TWENTY-THREE.	The Pride of Achill Island: Johnny Kilbane	194

Epilogue	199
Appendix: The Rules of Boxing	203
Chapter Notes	207
Bibliography	221
Index	229

Preface

In 1903, the *National Police Gazette*, the foremost chronicler and booster of boxing in the United States at that time, wrote of the reception received by fighters of different ethnic backgrounds when they entered the ring, "There is always a hearty cheer and earnest backing for the Irishman; grins and good-humored tolerance for the German, and virulent hostility to the Italian and the negro."[1] It was little wonder, then, that many fighters during the first three decades of the twentieth century opted to compete under Irish aliases or that Italians were at the forefront in this regard: Andrew Chiariglione assumed the moniker "Fireman" Jim Flynn, Peter Robert Gagliardi changed his name to Bobby Gleason, Vincent Esposito to Jimmy Dugan, Stefano Tricamo to Steve "Kid" Sullivan, and Ugo Micheli to Hugo Kelly, while Tony Caponi changed his poetic birth name to the rather more prosaic T.C. O'Brien. Jewish boxers also saw the advantages of posing as Irish men; Alexander Rudolph fought under the name Al McCoy, Vincent Morris Scheer appeared in the ring as "Mushy" Callaghan, Seymour Rosenbaum as "Irish" Eddie Kelly, and, most famously of all, Lithuanian-born Joseph Paul Zukauskas became better known to the wider world as Jack Sharkey.[2] The Irishman had become the idealized boxer in the United States: the apotheosis of masculinity. The "Emperors of Masculinity," as author Randy Roberts described the leading heavyweight boxers of the era, had become Emerald Emperors. The Great White Hope was, for a significant period, the Great Irish Hope.

How had this glorification of the Irishman come to pass? Remarkably, boxing was not a sport with deep roots in Ireland; it had long been popular in England before eventually gaining traction in America. However, for the majority of the nineteenth century, boxing, or bare-knuckle fighting as it was then, was virtually universally publicly deplored, morally condemned, and legally outlawed in the United States. It was viewed as a barbaric pursuit, confined to the marginalized of society, identified with criminal elements, low culture, and, in particular, impoverished Irish emigrants. It did not chime with a shining new Republic built on Enlightenment principles and Puritan stoicism.

Things had long been different in England. There, bare-knuckle fighting had enjoyed the patronage of the aristocratic classes, although the popularity of the sport had waxed and waned over time; its most admired periods were during the mid-eighteenth century, the early decades of the nineteenth century, and again in the mid-nineteenth century. During these eras bare-knuckle boxing embodied the fighting spirit of the nation, the "John Bull" doggedness which had built an empire. "Toe the line," "up to scratch," and "throwing one's hat into the ring" all came to the English language from the prize-fighting ring. On the other hand, the mere fact that boxing was championed by English nobility reinforced the sport's decadent and effete nature in the eyes of the Founding Fathers of the United States.

For the two decades prior to the American Civil War, bare-knuckle fighting boxing did become popular in certain quarters, largely as a result of the so-called penny press. The likes of Benjamin Day's *New York Sun* and James Gordon Bennett's *New York Herald* discovered an inexhaustible thirst for murder, mayhem, and bloodshed among certain demographics. Prize-fighting fitted squarely within the rubric of what they considered marketable news, and it was they who defined what was newsworthy. Bare-knuckle fighters, including James "Yankee" Sullivan, Tom "The Bowery King" Hyer, John "Old Smoke" Morrissey, Mike "The Terror of Mississippi" McCoole, Joe "The Adopted Son of America" Coburn, and John C. "The Benicia Boy" Heenan, were breathlessly followed by avid readerships. All except Hyer were Irish born or of Irish parentage. During this period of America's history, bare-knuckle fights became war by proxy between nativist and emigrant alike and the reading public was entranced. This phase of the sport reached its zenith when American champion John C. "The Benicia Boy" Heenan traveled to England to take on Tom "The Brighton Titch" Sayers, a fight which garnered international attention in the press.

With the doings of Billy the Kid, Jesse James, and their ilk, the press found more exciting things to write about and boxing fell into something of a despond in the United States. Then John L. Sullivan, "The Boston Strong Boy," stepped forward. It was as if a comet had landed on American soil. Sullivan, the son of Irish emigrants, became the country's first true sports celebrity, an American icon. Novelist Theodore Dreiser called him "a sort of prize fighting J.P. Morgan," while Ernest Thompson Seton, founder of the Boy Scouts of America, noted approvingly that he "never met a lad who would not rather be Sullivan than Leo Tolstoy."[3] John L. Sullivan came to represent the apotheosis of manhood at a time when a "cult of masculinity" was redefining the role of men in American culture and the Gilded Age created the perfect nexus of factors to spread his fame. He was the first true "Emerald Emperor." In addition to a newfound interest in physical culture and sports, the ever-expanding press, and the huge development in the rail network and telegraph technology, there was a burning desire to have heroes and celebrities in a country with vast ambitions. Sullivan was an example of a man from a humble background and a member of a frequently marginalized and discriminated ethnic group using sport as a means of climbing the social ladder. After Sullivan, successful heavyweight fighters were to achieve god-like status in American popular culture. To be the heavyweight champion was to be the supreme embodiment of male virility, the "Emperor of Masculinity." There, at the center of this new dispensation, as they always had been, were the Irish. After Sullivan, the roster of heavyweight fighters was replete with Irish boxers and those of Irish descent: James "Gentleman Jim" Corbett, Eugene "Gene the Fighting Machine" Tunney, James J. "Cinderella Man" Braddock, Billy "The Pittsburgh Kid" Conn, and Gerry "The Easton Express" Cooney were among the best known and most celebrated. All were different in their own ways; each of them told a part of the Irish experience in the United States. While the heavyweight title has always been viewed as the apotheosis of fighting manhood, American boxing history has been studded with stars of Irish and Irish American descent in all weight divisions at some point in time, and their story is told here as part of the warp and weft of the fabric of American society.

Introduction

The Fighting Irish

June 29, 1919, Fenway Park, Boston

THE TALL AND ANGULAR MAN ON the podium adjusted his distinctive pince-nez and began to address the estimated crowd of 50,000 people in his high-pitched nasal tone. He seemed a little nervous and looked like he had not expected so many people. The vast crowd, shoehorned into a stadium designed for 33,000, was more than three times the number that had witnessed Babe Ruth's Red Sox in the 1918 World Series nine months previously. Later there were reports that a number of women had fainted when the man first entered the stadium. The gates had been closed an hour before he took to the podium because the authorities were worried about overcrowding. Despite the several megaphones attached to the makeshift stage, the man's reedy voice did not carry well, and the crowd strained to hear what he was saying. He began by apologizing for reading from a prepared script. This was necessary because he did not want the British press twisting his words and making out he had said things which he had not. The man, whom American papers had been calling the "Irish Lincoln," said something about the failure of the nascent League of Nations to act and how Ireland needed America's help now. The Versailles Treaty, signed the previous day, was worth nothing while twenty-three wars still raged across the world. The recent uprising in Ireland might not have brought the freedom he so desired for the country but it would come someday, he told them. He reminded the crowd that they should never turn their hearts and minds from Ireland or allow themselves or the country to sink back into what he termed "sullen despair." He wanted to make something clear about what he had heard people saying in America. He had heard the phrase many times since he had come to the country. "The language you use here," he said, "the Fighting Irish … what we actually mean mostly when we talk about it is an indomitable spirit, a commitment, never tentative, always fully committed, to life itself … that's really the spirit of the Fighting Irish."[1] There was a deafening roar from the crowd and a brief smile crossed the man's thin ascetic face.

Éamon de Valera, freedom fighter and future president of the Republic of Ireland, was in the United States to raise money for the cause of Irish freedom from British rule and reach out to the American authorities to help plead its case. He had come to Fenway Park at the invitation of Mayor Andrew J. Peters, and the legions of Irish who had made the city their home had made "Dev" proud. The dozens of marching bands, the multiplicity of stars and stripes flags, and the abundance of orange, white, and green banners, proclaiming a nascent Irish Republic, reassured him that he had been correct in accepting the mayor's invitation. He had seen one banner with the words "We demand England withdraw from Ireland" and another with "England is disqualified and unfit to rule Ireland."[2] He had seen men in uniform beneath banners advertising themselves as stalwarts of outfits like Charlestown's John Boyle O'Reilly Guards, Lowell's Wolfe Tones, and the Sheridan and Meagher Guards. As he stepped away from the podium the American-born de Valera gave a slight wave to his people.

By the time Éamon de Valera got to Fenway Park, the term "Fighting Irish" had gained common currency in the United States. Although the phrase is now primarily associated with the University of Notre Dame and its sports teams, the term was first coined to describe Irish immigrant soldiers who fought for the Union side during the American Civil War. The 69th New York Infantry Regiment was reputedly given the designation by General Robert E. Lee for its bravery and valor. George Pickett famously wrote to his fiancée describing the steady advance of the Irish soldiers against murderous fire at Marye's Heights on December 11, 1862. "Your soldier's heart almost stood still as he watched those sons of Erin fearlessly rush to their deaths. The brilliant assault on Marye's Heights of their Irish Brigade was beyond description. We forgot they were fighting us and cheer after cheer at their fearlessness went up all along our lines."[3] Even then, there was a link to the venerable educational establishment, as the brigade's chaplain, Father William Corby, CSC, subsequently became the third president of Notre Dame and famously granted general absolution to the troops in the midst of battle, an event commemorated in the painting *Absolution Under Fire*, now part of Notre Dame's permanent art collection.

Sporting logos have frequently caused contention in America. In 2018, after interminable soul-searching, the Cleveland Indians finally removed their Chief Wahoo logo, a feature of all club uniforms since 1947. Calls had been made for the image's removal as far back as the 1970s. The demise of the red-faced, buck-toothed caricature of Chief Wahoo was not without precedent. St. John's University Redmen became the Red Storm in 1994, while the University of North Dakota Fighting Sioux were rebranded as the Fighting Hawks in 2015. With the retirement of Chief Wahoo and the increasing grip of "cancel culture" it was inevitable that Notre Dame's famous Irish fighting leprechaun would come under the public spotlight. Max Kellerman of ESPN got the ball rolling when he stated that the image perpetuated "pernicious and negative stereotypes of marginalized people that offend."[4] Brian Kenny, of MLB Network, added his weight to the argument when he tweeted that the mascot was an embarrassment and painted Irish people as "a bunch of foolish, drinking, fighting, singing, dancing, & lying gnomes."[5] When the Washington National Football League franchise announced it was getting rid of its long-time nickname "The Redskins," the debate escalated further. Washington's logo was no longer acceptable because of the negative connotations implied against Native Americans. What, then, for a university which used the image of a fighting leprechaun as its mascot? What was Notre Dame to do?

Dave Hannigan, an American-based sports journalist with *The Irish Times*, Ireland's self-proclaimed paper of record, was in no doubt. The image of a small man with "fists raised, hat askew and chin curtain beard" was, he wrote, "a replica of the simian-featured caricatures deployed by *Punch* magazine when mocking the Irish throughout the 19th century."[6] Hannigan described some Irish Americans as "a constituency famous for clinging to an archaic version of the land of their ancestors" and who took perverse pride in Notre Dame's mascot. In his opinion, every time there was a controversy about pejorative team names, Notre Dame's leprechaun too often seemed to skulk beneath the radar.

The University of Notre Dame was not best pleased with the criticism and explained its position at some length in the media. It outlined how the term "fighting Irish" had once been a cry of derision directed at the institution's sports teams and described an occasion in 1899 when Northwestern University students were heard chanting "Kill the fighting Irish" at a football game against Notre Dame.[7] At the time the student body of Notre Dame was largely Catholic and, while many were Irish, there were also Germans, Italians, and Poles in attendance. There are, however, competing stories of origin for the famed catch cry. One narrative suggests that a player's speech during the halftime period of a football game against Michigan in 1909 inspired a furious comeback in the second half by Notre Dame. The inflamed player allegedly yelled at his teammates, whose names included Dolan, Kelly, Glynn, and Ryan, "What's the matter with you guys? You're all Irish and not fighting worth a lick."[8] Subsequent reports in the press repeated the story and attributed the victory to the "Fighting Irishmen." Murray Sperber noted in *Shake Down the Thunder: The Creation of Notre Dame Football* that, after a 1919 game against Army, a student journalist wrote in the university magazine, *Scholastica*, that the encounter unmistakably rebranded the Notre Dame warriors as "the Fighting Irish," with Sperber contending that this might have been the first time the words were committed to print.[9] However, not all of the alumni were happy with the designation. Another issue of the university magazine from the same year carried a letter from a graduate criticizing the term because not all of the players were of Irish descent. He received a pithy reply from a "disgruntled" alumnus in a subsequent edition of *Scholastica*, who claimed, "You don't have to be from Ireland to be Irish!"[10]

Whatever the exact origin of the name, Notre Dame came to national prominence as a footballing power during the first three decades of the twentieth century and it was journalists, particularly ex–Notre Dame student Francis Wallace of the *New York Daily News*, who began to popularize the tag "Fighting Irish" in the press. (The nascent sporting dynasty was also known as the "Rovers" and the "Ramblers" due to their frequent traveling. For some, this was an insult with the implication being that the university was more interested in sport than in the academic program.) In 1927 Father Matthew Walsh, then the president of the university, thought it a suitable tribute to the qualities of his charges and officially adopted the term. Given that other names used for the university's teams at the time included "the Papists," "the Vagabonds," "the Horrible Hibernian Warriors," and, almost inevitably, "the

Dirty Irish," it was, on balance, a relatively benign choice. Father Walsh told a *New York World* reporter that the university authorities were in no way averse to the name "Fighting Irish" being associated with the university's athletic teams and that it seemed to embody the kind of spirit carried into the field of action by various teams representing the university. Furthermore, he hoped that the institution would always be worthy of the ideal embodied in the term.[11] The more recent statement issued by Notre Dame was much longer and more detailed than that of Father Walsh. It first addressed the use of a leprechaun, explaining that it was an intentional caricature and originated in England as "a derisive symbol of Irish people, which Irish-Americans—including those at Notre Dame—again have turned back on former oppressors as a sign of celebration and triumph." In both the upraised fists of the leprechaun mascot and the use of the word "fighting," the intent, it contended, is to recognize the determination of the Irish people and, symbolically, the university's athletes.[12] It used the case of the Washington Redskins, which was not in any way analogous, it believed. There was no comparison between Notre Dame's nickname and the "stereotypical images of Black people" used by several corporations, and the Indian and warrior names bore no resemblance to the case. "None of these companies or institutions were founded or named by Black people or Native Americans who sought to highlight their heritage by using names and symbols associated with their culture or heritage."[13] The statement noted the integral role Irish people had played in the history of the university and pointed out that four of the original founders were born in Ireland while fifteen of the seventeen presidents of the institution had been of Irish descent. It also explained that there are more students studying the Irish language in the university than anywhere outside of Ireland itself, while the Irish Studies program at Notre Dame is widely regarded as the best in the United States. The statement concluded that, unlike companies or organizations which had expropriated others' cultures, its symbols "stand as celebratory representations of a *genuine* Irish heritage … a heritage that it regarded with respect, loyalty and affection." There were others who supported the position of Notre Dame. Neil Cosgrove, chairperson of the Ancient Order of Hibernians National Anti-Defamation Committee, questioned the accuracy, logic, and motivations behind the analogies made between the use of Notre Dame's mascot and other contentious images. The leprechaun, he argued, is a "mythical character, not a caricatured representation of a real person with a real history."[14] Cosgrove acknowledged that the exact origins of the term "Fighting Irish" were a matter of debate and pointed to a further possible answer. It might have originated, he said, in conflicts between students of the university and members of the Ku Klux Klan during resurgence in anti–Catholic nativism after World War I, which was coincident with the rise of the team to national prominence. In this regard the Ancient Order of Hibernians argued that there was no shame and much to be proud of in the appellation "fighting." Similarly, Lou Holtz, legendary coach of Notre Dame, believed they were named the Fighting Irish because of conflict with members of the Ku Klux Klan. Soon they would topple the statue erected in his honor at the university and that's when he would "get really mad."[15] Fighting talk, indeed.

There is no doubting the long association between Ireland and the university. Éamon de Valera, future Irish leader, made it to Notre Dame on October 15,

1919, when he planted a tree of liberty there, a sapling which was unceremoniously uprooted and thrown into a nearby lake the following week by a student of "Unionist persuasion," according to some sources.[16] The logistics of de Valera's visit to the university had been arranged by the local chapter of the Friends of Irish Freedom, while he had been invited to speak to the student body by the Reverend James Burns, then president of the college. Appropriately, Notre Dame's first mascot was an Irish terrier with the catchy moniker "Tipperary Terrence" and was followed in the role by other similar canines, including the famous "Clashmore Mike," a 1933 incumbent that performed tricks to entertain fans at breaks in the game.

The association between Notre Dame and Ireland is not without a hint of irony, however. Father Edward Sorin, CSC, the French founder of the university, was undoubtedly biased against those of Irish ethnicity, and he wrote in his *Chronicles of Notre Dame du Lac* that the Irish were by nature "full of faith, respect, religious inclinations" but had a great defect in their lack of stability and changed more readily than any other nation.[17] During his tenure Father Sorin banned the celebration of St. Patrick's Day on the campus, including the wearing of all green clothing, with those who defied his fiat expelled.

Whether the little green man stays or disappears, Notre Dame still stands as one of the most successful athletic programs in the world, with a 73.6 percent winning percentage, eight Heisman Trophies, and eleven NCAA football championships. While the Fighting Irish have had fantastic success through the decades in football, there is another sport where the words fighting and Irish were once virtually synonymous: boxing.

Part 1
The Heavyweights

One

When Two Worlds Go to War
James "Yankee" Sullivan and Tom "The Bowery King" Hyer

The man born James Ambrose on March 10, 1811, in Bandon, County Cork, the southernmost county of Ireland, was to assume numerous identities before his death on May 31, 1856, by the hand of San Francisco vigilantes at the age of forty-five, but of all the names Ambrose operated under throughout his tumultuous life, it was the moniker of James "Yankee" Sullivan which was to live longest in the public imagination.

While the reasons he was first given the sobriquet "Yankee" remain obscure, it may be that he acquired it in the age-old tradition of calling Irish people returned from the United States a "yank." As a young boy Ambrose emigrated with his family to the rough-and-tumble environs of London's East End, and it was in this seething cauldron of humanity and vice that the Irish youth learned how to defend himself with his fists. The finer details of his young life are lost in the mists of time,

Yankee Sullivan was born James Ambrose in Bandon, County Cork, around 1810 and was the first Irish boxer of note in the United States. Operating under various aliases, including Frank Murray and Frank Sullivan, he spent time in the East End of London and in a penal colony in Australia before crossing the Atlantic in 1841 (Prints and Photographs Division, Library of Congress).

but what is certain is that by the age of twenty-five, he found himself on a ship bound for Australia's Botany Bay as a convicted felon. Perhaps he had murdered his wife, as some have speculated, or, more likely, he may have been caught in the act of aggravated burglary. Whatever the exact nature of his crime, Sullivan was sentenced to twenty-five years of penal servitude at the other end of the world but ended up only serving four, as overcrowding in the colony resulted in his release under the proviso that he stay in Australia. Sullivan settled in the Rocks area of Sydney, then notorious for its rough-and-tumble ways, where he became head of a gang infamous for aggravated robbery and arranged fist fights which generally took place on Observatory Hill. After one too many close encounters with razor-blade-wielding adversaries, Sullivan decided discretion was the wiser part of valor and stowed away on a ship bound for the United States. The arrival of Yankee Sullivan in America was subsequently viewed by *Fistiana* as a seismic change in the boxing landscape in the country. While it could not be certain the Irish man's arrival was single-handedly the reason for the upswing in interest in the sport, *Fistiana* noted that Sullivan was looked up to on all sides, not only as a "personage to be revered, but as an oracle whose opinion was infallible ... on all aspects connected with the Prize Ring."[1] Once in the New World the Irishman did not waste any time in furthering his reputation as a pugilist under his newly acquired sobriquet. After just over a year in America, Sullivan decided to cross the Atlantic to the British Isles with the intention of making his fortune in the booming underground prize-fighting scene. His status in England must have been dubious, as he had broken the conditions of his release from Botany Bay and would have been considered an escaped convict under the laws pertaining at the time. Nonetheless, Sullivan placed a newspaper ad in *Bell's Life,* the premier chronicler of prize-fighting in England at that time, challenging Hammer Lane, the reigning middleweight champion.[2] The Englishman duly obliged and was beaten by Sullivan on February 2, 1841, at Crookham Common in a typically brutal nineteen-round bout fight over thirty-four minutes. According to some sources, Sullivan, with a large purse under his arm, once again stowed away on a ship bound for the United States after his true identity was uncovered. In New York, Yankee joined the fire department and, like other Irish strongmen before and after him, found additional gainful employment as an enforcer for Tammany Hall, the Democratic Party political machine in New York. Sullivan became one of the most feared members of the Spartans, a vicious gang who worked for Mike Walsh, a radical within the Democratic Party ranks who pushed for workingmen's rights. When he wasn't running with the Spartans, Sullivan used his fighting skills in support of Matthew T. Brennan, an influential saloonkeeper who also acted as the foreman of one of the neighborhood's several fire companies. Sullivan would often switch allegiances between the various political factions of the Five Points but would remain a feared New York gangster into the early 1850s, regardless of which side he was on.

On September 2 of the same year Sullivan fought Vincent Hammond at League Island near Philadelphia, where over eight short rounds in fewer than ten minutes the Irishman triumphed.[3] *Fistiana* observed an incident in the first round which perfectly demonstrated Sullivan's wily ability to manage fights and his penchant for playing fast and loose with the rules. Many of those in attendance had wagered that the Irishman would draw first blood. However, *Fistiana*'s Patrick Timony noted that Hammond caught Sullivan with a blow to the mouth, which caused his teeth to penetrate his lips and blood to appear. Timony, being close to the action, saw Sullivan cover his mouth with one fist and hit Hammond with a blow which also drew blood. He then threw some of the blood and gore around and the ring and claimed "first blood."[4]

Sullivan was soon to run afoul of the law, however. With money accumulated from his prize-fighting, Yankee purchased a saloon called The Sawdust Horse at 9 Chatham Street in the notorious Bowery area of Lower Manhattan.[5] From this fastness Sullivan organized and promoted prize fights, one of which almost led to his ruination. In September 1842 Sullivan promoted a fight between Christopher Lilly, a son of English immigrants, and Thomas McCoy, a son of Irish immigrants, in Hastings, New York. According to a report in the *New York Tribune*, McCoy arrived "sick, and was evidently in an inferior condition for such an affray" and was "too high on flesh, showing that he had not been carefully trained for such brutality."[6] The paper described the crowd as unrefined and sinful, including gamblers, brothel masters, and keepers of "flash groggeries" who cheered for blood and pain and encouraged the men to fight on despite obvious warnings of life-threatening danger. It claimed that the originators and fosterers of boxing were almost entirely foreigners and that boxing was not part of true American culture and not native to the country. After nearly three hours of combat the Lilly–McCoy fight turned deadly, and the paper described the tragic results in vivid detail:

> At the one hundred and twentieth round, McCoy stood up as erect as ever, but with his eyes closed in funeral black, his nose destroyed, his face gone, and clots of blood choking the throat which had no longer the power to eject them. He could barely walk, but still sparred with some spirit, though unable to get in a blow at his still vigorous antagonist ... McCoy had been thrown or knocked down eighty-one times, his opponent falling heavily as possible upon him. For the last time this was repeated; and, when Lily was lifted off, McCoy was found lifeless, and sank inanimate in his second's arms.

At the end an official told the seconds to carry out their man and produce the next suitable opponent. Thomas McCoy was twenty years of age. What happened subsequently is not completely clear, with some accounts suggesting Sullivan was arrested and sentenced to five years in Sing Sing Prison but was released after ten months when Governor William Bouck granted him a pardon, while others contend that he received a pardon after two years on the condition that he stay clear of fighting for two years.

Whatever the correct story, Sullivan quickly set about reestablishing his reputation as a pugilist on his release and was particularly anxious to fight Tom "The Bowery King" Hyer, then widely regarded as the first true heavyweight boxing champion of America. Hyer, born on January 1, 1819, and of Dutch descent, spent his early working years as a butcher in Washington Market under the stewardship of his father Jacob, also a boxer of some repute.[7] An alleged fight between Jacob Hyer and Tom Beasley in 1816, in which Hyer Senior broke his arm and never fought again, is sometimes considered the first official boxing match fought under the Broughton Rules held in the United States.[8]

Hyer subsequently found work as a minder for the nativist Bowery Boys and became known as a master enforcer. By all accounts he cut a fine figure. Illustrations of Hyer in his prime depict a man with exceptionally wide shoulders, a huge chest, and long muscular arms. According to contemporary sources, his long legs and agile hips, combined with his impressive torso, helped give speed, leverage, power, and excellent placement to his punches.[9] As was the case with many of his contemporaries, Hyer was a brawler, eschewing the finer scientific points of the discipline, and was particularly renowned for his ability to land a crushing left-handed shot in the collarbone area of his opponent, frequently leading with a left swing and following through with a vicious short right uppercut.

Hyer had become the American champion by defeating George McCheester, more commonly known as "Country McCloskey," in a brutal fight over 101 rounds and two hours and fifty minutes at Caldwell's Landing, New York, on September 9, 1841.[10] Like so many encounters of the era it was a political battle by proxy. While Hyer flew the banner for the nativists, McCheester was a lieutenant of Isaiah Rynders and the infamous Tweed Ring of Tammany Hall, so called in honor of its venally corrupt leader William Magear Tweed. At the end of the contest McCloskey was so badly beaten that it was hard to recognize him, while it would be a full eight and a half years before Hyer took to the ring again.[11]

Yankee Sullivan had been in Country's corner at the encounter and was desperate to fight for the title, but, as was the wont of many fighters of the nineteenth century, Hyer rested on his laurels and Sullivan was forced to bide his time. In the interim, the Irishman defeated English fighter Robert Caunt in eight rounds over twelve minutes at Harpers Ferry, West Virginia, in 1847. In April 1848 Sullivan and Hyer crossed paths in a Hell's Kitchen saloon. When a half-drunk Sullivan entered the bar he immediately spied Hyer and attacked him. After a couple of minutes the American had the Irishman in a head lock and proceeded to administer a thorough beating to him, and according to *Fistiana* Sullivan was beaten into insensibility and had to be carried out of the cellar, leaving Hyer cock of the walk.[12] Word soon spread that Hyer had gotten the better of the famed Sullivan, and the Irishman, who had previously decided he would never take to the ring again, knew he would have to restore his pride and his rightful place in the pecking order among pugilists of the day. *Fistiana* thought the general tenor of the people of the city was one of contentment now that the upstart Irishman had been put in his place. Police authorities became worried that the shemozzle would spark faction fighting between the opposing groups of supporters, but Sullivan was averse to bowie knives and shooting irons and advised his boosters to pursue a more measured approach. A month later, Sullivan saw fit to take out an advertisement in the *New York Herald* in response to stories circulating that Hyers had called him an "Irish braggart," which included the words "I am no Irish braggart or bully, although I am an Irishman and believe I can show myself worthy of my country whenever I am required."[13] If Hyer thought he could make Sullivan cry like "a whipped child," the Irishman was of a mind to "flax" him out. Hyer responded in kind the following day indicating that he was happy to fight Sullivan anywhere and at any time. The *Police Gazette* subsequently printed Sullivan's offer and Hyer's response, commenting that the style and brevity of both missives should "be studied with improvement by all windy and wordy politicians."[14] The willing combatants, it concluded, had each defined their position "with the same rapidity and ease with which a colonel of the light-horse would perform the six cuts." Sullivan was standing for the Irish vote and Hyer for the suffrage of the real American, and the magazine would recommend them to political conventions for office on account of their expressed fighting qualities and bravery, for it was a time when the country needed all sorts of heroes.

On August 7, 1848, after the inevitable protracted wrangling, a contract for a fight between Sullivan and Hyer was finally signed at Ford's Tavern in New York. The encounter would take place within six months for a combined stake of $10,000, while the Articles of Agreement stated that the combatants agreed to have a "fair stand up fight … in a twenty-four feet roped ring, according to the new rules as laid down in the *Fistiana* for 1848." The contest would take place within the state of Virginia or Maryland if the parties could mutually agree on a location. The articles also decreed that the "sacred inclosure … shall be made on turf, and shall be four and twenty feet square, formed of eight stakes and ropes, the latter extending in double lines … in the center of the ring a mark be formed, to be termed a scratch … at two opposite corners … spaces be enclosed by other marks sufficiently large for the reception of the seconds and bottle-holders," to be entitled "the corners." The combatants were asked to conduct themselves with order and decorum and to confine themselves to the diligent and careful discharge of their duties.[15]

As was tradition at the time, both fighters put on exhibitions for the fancy in advance of the fight. Mr. Patrick Timony, writing for the *Police Gazette*, was at the Shakespeare Hotel on September 30 to witness Sullivan go through his moves, where, at the start of the evening, Hyer came in to view proceedings. He was, Timony wrote, "a splendid looking fellow … with regular and handsome features and a form that is a happy combination of Hercules and the Apollo Belvidere." His countenance was strikingly American but "the Emerald Isle never had a more unmistakable specimen of her hardy race."[16] Timony proceeded to give a lengthy account of the main exhibition fight between O'Sullivan and Hyer's trainer George Thompson, a fractious affair which threatened to get totally out of hand before wiser heads prevailed.[17] Mr. Timony was not a man who hid his light under a bushel, and in concluding his account of proceedings he noted that he had been moved to write of one of the great social movements of the year because of the many philosophers of all classes who read his column to obtain knowledge of every important movement that took place in the "vast Babel" of New York on a daily basis. They needed this information, he wrote, for the generation of religious and metaphysical theories and as an aid to the improvement of the then society and future generations.

On November 23 Timony attended an exhibition by Tom Hyer at Mager's Ballroom on Elizabeth Street, where he, too, sparred against his trainer George Thompson. On this occasion Timony was not entirely convinced by Hyer, and, while he admired the American's ability to counterpunch, he wondered why the sweat ran from him like rain and whether it was a result of careless training. Whatever the cause of the excessive perspiration, it created evident uneasiness in the faces of his backers, he concluded.[18] Timony subsequently went to view both men in training.

Yankee had decamped to a house beside the Union Race Course on Long Island. After running laps of the course, estimated at seven or eight miles by Timony, Sullivan proceeded to work with dumbbells before having a breakfast of a large beefsteak of the finest cut covered with a sauce of old English ale. After his repast he went for a nap before repeating his exercise regime. Following dinner he rested again and performed his exercise regime for a third time. Timony was impressed with his virtuous and abstemious life and noted that Yankee did not drink, take a car, or see Mrs. Sullivan other than in a "Pickwickian sense."[19] He ventured the time-honored opinion that one incidence of the latter could set a boxer's training back weeks. Some things in boxing have never changed. Timony summed up his description of Sullivan thus: "He is as strong as a lion, as gay as a lark, with a free conscience and a cheerful spirit and in all respects in that high condition of animal perfection which enables a man to set at naught all manner of disease or ailment except, perhaps, such as proceed from a hostile collision with some other human machine in as splendid a condition as himself."[20]

Timony also visited Hyer and noted that he was in equally good condition. Both boxers were visited by legions of their supporters while in their respective training camps, and both sets of fans left with a conviction that their man would dispose of his opponent with as much ease as a "fourteen stone M.P. would of an apple woman." For Timony the fighters, with their single-minded focus on exercise abstemiousness and cleanliness, were the opposite of the shriveled and wilted debauchees found in towns and cities.[21] When the journalist visited Hyer at his training camp he found that the American's preparations were very similar to that of Sullivan, although the former liked to spend part of his day rowing on the Harlem River. After providing a detailed account of Hyer's daily routine, Timony noted that the American was a man of virtue and "a pattern to many who claim to lead up middle aisles and to sound the key note in sacred psalmistry."[22]

As was so often the case in nineteenth-century America, the staging of the encounter became a cat-and-mouse game between the law and the backers; multiple changes of location by the organizers were frequently necessary to keep one step ahead of authorities, and such were the obfuscations and evasions that it was reported that friends of the combatants turned themselves in to the hands of the law purporting to be the fighters, so that the encounter could go ahead unhindered.

On February 7, 1849, Hyer and Sullivan, accompanied by three hundred supporters, boarded a flotilla in Baltimore bound for Still Pond, Maryland, a location chosen for its relative inaccessibility. The party was chased by Maryland state militia under the instruction of Attorney General George Richardson but eventually got to their destination unhindered. Local law authorities raided the boardinghouse where Sullivan and his entourage were staying, but the wily Irishman managed to climb out a window and hide in a tree until the coast was clear. After further evasive actions the much-anticipated fight finally got under way on a snow-covered field on the Eastern Shore of Poole Island overlooking picturesque Chesapeake Bay. The arrangements were so hasty that the only ropes to hand were taken from the ship, while staves were fashioned from wood obtained from a nearby forest. The *New York Herald* reported breathlessly prior to the fight, claiming it had never seen so great an excitement among certain classes of society as has developed during the previous few days and comparing it to the agitation produced in the public mind by the first accounts of the Mexican War.[23] One account noted that the sons of Erin were in "extacies [sic] at the prospect of a fight between one of their own countrymen and an Englishman and were no way slow in backing their favorite to the last copper in their possession."[24] There was no love lost between the combatants. According to one source, Sullivan called his rival a big overgrown girl.[25] It was literally a tall order for Sullivan from the start, with Hyer having a four-inch height and a thirty-pound weight advantage, in addition to a significantly superior reach.[26] However, *Fistiana* was impressed by the physicality of both combatants when they entered the ring:

> They were as finely developed in every muscle as their physical capacity could reach, and the bounding confidence which sparkled fiercely in their eyes, showed that their spirits and courage were at their highest mark. Sullivan, with his round compact chest, formidable head, shelving flinty brows, fierce glaring eyes, and clean turned shoulders, looked the very incarnation of the spirit of mischievous genius; while Hyer, with his broad, formidable chest, and long muscular limbs, seemed as if he could almost trample him out of life, at will.[27]

The *Wilkes' Spirit of the Times* noted that Sullivan was a fierce competitor whose game and fighting powers had been tested in many lands, and who had never lost a battle, with his unflinching game and that "wary craft which distinguishes the vulpine breed."[28] After a series of Byzantine maneuvers the combatants finally made their way towards the ring, Sullivan wearing his trademark green and white colors and Hyer in red, white, and blue, his supporters vigorously waving the stars and stripes. Sullivan was the first to throw his hat in the ring—a dark green velvet one—which brought forth the inevitable lusty cheers from his boosters. A couple of minutes later Hyer followed, and as he neared the ropes "shyed his castor, a foggy looking piece of felt," into the ring.[29] On entering the ring both men tied their colors to their respective stakes: Hyer, a star-spangled banner; Sullivan's, a green fogle with oval spots of white. Sullivan won the toss for choice of corner and chose the one he had already assumed; the contest finally began at twenty past four. Yankee started strongly and seemed to be in control of proceedings; at the end of the third round he managed to knock Hyer to the ground with a blow to the neck. This seemed to wake the American up and he proceeded to down Sullivan in the fourth round and again in the sixth. After fifteen minutes Sullivan had to have his right eye lanced to prevent it from swelling shut. It was to prove the beginning of the end for the Irish challenger. At the end of the fifteenth round Hyer threw Sullivan to the ground and fell on top of him. At the start of the sixteenth Sullivan was slow to come to scratch, and for Timony it was evident that Sullivan's fighting star had set for the day.[30] After pummeling the Irishman with a flurry of left and right shots, Hyer fell on his opponent again. This time, when Hyer was lifted off his opponent, Sullivan "reeled half round and staggered towards the ropes" before being carried away by his seconds. It was all over and the champion had retained his title. After eighteen minutes Sullivan's self-proclaimed record of having never been beaten in the ring had been shattered. Hyer duly removed Sullivan's green and white silk banner from a nearby stake and raised it triumphantly above his head to his assembled supporters.[31] The stars and stripes of the nativist Know Nothings had triumphed over the Irish colors of

Tammany Hall. Hyer had, according to *Fistiana,* shown he was capable of matching any man of his size and weight from Britain or the United States.[32] Looking back at the contest later, Timony called it a "hurricane fight," as it was remarkably short by the standards of the time. He drew particular attention to Hyer's tactic of going short with the left as a "preliminary to the Paixhan discharge of the right, in the style of a half uppercut" and his ability to throw his opponent and lie on him until he had to be removed by his seconds, a perfectly legal tactic at the time.[33] If anything, the amount of time taken to remove Sullivan hindered his progress in the encounter, he believed. Ultimately, he noted that Hyer had earned all the laurels a man could from the "brutal soil of the arena" and hoped that he would move forward in his life as a peaceable and unassuming person and leave the prize ring behind him. Sullivan was taken to Mount Hope Hospital where he was treated for his injuries, which included an injured arm, badly bruised eyes, and a slight fracture to his skull, while Hyer returned triumphant to New York with his $10,000 purse, cheered on his way by fawning fans. When the victorious entourage got to the Fountain House, Hyer's drinking establishment of choice in the city, they were treated to a fireworks display. While Sullivan might have had his pride—and his head—dented, he also received a $10,000 payout. With his stock in the ascendant, rumors began to circulate that Hyer would run as a Whig candidate for President of the United States. Not all New Yorkers were equally pleased, however. Philip Hone, a former mayor of the city, opined with some distaste that James Gordon Bennett's *New York Herald* had praised the fight, noting that "the appropriate organ of such disgraceful recitals is filled this morning with the disgusting details."[34] The *Christian Advocate* described the scenes on the streets of New York as "painful and humiliating."[35] Other journalists were not so harsh. The *New York Evening Mirror* declared that in spite of the mawkish twaddle written in many newspapers, it believed the public feeling had been decidedly favorable to the fight and that there were much worse vices tolerated and encouraged by society than prize-fighting.[36] *The Milwaukee Sentinel and Gazette* did not concur, as for it the encounter between the two rowdies was loathsome and ran counter to the views of all right-minded people. It was simply a "humiliating exhibition of human depravity."[37]

Interestingly, the *American Celt,* a paper popular with those Irish who had moved up the social ladder, was disgusted by the encounter and believed that someone must have a terrible account to give of the neglected class of first- and second-generation Irish and Irish Americans in both the United States and England.[38]

Hyer retired to run a saloon on Park Row, where he remained a popular figure, even taking to the stage in April 1849 in Albany, where he performed in *Tom and Gerry,* a theatrical adaptation of the life of boxing historian Pierce Egan. Adjudging the title to be now vacant, Sullivan claimed it, but his tenure as champion is not universally recognized by boxing historians and soon another fearsome Irish contender would come to the fore to take the place of Yankee.

The circumstances surrounding the storied fight between Sullivan and Hyer mirrored the story of boxing in America for much of the nineteenth century. Boxing had been brought to New York by British sailors during the Revolutionary War, but

20　　　　　　　　　　　Part 1—The Heavyweights

Yankee Sullivan (left) contesting the world heavyweight title against Tom "The Bowery King" Hyer on February 7, 1849, at Still Pond Creek, Kent County, Maryland, a fight the Irishman lost in sixteen rounds fought over eighteen minutes. The fight took place in the unlikely location on a snow-covered river bank as the organizers and participants were evading the authorities at a time when the sport was illegal (Harry T. Peters, "America on Stone" Lithography Collection, National Museum of American History).

the pursuit was quickly outlawed after independence. Not only was it brutal but also was a vestige of British influence that had to be expunged. In a 1785 letter Thomas Jefferson complained that young Americans who learned "the peculiarities of English education" would be exposed to drinking, horse racing, and boxing. He also worried that they might acquire a fondness for European luxury and dissipation, and contempt for the simplicity of their own country.[39] With Calvinistic New Englanders ill-disposed toward skating and fishing, boxing was always going to be a pursuit of the marginalized. That is not to say that there were no fights. Moreau de Saint-Méry, a French emigrant to Philadelphia, described an encounter he witnessed in the 1790s:

> Boxing has its rules and regulations. The two athletes settle on a site for the fight. They strip to their shirts, and roll up the sleeves to the elbows. Then at a given signal they run at each other and swing on chest, head, face and bellies, blows whose noise can only be realized by those who have been present at such spectacles. At each new clash, they draw back, and start again from the mark. If one of the two has fallen in one of these attacks his adversary cannot touch him as long as he is on the ground; but if he makes the slightest movement to get up, the other has the right to hit him again and force him to remain on the ground. Nobody interferes to separate the combatants: a ring is made round them, and the spectators urge on their favorites.[40]

Saint-Méry described the brutal end of the fight thus: "The boxers are bruised, disfigured, and covered in blood, which they spit out, vomit out, or drip from the nose.

Teeth are broken, eyes are swollen and shut, and sometimes sight is completely obliterated."

However, for most of the nineteenth century, boxing was technically illegal in America. Notwithstanding, as in the case of Sullivan and Hyer, there were many celebrated fights down through the decades, often attended by large numbers of spectators and widely reported in newspapers. Contests were frequently raided by the police and participants arrested. Such brutal events often lasted for hours and were regularly organized under the patronage of neighborhood politicians and rival factions. Rules were conspicuous by their absence, with wrestling, brawling, biting, hair pulling, and eye gouging part of the armory of any fighter worth his salt. The authorities were not overly concerned with the physical consequences for those who participated, but they did take exception to the gambling and rowdy behavior which became an integral part of the spectacle. As the sport was deemed illegal, fights were often held in secret and only those in the know were provided with the relevant details, often the night before the impending bout. Admission was generally free, with the money generated entirely by betting. Unlike in England, boxing did not interest the Establishment in the United States. In a country founded on principles of Republican Democracy, Enlightenment ideals, and Protestant virtues, prize-fighting did not have mainstream appeal. Newspapers of the era sometimes reported on fights from England but usually managed to include implied criticism of the barbarity still encouraged by people who should know better. It was a pursuit of the idle rich permeated by gambling and drunken behavior. In America it was different. Boxing gained most traction among those in the margins of society, and it was here that Irish immigrants were found in their greatest numbers. In a country where they were often ostracized from more mainstream occupations by nativist motivated employers, it was one way of gaining a leg up in the New World where material success was the inevitable yardstick of progress. It could be a way from rags to riches for those who had the ability, drive, and physical attributes to make it to the top. Between 1840 and 1860, over seventy percent of all professional prize-fighters were Irish or Irish American, with major American boxing centers located in New York, Boston, Philadelphia, and New Orleans.[41] In addition to the Irish making up an overwhelming percentage of boxers, they also made up the highest quality of boxers. Until the 1920s, Irish pugilists held nine of the nineteen possible recognized championships. Many early fights in America were billed as English versus Irish or Native American versus Irish, and the encounter between Yankee Sullivan and Tom Hyer is generally considered the progenitor of the species.

After retiring from boxing, Sullivan moved to California, where he once again gained employment as a shoulder striker, guarding ballot boxes to deter supporters of rival candidates from casting their vote. It was this dangerous occupation which proved his ultimate downfall. Sullivan was guarding a polling station, but would appear to have been in dereliction of his duties as a ballot box was apparently tampered with, resulting in the election of James P. Casey, despite the fact that his name had not even been on the voting sheet. This blatant episode of corruption resulted in the formation of a vigilante group tasked with eliminating electoral fraud in the city. Newspaper editor James King was about to disclose details of the Casey fiasco but was shot dead by a corrupt city official before he got the chance to do so. On

May 25, 1856, Sullivan was arrested by the newly established San Francisco Vigilance Committee following a crackdown on criminal elements in the city. He was found guilty and sentenced to deportation. Four days into his incarceration, while waiting for the second deportation of his life, Yankee Sullivan was found dead in his cell with his wrists slit. It appeared to have been a suicide, but some reports suggested he was murdered by individuals who were worried that he was going to provide further information about political corruption in the city.[42] James Yankee Sullivan was buried in an unmarked grave in the Mission Dolores Cemetery on May 31, 1856. Two years later a grave marker was erected by one Tom Malloy, the words on which would seem to support the latter story of murder most foul: "James Sullivan, who died by the hands of San Francisco vigilantes, May 31st 1856, aged 45 years." The marker had the further inscription, "Remember not, O Lord, our offenses, nor those of our parents. Neither take thou vengeance of our sins. Thou shalt bring forth my soul out of tribulation and in thy mercy thou shalt destroy mine enemies." It is highly unlikely that Sullivan would have been buried in a Catholic cemetery at that time if he had committed suicide. The *New York Times* was not complimentary when it reported Sullivan's death on June 30 under the headline "Yankee Sullivan No More." Yankee Sullivan had gone to his last account. His last round was fought. His name passed away from among the ranks of the active "Fancy." Like many of the "fighting men," Sullivan had enough in him to make a smart man; but as it was, "he was smart and shrewd only in a bad way."[43] Like many sporting men, Sullivan was a drinker and, according to the *New York Times*, not a very good one. "Drink made Sullivan insane," claimed the newspaper. "When overcome by liquor, he was furious against everybody, never distinguishing friend from foe." However, even the *Times* admitted that "there was some good feeling, much overlaid by rascality and very difficult to be discerned." Another source confirmed his drinking behavior:

> Anyone who ever saw Jim Sullivan once could never forget him, and in every city he visited he became a conspicuous object of peculiar interest. His close-cropped, bullet-like head, not unlike the head of a ram, except the horns; fierce, glaring gray eyes; high cheek bones, flat face; reddish-brown hair, prominent ears and thick neck, made him the beau-ideal of a fighter. His close-fitting, bottle-green velvet cutaway coat, tight-legged corduroys, high cut vest, spotted scarf and cluster diamond pin, protruding shirt collar and straight broad-brimmed plug hat, were decidedly Sullivan-like. He carried very little flesh, had a jaunty, springy, devil-may-care air, and when not in liquor was a clever sort of man, with an open heart for those not always too worthy.... [Sullivan] was never so happy as when he had on the mittens.

Despite the attitude of the Old Gray Lady, that is, the *New York* Times, Sullivan was an important figure in the narrative of America and of Irish Americans in their adopted home. He was an example to the Irish of someone who could become part of American society but still keep his ethnic ties to the old country. He was an exemplar of a proud immigrant achieving a successful life in his chosen field, albeit not one to which all aspired, although one of the first published histories of boxing in the United States said that Sullivan "was looked up to on all sides, not only as a personage to be revered, but an oracle whose opinion was infallible and without appeal on the subjects connected with the Prize Ring."[44]

While prize-fighting may have been a marginal activity bordering on the criminal, the Irish dominated the sport and it made them visible in the melting pot that the United States was becoming. The next Irishman to come to the fore would end up playing a significantly larger role in American public life, despite being hewn from the same tough Irish cloth.

Two

No Smoke Without Fire

John "Old Smoke" Morrissey

"I have been a wharf rat, chicken thief, prize fighter, gambler and member of Congress, and if any gentleman on the other side wants his constitution amended, just let him step into the Rotunda with me."
—John "Old Smoke" Morrissey addressing the U.S. House of Representatives[1]

JOHN MORRISSEY WAS A MAN TO be reckoned with from a young age, and the manner in which he acquired his colorful sobriquet was indicative of the courage that was to bear him through a remarkable and tumultuous life. While fighting a notorious underworld pugilist called Tom McCann at an indoor pistol gallery at the Saint Charles Hotel in New York City, Morrissey found himself pinned on top of burning coals which had been thrown free from an upturned stove. The Irishman ignored the coals searing his naked flesh and managed to throw McCann across the floor of the premises before proceeding to batter him beyond recognition. The unfortunate McCann was almost killed, while the legend

The fearsome John "Old Smoke" Morrissey assumed the mantle of champion after he defeated Sullivan on October 12, 1853, in the hamlet of Boston Corners, then in Massachusetts. Morrissey reputedly acquired his colorful sobriquet during a fight in a hotel where he was thrown on a stove but still managed to defend himself and gain the upper hand on his opponent (Lithograph by Currier & Ives, c1860, Library of Congress).

of John "Old Smoke" Morrissey was born.² In 1883 Morrissey's family immigrated to the United States from Templemore, County Tipperary, in the southern part of Ireland, where the records show he had been born two years earlier on February 12, 1831, to parents Timothy and Julia.³ The poor Irish family settled in the town of Troy in upstate New York, where John worked in a mill from the age of twelve before gravitating to working in a foundry which manufactured cannonballs.⁴ The young Morrissey also became involved in the factional fighting which raged between gangs in Troy and soon came to be regarded as the kingpin of the lower part of the city. His questionable curriculum vitae included stints as a cargo thief, a collection agent for Irish crime bosses, and even a period working as a bouncer at a brothel. By the age of eighteen Morrissey had been arrested twice for burglary, once for assault and battery, and once for assault with intent to kill. The *San Francisco Call* was later to note that Morrissey was not a man who needed to resort to cudgels and flying missiles because nature had endowed him with a "frame of iron, two gigantic fists ... shrewdness and the force of the leader."⁵

Morrissey was not a man for hanging around; nor did he lack ambition. Despite his criminal predilections he managed to teach himself to read and write during his teenage years and, leaving behind his parents and seven sisters in 1848, the young Irishman moved to New York, where he obtained employment working as a deckhand on a steamer plying its trade between the city and Albany. Like so many other young men of his day, Morrissey found the lure of the gold fields of California irresistible and, at the age of twenty, made his way to San Francisco by stowing away on a series of boats in the company of his friend Daniel "Dad" Cunningham. On the final leg of their journey Morrissey was raised to anger when he saw the ship's captain berate a cabin boy. When the Irishman stepped in to defend the boy the captain asked to see his ticket. After Morrissey was revealed as a stowaway the captain threatened to drop him ashore, but when the passengers intimated that they would revolt, the captain wisely employed Morrissey as his personal protector and provided him with his own cabin and return ship fare. It was in the hard-bitten environment of the Californian goldfields and the tumultuous backstreets of San Francisco that Morrissey developed his pugilistic skills, winning more money through his fists than he ever found in a pan.⁶ He tried unsuccessfully to arrange a fight with Tom Hyer, but on August 31, 1852, Morrissey defeated George Thompson, Hyer's trainer, in his first professional boxing match at Mare Island, thirty miles from San Francisco. The contest lasted eleven rounds and twenty-two minutes and landed the Irishman the impressive sum of $5,000.⁷ Morrissey took a firm beating in the first ten rounds but refused to give up in front of a drunken and hostile crowd, and the referee awarded the fight to the Irishman at the start of the eleventh round after he judged two of Thompson's punches to be below the belt and deliberate fouls.⁸ John Morrissey was now the champion of California and parlayed his newfound fame into a successful gambling enterprise in his adopted home of San Francisco. He subsequently returned to New York and found employment as a heavy in the political underworld after impressing Tammany Hall stalwart Isaiah Rynders when he challenged anyone in the politician's saloon to a fight after Charley "Dutch" Duane failed to show up for a scheduled match. Morrissey repeatedly challenged Yankee Sullivan to fight for the title the Irishman claimed to hold, and on September 1, 1853, articles for a meeting were finally signed.[9] Five weeks later, on October 12, the pair met at Boston Corners, an obscure train stop just over the New York state border, out of reach of that state's law enforcement, secluded on the opposite side of the Taconic Mountains from Great Barrington, Massachusetts, the closest town with any substantial law enforcement. The contest took place in front of a crowd of 4,500 for a purse of $2,000 governed by the recently revised London Prize Ring Rules.[10] Morrissey trained assiduously at Macombs Dam, while his opponent prepared at the intriguingly named Hit-or-Miss Hotel on the Coney Island Plank Road (now Coney Island Avenue, Brooklyn).

When a journalist from the *San Francisco Call* first saw Morrissey on the morning of the fight he described him as a "rugged, compact, clean muscled gladiator, in perfect condition and spoiling for more trouble" and believed that "fighting was the breath of life to him."[11] Sullivan was filled with delight, the paper suggested, now that he had finally found an opponent worthy of his best efforts and one who would require every ounce of his fine young red-blooded strength to defeat. Although Sullivan was much shorter than his adversary, he was "hard-bitten and solid as a stone pillar." Forty years of age and veteran of many tough encounters, albeit many of them by his own admission, the journalist described Sullivan as "fresh, arid, active, depending not only upon his superior knowledge of the game, but upon a strength and endurance as yet unsapped by age." While the older man might have a little bit more science, there was unlikely to be a startling display of technique by either boxer, he noted, and, in fact, when the fight finally got underway the attitude of neither could be called graceful. The combatants stood upright with hands high and knees bent, ready for hard knocks rather than shifty play, and from the outset it was hit and take, ding and dong. Sullivan dominated the early exchanges and managed to cause damage to the area around his opponent's left eye; by the end of the seventh it was almost totally closed. Yankee was in the ascendant until the fifteenth round, having used the common spoiling tactic of the day of dragging his opponent to the ground to foreshorten the rounds. A pattern unveiled itself as the fight progressed, with Sullivan the more skillful, more wary, quicker and craftier, but Morrissey had the superior punching power. Yankee continued to go to ground when the opportunity arose, desperate to avoid the heavy punches of his opponent. By comparison, Morrissey never once sought to end a round in this way and was relentless in his approach. Although he had a careless guard and limited speed, his single purpose was to hit solidly, while Morrissey seemed totally unaware that such things as dodging, shifting, and retreating could be part of the game. No other man fought, the journalist observed, with the superb simplicity of Old Smoke, while Sullivan was slow for a scientific boxer but "as elusive as a moth at dusk." Morrissey stuck doggedly to his task, however, and by the thirty-third round Yankee was exhausted; Morrissey kept going, "steady as a rock, wholly unconscious of the fact that by all precedents he ought to consider himself defeated." The journalist believed it was only a matter of time before Sullivan was beaten. In the thirty-seventh round chaos broke out when Morrissey lifted Sullivan off the floor by putting his arm around his opponent's neck, but Yankee's supporters, sensing an impending defeat, rushed the ring and both fighters disappeared under the invasion. Great confusion followed and the men were separated and swept out of the ring. In the midst of the uproar the referee gave the decision to Morrissey because Sullivan had left the ring without awaiting further instruction, but, not all of the press reported a similar reason for the referee's decision.[12] One account suggested Sullivan had struck Morrissey with a foul blow, while another in the same paper was adamant that Yankee had not come to the line in time.[13] Sullivan protested the outcome, but the greater political influence of his opponent held sway and Old Smoke assumed the title. Morrissey did not go unchallenged by the law, however, as the Grand Jury of Berkshire County fined him $1,200 for his participation in the then illegal fight.[14] With money earned from the fight Morrissey invested in gambling parlors and assumed the leadership of the Irish and Irish American Dead Rabbits street gang in 1857 after Rynders was forced to leave the city when a riot with the Bowery Boys went awry. With the patronage of Grand Sachem William Tweed, Morrissey expanded his empire by opening brothels and illegal drinking dens, as well as organizing the protection of polling stations in the city to ensure his political backers retained power. Morrissey had never forgotten Susie Smith, a childhood sweetheart from his early days in Troy, and the couple was married in 1854. Morrissey promised his bride, a graduate of what is now the Emma Willard School in Troy, that he would give up fighting. She demanded better from Morrissey, and for a while, he complied with his wife's wishes. However, in the world in which Old Smoke operated, things were never going to be as straightforward and as pacific as his new wife might have wished. Ranged against him were the Bowery Boys led by the vicious Bill "The Butcher" Poole, and on Election Day 1854, Poole announced that he and thirty of his gang were going to destroy the ballot boxes of their opponents. Tammany Hall called on Morrissey to protect their interests, and with the help of John A. Kennedy, later to become New York City's Superintendent of Police, he assembled a gang of over fifty Dead Rabbits who awaited Poole's arrival at the polling station. When the Bowery Boys arrived they quickly realized that they were vastly outnumbered by Morrissey and his gang. Tammany Hall, delighted by Morrissey's achievements, awarded him a free gambling house with full police protection.

Having fought and defeated Yankee Sullivan, Morrissey was to find an even more formidable foe in the boxing ring in the shape of Bill "The Butcher" Poole. So called because he spent his early days working in the meat trade, Poole was born in Sussex County, New Jersey, on July 24, 1821. Over two hundred pounds in weight and six feet in height, Poole was infamous for the raw barbarity of his boxing style and, according to one report, was not averse to "biting off noses, gouging out eyeballs, or beating a man to jelly," while his professional calling rendered him adept with knives.[15] Sometime in the 1850s he closed the family's butcher business and opened a saloon called the Bank Exchange, where he became renowned for being one of his own best customers. It was here that the Bowery Boys had their center of operations in the notorious slums of Five Points in Lower Manhattan and, along with other nativist gangs such as the American Guards, the True Blue Americans, and the Order of the Star Spangled Banner, Poole and his boys waged constant low-grade warfare with gangs of Irish immigrants such as the Dead Rabbits whose presence in the city offended their nativist sensibilities. Poole's rise in the Know Nothing Party was fast and brutal. The organization's twin aims were to disenfranchise adopted citizens, with the particular objective of preventing them from achieving political office, while waging perpetual war on members of the Catholic religion. Originally known as the Native American Party, its members had to be born in America of American-born parents and could not be Catholic.

When the two men crossed paths in late July 1854, Morrissey challenged Poole to a fight for the sum of $100 at a time and place of the latter's choosing.[16] The Butcher promptly agreed to fight at seven o'clock the following morning at the Amos Street Docks (now West Tenth Street). Poole arrived in his rowboat at daybreak to be greeted by hundreds of eager spectators waiting for the fight, many of whom suspected that Morrissey would not show up. They need not have doubted the intentions of the Irish man; at half past six Old Smoke appeared, spoiling for the fight. The two combatants circled each other for about thirty seconds until Morrissey thrust his left fist forward. Poole ducked, seized his enemy by the waist, and threw him to the ground before proceeding to fight according to his reputation. Once on top of his opponent, Poole mercilessly bit, tore, scratched, kicked, and punched his unfortunate opponent. He gouged Morrissey's right eye until it streamed with blood and, according to the *New York Times*, the Irishman was so disfigured he was "scarce recognized by his friends."[17] Eventually Yankee could take no more punishment and was carried away by his supporters, while Poole celebrated his victory with a drink before leaving on his rowboat for a victory party at Coney Island. Morrissey retreated to a hotel on Leonard Street to lick his wounds, drown his sorrows, and plan for revenge.

The hostilities between the two men did not end there. On February 25, 1855, their paths crossed in the back room of Stanwix Hall, a saloon which, unusually at that time, catered to supporters of all political persuasions.[18] Morrissey was playing cards with friends when Poole entered the premises, and after hearing that his arch-nemesis was in the same room the Irishman went over to confront the Butcher. The narrative of what happened next is contested, but there is general agreement that guns were involved. Some accounts suggest Morrissey drew a pistol and snapped it three times at Poole's head but it failed to discharge, while others maintain that both men drew their pistols, daring each other to shoot. Some tellings recount that Poole drew his revolver and was about to shoot Morrissey when a man named Mark Maguire intervened with a question: "You wouldn't kill a helpless man in cold blood, would you?" In this version of events Poole threw his pistol to the floor, grabbed two carving knives from the lunch counter, and hurled them into the bar, inviting either Maguire or Morrissey to a knife fight. Both men declined, knowing Poole's skills and efficacy with knives. Whatever actually transpired, the owners saw fit to call the authorities and the men were taken to separate police stations. Neither was charged with a crime and both were released shortly afterward. Poole then returned to Stanwix Hall, where a number of Morrissey's henchmen entered sometime after midnight. The group included Lewis Baker, James Turner, and Patrick "Paudeen" McLaughlin, all of whom had had violent disagreements with Poole and his associates in the past. According to Herbert Asbury's *The Gangs of New York: An Informal History of the Underworld*, Paudeen tried to goad Poole into a fight, but the Butcher knew he was outnumbered and refused to engage, even though the Irish gang member spat at his face three times and supposedly called him a "black-muzzled bastard." James Turner then reputedly said, "Let us sail into him anyhow!," and unmasked a large Colt revolver from underneath his cloak, drew it out, and aimed it at Poole. Turner squeezed the trigger but, after one of the bystanders made a lunge for him, the bullet accidentally went through Turner's left arm, shattering the bone. Turner fell to the floor but managed to continue firing, hitting Poole in the right leg above the kneecap and in the shoulder. The Butcher staggered toward the door but was stopped and shot in the chest by Lewis Baker. Eleven days later, Poole succumbed to his wounds and his supposed last words were to become a standard closing line on the New York stage for many years: "Goodbye boys, I die a true American."[19] Morrissey and Baker were indicted for the murder, but the charges were dropped after three trials resulted in hung juries.

John Morrissey with his wife Susan moved back to Troy, where he attempted to pursue legitimate business interests but did not find immediate success or social acceptance. By then the couple had a child, John Jr., but despite his best intentions, Morrissey was pulled back into the world of prize-fighting in 1858 when he accepted a challenge from John C. "The Benecia Boy" Heenan.[20] Heenan's background and upbringing were uncannily similar to those of Morrissey. His family had emigrated from Templemore, County Tipperary, the same village where Morrissey had been born, and, remarkably, also settled in Troy, New York, where John C. was born on May 2, 1834.[21] In his early teenage years Heenan began his working career at Watervliet Arsenal but like so many others, including Morrissey, the young Irish American was enticed to cross the country in search of Californian gold.[22] When he got to the West Coast in 1849, at the age of seventeen, Heenan, like Morrissey, became involved in the lucrative pastime of bare-knuckle fighting and quickly established a reputation as a formidable opponent in the chaotic and lawless saloons of the time. While displaying his considerable fighting talents, Heenan also spent a period working in the Pacific Mail Steamship Company in Benicia, where he acquired his sobriquet, and, like Morrissey and many Irish heavies, dedicated some of his time working as a political enforcer.[23] Six feet two inches tall and weighing around 190 pounds, Heenan had all the physical attributes required for bare-knuckle fighting, and his burgeoning talent was soon spotted by English-born itinerant boxing trainer Jim Cusack, who brought him to New York in the fall of 1857.[24] Like Yankee Sullivan and John Morrissey before him, Heenan was to find gainful employment as a shoulder hitter in the city—in his case, working for the nativists.[25] The Benicia Boy was duly rewarded for his fealty with an undemanding position at the New York Customs House.

On July 3, 1858, Heenan and Morrissey signed a contract for a purse of $5,000, with the bout scheduled to take place on October 20 in a Canadian venue to be determined at a later point.[26] Morrissey hired the Australian champion Jim Kelly as his trainer, while Heenan acquired the services of Aaron Jones, an experienced English fighter, to assist with his preparations.[27] The fight took place at Long Point, a lonely stretch of beach on a peninsula jutting into Lake Erie, a location which could only be reached by chartered steamer from Buffalo, New York. Morrissey was in the condition of his life, while Heenan had not been as assiduous in his approach to training, going into the fight with an ulcerated right leg, according to Fred Dowling.[28] Betting on the outcome was intense, and in keeping with the dichotomous attitude of the press to prize-fighting during the era, the *New York Herald* devoted its front page to the fight while the *New York Tribune* carried an editorial saying its coverage of the encounter was a result of the obligation it felt to report crime in the same way it reported the hangings and the murders of the community.[29] The *New York Herald* reported that the spirit of the prize ring was prevalent in every bar room, bowling alley, and billiard saloon in New York on the eve of the fight.[30] The crowds around the various newspaper offices were particularly excited, waiting for information about the contest, much of which was false alarms. Newsboys took advantage of the fever and sold off out-of-date extras. Pickpockets and counterfeiters also took advantage, with one man losing a gold watch and chain, valued at $275, and another a breast pin valued at $125, according to the journalist. People fought in the streets over betting odds. Policemen were kept awake all night by roaring, and the journalists feared that some might resign due to sleep deprivation. The *New York Times* thought Heenan was by far the weaker contestant: Morrissey looked like a "magnificent animal … [with] a look of wear and tear about him which spoke volumes," while Heenan "looked pale and dull of eye, and his muscles, though large, lacked consistency."[31] Another journalist was concerned at the sallow appearance of Heenan.[32]

In the early exchanges, Heenan was in the ascendant and Morrissey was soon bleeding heavily. However, the Benicia Boy had the misfortune of punching one of

John Morrissey (left) retained his title when he defeated fellow Irishman John "The Benicia Boy" Heenan in the eleventh round at Long Point, Ontario, Canada, on October 20, 1858 (Wood engraving from *Frank Leslie's Illustrated Newspaper,* October 30, 1858, Prints and Photographs Division, Library of Congress).

the ring stakes in error, breaking two knuckles on his left hand; notwithstanding, his superior reach allowed him to keep Morrissey at bay, at least for a while. As the fight progressed, Heenan found it increasingly difficult to keep his guard up and eventually fell from exhaustion in the eighth round. He struggled on but the end was nigh; in the eleventh he went down again after a hard blow to the neck, and after twenty-two minutes, the fight was over and Morrissey was still the champion.[33] In the colorful words of one journalist, the Irishman held on to the "miraculous belly band."[34] He was informed that Morrissey had jumped over the ropes and walked to the house where they had prepared, while Heenan did not recover his consciousness for half an hour after the fight was over but believed the news was biased, as he had heard from another source that both men were shockingly mangled and bruised, and both were carried away on beds.[35]

The moral majority was not impressed with the encounter, with Lambert A. Wilmer describing the fight as the "most demoralizing, beastly, disgusting, and scandalous affair of the kind that took place in any half-civilized country."[36] The *New York Herald* also saw the fight as an opportunity to moralize, describing it as another of those brutal exhibitions which had disgraced the country in recent years and that it was nothing but a relic of the barbarism of old Rome and the Middle Ages.[37] It wanted to know what the fight said about the United States. Was the country at the height of progress in civilization that it claimed to be, or was it in a condition such that the laws, moral and legal, were powerless to prevent these occasional disgraceful displays of human brutality? This was an event which could have resulted in the death of either of the boxers, it thundered, even though the local authorities were in a position to prevent it going ahead. The efforts made by the forces of law had only ensured the fight moved to a more remote location, and the newspaper had its suspicions about the interest some members of the police were taking in proceedings. Surely, this was not something that could be condoned in a great Republic. However, in another article in the same paper, on the same day, a journalist noted that the excitement in the city had risen to boiling point the previous day and that for a few hours the great triumph of the successful gladiator clouded the sunlight of public favor which had sparked in the eyes of one of the most charming artistes that ever captivated our public, and "obscured the laurels placed on the brow of La Piccolomini."[38] It seemed there was a dichotomous attitude to prize-fighting within the organ. The front page announced its extensive coverage of the fight with the boast that it was giving the great gladiatorial event the prominence and importance to which it was entitled. It promised a full and graphic description of the preparations for the encounter, charming biographical sketches of the contending gladiators, an account of their preliminary training, and a copy of the rules under which they agreed as to the exact manner in which they would proceed to bruise and maul each other until one was pounded into an acknowledgment of the physical supremacy of the other. The fight was an instance of the progress of the age, and the journalist proceeded to outline a history of manly combat:

> In medieval times the trial of skill by combat and the duello was confined, as a matter of course, to nobles and gentlemen. The common people, who were not privileged to bear arms, resorted to their fists, or to the quarterstaff, which cracked many an English skull in the good old days when the Eighth Harry was King. A century later we find the journals of the day

recording the pleasing fact that any gentleman who was desirous to have his head battered, for the trifling consideration of a couple of shillings, might be accommodated on any day of the week at an agreeable establishment called the "Cockpit."[39]

In those days, it explained, there was little advanced preparation or training by combatants. A challenge was usually issued one day and the fight took place the next. Now things were organized more elegantly. However, it seems the paper was being somewhat facetious: "The ring has become one of the dearest institutions of the British realm, and has extended itself to our shores, where its influences have killed more of our young men than war or pestilence." This fight was being talked about by some as if it were some great achievement of science or wonderful exhibition of strategic skill on the battlefield. The paper suggested that the victorious fighter should be given a civic reception, "including congratulatory orations, complimentary resolutions, and grand muscle processions, after the fashion of the cortege at the funeral of the late lamented Mr. William Poole. There should be grand fireworks—no doubt some patriotic pyrotechnist will give them gratis—in fact, altogether a Roman triumph." Throughout the long article the journalist hints that the local political classes were involved in promoting and supporting the fight.

The *Springfield Weekly Republican* of October 3 had no time for the manifestation of the "muscle movement" which the fight embodied, and, not shying away from a pun, it could not bring itself to "fancy" the proceedings.[40] Nor did it care a penny which of the contestants won, and it had heard that the flash saloons and gambling halls of New York had been deserted. Indeed, it had also heard that those who had departed for the fight were the ugliest party that had left the city in a good many years, opining, "If the whole grand swell mob, while in Canada, could be induced to go into a general scrimmage and enact the tragedy of the Kilkenny cats" it would be willing to assist in crowning the survivor as the champion of America and heap upon his head the gratitude and honor of a relieved and thankful people. It too bemoaned the inability of the law to stop the fight.[41] "Canadian officers cannot prevent them, because the field is not known to them in advance, and the barbarians make an irruption, settle their hash [defeat] and retreat before a sufficient force could be brought to the spot to arrest the combatants or prevent the fight." There should be laws, it believed, that would treat prize-fighting as dueling was treated, and punishment for a challenge or preparation to fight. The paper could not see how this was a sport or how men who go long distances at great expense of time and money to see two brutes pummel each other, batter each other's noses, smash each other's eyes, break each other's ribs, and come as near to driving the soul out of the human body as possible, yet escape the guilt of absolute murder. It could understand that a man might have occasion to fight in an act of self-defense when attacked by a madman or a mad animal, or that he might have to defend his honor at some point, but it could not believe that men should deliberately set to work to bruise and maim each other in perfect cordiality and for mere amusement or rivalry. If human nature was "a cross between the bull-dog and hyena" it might understand the sport, but this was not the case.

Heenan immediately called for a rematch and placed a notice in the *New York Evening Express* claiming that he had lost the first encounter due to illness, but

Morrissey refused and signaled his retirement from the ring. Inevitably, there were those who claimed Morrissey jumped before he was pushed, arguing that he would not get the better of Heenan in a fair fight. Although it was his last fight, John Morrissey kept up his interest in prize-fighting, and in the spring of 1860 he crossed the Atlantic to attend the widely anticipated contest between Heenan and English champion Tom Sayers. While in England he visited the offices of the sporting newspaper *Bell's Life in London and Sporting Chronicle* and placed a £600 wager on Sayers to win the fight. Morrissey also visited Sayers at his training quarters, where he reputedly gave the Englishman valuable advice.[42] On his way back to America Old Smoke spent some hours in the port of Queenstown, County Cork, where he attracted a large circle of admirers and was presented with a handsome blackthorn stick, grown on the soil of his native Tipperary.[43]

Morrissey was to have further profitable ventures in his colorful life. At first he concentrated on gambling establishments and was reputed to have an interest in sixteen casinos at one point. By August 1860 it was estimated that he was worth $200,000, all of which he had gained "at hazard," according to one journalist.[44] In 1862 a police raid on one of his gambling establishments in New York revealed that the house had made over $2,000 in December of the previous year.[45]

Recognizing the increasing popularity of horse racing, Old Smoke set about organizing a four-day experimental thoroughbred meeting at an old trotting course in Saratoga, and once again, the ambitious Irishman was onto a winner. Even though there were only eight races over the four-day period, the event proved a remarkable success, and Morrissey, never one to shy away from an opportunity, immediately set about enlisting partners to develop a state-of-the-art racecourse where he had the sagacity to appoint the highly respected horse breeder William Travers as the first president, helping to distance himself from his dubious past.[46] With the help of Travers, Leonard Jerome, and John Hunter, Morrissey purchased 125 acres of land and opened "the most classic racecourse in this country, located among the pines, beautiful to the eye, and rejuvenating to the horse." The forward-thinking Irishman also had the nous to employ emerging telegraph technology to accommodate off-course punters. The racetrack was a resounding success, but Morrissey did not sit back and rest on his laurels, and in 1870 he opened his Club House, a gambling palace in Saratoga's Congress Park, another venture which was to prove remarkably successful. Morrissey's "Elegant Hell," as it was dubbed in the press, was patronized by the great and the good, including American presidents Chester A. Arthur and Rutherford B. Hayes. Ulysses S. Grant, a celebrated former Civil War general at the time and future president of the country, was known to take to the tables, while business tycoons such as Commodore Cornelius Vanderbilt and John Rockefeller were also among Morrissey's distinguished guests. Such was his success that Old Smoke's business empire was said to be worth a million dollars at one stage of his career, and luckily, when Black Friday decimated his finances, Commodore Vanderbilt came to his rescue. Morrissey parlayed his newfound respectability into a successful political career, serving two terms as a Democratic member in the U.S. Congress between 1867 and 1871 backed by the political might of the Tammany Hall machine under the stewardship of William Tweed. Inevitably, Old Smoke was renowned for looking out for the interests of the Irish community and, true to his fighting spirit, was not averse to telling the assembled politicians that he could lick any man in the house if the need arose. After falling out with his political mentors, he testified against the corrupt regime of Tweedy in a trial which resulted in the chief of Tammany Hall's imprisonment and went on to serve two terms as a Democratic state senator between 1876 and 1878 as an anti–Tammany candidate.

John Morrissey died on May 1, 1878, at the Adelphi Hotel in Saratoga Springs at the age of forty-seven after contracting pneumonia. His high standing in the establishment was evidenced by the fact that the state closed all offices on May 4, the day of his funeral, while the entire New York State Senate attended his funeral service, with 20,000 members of the public lining the streets of Troy to pay their last respect as the cortege made its way to St. Peter's Cemetery.[47] Morrissey's philanthropy lived on after him. As well as forming the Saratoga Rowing Association and owning a professional baseball team in Troy, Old Smoke endowed schools and funded church building, even sending a donation of $500 to aid the construction of the Cathedral of the Assumption in Thurles in his native Tipperary back in Ireland. Such was his generosity that Morrissey had nothing to leave to his wife Sarah on his death. The *San Franciscan Call* saw only good in his life: "Morrissey's political career, like that of his pugilistic days, was free from stain. While conscious of his limitations and refraining from pushing himself forward, he was always careful to act honestly and to the best of his judgment. For the rest he was, first and last, a fighter and a man."[48] The *New York Times* noted Morrissey's metamorphosis from gambler and ex-prize-fighter to an honest, clear-headed, right-minded legislator.[49] He was, according to the writer, a man of "common sense, clear perceptions and unbending rectitude." In 1954 John Old Smoke Morrissey was elected to the Ring Boxing Hall of Fame, and in 1996 he was elected to the International Boxing Hall of Fame.

John Morrissey served as a senator in the U.S. Senate from 1876 to 1878 (Library of Congress).

Three

"The Benicia Boy"
John C. Heenan

So cheer up, you lads of Erin's Isle,
And never be dismayed,
I'm the son of a true-bred Irishman,
And never was afraid;
I'll show these English boasting lads,
Now I've come over here,
How Donnelly conquered Cooper
In the county of Kildare.[1]

For a man now forgotten in the mists of time, John Camel Heenan achieved considerable fame at the height of his career. Celebrated in poems and ballads, drawn by famous cartoonist Thomas Nast, and portrayed on Broadway by the country's most beloved comic actor, Joseph Jefferson, his name was used to sell butter, tobacco, and Kellogg's flour in his fighting heyday.[2] Barbers recreated his hairstyle, and newborn boys were given his unusual name. After assuming the mantle of champion when John Morrissey refused him a rematch, Heenan embarked on a lucrative tour on which he traveled

After John Morrissey refused John Heenan a return fight, Heenan became world champion by default. Heenan subsequently traveled to England to fight British champion Tom Sayers in an encounter which was highly publicized on both sides of the Atlantic. The fight, held near the village of Farnborough in Hampshire on April 17, 1860, ended in chaos with the referee declaring a draw (Lithograph published by Currier & Ives, c. 1860, Prints and Photographs Division, Library of Congress).

as far north as Montreal and as far south as Mobile, Alabama. It was during this trip that he had an ultimately ill-fated meeting with a renowned stage actress called Adah Isaacs Menken in Cincinnati. She followed him to New York, and the two were married in April 1859. At the time, Jim Cusack was planning to bring Heenan to England to take on British champion Tom Sayers because he believed there was no fighter in America capable of providing the Benicia Boy with a realistic challenge.

As the championship fight neared, it was reported that Heenan's actress wife had not secured a legal divorce from her first husband. (Her ex told the newspapers that the actress was an "incubus and disgrace" whose "superlative impudence and brazenness … renders her unworthy of my further charitable silence.")[3] Menken fought back against the charges in language which suggested they were true—"I am proud and happy to be known as the wife of the bravest man in the world!"—and used her notoriety to further increase her fame. Changing her stage billing to Mrs. John C. Heenan, she appeared in scores of productions prior to her husband's big match. In Providence, she starred in a farce about her husband called *Heenan Has Come!* While in Richmond she took to the stage in a production entitled *Benicia Boy in England* alongside a journeyman actor named John Wilkes Booth.

After a series of meetings, details of the impending fight were agreed and Heenan left New York on board Cunard's wooden paddle steamer *Asia*, landing in Liverpool on January 16, 1860. It was an encounter which was to capture the public imagination on both sides of the Atlantic. *Harper's Weekly* noted that the majority of the public in England and America were so engrossed with the upcoming encounter that a "Spanish bull-bait is but a mild and diverting pastime," while the *Manchester Guardian* opined that "no pugilistic contest ever decided has excited so great an interest, both in this and other countries, as the forthcoming conflict between Sayers and Heenan."[4] Another paper observed that "the odds are your butcher asks you which man you fancy, and if you want to bet on it. Your newsman smiles as he hands you your daily paper, and informs you that 'there is something new about the great fight in it this morning.'"[5] Elliott Gorn believed the fight garnered more public attention than any other athletic event during the fifty years straddling the mid-century and that the American–British rivalry sanctioned Heenan–Sayers as a genuine test of national supremacy. In the lead-up to the encounter, the prize ring attracted new followers at an unprecedented pace, Gorn noted, with pugilism momentarily dropping the distinctive garb of workingclass street gangs, donning the stars and stripes, and marching boldly up Main Street.[6] Even the perennially restrained *Philadelphia Press* seemed to waiver in its opposition to the ring: "That the strength of muscle, power of endurance, and indomitable pluck, called for in the successful prizefighter need cultivation in our age, and particularly in our own country, no one will deny."[7] It questioned the American people's physical preparedness for military conflict, fearing the country lacked the physical powers of endurance needed in times of war. In the final paragraph the journalist tempered his assertions by encouraging readers to go to a gymnasium or play cricket instead of subjecting themselves to the "rowdyism, gambling, and brutality" of prize-fighting. *Wilkes' Spirit of the Times* saw fit to print a ballad called "Heenan: Ireland's Pride" from a reader, noting that three or four weeks earlier it had published a "bellicose ballad of some British bard" predicting the defeat of John Heenan. Balance needed to be restored.

Talk about the event even eclipsed the anticipation for the April 23, 1860, National Convention of Democrats in Charleston, South Carolina, where the party split over slavery.

The nexus of factors surrounding John Heenan is particularly interesting. On the one hand he was trumpeted as the pride of Ireland, but he also represented the essence of what it meant to be American as purported by nativists and gained work through their patronage. Heretofore all the boxers of Irish American heritage were on the outside looking in. The *London Saturday Review* took an inevitably jingoistic stance, telling its readers that in a country where it is known that honor and property are only safe as long as its citizens are ready to fight in their defense, the nature which loves fighting for its own sake will always command respect. It believed that a man like Tom Sayers, who left his business as a bricklayer to devote himself to boxing, possessed a character which would make England feared abroad and safe at home.[8] As was often the case, there was a dichotomous view in the press, with the so-called respectable papers treating the fight as a brutal anachronism.[9] The *Guardian* did not like the association of healthy "muscular art" with the "unhealthy excitement" surrounding prize-fighting. It was critical of the fact that prize-fighters performed for money and not to develop their manly energies. Nor did the fighting develop the physical powers of those around them. The paper believed men should don the gloves of and learn the art of boxing for its intrinsic merits.[10]

The Prime Minister also criticized the impending fight but noted that Sayers was first and foremost an Englishman and that if the fight went ahead, he hoped victory would come his way.[11] In a parliamentary debate held four days before the fight, one MP called for the Home Secretary and the Prime Minister to intervene and stop what he believed was a "meditated breach of the peace."[12] Heenan trained at Newmarket, where he impressed all and sundry, according to Miles, who thought the fighter's feats as a pedestrian were extraordinary. Heenan normally walked six miles and a "bittock" each day, providing a stiff challenge to the foremost English jockeys of the era, many of whom were "no mean specimens of fair toe-and-heel walkers."[13] On April 17, 1860, Heenan finally came face to face with his English opponent in the village of Farnborough in Hampshire, in what is now widely regarded as the inaugural world title encounter. On the morning of the fight, the scenes at London Bridge Station reminded Henry Downes Miles of the crush on Derby Day. Sayers arrived first, he noted, "his fresh, brisk, and natty appearance indicated a good night's rest, and especial pains with his *toilette*," while Heenan looked like he did not want to be recognized and instantly proceeded to a compartment reserved for him and his seconds.[14] Special trains left London's Waterloo Station at four o'clock in the morning, while members of the Metropolitan Police lined the track to ensure the fight would take place outside their bailiwick. It had cost the excited passengers three guinea to buy a ticket stamped with the gnomic words "To Nowhere."[15] There was no doubting the American's superior physical attributes; Sayers was eight years older, forty pounds lighter, and five inches shorter. Known as "The Brighton Titch," the Englishman had become champion of his country without having to fight (he claimed the title when no one would take on the challenge to fight him for it; he was champion by default) and was billed as the small, clever little ring general in the prefight publicity.[16] Only five feet eight inches tall, Sayers had defeated many fighters larger and taller than himself over the years.

The disparity between the combatants could be viewed as a reflection of the chasm that was starting to open up between the sport in the United States and Britain as well as their respective dynamism as counties: America was growing bigger and stronger all the time, while across the Atlantic the sun was gradually starting to lower on the empire.

The Benicia Boy was confident when he arrived to view proceedings: "We have a fine morning for our business. If a man can't fight and win on such a crisp morning, then he can't fight at all."[17] Miles thought those in attendance at ringside were the most aristocratic congregation ever assembled and noted that they included the bearers of names highly distinguished in the pages of Burke and Debrett, officers of the army and navy, members of Parliament, justices of the peace, and even brethren of the cloth.[18] Among those present were the young Prince of Wales, Charles Dickens, William Thackeray, and famed caricaturist Thomas Nast, who was sent over by the *New York Illustrated News*. The presence of so many British journalists was a sight to behold, Miles wrote, while the attendance of the editorial and pictorial staffs of *Wilkes' Spirit of the Times* and Frank Leslie's *Illustrated Newspaper* gave an international dimension to proceedings and demonstrated the huge interest generated by the contest in the United States. When the men stripped, a single glance at Heenan was sufficient to show that his condition was all that could be desired, while Sayers's physique also showed evidence of strict attention to his work but there was no hiding the difference in size; Heenan was a "horse" to Sayers's "hen," according to Miles. Every muscle on Heenan's broad back, his shoulders, and arms was well developed and gave evidence of enormous power. His legs were rather light but there was no lack here of "wire" and activity, while his skin was exceedingly fair and transparent, shining like that of a thoroughbred. Heenan looked older than Miles had expected but his "mug was hard" and dominated by prominent cheekbones. On the other hand, the Englishman looked brown and hard as nails and his well-knit frame seemed fitter than it had been for years, while the only points in which there appeared any advantage on his side were in his "loins and his legs, which were cast in a decidedly stronger mold than those of his towering opponent." There was no doubt in Miles's mind that Sayers had his work cut out. When the duel finally got underway it proved to be a monstrous, blood-soaked and chaotic affair. In the thirty-seventh round, after two hours and six minutes, the ring was surrounded by policemen and utter chaos ensued. With a ring half full of people a further five rounds somehow took place. In his account of the fight Miles had the unpleasant duty of reporting that Heenan engaged in unmanly and unfair conduct which should have seen him disqualified. In the fourth additional round Sayers was sitting on his second's knee when Heenan rushed at him in a very excited state, let fly left and right at Tom's seconds, floored them, and kicked at them when on the ground in desperate style. After a wild rally, the two protagonists fell to the ground together. A reporter from *Bell's Life* described the farcical end of the encounter thus:

> The final round was merely a wild scramble, both men ordered to desist from fighting.
> The Blues being now in force, there was, of course, no chance of the men continuing, and

adjournment was necessary. Heenan had rushed away from the ring, and ran some distance with the activity of a deer, and although he was as fit as ever, he was obviously totally blind. Sayers, although tired, was also strong on his pins and could have fought some time longer, although by then the authorities were up in arms in all directions, so it would be a mere waste of time to go elsewhere.[19]

(The "Blues" referred to were the police authorities who put a stop to proceedings.)

William Thackeray wrote a parody of Macaulay's "Lays of Ancient Rome" about the fight, calling it "The Combat of Sayerius and Heenanus," which was also published in *Punch* and made reference to the aforementioned blues:

> Fain would I Shroud the tale in night—
> The meddling Blues that thrust in sight—
> The ring-keepers o'erthrown;
> The broken ropes—th' encumbered fight—
> Heenanus' sudden blinded flight,
> Sayerius pausing, as he might,
> Just when ten minutes, used aright,
> Had made the day his own![20]

After forty-two rounds played out over two hours the referee had no choice but to declare a draw, with the fighters sharing the £400 purse. Henry Downes Miles thought the encounter was the very best championship fight he had ever witnessed until the unfortunate departure of the referee and that it had been conducted "with manliness, fairness, and a determination on both sides worthy of the highest commendation." The "gluttony and bottom" of Tom Sayers was remarkable and, despite rumors to the contrary, "a gamer, more determined fellow, never pulled off a shirt" than Heenan. Miles was willing to forgive the American's behavior at the end of the fight, suggesting that the fighter may not have been able to see properly. Both England and America had shown they possessed brave sons, and Miles called on his fellow Englishmen to subscribe to a trophy for Heenan in acknowledgment of his enterprise and boldness.

After the brutal encounter, Sayers retreated to The Swan, a pub on Old Kent Road, to drink champagne, while Heenan was forced to spend forty-eight hours in a darkened room in Osborne's Hotel. Elements of the American press believed that the English authorities had stopped the fight in order to save their money, with the *New York Herald* particularly outspoken. It believed John Bull was growing old and shaky around his pins and could keep his five-pound notes. America did not need his money and was now capable of defeating him in yachts, clipper ships, steamboats, India-rubber shoes, city railways, sewing machines, the electric telegraph, reading machines, pretty women, and unpickable bank locks.[21] In his memoirs, the statesman Henry Cabot Lodge recalled his reaction as a young boy. "The manner in which the English crowd broke the ropes ... filled me with an anger which I still think just. It was my first experience of what is called fair play in England, and I do not think that I ever wholly recovered from it."[22]

On May 30 the *Times* eloquently described the presentation of a championship belt to both men by Frank Dowling, Esq., editor of *Bell's Life*, and G. Wilkes, Esq., editor of the New York *Spirit of the Times*:

America and England shake hands cordially to-day. What our greatest diplomatists and engineers have failed to achieve has been accomplished by the Benicia Boy and Tom Sayers, whose fame will descend to future generations, and whose posterity will each be enabled to show a *fac-simile* of that much desired "belt," so boldly challenged, so manfully defended. The Atlantic cable has not linked the two nations together, but the good feeling which has been shown by the two gladiators, who on this day receive at the Alhambra their respective "belts," will be responded to by the two nations on either side of the Atlantic. We have been favored with a view of the old belt, "the belt" still open to competition, and of the two other belts to be presented to the "two Champions of England," for such is the inscription upon the case of each. Both are precisely similar in every respect, and the somewhat clumsy workmanship, in frosted silver, carefully copied from the original, is by Mr. C.F. Hancock, of Bruton Street.

Within a couple of days, Prime Minister Lord Palmerston was being asked some searching questions in the British Parliament about the barbarity of the event. The eventual outcome was the establishment of a new code of conduct, the "Dozen Rules," drawn up by the London Amateur Athletic Club and sponsored by John Sholto Douglas, the ninth Marquess of Queensberry. From then on there would be three-minute rounds with a minute interval between them, compulsory gloves, padded ringside stanchions, ten-second counts on knockdown and no further wrestling moves. Thus, the Queensberry Rules came into being.

Heenan demanded a rematch but Sayers could not accept the challenge because he had badly damaged his arm in the fight; in the end the boxers went on a joint tour of what was then the Kingdom of Great Britain and Ireland. When they fought in Dublin in June *The Irish Times* was less than impressed and noted that the extraordinary exhibition had engrossed the thoughts and occupied the hours of every "bully, sot, roué, and 'fast man' in the metropolis for several days."[23] Half a century later, the fight was mentioned in James Joyce's famous modernist novel *Ulysses,* where his alter ego Stephen Dedalus stops outside a Dublin shop in the Wandering Rocks episode: "In Clohissey's window a faded 1860 print of Heenan boxing Sayers held his eye. Staring backers with square hats stood round the roped prizering. The heavyweights in light loin cloths proposed gently to each other his bulbous fists. And they are throbbing: heroes' hearts."[24]

Heenan set sail for the United States on July 4 but was forced to leave his newly acquired championship belt behind as security against money advanced to the jeweler who had made it, although he may have been heartened when Sayers and his son Owen turned up at Southampton to wish him a safe return to America. *Bell's Life* noted that such cheering had never been heard before between the walls of the station.[25] The Benicia Boy was also greeted as a hero on his arrival home and given the princely sum of $10,000 which had been collected by public subscription while celebratory cannon salutes were fired in his honor on both sides of the Mason–Dixon Line. He toured the country for nine months, visiting scores of cities in the North and South and reenacting the fight for his adoring public. Heenan refused offers to run for Congress and to serve in the Confederate Army, but on his way to St. Louis he made a detour to meet with Abraham Lincoln in Springfield, Missouri.

In March 1862 Heenan again departed a Civil War-torn America for England, this time to fight Tom King for the world title. On March 17, 1863, the men signed articles to the effect that a bout between them would take place on the following

December 8 within 100 miles of London.[26] Inevitably, there were suspicions that the arrangements would come to nothing, but Heenan was assiduous in his training. When Miles saw him he thought the American was "a model for a sculptor" and that every muscle was developed to a gigantic size, every tendon and sinew distinctly visible; taken altogether, he doubted whether such a specimen of a Herculean frame had been witnessed in Britain for very many years. Miles was particularly impressed when he learned that Heenan had sent a message to his backers stating that if he did not defeat King he should be considered the greatest impostor who ever entered the ring. After the inevitable prevarications and stonewalling, the contest eventually took place on September 10, 1863, in Wadhurst, with the American an overwhelming favorite to take the title. Just as both men were stripped and ready to fight, an objection was lodged as to the choice of referee, and three-quarters of an hour passed as the authorities sought in vain to get a mutually agreeable replacement before a journalist from *Bell's Life* was eventually tasked with the job. George Henning was in attendance and contentedly noted that "never did a handsomer, finer brace of pugilists step into the arena."[27] King was the taller of the combatants but a stone (14 pounds) lighter, as Heenan had filled out considerably since his encounter with Tom Sayers. This fact, in the eyes of Henning, was to Heenan's detriment, for his efforts seemed clumsy and his limbs were unwieldy. Nor was his facial expression a good omen: "He ... wore a jaded expression upon closer inspection, although he kept up a cheerful expression," while King was as serious as a mute at a funeral. On balance, however, the Londoner looked better than Miles had seen him before, with his smooth, white skin, glistening like polished ivory in the morning sun. Miles thought there was a bloom and healthfulness about King which he put down to a good training regime allied to a good diet. Heenan started strongly but the wily English fighter soon landed a number of damaging blows to the American's face. In the fifth round, King landed a telling blow which "sounded like the splash of a wet fish thrown on a marble slab." In the fourteenth round many in the crowd thought the fight had come to an end when Heenan threw his arms around King and lifted him off the ground like "a bear or a boa constrictor." The Benicia Boy proceeded to throw his opponent to the ground, and when King's seconds rolled him over to take him back to his corner, his head fell back, and his half-closed eyes had a vacant, glazed look, with his arms swinging limply at his side. One of King's seconds rushed to the referee, claiming his fighter had been kicked, allowing the American crucial further seconds to recover. King's corner man whispered desperately into his fighter's ear that his mother was badly in need of the money, and although Heenan was virtually blind by then, he managed to hit King with a savage blow to the face, knocking him onto his back. The American proceeded to throw the Englishman to the ground a number of times, but his efforts seemed to take more out of Heenan than they did King. Eventually the boxers faced each other like two drunken men with the "Yankee apparently in a state of stupor," before King finally gathered his senses and knocked Heenan out in the twenty-fourth round.[28] Miles was deeply unimpressed by the fight, which had been characterized by "clinching, rushing, squeezing, and attempts at strangulating hugs" on the one side and "wild, desperate sledge-hammer defensive hitting" on the other. Heenan had merely shown that "sheer brute strength, seconded by weight, stature, and a certain amount of mere animal courage" were his only qualifications as a fighter. The American had little idea of sparring for an opening, or as a means of defense, while skillful feints, well-timed delivery, accurate measurement of distance, or getting close and then getting away, as practiced by professional boxers, were beyond him. It was not Tom King's fault that the fight had been such a poor spectacle, and if he had been presented with a better opponent he would have shown more of his art, according to Miles. As always, there was controversy. The American's corner men pointed out that King had been given longer to recover after the eighteenth round than was legal, while Heenan later claimed his collapse was a result of having been drugged by the English camp. Notwithstanding, the result entered the record books.

The Benicia Boy went on to establish himself as a racetrack bookmaker but was to have ill luck on June 9, 1864, when he was involved in a collision between two trains at Egham in Surrey. Newspaper reported that he jumped from the train when passengers were warned of the impending collision and that he damaged his spine so badly he suffered a series of fits.[29] By October 1861 there were press reports that Adah Isaacs Menken had been reunited with a previous partner named R.H. Newell. She successfully sued Heenan for divorce in Woodstock, Illinois, claiming that he had scrounged off her earnings, although he claimed the pair had never been married. Despite their divorce she continued to call herself Mrs. Heenan. A later biography of Isaacs noted that it was generally known that Heenan had treated her in the "most brutal and ignominious manner."[30] Some time after their divorce, newspapers uncovered the fact that she had not yet been legally divorced from her second husband, Alexander Menken. A woman called Josephine Heenan claimed that she, in fact, was John Heenan's wife, not Adah.

Heenan returned to the United States in 1865, where he found mixed success in the gambling business, as well as getting married to Sarah Stevens. In 1870 he appeared in *Hamlet*, taking the role of Laertes alongside English fighter James "Jem" Mace.[31] Eight years after his return to America, Heenan contracted tuberculosis and decided to move to the clearer air of Green River Station, Wyoming, where he died on October 28, 1873. Jim Cusack, his former manager, brought his body back to New York where he was buried at Saint Agnes Cemetery, Watervliet, on November 2, 1873. The *South London Chronicle* reported his death in a brief column, noting that he "never was and never could be a first-class fighting man. He was a brave and athletic man, but neither quick nor artful, nor capable of administering rapid punishment."[32] Perhaps his most lasting legacy to the sport came from the outcry generated by the sheer brutality of his encounter with Tom Sayers resulting in the development of the Queensberry Rules.

Four

"The Adopted Son of America"
Joe Coburn

> Let the Englishman no longer boast nor Paddy's son degrade / For now they must surrender to our gallant Irish Blade.
> —From *The Cowardly Englishman*[1]

WHEN JOHN HEENAN REFUSED TO FIGHT Joe Coburn in 1862, the County Armagh-born boxer claimed the American title and yet another Irishman became the Emperor of Masculinity. Coburn, born Joseph Henry Coburn on July 29, 1835, in a small farmhouse in the parish of Middleton, departed Ireland with his parents Michael Coburn and Mary Trainor at the height of the Great Famine in Ireland in 1850 at the age of fifteen.[2] Like his father before him, the young Coburn worked as a bricklayer, while also volunteering as a fireman with the Croton Engine Company on West Twentieth Street in the sixteenth ward in Manhattan.[3] As a fighter, Coburn was known for his speed and did not have to depend entirely on brute strength as many others of the time did. Weighing only 145 pounds, Coburn was considered a precocious boxing talent, and was adjudged to have skills comparable to the finest sparring instructors in America.[4] Furthermore, unlike many other fighters of his era, Coburn expressed a willingness to face any man, bar none, a

Joseph Coburn, born in County Armagh in modern-day Northern Ireland in 1835, claimed the title in 1862 when John Heenan refused to fight him (Mathew Brady Studio, Frederick Hill Reserve Collection, National Portrait Gallery, Smithsonian Institution).

bravery and bravado which greatly appealed to New York City's workingclass Irish population.[5] He first caught the wider attention of the prize-fighting cognoscenti by beating the notorious Hezekiah Orville "Awful" Gardner in six rounds at Hibernia Hall on Prince Street, although his official debut is recorded when, at the age of twenty-one, he took on an English lawyer by the name of Ned Price at Still Pond, Massachusetts.[6] Price, though "a game man," was not among the sport's elite and, according to one journalist, his punches lacked the necessary force to win a battle.[7] The *Brooklyn Daily Eagle* thought Coburn possessed "a blow like a pistol shot."[8] The fight lasted a grueling three hours and twenty-five minutes, played out over 100 brutal rounds, and when darkness descended, the referee was forced to bring proceedings to a halt and declare the match a draw.[9] Upon his return to New York, Coburn's marathon prizefight with Price was celebrated by fellow boxers who conducted a sparring benefit in his honor at the famous Kerrigan's Hall.[10] The injuries sustained by both men were so horrendous that they were forced to stay indoors for two weeks and, perhaps not surprisingly, Price refused a rematch and decided to concentrate on his legal career, never entering the ring again. At his postvictory benefit, Coburn sparred with Harry Gribben of Belfast, with whom he agreed to contest a prize-fight in Canada West for $500 a piece the following year. A veteran of five fights by that stage in his career, Gribben was ten years older than Coburn and had three victories to his credit, an indication of how rarely some of the bare-knuckle fighters took to the ring. Coburn insisted Gribben weigh in at 147 pounds for the contest, ten pounds below his typical competition weight. On the day, Gribben weighed in at exactly the requisite weight limit but looked tired and overtrained, while Coburn weighed in at 145½ pounds. Known for administering devastating uppercuts, Gribben did not manage to get his shots off with his normal power, and Coburn controlled the fight from the beginning with his counterpunching game. The twenty-first round was to prove decisive. Gribben led off with his left but missed, receiving in return a terrific left-handed hit immediately below the region of the heart, and as he was falling, Coburn caught him again, this time on the right side of the face. With their man in trouble, Gribben's corner threw in the sponge, admitting defeat.[11] Not all journalists were impressed, however. According to the *New York Clipper,* some within the sporting community considered Gribben a "stale, played out fighter," whose defeat reflected no credit or honor on his victor. While the journalist acknowledged Coburn's superior science, he contended that much of the result could be put down to advantages in size and strength. Following the match, Coburn was honored with a sold-out sparring benefit at Montgomery Hall in New York, where he offered to fight "any man in America at 148 pounds, for any amount of money," or Harry Gribben again at his own weight. Due to his propensity for criminal behavior, Coburn's career as a professional prize-fighter entered a hiatus following his victory over Gribben. On January 11, 1858, a warrant for his arrest was issued in New York City after he broke into a saloon and assaulted the female owner. When Coburn and fellow prize-fighter Jim Hughes viciously attacked a police officer the following month, Coburn was held on $500 bail for his January attack on the saloon proprietress and an additional $1,000 for assaulting the officer. Luckily for Coburn Councilman Thomas Dunn put up $1,500 required to bail out the prizefighter.[12] Coburn had agreed to fight "Australian" James Kelly in December, but his criminal impulses got the better of him once again when he stabbed a police officer on Houston Street on December 12, leaving the man struggling for his life.[13] Coburn forfeited his stake and went into hiding, only coming back into circulation when the police officer recovered.[14] When he turned himself into the authorities, Coburn was held on $3,000 bail, a sum paid by one Matthew Hilleck of Eighth Avenue.[15] On May 7, 1859, Coburn was brought before Judge Davies for sentencing and was tried by the Court of Oyer and Terminer, a body used only in serious criminal cases and intended to prevent any political interference. Coburn pleaded guilty to assault with a dangerous weapon and received a sentence of three years of hard labor at Sing Sing Prison.[16] Upon his release from incarceration it was evident that he had lost none of his love for the ring, and when a sparring benefit was organized for Coburn on May 26, 1862, at the City Assembly Rooms against English fighter Bill Clarke, it was evident that he still had the fighting goods. After positive reviews, Coburn and Clarke agreed to contest a gloved fight for $200 a side on January 28, 1863, at a time when gloved fights and sparring were considered the same by the authorities.

The gloves used at the fight in Mozart Hall were blackened with bone char, resulting in a mark left on the part of the opponent struck with a successful blow, while only strikes to the head were counted, with a strict thirty-minute time limit observed. Defensive boxing would thus be key. The *New York Times* enthusiastically reported that Coburn and Clarke performed before a group of spectators which "in point of respectability and social standing, would have compared favorably with any assemblage that has of late been gathered within the spacious auditorium of Mozart Hall," pointing out approvingly that the occasion was marked by patriotism and orderly behavior. Given Coburn's recent past, it almost amounted to giving him a free pass. The contest, not the contestants, was the big story. The *New York Herald* was equally impressed and urged further similar encounters because it thought the greatest order and decorum had prevailed in a contest devoid of the usual repulsive features of the prize ring. Coburn won the encounter on a count of eleven punches to ten and took home the $400 purse. However, his recidivistic criminal predilections were once more shortly in evidence when he was arrested for throwing a sixteen-pound dumbbell at a woman named Cecelia Lyon, striking her in the chest. Luckily for Coburn, she was unable to attend court to testify and he was released without charge.[17]

On May 5, 1863, Coburn, now billed as "The Adopted Son of America," defended his crown when he took on Mike "The Terror of Mississippi" McCoole in Charleston, Maryland.

Coburn started as favorite but McCoole, although a slower and less technically proficient fighter, had a distinct weight advantage. Once again the fight proved to be a brutal marathon and, despite being thrown to the ground several times and being at the receiving end of some shuddering thumps, Coburn managed to get in telling punches throughout the course of the bout. In the sixty-third round he looked like he was going to drop from exhaustion but managed to rally once again. Four rounds later McCoole finally gave up the ghost and had to be carried away on a cart by his supporters. The barbaric encounter had lasted sixty-eight minutes. The general consensus among the assembled journalists was that Coburn had been the better stylist, with the *New York Herald* noting that he had "fought with a coolness, judgment and science which surprised even his warmest friends." His straight, quick, and well-timed hitting and admirable judgment of distance prevented McCoole from establishing any momentum in the contest, it contended.[18] While some thought the contest a mismatch, the *New York Clipper* concluded that Coburn had proved himself a thoroughly clever, scientific, and game boxer and was entitled to be called the Champion of America.[19] At 152 pounds, Coburn became the lightest boxer to win the heavyweight championship in a bare-knuckle prize fight, significantly below John Morrissey's previous mark of 175 pounds.[20]

Like many an Irish immigrant before and after him, Coburn invested part of his winnings in a tavern, going into partnership with veteran Civil War Captain James Saunders, formerly of the 69th Regiment New York Volunteers. The White House, located at 113 Grand Street, just off Broadway, was, according to the *New York Clipper*, the finest saloon of its kind in the city and provided a separate private room for sparring, in addition to the main bar.[21]

An encounter between Coburn and British champion Jem Mace had first been mooted the previous year by *The Era*, the foremost weekly sporting publication of the time in England. Mace, it argued, had no opponent in the country worthy of the name and was on the lookout for a proper challenge; it believed Coburn was that man. Mace had been hoping to get a tilt at Tom King, who had beaten him in 1863, but King had retired after defeating Heenan in the same year. In March it was agreed in principle that a fight between Coburn and Mace would take place in the south of Ireland in October, with the finer details to be ironed out subsequently. Mace and his backers provided Coburn with $500 for travel and expenses, but additional money was needed to make the contest a reality, so Saunders put the White House tavern up for sale, including the alcohol and fixtures and fittings.[22] Coburn also raised money by conducting a sparring tour of the northeast with stops in Boston, Hartford, Philadelphia, and Pittsburgh.[23] He performed one last benefit in Manhattan on May 10, where, according to one journalist, he filled the City Assembly Rooms with a diverse crowd including "the army and navy, mechanic, tradesman, gentleman of leisure, gambulier, parson, and all classes," as well as "the Fenian Brotherhood and other patriotic societies."[24] Earlier in the year, saloon proprietors Bob Smith, Israel Lazarus, Ed Wilson, and Harry Hill had set about raising money for a championship belt for the Irishman, but an initial belt benefit held on February 26, 1864, at the City Assembly Rooms, with sparring, singing, and dancing, failed to meet its financial target, leaving the acquisition of a suitable belt in jeopardy.[25] Eventually a group of benefactors came up with the requisite funding, and Coburn was able to depart on the *City of Washington* steamer with 3,000 well-wishers crowded on the docks to see the champion set sail with an appropriate symbol of his pugilistic supremacy.[26]

According to *The Irish Times*, Coburn insisted the fight proceed, with a referee to be selected at ringside. Mace was less eager to consummate the contest, offering to pay Coburn's travel expenses to the United States back and offering to reschedule the fight for a future date in Canada West. Coburn had been in training in Ballingoola, County Limerick, and was disgusted with what he believed was cowardice on the behalf of Mace. During his stint in Limerick he took time out to visit his birthplace in Armagh. He stayed in the Charlemont Arms Hotel, where, according to the *Belfast Newsletter*, the foyer was stormed by a large number of citizens anxious to meet their hometown hero and regale him with tales of his forebears.[27] While in England, he gave lectures in the art of self-defense in Liverpool to help cover the expenses of his 3,500-mile trip, but after the proposed fight fell through, an out-of-pocket Coburn left Cork by an Inman steamship on October 20, 1864, never to return to his native Ireland.[28]

Following the fiasco, Coburn refrained from prize-fighting for the remainder of the Civil War era. Disgusted with the sport, he retired in 1865, leaving the title to Mike McCoole. However, when the opportunity arose to fight Jem Mace in 1871, he could not resist the call of the ring and once again traveled across the Atlantic Ocean prepared to do battle on behalf of his country. Once again there was high anticipation across the British Isles as the fight neared. Crowds went in droves to see Mace sparring in preparation for the encounter; over 400 people went to see him practice at Dundee's Corn Exchange Hall alone. After arriving in Liverpool on June 3, Coburn began his preparations, while also giving lectures in self-defense in an effort to defray some of his expenses. Henry Downes Miles was not impressed by the way Coburn's representatives negotiated the finer details of the fight, noting that the discussions were conducted with "a Yankee cuteness and caviling that were suspiciously suggestive of knavery rather than straightforward honesty of purpose." Miles's comments were reflective of an era when relationships between Britain and the United States were becoming increasingly tetchy.

Nor was Miles overly impressed with Coburn. His face, with its decidedly Roman arch of a nose and hatchet-shaped head, was not that of a proper pugilist, he believed. Miles also bemoaned the demise of the gentlemen and philanthropists who had once run boxing and believed they had been replaced by a "clamorous crew of sharp practitioners, loud-mouthed disputants, and tricky match-makers." In Britain, fighters were now backed by the "ill-gotten gains of the keepers of low gambling hells and night-houses," while the Americans were funded by "the proprietors of bar-rooms, drinking-saloons, and the large crowd of loungers, loafers, and rowdies who hang on the skirts of the Sporting World of the Great Republic," he fulminated.[29]

The editor of *Bell's Life* believed Mace had been treated harshly, that Coburn never had the slightest intention of fighting, that he had not even trained and that he was a mere instrument in the hands of others. The journalist also thought that the encounter would be marred by some trick of "Yankee juggling" and that the cunning American had no intention of exposing himself to Mace's "handy digits." The focus then switched to Ireland, where the two men were to fight. Cardinal Paul Cullen, the Archbishop of Dublin, issued a Pastoral Letter to his priests instructing them to call on their flocks to preserve Christian Ireland from "an exhibition so disgraceful, and so well calculated to degrade human nature."[30] The clerics were to tell their parishioners that the fighters, their seconds, and spectators would be excommunicated in accordance with Pope Benedict XIV's interpretation of the decrees issued by the Council of Trent. If they were firm in their denunciation of the "misdeeds of foreign gladiators" such action could be avoided. Miles was shocked that the letter was printed in a newspaper which also reported dispassionately on a savage assault in which a man had his nose bitten off. He could only agree with Lord Lyndhurst, who had described the Irish as "aliens in blood, in language, and religion." Miles believed the Pastoral Letter was a hoax and reprinted two pieces from English newspapers on the issue, the first of which was a letter sent by J.F.T. to the *Manchester Guardian* published on October 5.

In the buildup to the big match Coburn had victories over Joe Goss, Tom Allen, and Bill Rayel, three pugilists Mace had instructed the Irishman to fight before he deigned to take him on. In the eyes of the English bookmakers Mace was the slight favorite with odds of seven to four. When Coburn arrived in Ireland at the start of July he received a decidedly mixed response. While prize-fighting enthusiasts were delighted to see their native son return home as champion, the Catholic Church, an ever increasing power in postfamine Ireland, did not share these sentiments. There was also considerable confusion about the details of the bout. On September 20, Coburn failed to turn up for a scheduled meeting at Harry Brunton's pub in Dublin where the finer details of the impending clash were to be discussed. Brunton, who was acting as Mace's agent, suspected that Coburn might have had second thoughts. Some days later, Mr. E. James, editor of the *New York Clipper* and representative of Coburn, arrived in England and contacted the *Birmingham Daily Post* seeking to meet Mace's representatives. After establishing the desired link, James won a coin toss and the pair agreed to meet in Dublin at a later date, when a venue and referee would then be decided. It appeared, at that stage, that the contest would go ahead, and anticipation mounted in Ireland despite continued clerical admonitions. Newspapers reported that famous fighters Nat Langham and Jack "The Elastic Potboy" Hicks, due to work as ring keepers at the impending fight, were seen socializing in James Woodroffe's Tavern in Dublin. John Heenan was said to be on the island, while Prince Humbert of Italy, a well-known member of the fancy, was reportedly on his way to see the fight. When the location was finally unveiled as Powerstown in Tipperary, thousands thronged to the small village. However, Jem Mace refused to travel. He did not agree with the choice of referee, believing that the Mr. Bowler tasked with the job was actually a brother-in-law of his adversary.[31]

While Coburn insisted that a more honorable man had never stood on Irish soil, Mace retreated to England. Coburn was further aggrieved when Mace informed him that his representative, Mr. Brunton, had departed Dublin with the fight funds in tow. Bitterly disappointed, Joe Coburn set sail from Cork to New York, never to return to his native land.

"The Cowardly Englishman," a street ballad which acquired considerable popularity in Ireland, expressed the bitterness felt by Coburn's supporters:

> The Englishmen bet five to one that Mace would gain the day,
> But indeed they were mistaken for poor Jem he ran away,
> Our champion boldly stood the ring without either dread or fear,
> But he was disappointed Jem Mace did not appear.
> There were many of our cousins got ready on that day,
> And followed gallant Coburn in hopes to see some play,

> With gold and silver plenty both in pocket and in purse,
> Jem Mace for his great cowardice got many a heavy curse.[32]

Jem Mace and Joe Coburn eventually fought, a full seven years later, in Bay Saint Louis, Mississippi, but by then, few New Yorkers were willing to travel to see the fight. The prohibitive distance and expense of getting there, combined with the possibility that it could again be canceled at the last minute, meant many of the fancy were reluctant to risk going, although Henning noted that some of the "greatest roughs of New York were able to purchase tickets and spoil the select company that was supposed to have things all their own way."[33] In the end a crowd of around 1000 people assembled to see the contest. After three and a half hours in the ring the fight was nowhere near a resolution and the patient referee, Colonel Rufus Hart, warned the men that he would bring the contest to a conclusion if they did not make more strenuous efforts. After allowing them a chance to make amends, the official finally had enough and declared the fight a draw. The combatants met for a second time in the same venue on November 3, just over five weeks later. This time Mace injured his hand in the fifth round but continued to fight on. However, torrential rain forced the encounter to come to an abrupt end in the twelfth and the match was again declared a draw.[34]

On March 6, 1877, Coburn was sentenced to a ten-year stint in Auburn Prison for assault with intent to kill police officer William Tobias and ended up spending six and a half years in incarceration. After his release from jail, Coburn fought seven successful exhibition bouts with the highly popular champion John L. Sullivan from December 1882 through March 1883, as well as three with Herbert Slade in April.[35] However, trouble was never far away from Coburn, and on May 17, 1885, he was arrested on the complaint of Charles Carter, who claimed that he had been robbed of $950 by Coburn at his saloon on Broadway. Luckily for Coburn, the charge was later dropped when Carter refused to formally file the complaint.[36] At the age of fifty-four, Coburn had his last bout in the ring on December 14, 1888, against "Professor" William Clarke in Cleveland, a contest he lost on points.[37]

Joe Coburn was to spend his last years alcoholic, tubercular, and poverty stricken and died on December 6, 1890, at the age of fifty-five. A few days before his death a group of his friends raised $1,000 in a benefit for him at Lexon Hall. Coburn is buried in Calvary Cemetery, Queens, New York, and, despite his criminal predilections, was inducted into the International Boxing Hall of Fame under the pioneer category in 2013.

Five

Jimmy Elliot

When Jim Coburn refused to fight Jimmy Elliot for the heavyweight championship of America, yet another Irish man claimed the title. By all accounts, James "Jimmy" Elliot was a formidable character. Born in Athlone, County Westmeath, in March 1838, Elliot immigrated to New York with his family when only an infant.[1] Shortly after their arrival in the new world his father abandoned the family and Elliot was forced to work a series of casual jobs from a young age, before eventually gravitating toward street gangs. In time-honored tradition, it was in these environs that he quickly gained a formidable reputation as a fighter, which he soon parlayed into prize-fighting. Standing over six feet tall, the Irishman was once memorably described as having the appearance of an untamable bull and being the possessor of an uncontainable temper, perfect requisites for the barbarity often associated with the sport in that era.[2] Despite his impressive physicality, Elliot, just turned fifteen years of age, came out on the wrong side of his first major fight, a typically ferocious contest against Nobby Clarke which lasted just under an hour over thirty-four rounds in Palisades, New Jersey, on May 25, 1861. On January 6 of the following year he fought Hen Winkle at Bull's Ferry near Weehawken, New Jersey, for a purse of $500.[3] Given the illegality of bare-knuckle fighting in New York at the time, the venture had to be carefully planned. A small group of 100 spectators avoided police intervention by remaining "shady and quiet" when organizing their excursion to New Jersey.[4] In addition to the required secrecy, the day of the contest was marred by heavy snowfall, further reducing the number of spectators. Just as the bout was entering its second hour, after ninety-five punishing rounds, the crowd grew restless and rushed the ring. The ensuing all-out melee had to be broken up by the police. The unfortunate Elliot was kicked by a spectator, but afterward Winkle's backers claimed that the Irishman had used a deadly grasp about his throat to gain an advantage. Kicking Elliot, claimed Winkle's supporters, was the only way to break the Irishman's stranglehold. Hoping to avoid a general scrimmage between the spectators, seconds, officials, and pugilists, both sides agreed to declare the contest a draw.[5]

The nature of the contest did not deter Elliot from continuing with his fighting career. On May 13, 1863, he took on fellow Irishman James Dunn from Brooklyn in front of a drunken mob in New Jersey.[6] The men had originally intended to fight on May 11 on Staten Island, but were prevented from doing so by the Metropolitan Police. They reconvened on May 13 at Bull's Ferry. Local authorities were aware of the impending prize-fight, and when the sheriff of Hudson County appeared and ordered the crowd to disperse, the fighters, seconds, officials, and spectators ignored the warning. By dint of sheer numbers they knew a single law enforcement official would prove little deterrence. The sheriff made an abrupt about-face and the contest went ahead. As was so often the case at the time, arrangements were rudimentary and far from ideal. The ropes were so loosely hung from the posts that spectators were able to lean in over the ring. Some of the onlookers even had their feet inside the ring, and such were the numbers pushing from behind that some were unable to turn to follow the action. In the third round Dunn knocked Elliot to the ground, managing to repeat the feat in the eighth. Elliot scored his first knockdown in the ninth and repeated the action in the next. After twelve rounds of vicious fighting, controversy erupted when one of Dunn's corner men called foul. According to the *New York Clipper*, Elliot pinned Dunn to the edge of the ring and hit him several times when he was bent backward over the ropes.[7] Referee Michael "Crow" Norton agreed with Dunn's corner and gave their man the nod. The fight had lasted a brutal thirty-four minutes and, once again, the general consensus was that Elliot should have taken the laurels. As spectators made their way out of the venue, local police officers arrested many of them, much to the chagrin of the *Clipper*: "Our neighbors in the Sandy State are a little too severe on New Yorkers upon whom they lay their clutches. Surely there is no great offense committed in looking at an exhibition of the manly art of self-defense." The *Clipper* was particularly incensed given the background of the ongoing war: "Some of our pugilists, and a number of supporters of pugilism have served their country in the war now going on; there are many still in the ranks of the Union Army, assisting to defend the stars and stripes. Fight is now the word everywhere and why should the prize ring be tabooed." Many spectators were held by New Jersey authorities until bail, set at $500, was secured by each detainee.[8] Following the Dunn–Elliot fight, the *Trenton State Gazette* expressed its outrage by publishing the state's laws regarding prize-fighting, noting that any person engaging in a prize fight in the state, and any person aiding, assisting, or abetting one, was liable to a fine of $1000 or imprisonment at hard labor for two years, or both.[9] The police established a manhunt for Elliot but he managed to go to ground. He might have thought the authorities had given up the chase when he resurfaced to participate in a sparring benefit in Newark, New Jersey, on December 21.[10] He managed to travel between New Jersey and New York without harassment, a journey which may have made him overconfident. When Dooney Harris and Patsy Marley were matched for a prizefight to take place in Pennsylvania in 1864, Elliot volunteered his services as Harris's second, traveling through New Jersey bound for Pennsylvania. While Elliot was en route to Pennsylvania, the New Jersey police were informed of his whereabouts and he was duly arrested at Jersey City for the crime of participating in the prize-fight with Dunn the previous year. According to the *New York Clipper*, Elliot was most likely to have been turned in by some vindictive person or an enemy, because the paper believed the officer would not have known him from any other man in the normal course of events.[11] Thinking they would be able to buy his way out of difficulty, his backers set about establishing a fund, but they were soon disabused of this notion when a Bergen court sentenced Elliot to two years in prison and imposed a $500 fine. The *Clipper* cried foul and looked upon Elliot's sentence as severe and unjust because even murderous duels had gone unpunished over the previous two decades in the jurisdiction.[12] In June 1865, having served just two years of his sentence, Elliot immediately challenged James Coburn for the title, and when Coburn refused to fight, Elliot claimed the crown. He issued an open challenge to any man to fight him for any sum from $1,000 to $10,000, but found few challengers as the prize-fighting game had fallen into a slump in the meantime. Inevitably, Elliot became involved in petty crime and protection jobs to support a lifestyle which revolved around alcohol and gambling.

In 1866 he took part in a singular event in Irish American history when he joined the Fenians in an attack on British forts in Canada, one of a series of raids between 1886 and 1871. The Fenian Brotherhood, established in 1848 as an Irish government in exile, had its own constitution, senate, president, and capitol building at Union Square in Manhattan. Elliot was a trenchant Irish nationalist and saw the presence of English Protestants in North America as an injustice which needed to be addressed.

Under the leadership of Thomas William Sweeney, the Fenians set out with the avowed aim of capturing the colony of Canada for Ireland. They aimed to seize the transportation network, hoping this would force the British to exchange Ireland's freedom for possession of their Canadian territory. In early June, 850 Fenians led by John O'Neill crossed the Niagara River, establishing a bridgehead near Fort Erie. They then advanced westward toward Port Colborne. However, George T.C. Napier, the commander of British forces in Canada West, acted decisively. Within a short period, in total 20,000 Canadian troops were under arms and British regiments were on the march. Some 900 men from the 2nd and 13th Battalions as well as the York and Caledonia Rifle Companies, under the command of Alfred Booker, were sent to Dunville. Another column of troops, under George Peacocke, was en route to Chippawa, from where Peacocke assumed command of the British and Canadian troops. To contain the threat posed by the Fenians, Peacocke ordered Booker to Port Colborne. Booker found 600 Fenians at Ridgeway and deployed his men. The battle opened well for the Canadians, who, despite their inexperience, held their own under fire. It was not until someone ordered them to prepare for cavalry and adopt a defensive formation that the tide turned: The Fenians were able to exploit the situation, forcing the Canadians from the field. Nine Canadians were killed and thirty-two wounded, while the Fenians lost ten men and had an unknown number wounded. Later that day the steamship *W.T. Robb*, crewed by the Dunville Naval Brigade and carrying the Welland Canal Volunteer Artillery, landed at Fort Erie, where a fierce skirmish broke out with elements of O'Neill's army that left six Canadians injured with thirty-six taken prisoner. The Fenians lost nine men killed and had fourteen wounded. Shortly afterward, other Canadian troops and elements of the British 16th and 47th Regiments arrived, forcing O'Neill to withdraw his forces back to the United States, where they were promptly arrested. Arguably, the Fenian Raids on Canada did little to advance the Irish cause of nationhood. Instead, they galvanized support for a confederation of Canada and helped develop a sense of Canadian nationalism; Ireland would have to wait for other opportunities to strike for its freedom.

On September 19, 1867, Elliot defeated Bill Davis at Choteau Island, Illinois, in a typically vicious nine-round affair after which the Athlone man could now rightfully declare himself the heavyweight champion of the United States.[13]

On November 12, 1868, he went to battle with Charles Gallagher at the ironically named Peace Park in Detroit in what proved to be yet another contentious and savage encounter.[14] When Elliot started gouging his opponent's eyes in the sixteenth round, Gallagher began to complain to the referee, and as he was making his grievances known, the Irishman came up behind him and struck his opponent viciously in the head. The referee had no hesitation in disqualifying Elliot and, as was so often the case in the early days of bare-knuckle fighting, the local police force had to be drafted in to deal with the ensuing riot.

Jimmy Elliot's wild ways did not stop with his controversial fight with Charles Gallagher. In 1870 he assaulted and robbed the famous black minstrel singer, Hughey Dougherty.[15] When the police arrived on the scene they eventually managed to subdue and arrest the crazed Irish pugilist. Despite pleas from his defense that his mother, wife, and children depended on Elliot for their livelihoods, the judge took a dim view of his misdemeanors and on December 12 he was sentenced to sixteen years and ten months in Eastern State Penitentiary, Philadelphia. After serving eight years he was released in 1879 due to an eye condition (although, at a time when political corruption was rife, there have been suggestions that his release may have had something to do with the influence of New York politician "Big Bill" Dwyer).

Nothing would stop Elliot from returning to the ring, which he did against J.J. Dwyer, a brother of the aforementioned bigwig, in a ferocious encounter, even by the standards pertaining at the time. Some authorities recognize the fight as one for the American title. The vicious bout took place at Long Point, Canada, on May 8, 1879, in front of a paltry crowd of 500. Elliot was not fit and bit Dwyer on the neck in the eighth round. The incensed Dwyer proceeded to knock Elliot out, at which point the fight should have ended, but for some reason, the referee insisted that the Athlone native be brought back to consciousness and the grim encounter continued. The exhausted Elliot reverted to biting and eye gouging before the referee, finally seeing sense, brought the battle to a halt in the twelfth round, deeming Dwyer the winner after Elliot sustained damage to his ribs. Such was the pummeling the victor endured that many said his early death in 1882 was a result of the injuries sustained in the fight. Elliot's eyesight continued to deteriorate, and eventually he could not go outside in the daytime, as the level of discomfort caused by direct sunlight was too much to bear. As the light literally and metaphorically declined, Elliot consistently challenged the emerging John L. Sullivan to a fight. Sullivan refused the challenge on a number of occasions, but Elliot kept chipping away in the press. The Athlone native fought Thomas "The Troy Terror" Egan to impress Sullivan with his credentials and to emphasize the fact that he still had the required boxing smarts, but given that the encounter was Elliot's first fight in fourteen years, it was overwhelmingly likely to have been a fix. Sullivan eventually agreed to a four-round exhibition for which Elliot would be awarded $500 if he could last the distance. The encounter was a noncontest from the start and the 6,000 spectators were inevitably short-changed. Elliot was knocked down three times in the first three rounds and did not make it past the end of the third. Sullivan gave the defeated man $50 for his trouble. Despite his waning powers, Elliot fought Paddy Ryan in a sparring match and even had a knockdown win over Captain James Dalton in the same year. Perhaps inevitably, Elliot was to come to a sticky end. On March 1, 1883, the Irishman was drinking with a friend in the Tivoli Saloon in Chicago when Jer Dunne, a notorious gambler and fierce adversary of Elliot, walked in and approached the two men. An argument over money ensued during which Dunne took out a pistol and shot Elliot. Although a bullet went through the Athlone man's chest, he managed to stand up and throw the table he had been sitting at in Dunne's direction. It hit the assailant and knocked him to the floor. The pair then began to grapple on the ground, where Elliot managed to ready his own pistol and shoot Dunne in the head, but astoundingly, Dunne was only grazed and the pair continued to shoot at each other as they sought cover in the bar. When the shootout was eventually broken up by police, Elliot was placed in an ambulance but it was too late; riddled by bullets, he died in the vehicle before it pulled away, with his last words reportedly being the rather prosaic, "I think I'm killed."[16] Dunne survived and, after a questionably short trial, was found not guilty and released. Jimmy Elliot's funeral was an elaborate affair despite his penurious circumstances. With funding from friends, his corpse was brought in a week-long procession from Chicago to New York, stopping intermittently so that fans could have a final look at the face of their dead hero. The cortege eventually found its way to the house of Elliot's mother in New York, but a patrician journalist from the *New York Times* was not impressed by the funeral: "It was thieves' day on the east side, James Elliot the murdered pugilist, bully, blackguard and burglar was buried, and all the criminals in the city gathered to pay the last honors to his memory."[17] Elliot was forty-five years of age.

Six

"The Terror of Mississippi"
Mike McCoole

"Passage to the United States seems to produce the same effect upon the exile of Erin as the eating of the forbidden fruit did upon Adam and Eve. In the morning, they were pure, loving, and innocent; in the evening guilty."

—*The Liberator*, August 11, 1854

By all accounts Mike "The Terror of Mississippi" McCoole was not conversant with the finer scientific points of boxing. Born on March 12, 1837, in Donegal in the northwest of Ireland, McCoole came to the United States at the age of thirteen and, after spending some time in New York, moved west to lead a peripatetic lifestyle working on steamboats carrying freight on the Ohio and Upper Mississippi rivers.[1] What the Donegal man may have lacked in finesse he made up for with brute force and well-honed wrestling skills. McCoole's first recorded fight, according to the majority of sources, was against Bill Nary in April 1858. The encounter in Louisville, Kentucky, lasted eight rounds and seventeen minutes, with McCoole taking the victor's purse of $100.[2] On June 29, 1859, McCoole defeated William Blake on Twelve Mile Island on the Ohio River. It proved a more trying encounter, with McCoole triumphing in twenty-four rounds fought over thirty-seven intense minutes, despite receiving substantial damage to his nose and eyes. On May 2, 1861, McCoole tasted defeat at the hands of Tom Jennings in New Orleans, the city that was later to become his home. On September 19, 1866, a full five years later, Mike McCoole finally got his tilt at the title when he took on claimant Bill Davis at Choteau Island, Madison County, Illinois. At stake was a purse of $500 and a gold and silver championship belt. After a barbarous and brutal encounter lasting thirty-four minutes, McCoole, who had a fifteen-pound weight advantage over his opponent, was declared the victor when Davis's seconds finally threw in the sponge after their man had been rendered insensate by the Irishman's unrelenting barrage of heavy punches in the thirty-fifth round. McCoole's next fight was against English fighter Aaron Jones on August 31, 1867, at Busenbark's Station, Ohio, and once again, the Irishman had distinct advantages in the physical stakes. Jones was four years older, an inch and a half shorter, and eight pounds lighter. The *New York Times* sent a journalist on the train to the venue and he was happy to report that there was no disorderly conduct despite the fact that many passengers had to stand up in the carriages. While it was noisy, he thought the men were in the whole business for a "frolic," and it reminded him of people traveling to a political convention or a "genial stag picnic party."[3] When he got to the venue he saw 2,000 men behaving as if they were at a picnic, some of them reading newspapers while others were attempting to make seats from fence rails. The journalist expressed surprise at the remarkable respectability of many of those in attendance and noted the presence of many prominent citizens of Cincinnati. By the time the fight was ready to start he estimated that a crowd of 3,000 had gathered. After twenty-six brutal minutes fought over thirty-four rounds, Jones was knocked unconscious by a thundering blow between the eyes. According to the *New York Times* scribe he was still insensate ten minutes after the fight had finished with no sign of any doctor, while McCoole walked off the ground with a fresh step and a smiling face.[4] The Englishman never fought again, and some sources suggest that he died a few years later from damage to his lungs caused by broken ribs sustained in the fight.

McCoole was scheduled to fight Joe Coburn at Cold Spring Station in Indiana on May 27 of the following year, but the encounter never took place as both pugilists, as well as Coburn's manager, were arrested and imprisoned in Lawrenceburg, Indiana. The men were subsequently released on July 3.

McCoole married Irishwoman Mollie Norton on August 9, 1868, but their union was to prove brief and troubled. On June 15, 1869, McCoole fought American-born English contender Tom Allen on Foster's Island in the Mississippi over nine rounds.[5] McCoole had intended to finish his fighting career after having defeating Jones but was eventually prevailed upon by his backers and the consistent goading by Allen to take on the Englishman as a matter of national pride. According to one journalist, Allen looked much the better, and McCoole's friends were greatly disappointed at his condition as he was fat and showed signs of unskillful training.[6] The fight was ended by the referee when Allen was adjudged to have gouged McCoole in the eyes, but the *New York Herald* believed Allen would have won the fight if it had been fought to a natural conclusion.[7] Allen out-fought McCoole all the way through, it noted, and the Irishman was "much blown, badly punished, and in reality, whipped." The most newsworthy aspects of the encounter, according to Fred Henning, occurred after the fight, when members of McCoole's supporters cut the ropes, stormed the ring, and demanded the referee call the fight in their man's favor. Discretion being the wiser part of valor, the referee fled the scene, informing all that he would make his decision the following morning when he was safely back in St. Louis. Despite his victory, Allen's glory was short-lived, as he was defeated by the English champion Jem Mace on May 10, 1870, in Kennerville, Louisiana, in what is considered by many boxing historians as a heavyweight world championship title fight, in addition to being a decider of the American title. Mace defended the heavyweight title against Joe Coburn on November 30, 1871, in a ten-round draw at Bay St. Louis, Mississippi, forty miles from New Orleans.

On September 23, 1873, exactly four years after their previous battle, McCoole once again fought Tom Allen for the championship at Chateau Island, Illinois, with Jem Mace having retired from the fray and having left the title vacant. As was often the case in those days, Allen and McCoole were arrested on the eve of the fight and required to post a bond of $1,000 to keep the peace.[8] Notwithstanding this inconvenience, the fight went ahead in front of a crowd of 2,000. Allen, despite being at a sixteen-pound weight disadvantage and three inches shorter, administered a shocking beating to McCoole, and by the end of the fifth round some of the crowd was beseeching his seconds to throw in the towel. The fight continued but, according to one journalist, by the end of the sixth round McCoole presented a horrible appearance and seemed scarcely able to hold up his hands—his left eye closed, a terrible cut under the right eye, the right side of his upper lip also cut off, his nose broken.[9] Before toeing the mark for the seventh, Allen told the referee that it would be a sin to punish McCoole further and that if he was not taken from the ring he could become disfigured for life. However, the referee refused and McCoole's seconds insisted the round go ahead. Allen refused to punish the Irishman anymore and the fight was stopped at the start of the eighth round, when Tom Kelly, one of McCoole's corner men, threw in a white handkerchief. The one-sided contest had lasted all of twenty minutes in what was the high point of Allen's career.[10] When McCoole later looked back on the fight, he described Allen as the most magnificent tactician he had ever seen and the encounter as the toughest he had ever been in. Tom Allen's victory was to usher in a decade of British dominance.

Mike McCoole went on to open a saloon in St. Louis, an establishment which, perhaps inevitably, garnered a reputation as a den of iniquity and violence and was frequently mentioned in local papers as the location of assaults, shootings, and thefts. The trajectory of the Irish man's life was to continue on a downward arc after his defeat by Tom Allen. On October 30, 1873, McCoole was arrested outside his saloon, charged with murdering lightweight boxer Patsy Manley. McCoole was jailed after his arrest, but was later acquitted on February 17, 1875, as the prosecution could not locate the principal witnesses to testify.[11] Despite the lack of a trial, it was widely believed McCoole was the guilty party.[12] In 1879 McCoole lost his business in St. Louis and relocated to New Orleans, where he spent time working as a shipmate, as a wharf laborer, and on a sugar plantation.[13] He still believed he had the ability to fight and had issued a challenge to Tom Kelly the previous year, a challenge Kelly refused because he thought the stake of $100 too low.[14] McCoole was to have further colorful episodes in his tumultuous life. On September 25, 1880, he was working as a mate on the stern of a cotton-laden freighter called *Florence Meyer* when she was snagged and sunk on the Mississippi near Bullitt's Bayou, Louisiana.[15] McCoole did not drown, as several newspapers reported at the time, although he was washed overboard as the ship was sinking. Luckily, he was able to grab on to a barrel and pull himself back onboard using a guard rope to wait for rescue.[16] After working on steamer boats for a further number of years, Mike McCoole died of malaria at Charity Hospital in New Orleans on October 17, 1886, and is buried at Saint Patrick's Catholic Cemetery on Canal Street.[17]

Seven

"The Trojan Giant"
Paddy Ryan

"All the fighting done here, I do."
—A sign behind the Side Cut bar owned by Paddy Ryan in West Troy, New York[1]

AFTER HAVING BEEN IN IRISH HANDS for almost thirty years, the heavyweight title was monopolized by British-born fighters between 1873 and 1880 during what was a much-disputed era. On November 18, 1873, Tom Allen drew with Ben Hogan in a championship fight at Pacific City, Iowa, while on September 7, 1876, Allen lost his title to fellow Englishman Joe Goss in a fight which took place in two locations in Kentucky over a total time of one hour and nineteen minutes.[2] At the end of the contest each of the participants was awarded $5,000. Allen was not best pleased with the result, claiming that he could not get fair play in America, and duly resigned from the ring.[3] He returned to England to spend his time fighting and gambling at racetracks. He briefly returned to the United States in 1878

Paddy "The Trojan Giant"' Ryan became the bare-knuckle American heavyweight champion on May 30, 1880, after he won the title from English fighter Joe Goss, and retained the title until losing it to the exceptional John L. Sullivan on February 7, 1882 (Prints and Photographs Division, Library of Congress).

hoping to challenge the emerging John L. Sullivan, but the fight never materialized. Joe Goss held the title until he met a stronger force in yet another Irishman, Paddy Ryan. Born on March 15, 1851, in Thurles, County Tipperary, Ryan moved to Troy, New York, at eight years of age. There his physical power helped him find work as a blacksmith and he later labored on the construction of the Erie Canal.[4] In 1874 Ryan opened the Side Cut, an appropriately named saloon in the tough environs of West Troy and mostly frequented by his fellow Irishmen. By all accounts Troy was a tough town. Within a two-block radius of Ryan's establishment there were twenty-nine pubs, including the ominously named Tub of Blood. Ryan laid his cards clearly on the table in his premises; a shingle behind the bar read "All the fighting done here, I do." Stories of his pugilistic ability were legion. In one encounter Ryan allegedly took on twelve men in a pub called Collins House, defeating them all with the help of a stove shaker.[5]

Jim Killoran, a director of sports at the nearby Rensselaer Polytechnic Institute, saw Ryan's impressive ability to deal with miscreants in his premises and suggested that the sport of prize-fighting might benefit from his talents. The "Trojan Giant," as Ryan was now called, took to the boxing scene like a duck to water. Killoran was a hard taskmaster and during one of Ryan's early amateur fights he struck his protégé with the leg of a chair between rounds in an effort to stir him to greater efforts. Ryan was as much an all-around fighter, grappler, and wrestler as he was a boxer, and on May 30, 1880, he fought Englishman Joe Goss for the bare-knuckle championship of the United States at Collier's Station, West Virginia.

The encounter had originally been planned to take place in Pittsburgh, but, as was so often the case in many jurisdictions, the mayor declared his opposition.[6] The fighters only arrived at the venue the night before under a veil of secrecy. The date and location had been kept a secret; until the day prior to the fight, the only details the fight organizers shared was that it would take place within fifty miles of Pittsburgh, which boxing fans assumed meant Collier's Station, as clandestine matches had been held there in the past.[7] The railroad town was easily accessible from Pittsburgh and Steubenville, Ohio, but far enough from well-organized urban police forces who might want to shut down the fight.[8] The Irishman was thirteen years younger than his opponent with Goss having a twenty pound and six inch advantage. While it definitely was not Paddy Ryan's first ever prize-fight, it was likely to have been his first competitive bare-knuckle encounter and was certainly one that exemplified the ethnic rivalry between those of Irish American and British stock. Goss even chose to fight on Tuesday because of the English belief that it was a lucky day.[9] Ryan's fans outnumbered Goss's by ten to one; some of the latter claimed that Ryan had come with "a gang of murderers and cutthroats."[10] At first Goss and his party refused to go ahead with the proposed fight but the crowd surrounded and threatened them, and Ryan, showing an admirable degree of sportsmanship, escorted his opponent to the ring.[11] A correspondent for the *National Police Gazette* was impressed by the physique of the Irishman, describing him as a "a giant, with muscles of iron and long, active arms."[12] Ryan was unfazed by Goss's seniority. "This is my first appearance in any ring," he told the assembled crowd, "and I rather feel glad to meet Goss, and see what I can do."[13]

The barbaric fight lasted eighty-seven minutes, until Ryan finally knocked Goss out in the eighty-seventh round. Goss was in terrible shape by the end and Ryan was only slightly better. News of the match traveled quickly through the wire,s and even readers in Scotland were able to read round-by-round accounts the following day.[14] As was so often the case at the time, the participants, their retinues, and the crowd rapidly dispersed before the authorities found evidence of the fight.[15] On the train back to New York, the misfortunate Ryan was attacked and stabbed by a gang of thugs.

During the course of 1881 Paddy Ryan fought eight exhibition matches, including bouts with Goss, John Dwyer, and Captain James Dalton, but ultimately he was to come up against an unstoppable force and the most celebrated boxer of the era, the imperious John L. "The Boston Strong Boy" Sullivan. Their encounter was to prove an event which reverberated around the world, and Sullivan was to change the face of the sport forever.

Fred Henning was happy to conclude that the axis of boxing had definitively switched to the United States by the end of the nineteenth century, and he had no doubt that the man who deserved the most praise was Mr. Richard K. Fox, proprietor of the *National Police Gazette,* a magazine founded in 1845 and more commonly known as the *Police Gazette.* The seminal publication was the first illustrated sports weekly in the United States and is now widely considered the progenitor of celebrity gossip columns and sensationalistic tabloid style reporting.[16] Originally established by attorney Enoch E. Camp and railroad magnate George Wilkes, it initially focused on reporting crime. In 1886 George W. Matsell bought it from the founders before selling it on in 1877 to Fox, who would remain the proprietor and editor until his death in 1922. Despite its avowed aim of covering matters of interest to the police, it became better known for lurid coverage of murders, celebrity gossip, engravings and photographs of exotic dancers, and sports material. Fox had emigrated from Belfast in 1874, where he had cut his journalistic teeth working on the *Banner of Ulster* and the *Belfast Newsletter.* From the start of his time in America he had an uncanny knack for promotion and self-publicity, years before Joseph Pulitzer's *New York World* and William Hearst's *New York Journal* he had mastered the techniques of what would later be termed "yellow journalism."[17] Printed on pink paper, and often featuring frolicking females on its front cover, the *National Police Gazette* was frequently referred to as the "barbershop bible." According to Matthew T. Isenberg, Sullivan's preeminent biographer, the *Gazette* became "the most lurid journal ever published in the United States, an endless weekly panoply of buxom showgirls, crime, sex and murder."[18] Anthony Comstock, a special agent for the United States Postal Service and founder of the New York Society for the Suppression of Vice, had Fox prosecuted on many occasions for publishing immoral material, but all of his efforts only helped to increase the *Gazette*'s circulation. Among the many things which troubled Comstock—and many others of his ilk—were advertisements for "private troubles," including "Dr Young's Patent Electric Belt," a device which "guaranteed to restore manhood," while "rubber goods," illustrated French playing cards, and imported pictures of men and women together could be delivered discreetly to all parts of the country, much to the distress of moral police.[19] However, it also provided coverage of current affairs, albeit of a sensationalistic nature. When President James A. Garfield was shot by Charles Julius Guiteau at the Baltimore and Potomac Railroad Station on July 2, 1881, the *Gazette* kept readers informed of the ailing president's condition on a weekly basis right up to his death in September, while the subsequent murder trial was also given the famous Fox "live journalism" treatment. Competitions of all types were also stock-in-trade of the *Gazette*. Those with talents in bridge jumping, oyster opening, one-legged dancing, rat killing, wood chopping, steeple climbing, and even water drinking could compete against likeminded individuals. Above all else, the *Gazette* devoted extensive resources to its sports department, and between 1896 and 1918 it published a Sporting Annual which provided a yearly summary of sporting statistics impressively entitled "Best Performances in Pugilism, Athletics, Bicycling, Rowing, Baseball, Trotting, and Racing."[20] It promoted sport as an antidote to the ills of the Gilded Age and the hustle and bustle of the modern era where the newly described disease of "neurasthenia" seemed to be growing ever more prevalent among men engaged in sedentary clerical work. In 1879 Fox changed the tagline of the *Gazette* to "The Leading Illustrated Sporting Journal in America," hiring William Harding as sports editor. The paper came to cover the entire gamut of sporting pursuits: billiards, rowing, horse racing, lacrosse, tennis, football, cricket, baseball, cycling, pigeon shooting, dogfighting, and even reported upon shin-kicking contests, where two men booted each other's legs until they were bleeding and as "raw as beefsteaks."[21] While the *Gazette* was not the pioneer of sports coverage (an honor given to William T. Porter with his launch of *Spirit of the Times* in 1831), it fervently embraced this as the commercial future. "Writer Tom Wolfe astutely observed that the magazine's interest in sport had nothing to do with the high Victorian ideal of sport and everything to do with gambling."[22]

When the paper sold 4,000 additional copies in the week it reported on the boxing match between Goss and Ryan in 1880, the die was cast for Fox, and boxing became the focus of the magazine's sporting coverage. Circulation gradually rose from 150,000 to 400,000 copies a week, prompting the Belfast proprietor to immediately engage more extensively in prize-fight promotion. The *Gazette* was immensely influential in the world of bare-knuckle fighting, and it became an accepted fact that the "World Champion" of different boxing divisions was the fighter it declared to be so. The magazine had first declared its intention to become the sanctioning body for bare-knuckle boxing in 1881 and issued its first championship belt in 1882 despite the fact that the sport was still illegal. It continued to be the de facto sanctioning body until 1894, and it was only in 1920 that the National Boxing Association began to sanction title fights. Fred Henning was in no doubt that Fox was the man responsible for bringing boxing back to life in the United States at a time when it had virtually died in Britain. It was to the eternal credit of Mr. Fox that he, his money, and his publication came along to revive interest in prize-fighting, and it was in the personage of John L. Sullivan that the sport had its savior, according to Henning.[23]

The Boston Strong Boy was, according to Henning, a "new prophet arisen as if by magic to lead the revival."[24] Sullivan arrived on the American scene when competing ideologies and world views were jockeying for position. The Founding Fathers had striven with all their might to build a republic founded on hard work, sobriety, probity, moral centeredness and suasion, self-control, nonviolence, and progressive reform. Reformation extended to humanitarian causes prohibiting the excessive display of violence and cruelty, the elimination of flogging in the army and the navy, the abolition of public whipping, and the prohibition of cockfighting, bullbaiting, bearbaiting, and the slave trade, while a wholesale penal reform was widely trumpeted if never quite achieved. Human nature, they believed, was divided between animal passions and the civilized, higher faculties of reason and self-discipline, and the Founding Fathers were firmly on the side of self-improvement, underpinned by a solid work ethic. The solution to the ills of society was persuasion, not violence. Boxing in any shape or form did not fit within this conception of the Republic, and moralists frequently stressed the retrogressive aspect of prize-fighting by relating it to a specific historical period which they regarded as an era of brutalism. The cultural relationship between prize-fighting and ancient Rome was a recurrent leitmotif in this regard. In an 1895 interview, R.G. Ingersoll made an analogy between modern prize-fighting and bloody gladiator shows of the old Roman days, claiming such fights were "enjoyed only by savages."[25] The religious were equally contemptuous of boxing. The Reverend Dr. T. De Witt of Brooklyn stressed that prize-fighting stood against civilization by making human beings comparable but inferior to animals, arguing that "the ox, the bear, and the lion are stronger than man, and the deer can outrun him, so that mere muscular force amounts to nothing unless it can be harnessed for the improvement and elevation of society."[26] All pugilistic contests were merely the exhibitions of uncontrollable brutalism as long as they involved violence, intended injuries, and pursued the goal of knocking another man unconscious, he fulminated. Similarly, another cleric, Dr. Hemphill of San Francisco, argued that boxing was not a "manly art," as many claimed, but a "brute's art."[27] A religious publication called the *Overland Monthly and Out West Magazine* similarly denied the claim of the manly art and viewed prize-fighting as "the highest exhibition of brute strength," rendering the participant nothing but a "vulgar false hero."[28] Anti-prize-fighting discourse also pointed out that the brutal entertainment pushed participants and their followers from a morally centered life to one of violent instinct and passion. The *New York Tribune* was representative of the attitudes adopted by the majority of the press toward boxing in the mid-nineteenth century when it described the crowd at an 1858 fight: "Probably no human eye will ever look upon so much rowdyism, villainy, scoundrelism, and boiled-down viciousness, concentrated upon so small a space.... Scoundrels of every imaginable genus, every variety of every species, were there assembled; the characteristic rascalities of each were developed and displayed in all their devilish perfection."[29] A report of a match between George Ducharme and James Dohagany in 1887 carried by the *Fort Worth Daily Gazette* similarly stressed the sheer brutality of the action: "The fight was so fierce and the blows so severe, many of the spectators weakened and were obliged to leave the room," while those who had the misfortune to remain until the final round were covered with blood from head to foot.[30] The *Milwaukee Daily Sentinel* observed the 1880 fight between Paddy Ryan and Joe Goss with horror. Under the headline "A Bloody and Disgraceful Mill" it noted that "deep gashes marred faces that never were classical, while swollen lips and black eyes evidenced the fierceness of the fight. Here and there over the naked breasts and arms of the men were stains of blood which gave them the appearance of painted savages."[31] In 1890, the editorial of the *New Orleans Daily Picayune* argued that the spectacle of two half-naked men mauling each other constituted "obscene brutality" which was "far from calculated to inspire thoughts and sentiments ennobling and purifying."[32] An 1891 report in the *Boston Daily Advertiser* was particularly direct: "It is seldom that many days elapse without the announcement of one of these vulgar contests in which one or both parties have suffered such maceration and mutilation as decent people cannot read of without a shudder; nor is it many days, usually, between one prize ring slaughter and another."[33] Some newspapers even sought to highlight their moral bona fides by placing fight reports in the crime and court reports sections.

However, as the nineteenth century progressed there was increasing support of sparring as a manly pursuit. Mark K. Frank, an instructor at the California Athletic Club, stressed the positive role of prize-fighting for men who followed "sedentary pursuits." He argued that seeing "two men trained to the pink of perfection struggling for supremacy" was a "great incentive" for these sedentary men. He noted that there were many medical men in the city who sparred as a form of exercise and that it would be a wonderful thing if every man in the city decided to do the same.[34] Boxing had been a popular form of recreation during the American Civil War: "a poignant if fleeting alternative to the ghastliness of battle," as Elliott Gorn described it.[35] After the passing of legislation to ban prize-fighting—in Massachusetts in 1849 and New York in 1851—there was a boom in sparring academies and cheap boxing manuals. Within this rubric, sparring was a healthy form of recreation for the middle-class man but prize-fighting was solely the preserve of the lower orders.

There was also evidence of changing attitudes in some quarters of the press, and some started to promote the qualifications and professionalism of their journalists with respect to critiquing boxing contests with less moralizing and more technical reportage. Some members of the press were beginning to recognize that boxing was a profession requiring skill and brain as well as brawn and muscle.[36] In 1897, the *Chicago Tribune* promised its readers quality professional boxing reports for the fight between Jim Corbett and Bob Fitzsimmons: "Trained observers told the story of the contest, ex–Senator Ingalls contributed his impression of the spectacle, both principals and the other pugilistic stars described their experiences, and all these, which were the essential features of the history of the occasion, were given to the Chicago public exclusively by The Tribune."[37] The *San Francisco Call* promised its readers a "Technical Story Dictated at the Ringside" by Walter Watson, a boxing instructor of the Olympic Club in San Francisco, although an editorial in the ever-staid *New York Times* thought the increased reportage on boxing across the nation one of the greatest achievements of "freak journalism."[38] However, it was one of the few dissenting voices. By 1910 the editor of the *Chicago Tribune* openly defined prize-fighting as a manly profession and sport. Those who criticized it were showing signs of effeminacy while it was, in reality, an exhibition of manliness.[39] There had been other voices of support, including poet Walt Whitman, who penned a thirteen-part series in the *New York Atlas* newspaper entitled "Manly Health and Training" under the pseudonym Mose Velsor.[40] Whitman believed there was a manly charm and a fascinating magic in the phrase, while there was a wonderful medicinal effect in the presence of a man who was perfectly well. He believed that the way to proper morals for a young man was by helping him to become healthy, clean-blooded, and vigorous, which could be achieved by plenty of outdoor exercise and an exclusively meat diet. In addition, men should grow a beard because it was "a great sanitary protection to the throat." In his 1860 "Poems of Joys" Whitman wrote that one of the delights of a "manly self-hood" was "the joy of the strong brawn'd fighter, towering in the arena, in perfect condition, conscious of power, thirsting to meet his opponent."[41]

Fiction writers also reflected this changing worldview embracing muscular Christianity as advocated by the likes of New England cleric Henry Ward Beecher, Thomas Wentworth Higginson, and Edward Everett. A robust physical existence married to a strong sense of Christian morality and duty was the formula for a well-lived life, according to these men. For journalist and novelist Jack London, fighting was a symbol of man's struggle to survive brutal realities. London did not praise prize-fighting unconditionally but did portray fighters sympathetically in his novels. Thomas Hughes's 1857 novel *Tom Brown's Schooldays,* with its didactic descriptions of physical development, fighting spirit, boldness, and male socialization, married to a strong sense of Christian morality, was both commercially successful and influential. The evolving attitudes adopted by elements in the press beg the question as to what changes in wider American society and culture reflected this gradual *volte-face* in some sections of the community. For one thing, the stultifying nature of the contemporary workplace was a significant push factor in the increasing attractiveness of physical sports like boxing and football. As historian John Higham noted, there was a strong desire to break out of the frustrations, the routine, the sheer dullness of an urban industrial culture. There was everywhere, he wrote, "an urge to be young, masculine and adventurous."[42] For many men life had become too predictable, too industrialized, too bureaucratic, too factory-bound, too corporatized. In the past a significant percentage of middle-class men had worked the land or were involved in physical labor of some type, and were masters of their own domain, but American society had changed rapidly, and by the turn of the twentieth century the majority of middle-class men were employees, answerable to the authority of others. The number of corporate office jobs had seen a tenfold increase in the decades after the Civil War and the majority of men no longer controlled productive property or was involved in regular physical labor. One journalist noted that the average American man was "a pasty faced, narrow chested, spindle shanked dwarfed race, a mere walking manikin to advertise the last cut of the fashionable tailor." An English commentator looked disparagingly at what up to that point constituted sport in America when he wrote, "To roll balls in a tenpin alley by gaslight, or to ride a fast trotting horse in a light wagon on a very bad and a very dusty road seemed the Alpha and Omega of sports in the United States."[43] Women were an increasing part of the labor force and were capable of doing the same work as their male counterparts, leading to a further sense of emasculation for some. The profession of teaching, for example, was becoming increasingly feminized, while there were widespread calls to give women the right to vote. There were movements calling for the closure of saloons and gambling houses, bastions of male socialization. Phineas T. Barnum—never a man afraid to give public voice to his opinions—described the need for structured leisure activities when he said, "Men, women and children who cannot live on gravity alone need something to satisfy their lighter moods and hours."[44] With an eye on a possible future battle with England for world supremacy, N. Parker Willis, an eminent magazine contributor and public intellectual of the era, warned, as many others of the era did, that America must create a culture of masculine vigor and physical culture.[45]

For Theodore Roosevelt the Spanish American War had led to national revitalization through cultivating the martial ethic and rekindling the manliness of generations past. If Americans shied away from such hard contests, stronger and bolder countries would come to dominate the world. Such "splendid little wars" as the Spanish American one would prevent American men from growing soft and effeminate while protecting and strengthening the country. Where soldiers and sailors had once been viewed as members of one of the lowest social castes, now they were increasingly admired for their martial prowess and battling qualities. Roosevelt embodied the cowboy soldier he so idealized: a former asthmatic weakling once branded a "wimp" by his father who built himself up by exposure to the harsh conditions of the Western frontier. His code of masculinity was famously embodied in his Rough Riders, the band of fighters he formed to fight in the Spanish American War. On the other hand, Mark Twain later described Roosevelt as "clearly insane ... and insanest upon war and its supreme glories."[46] Notwithstanding his mental health, the concept of a new type of man with an iron will and animal magnetism, capable of violent adventure and master of his own fate, had considerable appeal for Roosevelt. He believed there was no place in the world for nations which had become "enervated by the soft and easy life" and had lost their fiber of "vigorous hardiness and masculinity."[47] "Powerful, vigorous men of strong animal development," he maintained, "must have some way in which their animal spirits can find vent." He also believed that boxing was an ideal sport for city dwellers based on his own experience: "When obliged to live in cities I for a long time found that boxing and wrestling enabled me to get a good deal of exercise in condensed and attractive form."[48]

Psychologist G. Stanley Hall wanted to see more of the raw side of life and was drawn to boxing for his fix. He had never missed an opportunity to attend a prize-fight and had seen most of the noted pugilists of his generation, always feeling the unique thrill of such encounters.[49] This desire for a return to a conception of the individual male as vital and masculine abounded at the latter end of the nineteenth century. Public intellectuals like Oliver Wendell Holmes and Thomas Wentworth Higginson, among others, became famous advocates of physical training. Holmes noted that "anything is better than this white blooded degeneration to which we all tend" and deplored the "Autocrat of the Breakfast Table," believing that such "a set of black-coated, stiff-jointed, soft-muscled, paste-complexioned youth" as he saw in the cities of the Eastern Seaboard "never before sprang from loins of Anglo-Saxon lineage."[50] Ironically, Holmes was a slight and asthmatic man, but he frequented the training camps of John C. Heenan to see what the apotheosis of masculinity looked like. The Victorian conception of manhood based wholly on self-discipline and winning the individual economic battle was on the wane; no longer could everything be resolved by propriety, rationalism, and self-discipline, while abstention from what moral arbiters considered dissipating factors was no longer the panacea for all societal and personal ills. The physique of prize fighters like John L. Sullivan became something to be desired. Dr. Henry Lessing was representative of an increasingly common viewpoint when he wrote, "As to Sullivan, I regard him physically as a wonderful specimen of manhood…. These [muscles] are not only perfect in size and proportion, but also admirable in quality and endurance. Much of this is due to sagacious training, but more, to my mind, is due to inheritance."[51] Now the physique of this rough-hewn son of Irish emigrants was something to be admired rather than shunned. While prize-fighting was considered affray, assault, and riotous behavior in law, the eddying currents were gradually starting to shift direction.

College football also allowed men to demonstrate aggressive masculinity in a codified and acceptable environment, but for some, this was too much. Harvard professor Charles Eliot Norton saw football as "the invasion of modern barbarism and vulgarity."[52] On the other hand, Theodore Roosevelt ridiculed moralists' cries against the brutality of football, believing it helped "convert feminized men … to brawny ones" because it was a sport in which "masculine supremacy" was incontestable.[53]

Some historians point to class differences in the choice of leisure pursuits. Those from the middle classes were more likely to choose individual, family-oriented, orderly, sober, civilized, reflective, politically solemn, and noncommercial activities. By contrast, workingclass men participated in collective, violent, hedonistic, vulgar, disorderly, riot-inclined, and present-oriented ones. It was clear where prize-fighting lay in this rubric.

While Roosevelt saw amateur boxing and sparring as acceptable pursuits, he frowned upon the professional ring with its focus on financial gain. To him, boxing was a first-class sport for young men and a vigorous manly pastime which had a distinct moral and physical value, but he did not agree with professionalism in any sport, believing it was the curse of manly athletics and the chief obstacle to their healthy development.[54] He was particularly appalled by professional prize-fights and those who attended them, noting they hovered on the borderline of criminality and, in his opinion, were no better than those who frequented rat-pits and dog-pits.[55] However, Roosevelt was a realist and believed that it was better to try and remove the criminal element from the sport than to abolish it, wryly noting that some big business interests were twice as brutalizing as boxing.

The writings of Irishman John Boyle O'Reilly are highly instructive in respect of this dichotomous attitude toward boxing at the latter part of the nineteenth century. O'Reilly had led a remarkable life before getting to America. Imprisoned for revolutionary activities in Ireland, he was sent to a prison colony in Australia from which he subsequently escaped to make his way to the United States. Settling in Boston, O'Reilly became a highly respected figure and a foremost spokesman for the "lace curtain Irish," those who had climbed out of the lower socioeconomic categories where the "shanty Irish" dwelled. O'Reilly became editor of *The Boston Pilot* and numbered poet Henry Wadsworth Longfellow and novelist and playwright William

Dean Howells among his many influential and cultured friends. He campaigned relentlessly for the betterment of Irish immigrants and famously exhorted them to try "honest hard work for one year" to help gain acceptance in their new home.[56] In particular, O'Reilly railed against poor working conditions and included African Americans, Native Americans, and Jews in his campaigns for better treatment. O'Reilly used the pages of *The Pilot* to campaign against discrimination and often reprinted advertisements from other papers which included the dreaded phrase "No Irish Need Apply." In publishing these free advertisements he pointed out to his readers that they implied Irish people should not use any of the services offered by the offending businesses or individuals. O'Reilly was a fervent supporter of the Democratic Party, and such was his standing in the organization that President Grover Cleveland saw fit to meet with him to discuss an impending extradition treaty with Britain. On the untimely death of O'Reilly in 1890, the *Boston Herald* was laudatory: "He was a paladin of chivalry, sent down into our generation, except that he drew no credentials from palaces; his commission was always from the people. He had both mental and physical bravery to rank with either ancient or modern heroes."[57]

He was also a consummate booster of his fellow Irish and frequently pointed to his country's excellence in a wide array of sports. When it came to boxing, O'Reilly was a realist and, like Roosevelt, differentiated between the amateur and professional codes. He argued that amateur gloved boxing was the best of all exercises for physical development but criticized professional prize-fighting for its evil association with betting and gambling. For him, prize-fighting appealed to the low lives of too many of its professional followers.[58] Ever the realist, he acknowledged the brutality that was inherent in the appeal of the sport and that the bruises, scars, and blood were the price of a precious and beautiful thing. The professional boxer who fought an honest fight with skill and courage and without the savagery of bare hands was not a moral monster. A clean fight was a "supreme test and tension of such precious living qualities as courage, temper, endurance, bodily strength, clear-mindedness."[59] He asked his readers to visit a Turkish bath to find evidence of the muscular collapse which had happened to so many American men. To him, fatness was "sensuous expressions, or symptoms of disease."[60]

O'Reilly was an ardent booster of John L. Sullivan and wrote that his superiority was due to his extraordinary nervous force, the unmatched variety and force of his punching, and his ability to move as quickly and purposefully as a lion. He could strike more blows in ten seconds than any other man could muster in a minute. Sullivan could "rush, hammer ... overmaster, overwhelm and appall" all others.[61] There were dissenting voices on the thoughts of O'Reilly; his close friend James Jeffrey Roche thought the publication of *The Ethics of Boxing and Manly Art* and his fondness of boxing isolated O'Reilly from the society of Irish American intellectuals.[62]

The Catholic Church was a central plank of Irish American society and did not see prize-fighting in a positive light. Archbishop John Ireland led the anti-prize-fighting movement in the Catholic Church during the 1890s, and under his leadership, St. Paul, Minnesota, became a center of anti-boxing agitation.[63] In 1891, Ireland tried to prevent an impending fight between Bob Fitzsimmons and Jim Hall at the Minnesota Athletic Club, denouncing prize-fighting as "savagery" and "animalism" which only had appeal for the "riffraff of the country." Ireland and other Irish middle-class figures like J.R. McMillan and Thomas Cochran collaborated with respectable Protestant citizens to prevent the municipal government from issuing a license for the fight.[64] In 1893, the fight between "Gentleman Jim" Corbett and the English champion Charley Mitchell at the Coney Island Athletic Club in Brooklyn also drew the agitation of the Catholic Church. The Most Rev. Mgr. Farley, one of the Vicars General of the Roman Catholic Archdiocese of New York, expressed his antagonism toward prize-fighting, and because he was second only to Archbishop Michael A. Corrigan in power and authority, his denunciation was seen as the formal opinion of the Archdiocese. He said, "Prize fighting is a crime against morality, humanity, and the law of the State. The Catholic Church frowns on it as sinful and brutal, and no words are too strong for me to say in denunciation of it." Mgr. Thomas J. Ducey also stressed that prizefights were "exhibitions of brutality, vulgarity, and bestiality" that only caused the degradation of "manhood and womanhood." Ducey believed that Irish American boxers could not be ethnic heroes or role models because they appealed to those who had the most vulgar of educations and only knew how to "drink, display and dress." To him, contemporary fighters were simply the different versions of old fighters like Yankee Sullivan, Tom Hyer, and John C. Heenan, who were known as thugs.[65] To Bishop S.M. Merrill of Chicago, prize-fighting made respectable citizens "ashamed for humanity."[66] In 1897, the Reverend T. Magill of Reno complained that prize-fighting disseminated "brutality in its worst form," and he believed the ethos of prize-fighting was "diametrically opposed" to the "moral teachings of Christianity, the public school and of every lodge and benevolent order in the land," which taught the humanities.[67] The Reverend John Tallmadge Bergen argued that prize-fighting was not only "a disgrace to civilized communities" but also "an outrage upon true athletics."[68] To him, prize-fighting was "savagery" and "barbarism," and it could never be considered a sport because a contestant aimed to make the other "helpless and mangled."[69] Reverend Dr. Reese F. Alsop, a New York pastor, argued that a prize-fight was "an encouragement to the brutal element in human nature."[70] Dr. E.P. Goodwin, a pastor of Chicago, saw prize-fighting as a "relic of the old barbaric times."[71] For the Reverend Dr. E. Horner Wellman of Brooklyn, prize-fighting inherited "the rough cruelty of the past generation," but, unlike other moralists, he did not deny that there might be refined skill for the sport. However, he still believed that prize-fighting, which originated from military exercises in the ancient times, had "degenerated into a beastly trial of strength and scientific bruising." Wellman also stressed the retrogressive aspect of prize-fighting, supporting old Victorians' distinction of moral and brute. "This is an age of mind rather than muscle: of arbitration, not brute force."[72] In his sermon "The Prize Ring and Its Brutality; or, Cruelty to Men and Animals," the Reverend Theodore Clifton of Milwaukee also made an analogy between prize-fighting and the Roman gladiatorial contests. According to him, not only did prize-fighting signify the "degeneracy" of human amusement, but its popularity also signified that humans were cruel by nature and that the artificial control of human nature by humanity, pity, and religion was failing. He saw the popularity of prize-fighting as a signal of the defeat of civilization.[73] There were some countervailing views in religious circles, however. The Reverend S.J. McPherson argued that there was a "good and bad side to pugilism." He said, "I think that the chief objection to prize fighting is that it tends to make with less proof upon brutality: but it is, to my mind, better for humanity to have the men of the world leaning toward a condition tinged with brutality rather than effeminacy."

Whatever about the attitudes of the clergy, nothing was going to stop the phenomenon that was John L. Sullivan, a man who was to become the greatest sporting star in American popular culture.

Eight

"The Boston Strong Boy"
John L. Sullivan

"I believe in having a little fight in most everything except funerals. Anything that ain't got some fighting in it is like a funeral and I don't like funerals."
—John L. Sullivan

"I like his confidence, his arrogance … I like the way he used to say 'I can beat any man in the house.'"
—Mike Tyson[1]

IN LATER LIFE, WHEN ASKED TO account for the disappearance of his wealth, John L. Sullivan gave the immortal answer, "Well I guess I gave away about $200,000. I spent $200,000 on wine and general carousing. I blew about $100,000 on gambling…. That's half a million, ain't it? It cost me about $200,000 for legitimate living expenses, and my training cost me about $100,000. Trying to be a businessman without any experience cost me another $200,000. That's another half a million, ain't it?"[2]

It was a vastly different life than that envisioned by his Irish-born parents. Mike Sullivan from Laccabeg, Abbeydorney, County Kerry, and Catherine Kelly from Kiltoom, County Roscommon, settled in the South End area of Boston, a part of the city almost wholly occupied by Irish emigrants and their descendants at that time. Boston might have had a large immigrant Irish population, but of all the cities the couple could have gone to it was one of the least welcoming. In 1854 the Know Nothing party, running on a platform of Temperance, Liberty, and Protestantism, captured all state offices, the State Senate, and all except four seats in the House Chamber in Massachusetts. Even Catholic priests were banned from visiting sick members of their flock in the city hospital until 1859, while in the same year hundreds of Catholic students were expelled from Boston schools for protesting against the beating of a ten-year-old boy by a teacher when the boy refused to recite the Protestant version of the Lord's Prayer. It was a city ruled by the "codfish aristocracy," where the Irish were once infamously described as "a massive lump in the community, undigested, indigestible."[3] There was an irony in Sullivan being from Massachusetts, too. Of all states, it had long been bitterly opposed to boxing, and the sport had been banned by statute in 1849. In an 1876 legal case titled *Commonwealth v. Colberg* the Massachusetts Supreme Judicial Court ruled that prize-fighting was still illegal even if both participants were willing combatants, as it served no useful purpose.[4]

John L. Sullivan was born on October 15, 1858, according to family sources, although Church records note his birthday as October 12. Mike and Catherine had fervent hopes that their son would become a priest after his studies in the Jesuit-run Boston College, but he dropped out of formal education and, after trying his hand at a number of trades and spending a short stint as a baseball player, he joined up with manager Billy Madden and set about his dominance of the boxing ring. Despite the fact that his father only stood five feet and two inches tall, John L. was a broth of a boy; by the age of seventeen he weighed over 200 pounds. He always claimed his height came from his mother's side of the family and that he had also inherited his fighting skills from her, as some of her relations back in Ireland were given to wrestling.

Madden, born in England to Irish emigrant parents in 1852, had come to America virtually penniless but had managed to find his way to New Orleans to see the fight between Joe Goss and Jem Mace. Having walked the final twenty miles to the venue, Madden won a grand total of twelve dollars and fifty cents when he took up the challenge of boxing Tom Hart in a preliminary bout. He continued to fight as a lightweight and became a respected and knowledgeable figure in the game, and was to prove the perfect manager for Sullivan, familiar with the machinations of the fight game inside and outside of the ring. Madden helped Sullivan hone his fighting techniques and taught him how to concentrate on straight hitting, eliminating his self-taught roundhouse punching. Despite his relatively short legs, Sullivan's upper body was exceptionally well sculpted, a physique once memorably described as "a wonderful engine of destruction."[5] While his physicality was intimidating, many commented on the penetrating intensity of his dark eyes shielded by heavy eyebrows; some said his intense stare could defeat an opponent before the fight even began. With his tightly cut short hair, Sullivan looked every inch the Irish warrior.

In most accounts of Sullivan's career, his first ever fight took place in 1877 at Roxbury's Institute Hall (later to become the Dudley Street Opera House), where with a number of his friends he was attending a variety evening honoring an Irish sporting man called George Fogarty. As part of the proceedings, a young Irish boxer by the name of Jack Scannell took to the stage and challenged anyone in attendance to take him on in a three-round exhibition. The nineteen-year-old Sullivan duly stepped forward. When Scannell pretended to shake Sullivan's hand but proceeded to thump him on the back of the head instead Sullivan was raised to anger and duly knocked his opponent over the onstage piano and into the orchestra pit. He was later to recall the contest with the brusque words, "I done him up in about two minutes."[6] From the start it was Sullivan's preferred approach to fights. His mantra was simple: "I go in to win from the very first second. Win I must, and win I shall." Sullivan invariably fought off the front foot and went in for the kill at the first opportunity. The redoubtable John Boyle O'Reilly eloquently described the fighter's style: "Sullivan is as fierce, relentless, timeless as a cataract. The fight is to wholly go in his way, not at all akin to the other man's. His opponent wants to spar; he leaps on him with a straight blow. He wants to breathe; he dashes him into the corner with a drive in the stomach. He does not waste ten seconds of the three minutes of each round."[7] Other boxers began by sparring, but Sullivan's style was "as distinct from them as a bull dog is from a spaniel," Boyle memorably wrote.[8] Looking back on his first fight at a later point, Sullivan was honest about his lack of knowledge: "I didn't know the first thing about boxing then but I went at him for all I was worth and licked him quick."[9] On another occasion Sullivan expressed his straightforward approach this way: "There's nothing to fighting. Just come out fast from your corner, hit the other fellow as hard as you can and hit him first."[10] Sullivan believed the jaw was the most vulnerable part of a man's facial anatomy and claimed to have confirmed this with a number of doctors, all of whom told him a hard blow on the point of the jaw would render a man unconscious, and at the same time would not effectually damage him otherwise.

On December 24, 1880, a crowd of thirty people watched Sullivan demolish John Donaldson in a boarded-up Cincinnati saloon. His next opponent fared little better; The colorfully named John "The Bull's Head Terrier" Flood survived just eight rounds in a prize-fight that took place on a barge in the Hudson River to avoid detection by the law. As one reporter noted, "Sullivan didn't possess much science. But what a wallop he packed."[11] From the very start of his boxing career, Sullivan's avowed aim was to take the championship title from Paddy Ryan. With this mission in mind, he gravitated to New York City and announced himself to the wider world at the famous Harry Hill's Gentlemen's Sporting Theatre and Boxing Club on March 31, 1881, where he offered $50 to any man who could last four rounds with him under the Queensberry Rules. Harry Hill's, located on the corner of Houston and Crosby Streets, had opened in 1854 and was renowned for the variety of stage entertainment on offer, as well as its famously pretty waitresses. It was dubbed the most reputable den of vice in New York, with signs on the wall warning patrons that foul language and anything that could be construed as misconduct were prohibited. Hill proudly boasted that no one was ever robbed in his "dead respectable place."[12] While everything from Indian-club swingers to fighting dwarfs took to the stage in Harry Hill's, it was the nightly boxing that appealed most to his clientele. Hill, an Englishman who had first come to America in 1850 to care for the horses of a sugar magnate in Queens, had become a New York institution and a very rich man.

The gauntlet thrown down by Sullivan was accepted by Steve Taylor—born John Mahan—a grizzled Irish veteran who worked as a hard shoulder for William Tweedy's Tammany Hall political machine.[13] Taylor was a seasoned campaigner and had once fought the English champion Jem Mace, as well as training Paddy Ryan for his fight against Joe Goss. After an incessant barrage of power punching from Sullivan, Taylor was duly dispatched in the second round. Sullivan inevitably met Richard Kyle Fox at Harry Hill's Saloon but their first encounter proved inauspicious. According to boxing lore, their paths crossed two nights after Sullivan's demolition of Taylor. When an inebriated Sullivan refused to join Fox, who had invited him over to his table through an emissary, and responded with the blunt statement, "It's no farther from him to me than it is from me to him…. If he wants to see John L. Sullivan he can do the walking," it was to prove the beginning of a long-running feud between the two men, much of which played out in public through the press, particularly in the Police *Gazette*.z It was almost inevitable that Fox and Sullivan would not see eye to eye.

As Klein wrote, the forces of their personalities were like "powerful magnets with the same polarities, so identical that they repelled each other." They were both "arrogant, egotistical, self made products of Irish stock who rose from the working class to make it big in America." They were both relentlessly ambitious and vain self-promoters with the utmost confidence in their abilities to make men submit to their wills: "one by the power of his fists, the other by the power of the pen."[14]

Fox persistently called on Sullivan to take on Paddy Ryan, goading him that he was afraid of The Trojan Giant, a strategy which provided the wily Belfast native with the opportunity he needed to further promote boxing and sponsor bouts with belts, cash, and other prizes, as well as campaigning against anti-fighting legislation. Adding further hype, Fox displayed Ryan's fighting colors in barbershops and saloons where his magazine was particularly popular. In July 1881 Sullivan and Madden set off on an exhibition tour of the science of boxing. They traveled through a number of cities in the northeastern and midwestern parts of the country where Sullivan offered $50 to any man who survived four rounds in the ring with him under the Queensberry Rules. The tour, the first of its kind in American sport, established John L Sullivan's national reputation. On December 9 Sullivan finally challenged Ryan when he announced in the *Cincinnati Enquirer* that he was prepared to fight any man for any sum from $1,000 to $10,000, a challenge which would remain open for a month.[15] The encounter was finally announced by Fox in October 1881, and in the ensuing extensive press coverage there was a consensus that the wrestling skills of the bigger Ryan would carry him to victory over the lighter Sullivan. The encounter was penciled in for February 7 of the following year, to take place in New Orleans. While Ryan was the prematch favorite, reports began to circulate that he had suffered a hernia and had been forced to wear an uncomfortable truss as a result. He might have been aware of his diminishing powers when he spoke to a journalist before the impending bout, saying that his fight with Sullivan would be his last. He had meant to retire before, and this would be his last, he explained. There was always somebody else turning up who wanted to try his hand, he explained.[16]

Richard Fox ramped up public expectations by telling reporters that he would sponsor Ryan to the tune of $10,000 if he won, money the boxer could then use to travel to Europe to fight for a world crown. Fox assured readers that the fight would take place despite the state of Louisiana's attempt to hasten a legislative bill in order to prosecute those involved in prize-fighting. The encounter, he claimed, would be done and dusted before any law was actually in place. The *Gazette* highlighted Sullivan's lack of bare-knuckle fighting experience, pointing out that most of his boxing had been of the gloved variety and that fighting with "pillows on the hands" and contending with nature's weapons unadorned are two very different things.[17] Such was the hype developed by Fox's constant coverage that one authority noted that the upcoming fight was of more interest to the American public than the Garfield–Hancock Presidential election.[18]

Ryan, aged thirty-seven, was six years older than Sullivan and ten pounds lighter but a couple of inches taller. When the referee gave the nod to start, Sullivan immediately went on the offensive, breaking down Ryan's guard with thundering blows and following up by clinching and wrestling. The first round lasted a mere thirty seconds; the opening three rounds were over in less than a minute. Ryan took a ferocious beating from the very start, and according to the *New York Times* it became clear by the sixth round that he was not only suffering but was somewhat afraid of his opponent. The defending champion landed a solid punch in the eighth but it had little effect on the bullish Sullivan; it was just a matter of time before the end came. At the start of the ninth Sullivan hit the now defenseless Ryan with a flurry of punches to the face, and when the Trojan Giant collapsed to the floor, his seconds promptly threw in the sponge. In just under eleven minutes John L. Sullivan had become the champion of America, earning the princely sum of $10,000. The *New York Times* was pithy in its summation of the fight when it noted that it was "short, sharp and decisive" with Ryan looking weary from the first round on.[19] When all expenses were deducted, Sullivan cleared a profit of $4,500 and received a further $600 for his share of the excursion fares. The unfortunate Ryan, in an era when the winner took everything, ended up with a mere $85 from his share of the excursion fees. The bout had been disappointingly one-sided, and some wags suggested that the only interesting thing about the encounter had been the presence of Frank and Jesse James in the crowd. In retrospect, it was the birth of the modern sports age and the launching pad for America's first true sporting celebrity. After the fight Ryan was magnanimous in defeat: "I never faced a man who could hit as hard. I don't believe there is another man like him in the country ... any man that Sullivan can hit he can whip."[20] When Ryan was asked to describe what it felt like to be at the receiving end of a punch from Sullivan he replied that it was like a telegraph pole had been shoved against him sideways.[21] While Ryan accepted his defeat manfully at the time, he was later to claim that the accidental undoing of his truss early in the fight proved a significant handicap.

Afterward, Ryan vowed to never fight again, but news of his defeat was met with disbelief by many, including his supportive mother-in-law, who learned of it from journalists she clearly considered to be the purveyors of fake news. Rolling up her sleeve to expose her bare forearm, the Tipperary man's mother-in-law defiantly declared to the attentive pressmen, "I could lick that man Sullivan me-self."[22] Evidently she had not seen him in action.

The *New Orleans Times-Democrat* concluded that Sullivan was a wonder and had knocked Ryan about as if he were a football.[23] When the *Police Gazette* issued an illustrated extra edition with extended coverage of the fight, public demand was so great that the presses continued to roll for weeks. Crowds flocked to see Sullivan in Chicago, Detroit, Cleveland, Pittsburgh, Philadelphia, and New York. When he arrived back in Boston Sullivan received an ecstatic reception at the Dudley Street Opera House, the venue where he had his first ever fight three years earlier. Elements of the press which had previously looked askance at boxing now changed their tune. The perceptive John Boyle O'Reilly noted that every paper in the country published a detailed report of the fight, although many of them carried editorials critical of the sport.[24]

After the title fight with Ryan, Sullivan fought what the *New York Sun* called "a series of picnics."[25] On May 13 he took on British boxer Charles Mitchell at Madison Square Garden in an encounter where it was expected he would have an easy

Eight. "The Boston Strong Boy"

victory over a significantly smaller opponent, described by *The Enquirer* as only "five feet eight inches to his stocking feet," who looked more like a young London man of fashion than a fighter.[26] Members of the boxing cognoscenti came to see Mitchell on his arrival at the docks and were convinced Sullivan would be able to account for him, but when one journalist saw him at the arena he thought he presented a different proposition: "When Mitchell stripped and stood with hands up, in fighting position, he looked altogether another man. He is all muscle. His wrists and hands are small, but his arms are solid as a rock."[27]

On the day of the encounter a New York paper called *The Truth Teller* colorfully previewed the contest, believing the fight would be a new departure for Sullivan, whose reputation was associated with "*coups de grace* rather than elegant thrusts and parries," but sure that should the Irishman's blows be accurate, "Mitchell's dance would suddenly alter from a schottische to a minuet."[28]

The Enquirer had a question: "If Charley Mitchell, the English champion pugilist, could beat all the English pugilists from John O'Groat's house to Land's End ... what is going to prevent him from doing the same thing in this country?"[29] Twelve thousand spectators gathered that night in the first incarnation of Madison Square Garden at Fifth and Broadway, with *The New York Sun* reporting that "judges, lawyers, politicians, pugilists, theatrical celebrities and eminent statesmen were among them."[30] *The Sun* noted that Sullivan went at Mitchell like a maddened bull and that his fist flew out like a stone from a catapult. In the end Sullivan did emerge victorious, but not before the plucky Englishman had given it a good shot, even managing to put Sullivan on the canvas at one point. It was a much closer contest than the Irishman had envisioned and one he would remember for future reference.

When Sullivan set off on a tour around the country in 1883 it was an unprecedented event. He visited twenty-six of the then thirty-eight states in addition to the District of Columbia and British Columbia, where he demonstrated his manly art of self-defense to all and sundry. He was scheduled to hold 195 fights in 136 cities and towns over 238 days. No one in any walk of American life had previously undertaken such an ambitious venture. For a start it had not been possible, but now the ever-burgeoning railway network had opened up the continent. Only fourteen years earlier the driving of the Golden Spike had married the Union Pacific to the Central Pacific and brought the nation's railway system together. In the decade between 1870 and 1880, railway mileage in the United States almost doubled, from nearly 50,000 to over 87,000, with that in the West more than tripling.[31] Sullivan also benefited from the exponential development of the printing press and the increasing use of photography. His tour even chimed with the introduction of the new time system on November 18, 1883. No American had so embodied his times like John L. Sullivan. The United States was, by then, the fastest growing country in the world. Its population would soon eclipse that of Great Britain, and it was on its way to becoming the world's leading industrial superpower.

Wherever he went, the Irishman claimed he would box any man under the Queensberry Rules for a prize of $250. The so-called "knocking out tour" opened in Baltimore on September 28 before 3,500 eager fight fans who filled Kernan's Theatre. No audience member challenged Sullivan on opening night, but a "flutter of excitement" palpitated through the boxing fancy when the champion donned gloves to spar with the constellation of boxing's brightest stars who comprised the "Great John L. Sullivan Combination."[32] John L. finally encountered his first challenger in McKeesport, Pennsylvania. James McCoy looked like a suitable protagonist with tattoos of snakes, flowers, and a wide-mouthed dragon on his broad chest, but after he opened with a weak blow the champion needed only a right and a left to end the contest. "I never thought any man could hit as hard as he does," McCoy said afterward. "But I can say what few men can, that I fought with the champion of the world."[33]

In Davenport, blacksmith Mike Sheehan, the "strongest man in Iowa," told his family that he was going to beat the champion. Sheehan's wife visited Sullivan before the fight and beseeched him not to fight her husband. "We've got five small children, and I don't want them to have a murderer for a father. If you get into a fight with him, he'll surely kill you," she warned the champion. John L. entered the ring and started by smashing the nose of the stunned challenger, and Sheehan's surprise quickly turned to rage. He charged at Sullivan, but a second belt to the jaw by the champion sent his foe spinning to the back of the stage, and the challenger decided he had taken enough punishment. Sullivan sent Sheehan away with $100 for being game.[34]

Reports of drunkenness and brawling appeared with increasing frequency as the trip proceeded. On Christmas Day in Denver, Sullivan almost killed a fellow fighter while playing around with a double-barreled shotgun he was told was unloaded. Two days later, in Leadville, a drunken Sullivan staggered through his performance and hurled a lit kerosene lamp at another fighter following a backstage argument. In Victoria, British Columbia, he was in "a state of beastly intoxication" and refused to stand for a toast to the health of the city's namesake, Queen Victoria, explaining that he "hadn't been brought up … drinking to the health of English monarchs."[35]

When Sullivan arrived in Galveston, Texas, he faced perhaps his toughest foe, an imposing cotton baler named Al Marx who was considered the champion of Texas. The challenger wanted to send an early statement, and just after shaking hands, he nailed Sullivan in the jaw. The Texas giant gained confidence after landing several hard blows on Sullivan in the first two rounds, and he was convinced John L. had met his match.

Sullivan had spent the day drinking, but when he came out in the third round, the "cowboy pugilist" noticed a change in the champion's eyes. John L. glared "like a wild animal" and launched an uppercut that almost lifted the giant off the floor followed by a left smash to the jaw. Marx sank "down like a bag of oats." Sullivan lifted him up and threw him over the footlights and into the orchestra pit, which broke two chairs, three violins, and a bass drum. As the Texan lay unconscious, the tour's financial manager reached into the gate receipts to scrounge for $24 to pay for the destroyed drum.

In Memphis a bricklayer named William Fleming took the stage with the champion. At the opening signal Sullivan charged, feinted with his left, and struck a blow on the lower part of Fleming's left jaw that knocked him unconscious for fifteen minutes. Fleming was lifted over the ropes and helped out of the building to his home. When he came to, he asked, "When do me and Sullivan go on?"

Eight. "The Boston Strong Boy"

On May 23, 1884, "Sullivan's Sluggers" pulled into Toledo, Ohio. Nearly eight months after they had started in Baltimore, the combination had reached its final stop. In spite of Sullivan's drunken exploits, the tour had been a success, and somehow, through all the debauchery, everyone in the traveling party made it through without any lasting damage. According to some accounts, thirty-nine men had stepped into the ring seeking to go four rounds with the champion and all had failed. During the trip he knocked out eleven men and earned an estimated $80,000. Those who were at the receiving end of his punches were often traumatized. Minnesotan Morris Hefey said it was like being struck by lightning.[36] People were desperate to see Sullivan in the flesh; some were just happy to hear a secondhand description from someone who had met him. "Let Me Shake the Hand that Shook the Hand of Sullivan" became a popular song of the era. It did not matter how well he boxed. As Nat Fleischer wrote, "Fighting well or fighting badly, sober or drunk, benign or even tempered, John L. was always the hero."[37] As well as generating income from his knocking-out tour, Sullivan made personal appearances at baseball games and endorsed everything from boxing gloves to beef soup. In conjunction with his stage shows, Sullivan had effectively become a professional showman with all the requisite characteristics: garrulity, loquaciousness, spontaneity, bonhomie, and a live-for-today attitude. He was the very embodiment of the Gilded Age, representing the achievement of sensual fulfillment that so many lusted after. He was, in the words of Elliott Gorn, "a hero and a brute, a bon vivant and a drunk, a lover of life and a reckless barbarian ... he epitomized action in an age that feared inertia."[38] Sullivan knew that he was a media celebrity and was aware of the consequences, good and bad, but believed his excesses were grossly exaggerated and when he had one drink it turned into one hundred.[39] Even one of Sullivan's former school teachers ruefully noted that he got more kudos for knowing Sullivan than for his fifty-year teaching career.[40] As one Irish American newspaper editorialized, "There are moments in every man's life, I don't care who he is, when he wishes he were John L. Sullivan, if only for half an hour."[41] A famous image of Sullivan by Charles Dana Gibson called *The Champion* depicting a powerful man dressed in a top hat and sports coat with a cigar in his mouth, surrounded by a mob of adoring children, was to be seen everywhere. "Dana represented a view that saw beauty in the achievement of muscular manliness and noted that any person who succeeded brilliantly in anything—even prize fighting and wrestling—was an artist."[42]

When Ulysses S. Grant was introduced to Sullivan in the lobby of a New York hotel he told the Irish American that his style of fighting was the model he had tried to put in operation during the Civil War.[43] In 1887 Sullivan was even invited to the White House by President Grover Cleveland. From the back streets of Boston to the house of the most powerful man in the country was a remarkable journey for a child of impoverished Irish immigrants.

A planned trip to Ireland had been eagerly awaited by the majority of the Irish public. On October 1887, Sullivan, at the height of his fame, and with a mistress in tow, sailed from Boston aboard the steamer *Cephalonia*. On November 6, after a brief stop at Queenstown, County Cork, in the south of Ireland, the ship docked at Liverpool. After a month or so of being feted at the various sporting clubs of London,

Sullivan was formally invited to a breakfast in the mess room of the Scots Guards at St. James Barracks. Later the same day, December 9, Sullivan met the Prince of Wales, the future King Edward VII, at the nearby Fencing Club. Sullivan had been his inimitable self when he met the British royal, saying, "Well, Prince, next to Jem Smith, your champion, who I'm so anxious to whip, the Prince of Wales is the man I most wanted to see when I came to England."[44] The meeting went well and the Prince of Wales presented Sullivan with a matching set of emeralds. Sullivan, who sparred briefly for the Prince, thanked the future king and reminded him that if he ever came to Boston, to be sure and look him up and he would show him around. It was a proud day for the country to welcome a man of Irish stock viewed by many in the United States as a physically indestructible symbol of one of their own made good. Here was a world champion and a wealthy man who had come to national prominence in America, long the Holy Grail for decades of Irish emigrants.

After arriving by ship at Carlisle Pier, Kingstown, on December 11, Sullivan traveled by train to Westland Row in Dublin city center, where he found himself in a state of complete siege. The party proceeded to the Grosvenor Hotel, where he was prevailed upon to speak to the assembled masses outside. Sullivan informed the crowd that he was delighted to be in the country of his parents' birth and felt like one of their own and, while he would not be able to show the Irish people anything wonderful during his all too brief stay, he hoped he would be able to demonstrate a little of his abilities. He would, he told them, always remain their faithful friend.

On the following evening, Fred Gallagher, editor of *Sport,* introduced Sullivan to the crowd at Leinster Hall in Dublin. Even the Prince of Saxe-Weimar, Commander of the Forces in Ireland, was in attendance and made a point of visiting the famous boxer in his dressing room before he took to the stage.

With the strains of "See the Conquering Hero Come" and "Yankee Doodle" playing in the background, Sullivan gave a brief speech to the assembled worthies and was given a particularly spirited round of applause when he spoke about his sympathy for the cause of Irish freedom. No record would appear to exist of how the Commander-in-Chief reacted to Sullivan's words. John L. then stripped to the waist and provided the crowd with a demonstration of his fistic skills with the aid of Jack Ashton, his regular sparring partner when on tour. The following day, Tuesday, December 13, 1887, Sullivan left for Waterford on the nine o'clock train from Knightsbridge. According to reports he was greeted warmly at all the intermediate stops but most particularly at Maryborough and Kilkenny. During this part of the trip Sullivan visited "Donnelly's Hollow," a natural amphitheater at the Athgarvan end of the Curragh, County Kildare, where in 1815 Ireland's most famous boxer of the era, Dan Donnelly, fought and defeated England's George Cooper. Donnelly's footprints on leaving the hollow had reputedly been preserved by being retrodden, and Sullivan was only too happy to add his imprint. In Waterford, hundreds gathered along the quays to catch a glimpse of Sullivan as he made his way to the Imperial Hotel. Later that evening he sparred in another exhibition with Ashton at the Theatre Royal, during which the audience were spellbound, according to a correspondent from *The Freeman's Journal*.[45] Sullivan told the audience that he had hoped to fight the English champion, Jem Smith, but that he had been "blackguarded" out of that fight and would soon face Charlie Mitchell instead. He was not particularly worried about that encounter but, with his tongue-in-cheek and promotional skills to the fore, expressed reservations about the challenge he was to face the following day in Cork in the form of a highly rated local amateur, Mr. Frank Creedon. Sullivan arrived in Cork on the following afternoon where he was met by a large crowd at the Great Southern & Western terminus, after which he was taken to the Victoria Hotel. Later in the afternoon he visited Blarney Castle and kissed the famed Blarney stone.[46] He also visited Mahony's Mills, where the firm presented him with a suit of Irish tweed. That evening Sullivan appeared at Cork Opera House to take on Creedon. The local man was twenty-three years of age, five foot seven in height, and weighed a mere eleven and a half stone (161 pounds). Sullivan took one look at Creedon and declared, "He is not in my class," and refused to fight. However, one of Sullivan's party obliged Creedon, and "after a protracted spar he dusted Creedon considerably."[47] Later, prior to another exhibition with Ashton, Sullivan presented Creedon with a gold medal and commended him on his bravery. On the afternoon of Thursday, December 15, 1887, he traveled to Limerick city, where he received his customary reception by enthusiastic followers. On that evening Sullivan and his troupe appeared at the Theatre Royal with a full house sign on the front doors an hour before the performance. After a number of amateur bouts, Sullivan took to the stage with the No. 1 National Band playing "See, the Conquering Hero Comes." After a brief speech he sparred for four rounds with Jack Ashton. A *Limerick Chronicle* reporter was very impressed with Sullivan's fighting style and particularly with the "swiftness of hands, eyes, and feet."[48] Then, to tremendous applause Sullivan exited the stage. After traveling back to Dublin that evening, he made an appearance at Leinster Hall for the finals of Monday's amateur boxing promotion, where he acted as a referee and subsequently had his usual four-round joust with Ashton. Afterward, Sullivan's personal manager, Harry Phillips, presented Fred Gallagher, the editor of *Sport,* with a gold locket, surmounted with a diamond horseshoe, as an acknowledgment of the manner in which Gallagher had organized the Irish tour. Sullivan and his party then retired for dinner at the exclusive Sheridan Club on St. Stephen's Green. The next day, Sullivan traveled to Belfast for yet another exhibition where he was once again enthusiastically received. Although Belfast was a predominantly Protestant city and Sullivan a Boston Catholic, boxing had long been a popular sport spanning the political divide.

John L. Sullivan had found the Irish people kind and generous and later claimed that he made more money in the week he spent in Ireland than in the six he had in England. In addition to hard currency he was gifted a tweed suit, four jugs of whiskey, seventeen blackthorn sticks, and a grand total of forty-five letters asking him to underwrite charitable organizations during his time in Ireland. He would later note that the reception he received in Dublin was "marvelously enthusiastic and brought forcibly to my mind the fact that I was in the midst of the warm-hearted people who I am proud to claim descent."[49]

On March 10, 1888, Sullivan went into the ring to defend his title against Charles Mitchell at the unlikely venue of Chateau de Laversine, the stately home of Baron Gustave de Rothschild on the banks of the River Oise three miles north of Chantilly in the

Picardy region of northern France. There had been bad blood between the two men from their previous encounter in New York, and when Sullivan had visited England the previous December Mitchell had taunted Sullivan in the press, reminding him that he had knocked him down in the first round of their fight in Madison Square Garden. Sullivan always maintained that he had just slipped in that fight and later referred to the Englishman in his autobiography as "a bombastic sprinter boxer."[50] Fought in driving rain, their second bout was to prove an epic and brutal encounter. Mitchell insisted on a twenty-four-foot ring, while Sullivan wanted to fight in a sixteen-foot area to limit the Englishman's evasive tactics, which he deplored. After much wrangling, Sullivan conceded to Mitchell's wishes and the fight got underway just before one o'clock in the afternoon in an outdoor ring erected adjacent to the estate's livery stables. Sullivan later noted in his memoirs that he did not like the approach taken by his foe, with his constant running and dropping, so much so that there was a "track like a sheep run" visible on the floor of the ring at the end.[51] After three hours and eleven minutes fought over thirty-nine rounds, neither of the men could lift their hands and the contest was declared a draw. Because the fight was considered illegal, Mitchell was arrested by the local police while Sullivan, wrapped in bandages, was spirited across the English Channel where he spent a number of weeks convalescing in a Liverpool hospital. When Mitchell got back to England he was hailed as a hero by his supporters and presented with an ostentatious sterling silver and velvet belt ornately embossed with the words "Presented to Charles Mitchell to Commemorate His Gallant Fight with John L. Sullivan for the Championship of the World on March 10th 1888 near Paris Resulting in a Draw, 39 Rounds being Fought, in 3 Hours 11 Minutes."[52] There was no doubting the diminution of John L. Sullivan's formidable strength, and as Arthur Brisbane of the *New York Sun* noted, his talents had wilted "under the double bombardment of French champagne and American whiskey."[53]

Sullivan lived life to the full and his health inevitably suffered from the many excesses he subjected his body to. At various times he claimed to suffer from typhoid fever, gastric fever, inflammation of the bowels, heart trouble, liver complaints, and incipient paralysis, but alcohol abuse was undoubtedly his Achilles' heel. He would later say that "an ocean would scarcely hold the liquor that was pressed upon me by good fellows."[54] When once asked by a journalist as to his daily consumption he replied, "I don't drink much. Say five or six glasses of ale a day and a bottle for dinner, if I feel like it."[55] One of his best known mantras was "we are going to be a long time dead and only a few of us know how to enjoy it as it goes."[56]

While drinking may not have killed him at a young age, it did destroy his marriage to Annie Bates, a chorus girl he had married in 1883. Their only child, John Junior, died in 1886. In her divorce proceedings Bates referred to Sullivan's "cruel and abusive treatment and gross and confirmed habits of intoxication"[57] Given that the rate of alcoholism among the Irish community in Boston was four times that of any other ethnic group during the last two decades of the nineteenth century, it was perhaps inevitable that such a publicly celebrated character as the Strong Boy would succumb to alcohol addiction.[58] The Irish had brought their drinking culture to the United States; between 1846 and 1849 the number of saloons in Boston increased from 850 to more than 1,200.[59]

Sullivan was always aware of the necessity of capitalizing on his fame while he could, and avoided defending his title for as long as possible. When the *Police Gazette* declared Jake Kilrain the champion in light of Sullivan's continued absence from the ring, a ferocious public backlash ensued. Kilrain, born John Joseph Killion on February 9, 1859, earned his fighting chops working in the mills of Somerville, just outside Boston. The men had much in common; there was only four months between them in age and both were sons of Irish immigrants. A keen sportsman, Kilrain was also a champion rower and won the National Amateur Junior Sculling Championship in 1883 but was later stripped of his title when it was discovered that he was a prize-fighter and could not be considered an amateur sportsman. Kilrain took up professional prize-fighting in the same year as his rowing success and quickly established a reputation as a formidable foe. Inevitably, Richard K. Fox took an interest in Kilrain, declaring him the new heavyweight hope in the *Police Gazette*. In 1887 Fox challenged Sullivan to fight Kilrain, and after the inevitable wrangling the two sides agreed on terms, but when Sullivan took on a fight against Paddy Cardiff in the interim, Fox was incensed and deemed Kilrain the new champion, claiming Sullivan had forfeited the title by fighting Cardiff. Fox promptly commissioned a diamond-studded belt and presented it to Kilrain, but Sullivan's financial backers responded by presenting their man with his own championship belt, a fourteen-carat gold affair, encrusted with 256 diamonds and engraved with the words "Presented to the Champion of Champions, John L. Sullivan, by the Citizens of the United States" and valued at $10,000.[60] When presented with the belt, in front of a crowd of 3,500 of his ardent supporters at Boston Theatre on August 8, 1887, Sullivan reputedly roared, "I wouldn't put Fox's belt around the neck of a goddamn dog."[61] Later the same year, Kilrain fought British Champion Jem Smith for what Richard Fox declared the world title on the island of Saint-Pierre-d'Autils on the River Seine near Paris. After two and a half hours of intense fighting the bout was declared a draw when darkness forced a halt to proceedings. Meanwhile, Sullivan was also in Europe, where he sparred against a series of inferior opponents in England, Scotland, and Ireland, with his only legitimate fight being the encounter with Charles Mitchell in France.

On his return to the United States, Sullivan's backers put him under the care of the famed wrestler William "The Solid Man" Muldoon to whip him into shape for the proposed fight with Kilrain. Muldoon, another son of Irish emigrants and a keen physical culturalist, had been a Greco-Roman Wrestling Champion and would later become the first chairman of the New York Athletic Commission. In 1876 he had accepted an appointment with the New York Police Department when invited to do so by the redoubtable ex-brawler Senator John "Old Smoke" Morrissey. Muldoon had taken on the task of training Sullivan on a friendly wager and undertook to absorb any expenses if he lost. As part of the boxer's preparations, the two men fought an exhibition wrestling match under London Prize Ring Rules on May 28, an encounter which ended in a draw. Based in Belfast, New York, a town heavily populated by Irish immigrants in the west of the state on the banks of the Genesee River, Sullivan assiduously followed the program designed by Muldoon, a routine which included wood chopping, cow milking, field plowing, and rope jumping. Fox had continued to trumpet his support of Kilrain and even commissioned a four-verse song in his honor, sung by Irish American star Maggie Cline, which included the line "Hail to the most straightforward and the most unassuming champion the world ever had."[62] He contended that Kilrain was champion of the world, although he had only ever drawn with English fighter Jem Smith.[63]

New Orleans, the city chosen to host the fight, was agog in advance of the boxers' arrival. "The city is fighting mad.... Everybody has the fever and is talking about Sullivan and Kilrain. Ladies discussed it in street cars, men talked and argued about it in places which had never heard pugilism mentioned before," reported the *New Orleans Picayune* on the eve of the fight.

The *New York Times* compared the level of excitement to that of a presidential election, while the *New York Herald,* dismissive of Sullivan's chances, believed the superior fitness and wrestling skills of Kilrain would carry the day over Sullivan and his debauched lifestyle would fail him after twenty minutes of fighting.[64]

Once again the fight was pushed to the hinterlands because of official disapproval. The chosen location was the farm of timber baron Charles Rich in the township of Richburg, 100 miles distant from New Orleans. Three trains departed the city under the cover of darkness to avoid the forces of the law, with the first carrying the pugilists and their entourages while the others were packed with the hordes of ticket holders. The fans traveled through the night holding tickets with nothing but the words "Destination" and "Return" printed on them. Bare-knuckle boxing was still illegal in thirty-eight states, including Mississippi, where Governor Robert Lowry had offered a $1,500 reward for the arrest of the fighters. The ring had been erected the night before by a crew working by torchlight. Some of the fans had paid $15 for ringside seats, while the rest paid $10 for general admission.

Finally, at thirteen minutes after ten on the morning of July 8, 1899, with an already scorching hot sun beating down on the exposed venue, the two fighters came to the line for what would prove to be the last great bare-knuckle fight contest in history. Charles Mitchell was in Kilrain's corner, desperately hoping that his man could take down the Strong Boy, while Sullivan, his hair cut short and his customary mustache absent, looked in fine fettle, as the referee, John Fitzpatrick, later to become the mayor of New Orleans, called the men to scratch. The *New York Times* thought Kilrain looked ill at ease, as if he felt that there was hard work before him.[65] However, Kilrain ended the first round in a mere fifteen seconds when he threw Sullivan to the ground, landing on him for good measure. Proceedings evened out over the next five rounds.

The fourth lasted a draining fifteen minutes, most of which consisted of prolonged grappling and wrestling. In the sixth round Kilrain drew first blood when he opened a cut on the champion's ear with a vicious right, but Sullivan, unbowed, proceeded to floor Kilrain. The fight dragged on, round after relentless round. William Edgar Harding of the *Police Gazette* was impressed with the physical condition of Sullivan despite his famously dissolute lifestyle, noting that his "old time ferocity seemed to come back ... he rushed at Kilrain like a tiger at its prey. His eyes flashed, his lips were set and he seemed to become larger and more massive than he was."[66] The sun was so hot that spectators' clothes stuck to the pitch bubbling forth from the newly constructed pinewood stands. Sullivan goaded Kilrain: "You're a champion. A champion of what?" The fight ground relentlessly on. At the end of the seventeenth round Kilrain's seconds had to carry him to his corner: Sullivan was not much better. The fighters were wearing high-topped cleated shoes to help them gain traction in the dirt, and at some point Kilrain stepped on Sullivan's feet, accidentally or otherwise, causing blood to seep through the tops of his shoes as he prepared for the eighteenth round. At the end of the thirtieth round Sullivan's trainer asked him how long he thought he could keep going, to which the fighter replied, "I can stay here until daybreak tomorrow."[67] Notwithstanding his verbal bravado, Sullivan was visibly tiring. For the start of the fortieth round his seconds had to carry him to the scratch line, while in the forty-fourth Sullivan

"The Boston Strong Boy": John L. Sullivan (*The New York Illustrated Times*, Currier and Ives, Library of Congress).

"Sullivan–Kilrain boxing match, Richburg, Mississippi, 1889." Sullivan (left) faces up to Kilrain in the first round (Ernest Marx, Prints and Photographs Division, Library of Congress).

began to vomit uncontrollably. Kilrain's trainer, Mike Donovan, implored his fighter to take advantage of the situation, but Jake refused; "No, I won't Mike, I won't.... John, I won't hit you while you are vomiting." Kilrain asked Sullivan if he was agreeable to drawing the fight but the Boston man refused and the contest dragged on. In the seventy-fifth round Sullivan punched his dazed opponent at will and one of Kilrain's seconds asked the Irishman if he would take $1,000 if his man conceded. Sullivan looked at the state of his opponent and agreed, only to be overruled by his backers, who insisted he fight on. Mike Donovan had seen enough, however. One of the doctors in attendance told him that his man would die if the fight was not stopped and he was not going to be party to manslaughter.[68] It was finally over.

Those in attendance knew they had witnessed a historic event, and everything on view became a valued souvenir. The hat which Sullivan had thrown into the ring

"The Sullivan and Kilrain fight—John L. Sullivan, champion of the world." The large crowd is watching the seventh round of the contest (Thomas Pye, New Orleans, Louisiana, Prints and Photographs Division, Library of Congress).

"Sullivan–Kilrain fight. The last round—victor and vanquished" (Geo. Barker, Prints and Photographs Division, Library of Congress).

to signal his intention to fight was auctioned for $50, while ice buckets went for $25; even slivers of the ring post commanded $5. Reporters' desks were splintered, fences went down, and all restrictions were swept aside.[69] Kilrain had stayed in the fight for a brutal two hours and eighteen minutes, seventy of the scheduled eighty rounds.

Details of the contest were front-page news across the nation; even the *New York Times* led with the ambivalent headline "The Bigger Brute Won." Its disdain for prize-fighting had not gone away, and it explained to its readers that the brute might be good at fighting other men but they were unlikely to be of any use for anything else. "A prize fighter, however, is merely a muscular person who is capable of giving and taking very hard knocks. There is no productive industry in which Sullivan or Kilrain could earn two dollars a day more than a man of ordinary muscular power."[70] Sullivan just about made it to a train returning to New Orleans and spent the night at the Young Men's Gymnastic Club, where he celebrated in his usual style. As was his wont, the Strong Boy demonstrated his largesse by throwing money from a window to his adoring fans. There were to be further unforeseen difficulties. Sullivan was arrested in Nashville as he traveled back to New York, while Kilrain was detained in Baltimore. The former was released without charge but was further detained in Purvis, Mississippi, where he was found guilty of illegal fighting and sentenced to a year in jail. He appealed; the verdict was overturned after he paid a $500 fine. Kilrain was not as lucky; he received a two-month jail sentence, which he served on Charles Rich's farm. Kilrain had fifteen more professional fights but never fought for the world title again and died at the age of seventy-eight in Quincy, Massachusetts, where he is buried in St. Mary's Cemetery, just a few miles from his old foe.

The historic fight was famously celebrated by troubadour poet Vachel Lindsay in "John L. Sullivan, the Strong Boy of Boston."

"When I was nine years old, in 1889 / I sent my love a lacy Valentine / Suffering boys were dressed like Fauntelroys / While Judge and Puck in joint humor vied / The Gibson girl came shining like a bride / to spoil the cult of Tennyson's Elaine. / Louisa Alcott was my gentle bride… / Then I heard a trumpet sound. / Nigh New Orleans / Upon an emerald plain / John L. Sullivan / The strong boy / Of Boston / Fought seventy five rounds with Jake Kilrain."[71]

For three years after the Kilrain match, Sullivan did not fight. He toured as the hero of a play called *Honest Hearts and Willing Hands,* boxed in occasional exhibitions, and drank. The comedy-drama, written specially for Sullivan by Duncan B. Harrison, was set in Ireland with the Strong Boy in the starring role of the boxing village blacksmith who vies for the heart of a girl. The production toured for two years and took Sullivan to theaters as far away as Canada and Australia, and while John L. was not a good actor by most accounts with a propensity for bawling out his lines in the same way as he offered to lick all comers in the nation's taverns, indulgent

"The champion of all champions—'Hoping to deserve your appreciation, I remain yours truly—John L. Sullivan'" (Prints and Photographs Division, Library of Congress).

audiences were happy to watch, holding back their loudest cheers for the end when he floored the villain with a knockout punch. Sullivan even entertained thoughts of running for political office and wrote an open letter to newspapers outlining his suitability to the role: "I feel to be more important than all else is the work which I have done to keep up the reputation of America among other nations."[72] He soon forgot about his political notions and continued on his travels. When he returned from a theatrical trip to Australia, boxing fans desperately wanted to know if he would fight to prove his abilities to all the naysayers who believed he was past it. Sullivan answered in no uncertain terms: "I hereby challenge any and all the bluffers who have been trying to make capital at my expense to fight me, either the last week in August or the first week in September, this year, at the Olympic Club, in the city of New Orleans, for a purse of $25,000 and an outside bet of $10,000, the winner of the fight to take the entire purse...The Marquis of Queensberry rules must govern this contest, as I want fight, not foot-racing, as I intend keeping the championship of the world."[73] Sullivan had begun his bare-knuckle fighting on a barge on the Hudson River in order to get away from the forces of the law and ended his career fighting under Queensberry Rules in arenas watched by crowds which included middle-class business men and their wives.

James "Gentleman Jim" Corbett, the next great Irish American boxer, immediately accepted the challenge. In a sign of the increasing commercialism of boxing, the articles of agreement were signed at the offices of the *New York World* and not at those of the *Police Gazette* as had previously been the custom. For some this proprietary stamp was too much to take. E.L. Godkin, editor of *The Nation,*, fulminated against organs of the press who, he believed, were pandering to the "offscourings of human society—gamblers, thieves, drunkards and bullies.... persons whose manners and morals are a disgrace to our civilization."[74] On the other hand, Joseph Pulitzer, editor of the *World,* saw where public taste and commercial opportunity lay, and added a sports supplement to his paper, a development soon copied by many others. The arrangements made for the fight were equally instructive. In 1889 some of New Orleans's up-market athletic clubs began to sponsor professional prize fights, building new venues to accommodate them. Boxing was entering the mainstream. As one newspaper put it, "Steady businessmen, society bloods, and in fact, all classes of citizens are eager and anxious to spend their wealth to see a glove contest."[75] On March 14, 1890, the New Orleans City Council authorized Queensberry fights with the provisions that no liquor be served, no bouts be staged on Sundays, and that promoters must contribute a sum of $50 to charity. Boxing was becoming a business, and the fight between Corbett and Sullivan was going to be box office. As the *New Orleans Picayune* noted, it would be "the old generation against the new ... the gladiator against the boxer."[76]

Nine

A Changing of the Guard

James "Gentleman Jim" Corbett

"You become a champion by fighting one more round. When things are tough, you fight one more round."
—James J. Corbett

"Why a fighter can't be careful about his appearance I don't understand."
—James J. Corbett[1]

JOHN L. SULLIVAN AND JAMES CORBETT were active athletes at a crucial period of time for Irish Americans. The majority of postfamine Irish emigrants had gradually assimilated into American society and were, bit by bit, climbing the socioeconomic ladder. While Sullivan was only eight years older than his adversary, the fighters were polar opposites in many ways: John L. Sullivan did his best to project an aura of refinement and decorum at certain times during his life, but Jim Corbett had an uncanny ability of perfecting the art. The literary critic John V. Kelleher once wrote of him that he "was a prophetic figure: slim, deft, witty, looking like a proto–Ivy Leaguer with his pompadour, his fresh intelligent face, his well-cut young man's clothes. He was, as it were, the paradigm of all those young Irish Americans about to make the grade."[2] Corbett certainly took his appearance seriously, once stating, "Why a boxer can't be careful about his appearance, I don't understand."[3] From the start of his career he was aware of the tight control he needed to exert over his celebrity. On meeting Mark Twain in 1894 the celebrated writer challenged Corbett to a fight. Twain later wrote that Corbett declined "so gravely that one might easily have thought him in earnest." The Irishman was worried that Twain could knock him out with a "purely accidental blow." If that happened he would lose his reputation and Twain would double his: "You have got fame enough already and you ought not want to take mine away from me."[4]

In his 1925 memoir *The Roar of the Crowd*, Corbett openly criticized the brash behavior of Sullivan and recounted a particular incident where he felt compelled to challenge Sullivan's boorish and drunken behavior in a bar in San Francisco. Sullivan was on tour with his play *Honest Hearts and Willing Hands* and Corbett bumped into his entourage in a bar called Mat Hogan's, where, according to Corbett, Sullivan banged his fist on the counter and made his old boast that he could lick any man in the world, giving him a ferocious and contemptuous glance.[5] The teetotal Corbett

Nine. A Changing of the Guard

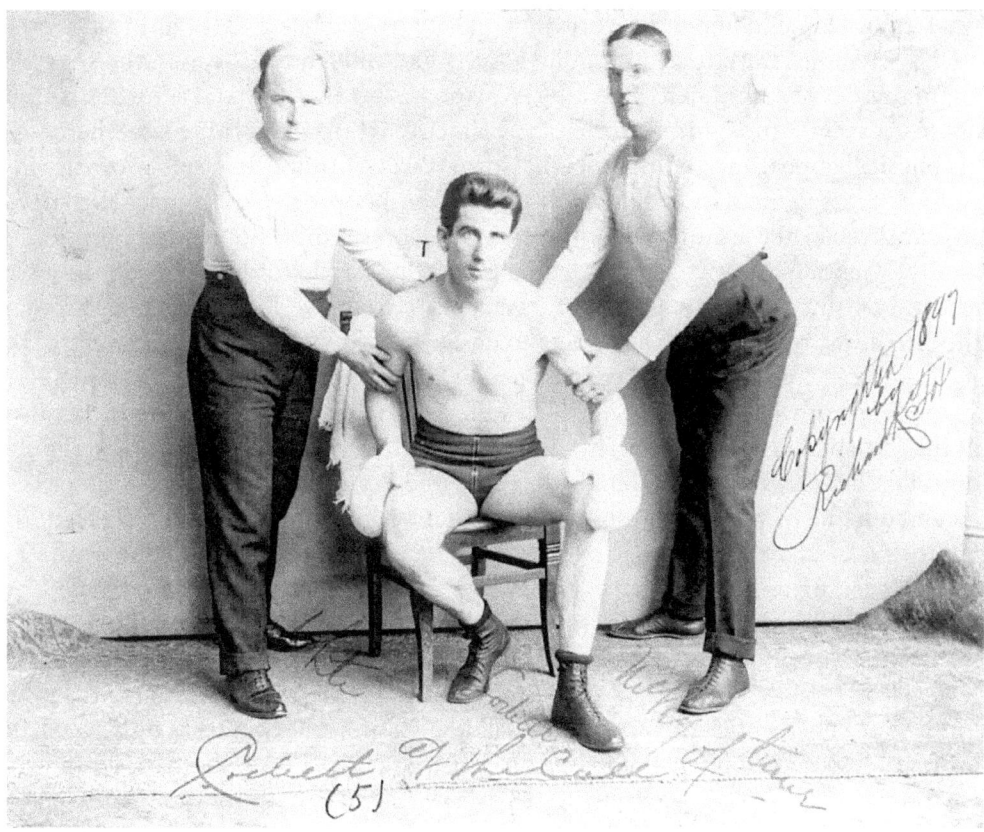

Born the son of an Irish father and Scottish mother in San Francisco in 1866, Corbett (center) was given the sobriquet "Gentleman Jim" for his ostensibly suave and sophisticated manner and is widely regarded as the first fighter to bring "science" to the sport. He won the heavyweight title on September 7, 1892, at the Olympic Club in New Orleans, Louisiana, by knocking out John L. Sullivan in the 21st round (Photo print copyrighted by Richard K. Fox. Prints and Photographs Division, Library of Congress).

informed Sullivan that his lewd pronouncement was "hardly courteous" and that he did not want to hear such talk in his presence again. Somewhat surprisingly, Corbett noted that Sullivan listened to reason.

By his own account, Corbett was dedicated to his parents and, with money made from fighting, paid off their mortgage and later brought his mother back to Ireland. He, in his own mind at least, was the perfect Irish son. In reality, James Corbett was no shining light of virtue. While he may have had good manners, a fine dress sense, and a preference for stylish boxing, he was also arrogant, bigoted, and a serial philanderer. His parents, Patrick Corbett from Ballycusheen, Ballinrobe, County Mayo, and Kate McDonald from Dublin, emigrated to the United States in 1854 and settled in San Francisco, where they established a successful livery stable. James was born on September 1, 1866, one of ten children, and like John L. Sullivan's before him, his fervently Catholic parents entertained hopes that their son might join the priesthood; he was even named after his father's brother, a priest back in Ireland. It was not to be for the feisty young Corbett. After being expelled from two schools, James entered the world of work as a bank teller, and it was in San Francisco's Olympic Athletic Club that he got his first official coaching in the sport of boxing under the guidance of Walter Watson. From the very start Corbett stood out in the rough-and-tumble world of the ring. Apart from anything else, there was his physical appearance and decorum. Corbett wore his hair in a full-grown pompadour, dressed smartly, and prided himself on his precise grammar. His suave appearance earned him the nicknames "Handsome Jim," "Pompadour Jim," and finally, "Gentleman Jim." Corbett had a perfect physique for boxing, standing six feet and one inch tall with a reach of seventy-three inches. His progression through the ranks was rapid; by the age of eighteen he was the club's best heavyweight. In 1886, at the age of nineteen, Corbett eloped to Salt Lake City where he married Olive Lake Morris in what he later ruefully described as "a mad act of youth."[6] It was also in the state of Utah that the Irishman was to get his first taste of professional boxing when he answered a challenge issued by one Frank Smith. Fighting under the assumed name of Jim Dillon, so that news of his whereabouts would not reach his family back in San Francisco, Corbett pocketed a badly needed $460 for winning. After returning to his home city the newly married boxer found work as a clerk at an insurance company while continuing to ply his trade in the boxing world as an instructor and fighter. On May 30, 1889, Corbett made his professional debut against Jewish boxer Joe "Chrysanthemum" Choynski in a remote barn in Marin County. The son of Polish emigrants who had settled in California, Choynski only weighed around 170 pounds but was renowned for his punching power relative to his size. Corbett subsequently wrote of the class difference between himself and his opponent, describing Choynski as a candy puller in a factory while he was supported by wealthy bankers.[7] Corbett was always a man who wanted to be seen in the best possible light, and whether or not those bankers even knew he was fighting is a question which cannot be answered at this remove. Five rounds into the contest the local sheriff turned up and brought proceedings to an abrupt halt, but the combatants met for a rematch a week later on June 5, this time on a barge north of San Francisco Bay, a venue outside the jurisdiction of the law. The men had agreed to use two-ounce gloves, but Choynski was aware that Corbett had hurt his hand in the first fight and turned up at the rematch claiming he had forgotten to bring his gloves and asked the Irishman if he would be amenable to a bare-knuckle fight. Gentleman Jim declined to fight without gloves but allowed the bout to go ahead when Choynski borrowed a pair of leather riding gloves from a spectator. It proved to be a barbaric encounter. In the third round the seams of Choynski's gloves cut Corbett badly, and such was the level of blood loss that sawdust had to be placed on the floor to enable the combatants to remain standing. Corbett was also competing with badly blistered feet. After damaging two of the knuckles on his left hand in an early round, Corbett was forced to improvise with a shot he had rarely used previously, a left hook. In time it was to become his trademark. After twenty-seven brutal rounds Corbett finally knocked out his opponent and would later claim it was the toughest battle he had ever fought.

Most boxing historians consider Corbett to be the first truly "scientific" boxer and a pioneer in the development of daily boxing training regimes. While not gifted with heavy punching power, Corbett used his speed of foot, boxing skills, and tight defense to frustrate rivals who concentrated on landing a knockout blow on his chin. Corbett's professional career took off in earnest when he defeated Irish American Dominick McCaffrey at Brooklyn's Casino Rink in April 1890, and he then had his sights firmly set on a tilt at the world title. On May 21, 1891, Corbett took on the formidable Peter "The Black Prince" Jackson at the Californian Athletic Club in San Francisco for a purse of $10,000. John L. Sullivan had refused to fight the Australian on color grounds. Corbett would later refer to Jackson, also known as "Peter the Great," as "one of the most intelligent pugilists that ever stepped into the ring."[8] The Australian had immense difficulty in getting any opponents to take him on and at one stage offered to fight with only his left hand. Anticipation of the Corbett–Jackson meeting was intense; promoters were able to charge the unheard-of sum of $50 dollars for tickets. Coming into the fight

On August 14, 1903, world heavyweight champion James Jeffries made his sixth defense of the title he had captured in 1899 from Bob Fitzsimmons against Gentleman Jim. The soon-to-be thirty-seven-year-old Corbett fought gamely, but was no match for the bigger, stronger, and younger champion. Corbett was stopped in the tenth round and never fought again (Photo print copyrighted by Paul Thompson, Prints and Photographs Division, Library of Congress).

Gentleman Jim was the decided underdog. At six feet one inch and 210 pounds, Jackson was an intimidating presence. In a demonstration of bravado, Corbett refused the Australian's request to enter the ring second. From the start of the fight the Irishman showed all his customary evasiveness, and it was only in the sixteenth round that Jackson managed to land one of his trademark heavy rights to Corbett's body. In the twenty-fifth Corbett was almost knocked out by a right from Jackson but managed to reply with a short barrage of his own. After an unrelenting four hours and sixty-one rounds a no-contest decision was eventually recorded, as both men were so exhausted that neither could muster a further blow. It was not the result that most of the cognoscenti had foreseen. The Australian had been a firm two-to-one favorite to win, but by the end of proceedings the general consensus was that the Irishman was looking the most likely winner and would have taken the laurels if the fight had been allowed to continue.

A few months before their famous meeting in New Orleans, Corbett and Sullivan had briefly sparred in full evening dress at an exhibition bout in San Francisco. The clothing had been donned at Sullivan's insistence, ostensibly to bring decorum to proceedings, but more likely to have been an effort to disguise his ever-burgeoning girth. Although a tame affair, it provided Corbett with a good opportunity to weigh up his opponent for the forthcoming title fight. With his superior fitness and more advanced ring skills, he felt confident he could take the aging Sullivan and informed his seconds that the Boston Strong Boy was made to order for him.[9] Sullivan was also bullish in advance of their meeting in New Orleans and believed the genteel Corbett would not survive in the ring with him. How could a counter jumper be a decent fighter? Sullivan would punch holes in handsome Jimmy.[10]

There were countervailing viewpoints, however. Dr. Dudley A. Sargent of Harvard University, America's first professor of physical education, followed Sullivan's regime prior to the fight. He noted that the Strong Boy had shed twenty pounds over two months in a training regime which involved running, walking, playing handball, lifting dumbbells, skipping exercises, pounding a punch-bag for an hour each day, bathing, and swimming. Despite this, the professor still had doubts as to whether Sullivan would be able for a fight at the highest level, noting that the Strong Boy's weight of 216 pounds for his height was considerably in excess of what it should be for a man in good condition. Jake Kilrain, perhaps remembering his own chastening experience with Sullivan, backed the Strong Boy to win, believing that the science of Corbett would not survive one of Sullivan's stiff punches.[11]

Before the fight some members of the press marveled at the change in attitude toward the sport. *The New York Herald* noted that the odium which rested upon the prize ring and the majority of its exponents a decade or two previously because of the disgraceful occurrences connected with it had now been removed to a certain extent and the sport was now of national and international importance.[12] The *Chicago Daily Tribune,* reminiscing on the old bare-knuckle days, was wont to agree, writing that men were now traveling to great boxing contests in vestibule limited trains, sleeping at the best hotels, and attending fights in grand, brilliantly lighted arenas.[13] Even Grover Cleveland and Benjamin Harrison's presidential campaigns were reduced to the status of secondary news as the fight neared.

It was like Mardi Gras in New Orleans, according to Elliott Gorn: "Fans from across the country swelled New Orleans to bursting, and the festive crowds in the French Quarter evoked Mardi Gras. Colorfully dressed sportsmen, solid planters, ragged black roustabouts, and Italian street vendors paraded the teeming thoroughfares. Merchants' windows were filled with pictures of the pugilists and replicas of their fighting colors."[14]

The fight was the highlight of a three-day boxing extravaganza. On September 5 Jack McAuliffe knocked out Billy Myer to retain his lightweight world title, while on the following day George Dixon won the featherweight title by defeating Jack Skelley. The fact that Dixon was black and Skelley white added an extra frisson to the encounter, and the fight was so bloody that it was cited in a Louisiana court in November of the following year when a commission was established to discuss the banning of prize-fighting in the state. One newspaper graphically described the brutality of the bout: "What with bruises, lacerations, and coagulated blood Skelley's nose, mouth and eye presented a horrible spectacle, and as the poor fellow staggered around almost helpless, even some of the most blase at the ringside were heard to shudder and some even turned away at the face already disfigured past recognition and heard the ugly half splashing sound as his blood filled gloves again and again visited the bleeding wounds that had drenched them."[15] Nothing, however, could have engendered the excitement generated by the encounter between Sullivan and Corbett on September 7. On the night of the fight, former New Orleans Mayor Guilotte announced the contestants' weights to 10,000 fans in the Olympic Club arena, with Sullivan hitting the scales at 212 pounds while his opponent was twenty-five pounds lighter. Fifty Western Union telegraph operators sat ringside, dictating blow-by-blow accounts to the nation, with Sullivan four to one to win. Even Corbett's manager had a bet on the Strong Boy. The nation was on tenterhooks. A beacon was poised on top of the Pulitzer Building in New York to signal red if Sullivan won and white if Corbett triumphed. Some years later the famous trainer and referee Billy Roche described the appearance of the fighters when they entered the ring:

> Sullivan, whom my father trained for his fight with Paddy Ryan, was fat and terribly out of condition, I'll never forget the look of Corbett. He was the finest specimen of a man I had ever seen in a ring. He had fine broad shoulders and long, trim legs. His skin was white and his long face was thin. The contrast with his black eyes and dark heavy pompadour was striking. Years before, when first I had seen Sullivan he had looked something like that. Originally he was a lean-faced, dark Irishman, very trim and lithe, with high cheekbones.[16]

It was clear from the start that Sullivan was unfit and no match for the better conditioned and more talented Corbett. The younger man easily danced away from all of Sullivan's lumbering punches and had no difficulty in regularly landing his impressive jab. Corbett provided a technical masterclass and time and time again managed to avoid the bullish charges of Sullivan. Then came the twenty-first round. Corbett described it thus in his autobiography:

> When we came up for the twenty-first round it looked as if the fight would last ten or fifteen rounds longer. Right away I went up to him, feinted with my left and hit him with a left-hand hook alongside the jaw pretty hard, and I saw his eyes roll.... Summoning all the reserve force I had left I let my guns go, right and left, with all the dynamite Nature had given me, and Sullivan stood dazed and rocking. So I set myself for an instant, put just "a little more" in a right and hit him alongside the jaw. And he fell helpless on the ground, on his stomach, and rolled over on his back! The referee, his seconds and mine picked him up and put him in his corner; and the audience went wild.[17]

The *New York World* wrote that Sullivan fell like an oak tree, "slowly and majestically."[18] Youth, skill, and science had inevitably triumphed over age, dissipation, and brute strength. The *New York Times,* for one, was content to see the back of Sullivan: "The dethronement of a mean and cowardly bully as the idol of the barrooms is a public good that is a fit subject for public congratulations."[19] Another magazine termed Sullivan a "vulgar false hero" who appealed to those still living in barbarian times and wrote that his glorification had been in every way "demoralizing." He taught people that his "coarse preeminence" was "not to be maintained without paying the price in self-control and industry."[20] Reflecting upon the bout some years later, the *Washington Herald* recalled it as a "triumph of youth, agility and skill over advancing years, over-confidence and strength. It was a victory of mind over matter."[21] Sullivan admitted as much to reporters after the fight when he said, "It's the old, old story. I am like the pitcher that went to the well once too often."[22] Years later, Billy Madden, Sullivan's former manager, insisted the Boston man would have defeated Corbett if he had still been in his prime: "When they tell me that Corbett at his best could have mastered the skill of John L. Sullivan in John's prime, I must take more than a modicum of salt to swallow such a yarn."[23]

Despite his loss to Corbett, Sullivan's fame and popularity continued unabated. As the *Police Gazette* noted in 1905, he was better known in America than George Washington.[24]

However, Sullivan later became a figure of fun in some quarters. When he had earlier declared his interest in running for political office, the *Boston Investigator* reminded Bostonians of Sullivan's profession. "Boston has been represented at Washington heretofore by more or less brains.... The funniest thing in his letter is that he speaks of himself as a man. Every individual of the human race, every grownup male person, is not a man.... Let this fellow stick to prize-fighting and whiskey drinking. He is an ornament to the ring and the bar-room, but a disgrace to any other place." In this critical comment, the *Investigator* stressed Sullivan's ethnicity, describing him as the "most famous Catholic in America."[25]

In 1906 the *Paterson Morning Call* reported that Sullivan had recently been living in St. Louis instead of his "dear classic Boston" and had "withered away like a rare orchid engrafted on the root of an unromantic cauliflower." However, Sullivan had plans to take back the world title and had contacted the paper to outline his intentions. His face would once more be seen on the walls of the nation's barbershops and whiskey would flow from distilleries when his name was mentioned, he told them. The world's championship belt, studded with precious stones, would once more come home "to roost on papa's tummy" and the voice of the happy newsboy would once again proclaim his greatness. Through the newspaper he issued a challenge to prominent fighters Tommy Burns, "Philadelphia" Jack O'Brien, Marvin Hart, and James J. Jeffries, claiming he would account for all of them in one night. If any of them lasted four rounds he was willing to reward them with a sizable sum. The challenge went unmet and the journalist wryly noted that the only rounds Sullivan was now familiar with were those bought in bars.[26]

Despite having declared bankruptcy in 1902 and pawning his beloved championship belt, Sullivan traveled to Ireland for the last time in 1910 accompanied by his second wife, Kate Harkins, who had been born in County Donegal and brought to Boston by her parents. When they returned to America the couple bought a cottage and farm outside Boston which they named "DonLeeRoss," derived from Donegal, Tralee, and Roscommon, the latter in honor of his parents' places of birth. In his later years Sullivan became an unlikely convert to the Anti-Saloon League. Among his pithy aphorisms were "the booze wasn't afraid of John L. Sullivan" and "now,

I want to tell you something from the book of experience of John L. Sullivan. The booze has more ways of hitting you than you have of dodging, no matter how successful an individual you may be."

Beyond his flag-waving for the cause of sobriety, Sullivan was an ardent nationalist. In an 1889 public speech he cast himself as a patriotic symbol of American athleticism, opining that no self-respecting American could do other than take pride that a native son could beat any man in the world. Earlier in his fighting career he had ended his 1892 challenge to Charles Mitchell of England with the words, "I prefer this challenge should be accepted by smoke of the foreigners who have been sprinting so hard after the American dollars of late, as I would rather whip them than any of my own countrymen.... I intend to keep the championship of the world where it belongs in the land of the free and the home of the brave."[27]

Sullivan also famously addressed an eager public at Faneuil Hall in Boston in May 1917, telling them that he had no difficulty in going to war if called up for military duty and no fear of death in the name of democracy: "If the time prevails and the opportunity avails, your uncle, John L., will be there. I've got to die sooner or later, but I have no fear of death in this fight for democracy."[28]

Even Richard K. Fox, with whom he had many differences during his lifetime, noted that Sullivan's fist was "like a clapper of some great bell that ... boomed the brazen message of America's glory as a fighting nation from one end of the earth to the other."[29] Unfortunately, John L. never did get to see any battlefield and was dead by the end of World War I. On February 2, 1918, at the age of fifty-nine, Sullivan died of a heart attack at his home in Abingdon, Massachusetts, as he was preparing to leave for Boston, where he was to announce his upcoming role on a circus tour for which he would receive $1,000 to enter the ring in an Irish jaunting car and deliver a short speech. When James Corbett was informed of Sullivan's passing he commented:

> John L. Sullivan was the greatest of all fighters in his day. The world will bear me out on that statement ... I can honestly say he was the best man and the most admired of the heavy-weight fighters. In his day he could have bested any man. Even though I won the championship from Sullivan I could never have won nor could have won had I faced him in his prime. His fairness in the ring and his true sportsmanship made him the most loved of all in the ring, not only by the fans, but by the men he fought as well.[30]

For many, including novelist Theodore Dreiser, John L. Sullivan had been the apotheosis of American manhood:

> John L. Sullivan, raw, red faced, big fisted, broad shouldered, drunken, with gaudy waistcoat and tie, and rings and pins set with enormous diamonds and rubies ... what an impression he made! Surrounded by local sports and politicians of the most rubicund and degraded character.... Cigar boxes, champagne buckets, decanters, beer bottles, overcoats, collars and shirts littered the floors, lolling back in the midst of it all in ease and splendor in his very great self, a sort of prize fighting J.P. Morgan.[31]

Dreiser recalled that he was once jokingly rebuffed when he sought to ascertain the future plans of the renowned fighter: "Write any damn thing yuh please, young fella, and say that John L. Sullivan said so. That's good enough for me. If they don't believe it, bring it back here and I'll sign it for yuh. But I know it'll be all right, and I won't stop to read it either." Dreiser noted that he would have written anything Sullivan asked him to because he adored him.[32]

John L. Sullivan had been many things to Americans during his storied life. For some he represented the triumph of the individual, while for others he was the very embodiment of the emigrant child made good. For those of a political bent he represented the superiority of American and Irish fighters over those of British stock, but he was far from perfect. For one, Sullivan had the prejudices of his time and did not countenance fighting against a black opponent. As he once stated, he was prepared to defend his heavyweight title against "all fighters, first come first served, who are white. I will not fight a negro. I never had and I never will."[33] He informed a reporter at one point that he had no respect for any white fighter who went into a ring against a Negro, and throughout his career he simply ignored challenges issued by black fighters.[34] It was not for the want of contenders. Canadian George Godfrey would have proved a severe challenge if Sullivan had deigned to fight him, while the Australian fighter Peter Jackson was yet more formidable. Richard K. Fox even put up a $10,000 guarantee if Sullivan would take on Jackson but the Bostonian simply ignored the offer. Many years later, William Muldoon, Sullivan's manager at the time of the Corbett fight, admitted that it was he who made the decision to ignore the Jackson challenge as he believed his fighter would have been defeated. He wished, he said, to save his man from the humiliation of being defeated by a negro.[35] At the turn of the twentieth century there was no way that the title of Emperor of Masculinity, as writer Gerald Early put it, was going to be allowed to fall into the hands of a black man. As far back as 1895, Charles A. Dana, editor of the *New York Sun,* was warning the paper's readership of the coming "menace" of black fighters when he wrote that the black man was rapidly forging to the front ranks in athletics, especially in the field of fisticuffs. He believed, like many others, that the country was in the midst of a black rise against white supremacy.[36] Dana would have seen the impressive skills of George "Little Chocolate" Dixon, who had taken the bantamweight title in 1890 and the featherweight title in 1891, and the lightning reflexes of Baltimore's Joe Gans, who had amassed thirty-one straight victories by the end of 1895. Dana also foresaw the appearance of a black heavyweight in the not too distant future.[37]

Perhaps Elliott Gorn best summed up the life of John L. Sullivan when he wrote that he was a "bon vivant and a drunk, a lover of life and a reckless barbarian.... He cut through all restraints, acted rather than contemplated, and paid little regard to the morality or immorality of his behavior. He was totally self-indulgent, even in acts of generosity, totally a hedonist consuming the good things around him and beckoning others to do the same."[38]

Gorn continued:

> Sullivan rejected the routine world of work and family to live by his fists and his wits. If one may think of culture in terms of gender, then John L. Sullivan, the greatest American hero of the late 19th century, represented a remasculinization of America ... the Strong Boy of Boston embodied a lost era of genuine heroism, betrayed now by the complexity of modern life. To turn-of-the-century American men, Sullivan symbolized the growing urge to smash through the fluff of bourgeois routine and the ensnarement of corporate dependencies to the throbbing heart of life.

John L. Sullivan earned and squandered several fortunes, drank champagne by the bucket, left his wife in order to live with a chorus girl, and was a consistent thorn in the side of Victorian morality. From reading his first autobiography, none of this was immediately apparent. In his 1892 autobiography, *Life and Reminiscences of a 19th-Century Gladiator*, Sullivan was at pains to emphasize his Irishness. The book glorified sobriety, pious Catholicism, a home life focusing on idealized motherhood, and a preoccupation with good appearances. This did not chime with Sullivan's famous saloon entry whereby he entered the premises, struck the bar with his hand, and told those assembled that he could lick any son of a bitch in the house. Both of his parents were Irish and he had always sought to uphold the honor of the Irish people, whom he considered a brave race. He also wanted people to know that he was more than just a pugilist and could give an opinion on almost everything, as well as being a gentleman in company.[39] John Boyle O'Reilly, always a balanced voice of reason, acknowledged Sullivan's shortcomings but believed he deserved immense credit for advancing the sport of boxing into the professional era and that, while he had his faults, this should always be remembered.[40]

The ground in the graveyard had to be dynamited so that Sullivan could finally be laid to rest, an action thought most fitting by his former foe Jake Kilrain.[41] Nat Fleischer, founder of *Ring* magazine, summed up the impact of John L. Sullivan when he wrote that the Irishman was something more than the greatest figure in boxing. He was the man who, more than any other, made boxing reputable. This he succeeded in doing largely through accident, because he was a great popular hero.[42]

Corbett's Career

Corbett was not a man who liked to enter the ring on a frequent basis, and his only successful title defense took place against British boxer Charley Mitchell over three rounds on January 25, 1894, in Jacksonville, Florida. Sandy Griswold, a journalist with *The Lincoln Call*, described Mitchell as a high school kid compared to the Herculean American champion and stated that he had more chance of being elected the president of the United States than the Briton had of defeating Gentleman Jim.[43] Corbett was, according to Griswold, "a physical hurricane, quick as lightning's flash and as powerful as a grizzly bear, clever as a magician and ferocious as a hyena." However, the journalist thought it one of the foulest and dirtiest prize-fights in the annals of the ring, and that Corbett should be "cringing under the sting and disgrace of ignominious defeat," while Charley Mitchell should be "trotting about with a crown of laurel leaves resting on his brow." He described proceedings as "a go-as-you-please, free-for-all after the first round" and reported that Corbett, having knocked the Briton to the floor with the smash of his wrist across the bridge of the nose in the second round, repeatedly fouled his adversary while "referee Kelly stood by like a big cigar sign." While Corbett's seconds were frantically attempting to keep him from killing Mitchell while he was down, Mr. Kelly did little else but flourish his arms and bellow "break away." Another journalist was happy to report that "the tail of the British lion has been severely stepped upon by the foot of the mighty bruiser from the West."[44]

Gentleman Jim Corbett pursued a path different from John L. Sullivan's. Shortly after his victory over Sullivan, he appeared in a play called *Gentleman Jack*, in which he portrayed a college student with a convict father. The play had been commissioned from Charles T. Vincent by Corbett's manager, the sometime theatrical impresario and later film producer William A. Brady, who also took a role in the play.[45] In the course of the narrative, as for other vehicles specifically designed for him, Corbett has to overcome a false criminal charge and defeat a rival to retain the heavyweight title. Other plays written specifically for Gentleman Jim included *A Naval Cadet*, *Pals*, *After Dark*, and *Neither Maid, Wife or Widow*. Corbett went on a European tour with *Gentleman Jack*, and when it played at Dublin's Queen's Theatre in July the *Irish Times* opined that he played the part of Jack Royden with very good effect, "his manner being quiet and honest."[46] Corbett was worried about the reception he would receive from the Irish public and was all too well aware that he had toppled a national hero with his defeat of Sullivan. When he arrived in Westland Row train station in Dublin, the wily Corbett prevailed upon his sparring partner, Con McVey, to take his place in the first horse-drawn carriage in the procession to the center of the city in what was, he later wrote, a move to "test the water."[47] Corbett need not have worried. The crowd, believing McVey was the world champion, cheered him all the way to the Metropole Hotel in O'Connell Street. Corbett was both relieved and delighted. After a short speech from the balcony of his hotel, he was left in no doubt about the feelings of the Irish public toward him, and there followed a weeklong production of *Gentleman Jim* in the famed Queen's Theatre, after which Corbett went on to make successful presentations in Derry, Waterford, Limerick, and Cork. He also traveled to Ballinrobe, County Mayo, to put on a special one-night performance at the local town hall in aid of the Catholic Church at nearby Partry, where his Uncle James was parish priest. On September 7 of

Corbett frequently went on theatrical tours, where he performed shows based on his own life and gave lectures on pugilism (W.M. Morrison [William McKenzie], Prints and Photographs Division, Library of Congress).

the same year Corbett fought Peter Courtney in what was only the second boxing match to be visually recorded. Filmed at the Black Maria studio at West Orange, New Jersey, it was produced by William K.L. Dickson.

James Corbett was to eventually meet his nemesis in the shape of British boxer Bob "The Freckled Wonder" Fitzsimmons in Carson City, Nevada, on March 17, 1897, in an encounter famously captured on film by Enoch J. Rector, a recording which some consider the first ever feature film, and its nationwide screenings could also be regarded as the first pay-per-view media event in boxing history, for the fight produced more income in box office than in live gate receipts. Although prize-fighting was illegal in twenty-one states and many cities and states tried to ban the film, efforts to ban fight films were mostly unsuccessful.[48]

Gentleman Jim was adjudged to be in perfect condition when examined before the fight by Carson physician Dr. J. Guinan, who proclaimed that Corbett's "whole physical machinery" was in splendid condition and that he was the most perfect specimen of physical manhood he had ever seen.[49] Dr. A.P. O'Brien could not find one single flaw in his anatomy, which he believed was achieved by a hard and persistent course of training.[50]

There was a strong element of Irish against English sentiment in the press prior to the fight. Reprinting material from the *Daily Mail* and the Dalziel Agency, the British *Evening Telegraph,* for example, reported that Corbett intended to wear the American and Irish colors and might even sport a bunch of shamrock which an enthusiastic supporter had given him. The fact that the fight took place on St. Patrick's Day at Corbett's insistence was a matter of debate in some quarters. The decision rankled with some members of the Catholic clergy and middle-class Irish Americans. Jerome Deasy, one of delegates at a St. Patrick's Day convention in San Francisco, railed against prize-fighting as an immoral recreation and was instrumental in the body passing a resolution censuring the fight managers for desecrating the festival day of Ireland's patron saint.[51]

On the day, the bout was delayed by two hours because the cameraman needed the brightest conditions to use the new Verascope, which would record "an actual living picture of the fight," as one journalist described it.[52] Thirty percent of profits would go to the promoters and forty percent to Rector, with the remainder split between the two contestants. In an effort to ensure that none of the action would be missed, Stuart had carpenters reduce the width of the ring by two feet the night before. However, the referee spotted the change and had it put back to the normal size.

Fitzsimmons, also known as "Ruby Robert," always took to the ring wearing heavy woolen underwear in an effort to conceal the disparity between the length of his legs and that of his trunk. Born in Cornwall of an English mother and Irish father, Fitzsimmons had moved to New Zealand, where he worked as a blacksmith. Corbett seemed to get the better of his opponent for the first six rounds and even managed to floor Fitzsimmons for a count to nine in the last one. However, Fitzsimmons recovered and proceeded to wear down his opponent with body blows before scoring a knockdown in the fourteenth round with a vicious effort to Corbett's stomach, a belt subsequently referred to as the infamous "solar plexus punch."[53] While

Corbett did get caught with a hard blow it was the opinion of the referee that he had left his fight on the road and should have accounted for his smaller and much lighter opponent. At 165 pounds Fitzsimmons was a full seventeen pounds lighter than Corbett, still the lightest heavyweight champion on record. Wyatt Earp, who had been in Corbett's corner, wrote in the *New York Herald* that the encounter was the greatest gloved fight ever held in the United States or any other country.[54] It was a particularly notable achievement given that Fitzsimmons had previously ruled as world middleweight champion, and would also go on to win the light heavyweight title. In addition to going down in history as the lightest ever heavyweight champion, Fitzsimmons may have been the first three-division world champion, although this distinction would later be disputed by Michael Spinks.

An editorial item in the *Evening Herald* the day after the fight inaccurately summarized events with the announcement that "the Australian from Cornwall beat the Californian from Galway."[55] Dispensing with one half of each boxer's supposed ethnic affiliation, an editorial item in the *Irish Independent* earlier that day had described Fitzsimmons as "the Australian bruiser who defeated the Irishman, Corbett, at Carson City, Nevada, yesterday," and claimed that "Corbett was the favorite in Ireland, not only because he is an Irishman, but because of his undoubted skill and fine form."[56] Amid this confusion, no Irish newspaper appears to have pointed out that Fitzsimmons' blacksmith father was also an Irishman.[57]

Corbett thought the infamous punch was just a lucky blow and was deeply upset

Corbett–Fitzsimmons fight. "Gentleman Jim" Corbett fought Bob Fitzsimmons on March 17, 1897, in Carson City, Nevada (George Grantham Bain Collection, Library of Congress).

by the loss. He immediately demanded a rematch, but even a guaranteed purse of $30,000 put up by his manager William A. Brady could not tempt Fitzsimmons back into the ring. Fitzsimmons' refusal was most likely a result of the many insults Corbett had thrown his way over the years. Fitzsimmons instead opted to fight James J. Jeffries, a former sparring partner of Corbett's. However, after Jeffries defeated Fitzsimmons, Corbett again entered the frame. William Brady was now guiding Jeffries and, having seen his old protégé performing poorly against Tom Sharkey, decided that he was most likely past it at thirty-four years of age. As well as an age gap of seven years, Corbett was ceding advantages of size and strength and a weight difference of thirty pounds. Corbett trained assiduously while Jeffries did the bare minimum, confident that his superior attributes would help him coast to victory. In the interval between the two Jeffries fights, Corbett knocked out middleweight champion Charles "Kid" McCoy in the fifth round, but the contest was widely believed to be a fix.

On May 11, 1900, the two men met for a second time at Coney Island, New York, in front of a crowd of over 8,000 people. Originally scheduled for September, the fight was moved up because boxing was going to be outlawed in New York in autumn. Governor Theodore Roosevelt had called for the repeal of the Horton Law, which had legalized the sport in 1896. It passed the state senate twenty-six to twenty-two on a partisan basis, with all but one Republican supporting Roosevelt's arguments. The sport had garnered a bad reputation in the city; in 1899 alone, there were three Manhattan club fight fatalities. After one fight a riot had ensued after a boxer temporarily blinded his opponent and the referee by soaking his gloves in mustard oil.[58] The Lewis Law came into effect at the end of August, stipulating that boxing would only be allowed on a club membership basis, thus making prize fights criminal activities. (The Lewis Law would subsequently be repealed by the Frawley Act in 1911.)

In advance of the fight, Jeffries proclaimed that he was going to make Corbett look like a "cheap boxer" and prove that anything the Irishman had said about him was just "con talk."[59] Such was his confidence in his charge that William A. Brady had booked him to give boxing exhibitions and umpire baseball games two weeks later.[60]

Just before 10 p.m. the men entered the ring: Corbett wearing a blue sweater and trousers, Jeffries an open bathrobe to show off his physique. Corbett spent much of the fight successfully evading Jeffries in what was regarded by boxing experts as a fantastic demonstration of a scientific fighter managing an opponent with substantially greater brute force. In the ninth round Corbett landed two solid rights to leave Jeffries stunned in what the *Brooklyn Daily Eagle* noted was the only round where Corbett made his blows tell.[61] Subsequently, Jeffries "recovered like a lion at bay."[62] All Corbett had to do was last the twenty-five rounds, but it was not to be. In the twenty-third round he was badly caught when he leaned back on the ropes to avoid a punch, only to rebound directly into the path of a short right hook to the jaw from Jeffries. Even though the champion's face looked like "a raw hamburger steak" according to one source and Corbett only had bruising on his shoulder, brute force was to win the day when the Irish man went down like a "felled ox," as

Former heavyweight champions Robert Fitzsimmons (left) and James Corbett in later life (George Grantham Bain Collection, Library of Congress).

another scribe described the brutal end.[63] It was a victory for "bulldog tenacity and perseverance ... the old story of the magnificent boxer meeting a rugged, muscular heavy hitter, capable of taking all kinds of punishment in order to get a decisive smash."[64] One California journalist stretched his vocabulary when looking back on the fight, noting that the champion put the "soporific kibosh on the pompadoured ex-champion in the twenty-third round."[65] Despite the loss, the public lauded Corbett for his pluck and endurance, and for many, it was his greatest hour. Gentleman Jim later recalled that he had started to imagine posters in the city streets proclaiming him the recrowned champion as the fight progressed. Afterward, referee Charley White said he had never seen a squarer or fairer ring contest.[66] The boxers met for a third time in 1903 when Corbett, then thirty-seven and long past his prime, just about managed to hold on until the tenth round.

Following his retirement from boxing, Corbett returned to acting, appearing on stage and in film, as well as coaching boxing at the Olympic Club in San Francisco. He returned in 1909 to Dublin, where he spent a week at the Theatre Royal regaling the audiences with humorous stories of his travels and experiences. During his stay Corbett put an advertisement in a newspaper appealing for help in locating his late mother's former home. Paddy Gunning, a boilermaker at the Great Southern and Western Railway Company, wrote to Corbett after reading the article, and offered to show him his mother's house in Islandbridge in the city of Dublin. Afterward, Gunning brought the boxer on a tour of his firm's work site. The trip around the railway company finished up in the crowded dining hall, where Gunning turned to Corbett and said, "You have fought many rounds, but this is one round you probably won't stand."[67] To the Dublin man's delight his esteemed guest bought a drink for everyone in the room. At least Gentleman Jim was aware of one long-standing Irish tradition. Despite the reception he received in Dublin on both of his visits, Corbett was fully aware that many Irish saw him in a different light than they did John L. Sullivan. He also knew, even though he was equally Irish, that it was Sullivan's ebullient personality which carried the day. Corbett believed he was perceived as being too controlled and businesslike compared to the more outgoing Sullivan, and the fact he did not spend time standing up against the bars of the various cities he visited also counted against him. He was astute enough to realize that it was not possible to bring down a public hero without it being resented.[68]

His autobiography, *The Roar of the Crowd*, was serialized by the *Saturday Evening Post* in six weekly installments during October and November of 1924, while G.P. Putnam and Sons published it in book form the following year with the title *True Tale of the Rise and Fall of a Champion*. That Corbett was a man of some culture may be deduced from the fact that he was hired as a master of ceremonies by the radio station WGY with the tag, "'Gentleman Jim' CORBETT wants to meet you TONIGHT! He's thrilled a million women from the stage ... and millions of men from the ring ... now he's on the radio as Master of Ceremonies, presenting a prominent theatrical star each night."[69] Warner Brothers released the film *Gentleman Jim* in 1942 starring Errol Flynn and based on Corbett's autobiography *The Roar of the Crowd*. Timed to coincide with the fiftieth anniversary of Corbett's championship victory over Sullivan, Flynn later said it was one of his favorite celluloid outings.[70] Directed by Raoul Walsh, the film portrayed Corbett as a devil-may-care, happy-go-lucky fighter, who never lost his nerve or self-confidence and was widely regarded as a great evocation of the rough-and-tumble San Francisco of the late 1800s. Corbett was played by Ward Bond, an accomplished boxer in his college days. While the filmmakers took some artistic license in adding a fictitious scene in which

John L. Sullivan hands over his championship belt to Corbett, telling him that it was time for him to make way for a new breed of fighter, the public loved the movie. Errol Flynn was a good choice to play Corbett. They were about the same height and weight and Flynn had even been an amateur boxer in his earlier days. However, he found the role difficult; a heart condition rendered him unable to shoot fight scenes for more than a minute at a time. "Mushy" Callahan, a well-known boxer and trainer charged with getting Flynn in shape for the movie, found the actor a natural study despite his physical shortcomings. Mike Tyson later said that the film was the best boxing movie he had ever seen.

Corbett numbered film director John Ford, writers P.G. Wodehouse and Mark Twain, and actor Lionel Barrymore among his many high-profile friends while, in his later days, he sat on a number of committees tasked with trying to find solutions to the problem of mass unemployment. There is no doubting the fact that Corbett left a significant legacy to the sport of boxing and is widely regarded as the first to bring strategy, dexterity, and analytical thought to the discipline. He also brought a sense of refinement and attracted many new fans to boxing, including women. Asked to describe his approach to boxing, Corbett once famously replied, "From my first fight I started to run away."[71] Fellow boxer Bob Fitzsimmons pithily noted

Jim Corbett preaching a sermon on good health to Senate pages sitting on a wall outside the U.S. Capitol (Underwood & Underwood, April 1926, Prints and Photographs Division, Library of Congress).

that it was Corbett who had introduced "the leg qualities" to the sport.[72] His sidestepping and circling had never been seen before. For many he was quite simply the father of modern boxing. Gene Tunney, another future champion of Irish parentage, said Corbett was an inspiration to him and once told a journalist from the Associated Press that Gentleman Jim had the greatest knowledge of boxing technique of any man who ever entered the American prize ring and was also the most originally colorful figure in the fight game.[73]

There was tragedy, too, in the life of Corbett. His father went on to establish a hackney and undertaking business in San Francisco but was dogged by depression. On August 16, 1898, Patrick Corbett shot his wife Kate dead at their home before fatally turning the gun on himself. Corbett continued his extramarital affairs and was widely rumored to have had a liaison with Mae West. However, his second wife, Vera Standwood, stayed with him until his death at the age of sixty-six from liver cancer on February 13, 1933, at their home in Bayside, New York. Such were the numbers who turned up to pay their respects that the authorities were forced to put traffic controllers in place. His funeral service in St. Malachy's Church in Manhattan was a national event with many sportsmen, actors, politicians, journalists, and businessmen in attendance. There were notable tributes from his fellow boxers, including one from Jack Dempsey, who said that the world had lost one of the greatest champions and one of the finest gentlemen there ever was.[74] Future heavyweight champion Jim Jeffries told a journalist that Corbett was one of the finest fellows he had ever known.[75] They had their differences but they were always in good fun and he considered Corbett a "square shooter."

H. Montgomery Gerrans, a hotel proprietor in Buffalo and longtime friend of Corbett, told the *Buffalo Evening News* that it had always been a pleasure to watch his masterly blocking, clever slipping of punches, and beautiful jabbing. He believed that Corbett's gentlemanly behavior and polished appearance did more than anyone or anything else to elevate the game from the "rough-neck class," in which it had long been mired. Corbett had once told Gerrans that he would live to be one hundred years of age. While Gentleman Jim did not achieve that milestone, he had left an indelible mark on the world of sport and American culture.[76]

Ten

Only Non-Irish Need Apply

In 1903 the *National Police Gazette* wrote of the reception received by fighters of different ethnic backgrounds when they entered the ring, pointing to the particular hostility encountered by those of Italian origin: "Put a boy of any race in with an Italian and everybody in the house who is not himself of Italian origin at once begins to root frantically against the son of ancient Rome. It is to the credit of the Italians that they have pushed so far forward against such adverse influences."[1] It is little wonder that it has been estimated that more than 1,000 Italian professional boxers went by Irish pseudonyms in the early decades of the twentieth century in the United States. There were good reasons for this. Relations between Italian and Irish communities were frequently fractious. The Irish had got to America in the greatest numbers first, and the Italians were frequently forced to take a back seat, literally and metaphorically. The communities vied for the same jobs, while the Catholic Church, overwhelmingly dominated by Irish clerics, frequently gave Italian members of their flocks short shrift and even in some cases made them sit at the back of the church. Irish laborers complained that their Italian counterparts worked longer hours for lower pay and were distorting the labor market, with some claiming the Italians were anarchists and communists. In some workplaces crews had to be divided along ethnic lines to keep the peace. Italians might get a job in construction through the local padrone, but they were likely to have to answer to an Irish foreman. The Irish were everywhere the newly arrived Italians looked. Between 1840 and 1890 more than three million Irish immigrants entered the United States, and by the turn of the century more than five million Irish had made America their home. New York had more Irish people than Dublin, while there were more Irish in the United States than back in Ireland. In each decade between 1820 and 1869 the Irish accounted for more than 35 percent of the total number of immigrants to the United States, while in the four years after 1847, 1.8 million immigrants landed in New York, of which 848,000 were Irish. At the same time that Irish immigrants were streaming into America, the country was undergoing a rapid process of urbanization. In 1830 only 10 percent of the country's population lived in cities, with New York the only urban center with a population of more than 100,000, but by 1900 the situation had radically changed. By then 40 percent of Americans lived in cities, of which thirty-eight had a population greater than 200,000.[2] The Catholic Irish overwhelmingly settled in the cities of the Northeast. While earlier Protestant Irish immigrants had settled in Appalachia where they were happy to earn a living from the land, these newer Catholic immigrants had seen the hardship that a dependence on agriculture could bring and opted instead to live in the city. As social reformer Emily Greene Balch noted in 1910, "the newcomers, encountering Irish policemen, Irish politicians, Irish bureaucrats, Irish saloon keepers, Irish contactors, and Irish teachers could be excused for thinking that 'Irish' equaled 'American.'"[3] During a span of 100 years, from 1820 to 1920, 19 million immigrants entered the United States, of whom 4.5 million were Irish. While the Irish may have climbed the ladder of respectability in many areas of society, the experience of the first waves of Catholic immigrants was far from easy and mirrored that of the later Italian immigrants. In New York, for example, the vast majority of Irish immigrants ended up living in difficult circumstances. Huge numbers gravitated toward Lower Manhattan, the Five Points area in particular. When the famous frontiersman Davy Crockett visited the area in 1835, he thought the Irish living there "worse than savages ... too mean to swab hell's kitchen."[4] Two decades later Charles Dickens commented on the "hideous tenements which take their names from robbery and murder."[5] In the late nineteenth century, a report on tenement life in the Five Points area counted one bathtub for 1,321 families and an average of one water tap for each floor of apartments. It was an area heavily polluted by industry, where poisonous chemicals like naphtha, benzene, and other flammable materials made fire an ever present threat. Raw sewage flowed down the streets, while rodent infestation was endemic. Disease was inevitably rampant, and the Irish suffered disproportionate health problems and had the highest rates of cholera, typhoid, and typhus among all ethnic groups. Discrimination against the Irish was rife in the workplace, and the vast majority ended up in low-paid, low-skilled jobs where physical strength was the foremost requirement. In 1860, 46 percent of male Irish immigrants worked in the bottom tier of the labor market, with only one in a thousand having a white-collar job. The overwhelming majority of working Irish females found employment as domestic help and even then they were frequently discriminated against. The *Daily Sun* carried an advertisement in 1853 looking for a housekeeper of any color or nationality other than Irish.[6] The Irish were at the bottom of the social ladder, a place they shared with African Americans. The Irish were frequently referred to as "nigger Irish" and "white Negro," while African Americans were sometimes called "smoked Irish."[7] While not all Irish immigrants spoke English, those that did had a strong advantage over other groups, and acculturation was that little bit easier when you spoke the tongue of the host country.

The Irish in America had a fearsome reputation. They had come through a life-and-death experience with the Great Famine of 1845 to 1847 and were desperate to make a new home. The Famine had cost Ireland more than half its population between death and immigration, and the vast majority of those who had made their way across the Atlantic Ocean were traumatized and had witnessed the wholesale destruction of much of their traditional culture that an occupying political regime could cause. Their struggles, both in Ireland and in the great cities of America, according to James Barrett, produced a "culture that mixed aggressiveness, a sentiment of grievance, a sensitivity to slights and, above all, a strong instinct to survive."[8] As folklorist William Williams noted, the Irish seemed to understand that they had to succeed as a people, not just individuals.[9] Caroline Ware described relationships between Irish and Italians in Greenwich Village, New York, during the

1920s, noting that the Italians knew which streets to stay away from because they were the bailiwick of the Irish.[10] Some claimed a pseudo-scientific basis for their discrimination against Italians, claiming that they were "biologically incapable" and a "burden on America."[11] Street battles between Irish and Italians were frequent, reflecting those between Irish and nativists decades before.

Angelo Dundee, the legendary boxing trainer from Philadelphia who trained champions like Muhammad Ali and Sugar Ray Leonard, described the experience of Italian Americans at the turn of the century in his home city by noting that it was not advantageous to have an Italian name, as they were not held in high esteem by the host population. The prevailing view was that they lived in ghettos, held menial jobs, spoke funnily and ate spaghetti and ice cream, and were considered by the average American to be "gangsters" and members of crime societies.[12]

Interestingly, some gangsters of Italian extraction assumed Irish identities. Al Capone's infamous bodyguard "Machine Gun" Jack McGurn had previously been known as James Gebardi and had been born James DeMora, while Paola Vacerilli, a notorious heavy in the Five Points area of Lower Manhattan, was better known as Paul Kelly and, perhaps not surprisingly, was involved in boxing promotion.

Frederic Thrasher, a University of Chicago sociologist who studied gangs in the 1920s, noted that fighting was described as "a sort of national habit" of the Irish by some of those he interviewed. While the majority of ethnic gangs were defensive, he concluded that Irish gangs seemed to invariably look for trouble.[13] While there was a history of faction fighting in rural Ireland in the nineteenth century, whereby semi-organized gangs of peasants and farmers engaged in stick fights at fair days and other occasions, it cannot be put forward as the sole foundation for the Irish predilection for urban warfare in the America city and subsequent domination of boxing. It is true that the word "donnybrook" came in to the English language as a result of the reputation of Donnybrook Fair, which took place just outside Dublin and became infamous for particularly fractious fights. Certainly, these fracases did place a premium on physical prowess and courage, and the man who could take on all around him was a natural hero.

John L. Sullivan had set the template for the Irish American masculine hero. He had struck a blow for the Irish community and shown how sporting success could prove a ladder to social success. Elliott Gorn eloquently termed Sullivan's famous war cry that he could lick any son of a bitch alive as a "defiant cry for a downtrodden people who, in their first full post immigrant generation, sought a fairer share of America's opportunities."[14]

With the success of Sullivan, James Corbett, and other Irish fighters, some believed that to succeed in the business of boxing it would be wise to take an Irish name. Between 1870 and 1920 nine world champions were Irish or of Irish descent. In the best case scenario this would allow access to fight cards largely run by Irish promoters and help obviate the type of racial slur outlined by the *Police Gazette*. This was borne out by Italian boxers who opted to keep their names having more difficulty getting fights, while promoters also forced fighters to take Irish names to make them more appealing to Irish patrons.

While there was a significant number of Italian boxers who chose to operate under Irish aliases, there were few heavyweights. One exception was Andrew Chiariglione, who reputedly changed his name on the spot to Jim Flynn when a referee was unable to pronounce his name. Chiariglione was fighting in Utah and, after the referee garbled his surname, supposedly yelled "Oh, hell just call me Jim Flynn." It did not prove to be a hindrance; Jim "The Fireman" Flynn was the only boxer ever to knock out future champion Jack Dempsey.

Minnesotan native Tony Caponi, another heavyweight of Italian extraction, believed his name sounded more like a music master than a prizefighter and opted for the rather more prosaic TC O'Brien for a period of his boxing career. In the lighter divisions there were a significant number of Italian boxers who acquired Irish aliases. Thomas Frascella, American Bantamweight Champion in 1907, boxed under the name "Kid" Murphy, while Peter Robert Gagliardi changed his name to Bobby Gleason for boxing purposes and later opened his famous gym in the Bronx where many boxing luminaries, including Muhammad Ali and Mike Tyson, trained. The Calabrian-born Francesco Conte was given the name Frankie Conley by his Irish Catholic school friends in Wisconsin and decided to stick with it. It did not hold his career back either; he went on to claim the World Bantamweight Title when he knocked out Monte Attell in 1910. Vincent Esposito of Philadelphia became Jimmy Dugan, forging a highly successful career as a flyweight during the 1930s. Hugo Kelly, World Middleweight Champion, was born Ugo Micheli on February 10, 1883, in Florence, Italy, and took up boxing in Chicago in 1899. In 1905 he claimed the crown after defeating "Philadelphia" Jack O'Brien, losing it to Stanley Ketchel in 1908. Kelly went on to become a wealthy man through his involvement in the world of cinema. Raffaele Giordana, a world welterweight champion in 1933, had the intriguing boxing name Young Corbett III. Born in the Basilicata region of southern Italy on May 27, 1905, he reputedly acquired his fighting sobriquet after the ring announcer told him he would not present him as Ralph Giordano and dubbed him "Young Corbett III" because his fighting style reminded him of William J. Rothwell, known as Young Corbett II, an American born featherweight champion who had taken the name in honor of his hero, Jim Corbett. Other sources suggest Giordana acquired the name because of the similarity of his hairstyle to James J. Corbett. Guglielmo Papaleo found significant boxing success under the name Willie Pep, while Antonio Pillieteri, born on November 11, 1917, in New Jersey, fought under the name Tippy Larkin and took the light heavyweight title on April 29, 1946, when he defeated Willie Joyce by unanimous decision over twelve rounds. Known to his family as Tony, he came up with the name Tippy by combining the initials of his name while taking his boxing surname from Bobby Larkin, whom he had seen fighting his older brother Frank. Jack Delaney (March 19, 1900–November 27, 1948) was a world light heavyweight boxing champion and contender for the heavyweight crown. One of the most popular fighters of the 1920s, the French Canadian was born Ovila Chapdelaine in Saint-François-du-Lac, Quebec, Canada. The story goes that a great Jewish boxer, Benny Leonard, once fought an opponent called "Irish" Eddie Finnegan in a Pennsylvanian coal-mining town, where the latter's supporters urged their man on with shouts of "kill the kike" and other anti–Semitic jibes. An enraged Leonard took his anger out on Finnegan, who was increasingly outclassed until he grabbed his tormentor in a clinch and, pleading for mercy, explained in Yiddish that his real name was "Seymour Rosenbaum." The bout is not listed in Leonard's official record. But if the story isn't true, it's still a good one.

From the 1920s onward, the boxing landscape in the United States started to change and the assumption of Irish names by other nationalities became rarer. In particular, Italian communities began to root for their own, and it was not too long before names like Tony Canzoneri, Frankie Genaro, Fidel La Barba, and Mike Ballerino filled the boxing ring, but according to boxing historian Mike Silver, a significant 62.5 percent still used Irish or Anglicized names by the end of the 1920s. In the next decade this figure declined to 50 percent, while between 1940 and 1949 it was down to 36 percent.[15] More famous names like Jake LaMotta, Joey Giardello, Carmen Basilio, and Rocky Marciano would gradually fill houses. Like the Irish before them, the Italian emigrants had spent their time at the bottom of the social pecking order and were now becoming assimilated in American society. There would be others to take their turn in time. Like the Italian community, the Jewish people saw how the Irish had climbed the ladder. One Jewish writer recalled the Lower East Side Manhattan of his youth: "Though surrounded by Poles and Italians it was the Irish and the Irish alone we Jews admired ... we identified the Irishman not only with the English language but also with the image of what an American looked like. The Irish were the cops and the firemen and the ballplayers. Although the immigrant Jew and the Irish poor did not get along well, these Irish were still the figures Jewish immigrants wanted to emulate."[16] From 1901 to 1939 the Jewish community produced twenty-nine world champions, approximately 16 percent of the total.[17] From the early 1900s to the late 1930s Mike Silver estimates there were upward of 3,000 Jewish professional boxers plying their trade in the United States. Among the many that assumed aliases were Gershon Mendoloff, who was better known to the fighting world as Ted "Kid" Lewis and as the first boxer to wear a gum shield, while Beryl Rosofsky traded as Barney Ross. Jackie Fields was born Jacob Finklestein and won featherweight gold at the 1924 Olympics, later becoming world welterweight champion in 1929 and again in 1932. Boxing historian Mike Silver posits an interesting argument when he suggests that the power of the mother figure in Jewish families sometimes resulted in hiding their participation in boxing.[18] Benjamin Leiner was the real name of Benny Leonard, the World Lightweight Champion between 1917 and 1925 and ranked seventh in ESPN's "50 Greatest Boxers of All Time." By his own account, he changed his name so that his parents would not know what he was doing in his leisure time. He took the name in honor of the famous minstrel singer Benny Leonard. In 1983 he told Bud Greenspan of the *New York Times* that he was a "mama's boy" and told a tale of how he got home one evening after a fight to find out his parents had heard of his boxing exploits. His father called him a "viper" and a "tramp," but when he presented them with the money he had won from his fight they were happy to accept and wanted to know when he was fighting again.[19]

Alex Rudolph fought as Al McCoy but was not the "real McCoy" at all. Rudolph, born on October 23, 1894, held the World Middleweight Champion from April 1914 to November 1917. It has been speculated that his manager, Charley Goldman, changed his fighter's name to hide his participation in boxing from Rudolph's parents. Perhaps the most colorful of all of the aliases taken by Jewish boxers was that of "Mushy" Callahan, who was born Vincent Morris Sheer on November 3, 1904, in the Lower East Side of Manhattan, and was to hold the newly created World Light Heavyweight title from 1926 to 1930, as well as having a successful career as a referee and actor. At the age of two Sheer moved with his family to Los Angeles, where they settled in the predominantly Jewish area of Boyle Heights. He took the Mushy part of his *nom de guerre* from his Hebrew name Moishe (Moses), while his boxing surname was copied from an Irish promoter at the Newsboys Boxing Club where he trained. Callahan went on to have a successful acting career while he also worked as a stuntman and as a technical advisor on films with boxing themes, including Warner Brothers' 1942 movie *Gentleman Jim,* based on the life of James Corbett. Like the Italians, the Jewish gradually started to have more of their own heroes to cheer using their real names. The golden era of Jewish boxing is largely forgotten now.

Eleven

"The Fighting Marine"
Gene Tunney

"He was unloved, underrated, shunned by his own people, rejected by history. Still, he was the best advertisement his sport has ever had.... He was like no Irishman you ever saw, but he was the greatest Irish athlete who ever lived."[1]

—Jim Murray

THERE IS NO DOUBTING THE IRISH credentials of James Joseph "Gene" Tunney. His parents, Mary Lydon and John Tunney, immigrated to the United States from the small village of Kiltimagh, County Mayo, met in New York City, and married after a brief courtship. John Tunney, like many Irishmen before and after him, found employment as a longshoreman, loading and unloading freight at New York Harbor. Like so many other Irishmen of his generation and situation John Tunney was an ardent boxing fan, even fighting in some amateur matches in Owney Geaghan's famous boxing club on the Bowery. It would have been hard for the Tunneys not to have been fans of boxing; five of the seven championships were in the hands of Irishmen when they arrived in

Gene Tunney was known as "the Fighting Marine" because of his successful boxing career while in the military and won the heavyweight world title by defeating the highly favored Jack Dempsey in Philadelphia on September 23, 1926, via a ten-round decision (Kraus Mfg. Co., 1926, Prints and Photographs Division, Library of Congress).

America. As well as witnessing countless unofficial fights on the docks, John Tunney was a fan of Friday and Saturday night "smokers," illegal fight shows rife during the era. James Joseph Tunney, born on May 25, 1897, at 416 West 52nd Street, was the second of seven children and the first boy. He acquired the name Gene when his sister could not pronounce his full name. The story goes that John presented his son with a pair of boxing gloves on his tenth birthday so that he could learn to defend himself against school bullies who had been picking on the scholarly young Irish American boy as he made his way home in the evening. At the age of fifteen Gene dropped out of high school and found work as an office boy at the Ocean Steamship Company, where he earned the princely sum of $5 a week. Tunney was a quick learner and was soon promoted to the job of mail clerk, doubling his pay. A short time later he rose to the position of freight classifier, where he commanded a weekly wage of $17. Under the tutelage of former boxer and trainer Willie Green, a willing Tunney quickly learned the rudiments of the ring at the Greenwich Village Athletic Club, taking his first amateur title at the age of sixteen. Despite his parents' hopes that he might join the priesthood, Gene Tunney turned professional two years later and had his first professional fight, a seven-round knockout against the well-regarded Bobby Dawson, earning him the princely sum of $18 and a taste for greater boxing glory. When America entered the First World War, Tunney joined the Marines and while stationed in France won the American Expeditionary Forces' light heavyweight title. After his discharge, and, in his own words, wanting the "solitude and the strenuous labors of the woods" to help condition himself for the successful professional boxing career he yearned for, Tunney spent the winter of 1921 as a lumberjack in northern Ontario working for the J.R. Booth Company of Ottawa.[2] On his return to the United States he came under the management of Doc Bagley, the man most often credited with coming up with the sobriquet "The Fighting Marine." The wider boxing fraternity was soon made aware of Tunney's smooth fighting style, impressive speed, and devastating right hand, when he won seven straight bouts to earn a shot at Barney "Battling" Levinsky, a tough campaigner who had held the world light-heavyweight title between 1916 and 1920. Lewinsky, born Barney Lebrowitz, spent an earlier period of his career boxing under the name of Barney Williams, in keeping with the widely practiced tradition of taking an anglophone name for the purpose of career advancement. Battling Levinsky was past his best by the time he met Tunney and was comprehensively defeated in their January 13, 1922, meeting. The Fighting Marine was next penciled in for a fight against Harry "The Smoke City Wildcat" Greb, a fighter who also went by the sobriquet of "The Pittsburgh Windmill," a perfect description of his aggressive, fast, and swarming style. Combined with good footwork and a comprehensive knowledge of the darker arts of the game— including spinning his opponent and using the heels and laces of his gloves—the highly durable Greb was a dangerous foe, and it proved to be an infamously vicious and bloody encounter. On March 13, 1922, in front of a crowd of 13,000 at Madison Square Garden, the fighters topped the bill at a Milk Fund Show organized by Mrs. William Randolph Hearst and attended by members of the Astor and Vanderbilt families, among other society luminaries. From the outset it was a gruesome spectacle. Greb butted Tunney in the opening round and broke his nose. It was to go from bad to worse for the Fighting Marine. Over the course of fifteen brutal rounds the Irish American was beaten to a bloody pulp but somehow managed to survive to the final bell. Later the ringside doctor claimed Tunney lost at least two quarts of blood over the course of the fight, while journalist James R. Fair would note that it was the toughest fight he had ever seen and "maybe the bloodiest since the Romans fought with Cestus."[3] At the conclusion of the final round Tunney's face was an inch-thick mask of blood according to Fair, who did not hold back on graphic detail in his telling of the fight, writing of how Greb slammed Tunney into the ropes and smashed him with "knife-sharp blows" to the head and body, round after bloody round.[4] The referee used up half a dozen towels wiping the blood off Greb's gloves. After each cleansing, referee McPartland would move away from the fighters and Greb would leap to attack again. His fists would thud against Gene's face, the blood would gush, and McPartland would duck to avoid further splashing. As the fight wore on Tunney began to grow weak from the relentless pace. Time after time he used his forearms to wipe away the blood that was blinding him, but he refused to quit. From time to time he supported himself against the ropes and pawed at his tormentor with arms that were weary, aching, and leaden. Tunney even smiled during three of the bloodiest rounds, albeit those smiles were limited in their intensity, according to Fairs. At the end of the contest Greb was unmarked but his opponent was a mess. Tunney stumbled toward his dressing room, rivulets of blood from both cheeks meeting at the point of his chin and dropping onto his chest. He collapsed before he got there and his handlers had to carry him the rest of the way. The moment supporting hands left him he fell, with the back of his head striking the rubbing table. Fair had seen 10,000 fights by then, but never one so bloody. The crowd gave Tunney a standing ovation for his bravery and perseverance. The Irishman later described the experience: "He was never in one spot for more than half a second, all my punches were aimed and timed properly but they always wound up hitting empty air. He'd jump in and out, slamming me with a left and whirling me around with his right or the other way around. My arms were plastered with leather and although I jabbed, hooked and crossed, it was like fighting an octopus."[5] He also outlined how Greb had given him a "terrible whipping." "My jaw was swollen from the right temple down the cheek, along the chin and part way up the other side. The referee, the ring itself, was full of my blood. If boxing was afflicted with the commission doctors that we have now, the fight probably would have been stopped and no one would have heard of me today." It would prove to be the only loss of his professional career and was voted "Fight of the Year" in 1922 by *Ring* magazine. Fair later caught up with Greb at a city saloon where he was celebrating his victory. The journalist was puzzled when he found the champion in a downbeat mood and asked him what the trouble was. Greb informed Fair that, despite what people were saying, it was not an easy fight for him. In fact, it was one of his hardest and it was only the fact that Tunney had bled so much that made him look better. He had never come close to dropping Tunney, a fighter, he ventured, who must have an iron jaw and will. Tunney had hurt him in every round, and while there might have been a general perception that The Fighting Marine was only a counterpuncher incapable of hurting opponents, those who took this view were wrong. He was the most accurate puncher Greb had ever encountered. Greb excused himself to go to the toilet and when he returned to the bar he bluntly informed Fair that there was blood in his urine, the first time it had ever happened. He was not going to order steak because his face hurt so much after being constantly hit with the sledgehammer blows of Tunney that he would not be able to eat it.[6]

Tunney later wrote in his 1941 book *Arms for Living* that he had been in bad shape going into the fight; his hands were chronically ailing with imperfectly mended fractures and were sore and swollen. From the third round on, all he could see was a red phantom-like form dancing in front of him.[7] The defeat to Greb was to prove a turning point in Tunney's career. He reevaluated his tactics and techniques; when he met Greb in a rematch the following February it was clear that he had done his homework. Having taken advice from boxing coach Benny Leonard, Tunney sought to keep his opponent off balance from the start and landed as many punches to the body as he could. He outboxed Greb over another fifteen-round hard-hitting marathon, winning by a majority decision. Tunney would defeat Greb three more times before hanging up his gloves. By this point Tunney's fighting style was starting to become established. He preferred to think his way through a match, relying more on his fleetness of foot and quick jabbing than all-out punching. In this regard he took much from his fellow Irish American, Gentleman Jim Corbett. Tunney had an excellent left jab and usually preferred to stay outside and nullify any of his opponent's attacks using quick counterpunches to keep them off balance. He held his hands lower for greater power and used his fast footwork to adjust to his opponents' moves and counter with quick and accurate punches. Tunney wrote about his approach to boxing in *Arms for Living,* comparing his methods to those of a fencer or chess player. Those were both pursuits where the adversaries had to think their way through the encounter in a scientific manner, he noted.

After defeating Greb, Tunney expressed his desire to fight the heavyweight champion Jack Dempsey, but few took his words seriously. Dempsey was considered by many experts to be the most savage and brutal fighter who had ever taken to the boxing ring and had recently destroyed the giant Argentinian Luis Firpo in two rounds. But Gene Tunney was intent on his mission and gave fair warning when he defeated by knockout Tommy Gibbons, another Irish American heavyweight fighter whom Dempsey had only defeated on points in an infamous fight that had bankrupted the unfortunate town of Shelby, Montana. The vast majority of the public could not see the fresh-faced Tunney take down "The Manassa Mauler" and most did not want to see a hit-and-run artist defeat their popular hero. Part of the reason for Tunney's opportunity to fight Dempsey in September 1923 was his skin color. Famed promoter Tex Richard knew that a mixed-race encounter would not be a big seller. He had wanted to stage the fight at Yankee Stadium on September 16, but exactly a month beforehand, the New York State Athletic Commission decreed that they would not grant Dempsey a license until he complied with their order to defend his title against Harry Wills. On August 18 Rickard announced that Dempsey would fight Tunney in Philadelphia on September 23 in a contest worth $770,000 to the former and $200,000 to the latter. The lead-up to the fight was frenzied. A crowd of 2,000 people came to watch Tunney spar twelve rounds with two workout partners on August 15, while on the same day more than 1,000 people paid $1 each plus tax to watch Dempsey workout at Saratoga Springs, New York. Even the *New York Times*, once the leading critic of boxing in the country, published seven articles on the fight preparations in August and September.

On September 23, in Philadelphia's Sesquicentennial Stadium, the two men finally met in front of a crowd of 118,736 in a contest which generated an unprecedented $2,000,000 and was promoted as "the greatest battle since the Silurian age."[8] The attendance was to remain a record for sixty-seven years and was only broken when 132,274 paid to see Julio César Chávez against Greg Haugen in Mexico City on February 20, 1993. The great and the good were in attendance, including the mayors of Philadelphia and New York City, as well as Pennsylvania Governor Pinchot, Secretary of the Navy Curtis D. Wilbur, and numerous society luminaries. Extra trains brought crowds from New York, New Jersey, Chicago, and dozens of cities and towns across the country, while 39,000,000 tuned into their radios across the nation. A Mr. Bice, owner of an electrical shop, told the *Franklin Evening Star* that he was going to broadcast the fight from an amplifier on the roof of his premises if the weather was suitable, and if the evening proved uncooperative he would use a loudspeaker to keep the crowd abreast of proceedings.[9]

The men had been cast as opposites from the start. Dempsey was an iconic figure, viewed as the very apotheosis of male virility by his vast following, and had held the title since his defeat of Jess Willard on July 4, 1919, a fight in which he had destroyed his opponent, flooring him seven times in the first round. His boxing style was in keeping with his personality. Dempsey kept on the offensive almost continuously, bobbing up and down and moving from side to side as he delivered short swinging blows out of a crouch. His constant movement and the speed of his attack constituted his defense. For many, Dempsey represented the raw pioneering spirit that had tamed the American wilderness, the noble savage and rugged individualist. He was the John L. Sullivan of his day, fighting under the name "Kid Blackie" in his younger days and telling any man in the house that he could lick them for a dollar.

On the other hand, Tunney was the urbane Easterner with his scientific boxing and refined manners. He represented a society of business and capitalism, a regimented and organized twentieth-century man. By then Tunney had seventy-seven professional fights under his belt with his only loss to Greb. Dempsey had not fought in three years and had been occupying much of his time in Hollywood. Over that three-year period he had fought nineteen times.

Tunney stuck to his tactics and the fight went the full ten-round distance; the Fighting Marine took the first ever heavyweight title awarded by decision. The *New York Times* reported that Tunney was a complete master from first bell to last and that he outboxed and outfought Dempsey at every turn.[10] *Ring* magazine deemed it the "Upset of the Decade," with journalist Paul Betson describing Dempsey as being like a dance partner obeying a lead.[11] The people's champion had been defeated. The Chicagoan writer Studs Terkel, fourteen years old at the time of the fight, later explained the devastation felt by people at Dempsey's loss, noting that it was unbelievable that a boxer who read Shakespeare could defeat a man who defined the era.[12]

On September 22, 1927, Tunney and Dempsey met for a second time in Soldier Field, Chicago. Tunney was interviewed by the *Greenfield Recorder* prior to the rematch and told the journalist that he was confident he would defeat Dempsey again, before proceeding to outline his philosophy on life.[13] He believed in destiny and fate and that any man could only do his best to achieve this. Tunney pointed out that fate had made him a boxer almost against his will and that the same fate had provided the driving force to build up his body from that of a middleweight fighter to that of a heavyweight. Fate had also brought him all the way to the top of the boxing tree, despite the critics and setbacks he had encountered.

In an interview before the fight, journalist Clack H. Kelsey wanted to get to the essence of Tunney's character and concluded that the boxer was "just the sort of specimen that writers of yellow-backed thrillers for boys would make a hero of."[14] He despised crowds, liked kids, preferred to be called a boxer rather than a prize-fighter, was a man who relished society but abhorred being mentioned as a social climber, and was flattered when called an intellectual but pained when termed a bookworm. He was not girl-shy but simply not interested in the sort of girl who would be interested in a prize-fighter. He liked to spend much of his free time with Eddie Egan, a Yale graduate and Rhodes Scholar. Kelsey noted that after the fight Tunney was going to depart for Cleveland, where he would hobnob the Hanna brothers, millionaires and sons of the late Senator Mark Hanna. After one training session he told a group of journalists that he had never really liked boxing and that the constant talk of money was useless and disgusting.

The fight was to prove a singular occasion. In the first ever boxing encounter covered by a professional radio announcer, the legendary voice of the newly established National Broadcasting Corporation's Graham McNamee was heard as far away as the Arctic Circle. Once again, the great and the good of American society came to see the spectacle; among those seated in the front row were Charlie Chaplin, Douglas Fairbanks, and Irving Berlin, while a train chartered by James J. Corbett numbered George M. Cohan and Al Jolson among the celebrated passengers. The seats stretched a full one hundred and thirty-seven rows back from the ring, while twelve hundred journalists were in attendance to document proceedings for an insatiable worldwide audience. A crowd of 102,450 generated almost $3,000,000. Journalist Westbrook Pegler was sitting ringside and could not make out the last row of customers, only knowing that they were there from the "combers of sound that came booming down the slope of the stadium out of the darkness."[15] It was little wonder that Tex Rickard called the event the crowning achievement of his life; he had sold 42,000 "ringside" seats at $40 apiece. Hype Igoe of the *New York World* was sitting next to the ecstatic promoter, who boasted that in the first ten rows he had all the world's wealth, all the world's big men, all the world's brains, and all of Hollywood's production talent.[16] This time Dempsey's purse was $447,500, with Tunney due to take home $990,445. (Tunney paid Rickard the difference in order to get a check for $1 million.) Tunney opened as the betting favorite, but the odds were nearly even by the day of the fight. Gangster Al Capone told newspaper reporters that he had bet heavily on Dempsey after hearing that Davy Miller was going to referee the fight and that Miller's brother had also wagered heavily on the Manassa Mauler. Shortly before the fight, Illinois boxing officials, believing Miller might be in league with Capone, replaced him with Dave Barry. Racketeer Arnold Rothstein and former World Featherweight Champion Abe Attell allegedly offered Tunney $1 million to throw the fight.

When the fight finally got under way the first six rounds were even, but it was obvious that Dempsey's reflexes had slowed in the interim three years. Then, at the start of the seventh, Dempsey caught Tunney with a shuddering left hook to the jaw. As Tunney fell to the floor Dempsey followed on with a flurry of punches. For the first time in Gene Tunney's illustrious professional boxing career, the first time in twelve years and seventy-six professional fights, he had hit the canvas in the course of a contest. The crowd rose as one, the noise deafening: "Tunney is down. Tunney is down from a barrage of lefts and rights to the face," roared McNamee. The *New York Times* reported that Tunney's eyes were dull and, mouth agape, he groped with his right arm for a rope that seemed to escape his clutch.[17] Nine people allegedly died of heart attacks during the course of the fight, three of whom succumbed when Tunney hit the floor.[18] Under the recently amended Illinois Rules, Dempsey was supposed to go and stand in the most distant neutral corner but he continued to hover over his fallen opponent. Referee Dave Barry insisted Dempsey return to his corner but by the time he had retreated to his proper place Tunney had already been down for four or five seconds, and only then did Barry begin his count. With one arm draped across the rope, Tunney took as much time as he could getting to his feet, and by the time Barry had counted to ten Tunney was upright. Paul Beeler, the official timekeeper, later said he was at thirteen when Tunney got up. After the fight resumed, an irritated Dempsey stalked his opponent around the ring, wildly trying to land another decisive blow. However, Tunney rallied and dominated the last three rounds; the fight later became known as the infamous "Battle of the Long Count." Jack Dempsey was gracious in defeat, and after the decision was awarded to Tunney he raised the new champion's hand and told him that he was the best and fought like a smart kid.[19] The pair remained good friends for the rest of their lives. In the aftermath of the fight, Nat Fleischer, founder and editor of *The Ring* magazine and an official biographer of Jack Dempsey, believed it was "plausible" that Tunney could have risen with a normal count.[20] Fifty-one years later, sports writer Shirley Povich noted in the *Washington Post* that he still believed Tunney would not have regained his feet if there had been a proper ten-second count.[21]

The *Guardian,* after surmounting a number of difficulties in getting a copy of the film to England, found the evidence inconclusive but thought the speed of the boxing tremendous, similar to that of featherweights in the British Isles. It found the contrasts between the two men curious, with Tunney standing up like Jem Mace, while Dempsey, with his two days' beard, was "crouching ... with his chin tucked in almost beyond nature" and seemed to pull his punches right out of the ground.[22] The real miracle of the match, the paper thought, was the referee dancing all night in time with the boxers, prizing them apart and flashing between them as they broke, and the journalist would have liked to see a film of the umpire alone doing his dance in the ring.

Tunney retired undefeated in 1928 after his bout with New Zealander Tom "The Hard Rock from Down Under" Heeney on July 26 was stopped in the eleventh round by referee Eddie Forbes. Tunney had promised his wife that he would never

Gene Tunney (center) wearing a Native American headdress (Bain Collection, Library of Congress).

fight again and he stayed true to his word, announcing his retirement five days later. The only blemish on his exceptional record was the ban he received in New York for refusing to fight African American challenger Harry Wills. Despite his marvelous career, Gene Tunney never received the adulation he might have done during his lifetime. Some were suspicious of his bookish ways, while he was not a man to pander to the popular press. From a young age he maintained a little black book of unfamiliar words which he committed to memory after looking up their meanings and pronunciations. Additionally, he was a stickler for diction, with no trace of his New York street accent.[23] Among the words he frequently used were "ineffectual," "hitherto," and "cosmeticize." Tunney resented intrusion into his private affairs and berated those who cursed in his presence. He was given to quoting Shakespeare and once spoke at Yale University on the subject, while he was a personal friend of writers Ernest Hemingway and George Bernard Shaw. Norman Klein of the *New Yorker* outlined Tunney's plans to travel to Europe with Thornton Wilder to do some walking, after which they hoped to rent Henry James's old house in Rye, England, for a period of reflection and contemplation. Wilder hoped to work on a novel during their sojourn, in addition to a work of nonfiction which would record conversations on life, literature, and men's wills.[24] Wilder expected the work to be subtle and intellectual and not particularly marketable, but this did not concern him as he wanted to record the thoughts of Tunney for posterity.

Tunney was also firmly opposed to tobacco use, and when the manufacturer of Lucky Strike cigarettes asked him to endorse their product with the line "My friends all smoke Luckies so they must be good," he gave the company short shrift. "No. There are a million boys throughout the country who would feel that I had betrayed them. It is not proper that a champion should, even by inference, encourage cigarette smoking among American youth."[25] Tex Rickard had no such qualms and appeared in a 1928 advertisement for Lucky Strikes with the tagline "Lucky Strikes never injure my throat."[26] For many, there was something just too perfect about Gene Tunney. He was an exemplary student, a decorated soldier, and, to top it all off, found even greater material success when in 1928 he married Polly Lauder, a grandniece of the famous industrialist Andrew Carnegie. Tunney was everything that the overwhelming vast majority of boxers and their followers were not. In keeping with his bookish interests, Tunney contributed an entry on boxing for the *Encyclopædia Britannica* in 1945. He also penned three of his own books: *Boxing and Training, A Man Must Fight,* and *Arms for Living.* In the 1950s and 1960s he joined forces with his friend Jack Dempsey to argue before Congress for the creation of a national commission to oversee boxing. He was also invited to sit on the boards of several well-known corporations, including the American Distilling Corporation, Technicolor, and Schick. Additionally, he was a director of the Boy Scouts of America and the Catholic Youth Club. In 1940 Tunney made the headlines when he deemed the American Youth Congress to be pro-communist and helped establish the rival National Foundation for American Youth, lending his voice to a national radio campaign warning against the threat of communism. "Commies were a mad clique," he intoned, "devoid of principle, of honor, of truth. Lies, treachery, subversion, wholesale imprisonment and murder were their prime tools in their daily and untiring effort to conquer the free world." Communism posed the threat of a third world war, and from personal experience he knew that "war is hell" and had to be fought "above the belt."[27]

Perhaps his frequently quoted aphoristic words of advice rubbed some the wrong way. Among the many were: "Never eat less than four hours before boxing. Then eat only lightly"; "A boxer's diet should be low in fat and high in proteins and sugar. Therefore you should eat plenty of lean meat, milk, leafy vegetables, and fresh fruit and ice cream for sugar"; "Fat is one of the chief enemies of the heart because it has to be plentifully supplied with blood and thus needlessly increases the pumping load that the heart must sustain"; "The man who has allowed his body to deteriorate cuts a pitiful figure"; "We get plenty of exercise through games and running around, but as middle life approaches, we settle down, literally and figuratively"; "If all human lives depended upon their usefulness—as might be judged by certain standards—there would be a sudden and terrific mortality in the world"; and "Ever since boyhood I've made a religion of keeping in shape by regular, conscientious exercise."

Perhaps one of the most remarkable aspects of Gene Tunney's life was his friendship with Irish playwright George Bernard Shaw. Shaw had first become

Boxers Gene Tunney (left) and Jack Dempsey in 1964, their first meeting since the "Battle of the Long Count." The meeting took place in California, thirty-seven years to the day after the infamous bout (Photo by Cal Montney, UCLA Library, *Los Angeles Times* Photographic Collection, Creative Commons 4.0).

interested in boxing when he was introduced by his friend Pakenham Beatty to Ned Donnell, a "professor of boxing" who ran a gymnasium near Haymarket Theatre in London. After seeing Georges Carpentier fight, Shaw had been moved to write in his booklet *The Great Fight* that fighters were either geniuses like the Frenchman or poor fellows whose boxing was simply not worth looking at except by gulls who knew no better.[28] In 1924, after seeing newsreel footage of Tunney demolishing Carpentier at New York's Polo Grounds, Shaw was mesmerized. Tunney, he believed, was the embodiment of Cashel Byron, a character in one of his early novels called *Cashel Byron's Profession* who mastered the fistic arts and became the champion of the world, capturing the heart of an aristocratic heiress. The book proved widely popular, although Shaw was disappointed in the way it was interpreted by the press and many of its readers. He subsequently wrote that he had intended it to deal with the challenges and injustices of the modern world and as a "hymn to skill and science over incoherent strength," as well as a "daring anticipation of coming social developments."[29] Shaw was unhappy that the press focused on Cashel's professional performances. After it was pirated for stage in the United States, he penned his own dramatic version called *The Admirable Bashville*. However, after 1900 Shaw no longer had any interest in the novel—or boxing as a sport—as it frequently reduced him to "such a condition of deadly boredom that even disgust would have been a relief."[30] Despise his spurning of the sport he appeared to subsequently revive his enthusiasm when he wrote an article for *The Nation* on Joe Beckett's European heavyweight championship fight, describing him as a genius.

Before Tunney's first fight against Dempsey, an eagle-eyed reporter spotted a pile of books nearby and asked the boxer about his current reading matter. He was enjoying *The Way of All Flesh,* an autobiographical novel by Samuel Butler, a book he was drawn to, he said, because Shaw had written the preface.[31] Tunney attended the world premiere of Shaw's play *Saint Joan* in 1923 and had been highly impressed when the Irish writer had been awarded the Nobel Prize for literature in 1925. He thought the play a masterpiece and subsequently gave his only daughter the name Joan. The *Chicago Tribune* was delighted to point out that Jack Dempsey's preferred reading matter did not stretch beyond comic books and that he had once referred to Tunney as a "big bookworm." Even Paul Gallico, the Columbia-educated sports editor of the New York *Daily News*, considered Tunney's intellectual interests an irrelevance, believing his love of first editions and rare paintings did not further his fighting ability.[32]

Tunney was approached about starring in a Hollywood adaptation of *Cashel Byron's Profession* but turned it down because the central character, he maintained, was "a soap-box orator bore."[33] When Shaw heard this he was intrigued, and expressed a wish to meet this boxer with such refined literary taste. While the Tunneys were on honeymoon in London in 1928 they received an invitation from Shaw's wife, Charlotte, asking them to lunch. Among other luminaries present at the repast were author H.G. Wells and artist John Collier. Although Shaw was seventy-seven years of age by then—over forty years older than Tunney—the men found common ground and subsequently entered into a correspondence. Some months later the two couples holidayed together for three weeks on the Brionian Islands in the Adriatic.

On his return to England reporters asked Shaw what the two men had talked about for the duration of the trip, to which he replied they had discussed everything from ancient Egyptian wrestling to the theosophy of Madame Blavatsky.[34] The correspondence between the two men subsequently lapsed, but in 1946 Shaw made contact with Tunney by letter:

> I feel I must give you a mail to show that I have not forgotten our old, happy contacts. I have only some scraps of wit left and shall soon forget the alphabet and the multiplication table and be unable to walk more than a hundred yards without two sticks. I hear you and your lady are prosperous and well and have three sons and a daughter. Keep them off the stage and out of the ring if you can.[35]

At the end of his missive Shaw mentioned that their mutual acquaintance H.G. Wells had died earlier that year, pointing out that he and Wells had finished as great men but Tunney had started out as one.[36] In 1951 Tunney published the letters he had received from Shaw, noting in the preface that their friendship was one of the most precious gifts of his life and that he had been proud to know a man who lived "above personality in a sort of spiritual and intellectual world free from vindictiveness or malice, with a love for mankind but a shyness that only a few people were privileged to penetrate."[37] Shaw praised Tunney for winning by "mental and moral superiority."[38] One thing they certainly shared was contempt for most sports journalists. Shaw once suggested the passage of a legal bill to make it a punishable offense for a newspaper to publish any description of a prizefight until they had sent for a professional boxer and made the writer spar with the journalist and then obtained from a couple of competent judges a certificate that he at least knew his right hand from his left.[39]

Gene Tunney was comfortable with the rich and famous and, along with Shaw, included novelist F. Scott Fitzgerald and world-renowned Irish tenor Count John McCormack among his many celebrated friends. He wrote of the role of friendship in a man's life, terming it the most satisfying connection of all and that no one could go through life without it.[40]

Tunney was elected as *Ring* magazine's first-ever Fighter of the Year in 1928 and later was inducted into the World Boxing Hall of Fame in 1980, the International Boxing Hall of Fame in 1990, and the United States Marine Corps Sports Hall of Fame in 2001. His life was not without tragedy. Tunney's daughter Joan was committed to a mental hospital on June 6, 1970, after she murdered her husband.[41]

The Fighting Marine is fondly remembered in Ireland and reference to him is often heard on the stage, where he is mentioned in Tom Murphy's iconic play *A Whistle in the Dark* by a character who insists that a man must fight back at some stage in his life and that his father was a Mayo man, too.[42] As well as holding the world heavyweight championship from 1922 to 1926 Tunney held the world lightweight title between 1922 and 1923 and finished his career with a total of eighty-eight fights: eighty-two wins, forty-eight knock-outs, one defeat, three draws, and two no-contests. After his retirement from the ring Tunney and his wife moved to Stamford, Connecticut, where they raised four children. He is one of only four heavyweights to have retired as champion; the others are Rocky Marciano, Lennox Lewis, and Vitali Klitschko.[43] He is also one of only five champions to retire without ever suffering a stoppage defeat; the others are Marciano, Riddick Bowe, Sultan Ibragimov, and Nicolai Valuev.[44]

Gene Tunney died on November 7, 1978, at the Greenwich Hospital in Connecticut at the age of eighty-one, having suffered from a circulation problem for some time. He is interred at Long Ridge Union Cemetery in Stamford. The *New York Times* reported that Jack Dempsey was "broken up" by the news of his old foe's death and felt a part of him had died. Because he was three years older than Tunney, he thought he would have been the first to die.[45] Tunney once said that he had a dream to live in three centuries. He was born in 1898 and hoped to live until the year 2000 to fulfill his wish. While this did not transpire, he left a great mark on the world of American boxing and was the apotheosis of an Irish American made good.[46]

However, the paper did not sugarcoat its words when it came to write of Tunney's legacy. "Mr. Tunney had enjoyed little popularity among fight fans. He was a boxer in a time when punchers like Mr. Dempsey were idolized. After his retirement, the fans resented his blandness, his literacy, his wealth and his decision to retire undefeated." It did, however, note that he had a genuine love for learning and read extensively.[47] Polly Tunney lived to the grand old age of 100.

Twelve

"The Cinderella Man"
James J. Braddock

> Without doubt it is a great advantage to have intelligence, courage, good breeding, and common sense. These, and similar talents come only from heaven, and it is good to have them.
> —Charles Perrault, *Cinderella*, 1691[1]

James Walter Braddock, later to become James J. Braddock when his manager decided it would follow better in the list of his predecessors Corbett and Jeffries, was, in retrospect, the last of the line: the final heavyweight boxing champion born in the Irish American community in the United States. Born on June 7, 1905, on West Forty-Eighth Street in Manhattan's Hell's Kitchen to Elizabeth O'Toole and father Joseph, the young James was a heavyweight from the start of his life; he reputedly weighed seventeen and a half pounds at birth. Unlike the vast majority of Irish emigrants to the United States, his parents had been born of Irish parentage in England, where they had been raised in the hardscrabble environment of Manchester. The couple married in New York in 1893, and by the time James was born he already had two sisters and three brothers. The family subsequently moved to West New York, New Jersey, and later to North Bergen in the same state when the young James was ten years of age. Braddock attended Saint James Catholic School but did not distinguish himself academically and departed

Jim Braddock (Photograph by Alan Fisher, *New York World-Telegram* and the *Sun* Newspaper Photograph Collection, Prints and Photographs Division, Library of Congress).

from formal education without a qualification. He harbored ambitions to play football for Knute Rockne at the University of Notre Dame but was later happy to admit he had more brawn than brains.[2] While working as a messenger boy for Western Union he came to boxing at the relatively late age of eighteen, and at just over six feet tall and weighing 160 pounds, Braddock was light for the heavyweight division. On November 27, 1923, Braddock had his first official fight in Grantwood, New Jersey. He had gone to see his older brother Joe against a fighter called "Battling" Walker, but when promoter Harry Buesser found out that there was no opponent for one of his fighters, Braddock, fighting under the name Jimmy Ryan, borrowed his brother's gloves and shorts and was roundly beaten over four rounds. The defeat did not deter him, and on March 21, 1925, he knocked out Jimmy Emerson to take the New Jersey light heavyweight title. Two nights later he defeated Tom Bodman, a fighter forty pounds heavier, to take the heavyweight title. At nineteen Braddock already held two state titles and went on to defend both crowns the following year, the latter against Frank Zavita, who outweighed him by fifty pounds.

Braddock turned professional at the age of twenty-one in 1926 and on April 14 took on aging black heavyweight Al Settle in what proved to be an unmemorable no-decision draw. Braddock walked away with his first professional purse— the grand sum of $15—and went on to have a series of convincing wins during his maiden year. The *Jersey Journal* took a look at local prospects in its end of year boxing column and suggested that he might one day follow in the footsteps of Corbett and Tunney but described his style as awkward and crude. However, it noted that his sheer hitting ability might help him triumph over better fighters.[3] Early in 1927 Braddock caught the eye of Damon Runyon, the most influential sports writer in the country. Runyon noted that Braddock had considerable class and a strong punch but had doubts that he would make it as a heavyweight and believed that he might do better by staying in the light heavyweight division. Notwithstanding, Braddock looked to be on his way to the big time when he defeated Nebraskan Tuffy "The Pender Pounder" Griffiths in two rounds, leaving his opponent "as stiff as a frozen mackerel," according to renowned boxing writer Hype Igoe.[4] After a victory over the highly rated Jimmy "Slats" Slattery, the *Philadelphia Ledger* noted Braddock was developing into an aggressive two-handed battler but it still rated him as a glorified club fighter.[5] On June 18, 1928, he finally got a shot at a title fight when he took on the supremely talented, and fellow Irishman, Tommy Loughran at Yankee Stadium in what was to prove a disappointing outing. Not alone did Braddock lose the fight to the wily Loughran, he also fractured his right hand in several places in an extremely bloody contest.

At that point in his young life Braddock was in relatively good financial shape and had invested the rewards from his fight career in a taxi company and bar in Jersey City, but on Monday and Tuesday, October 28 and 29, 1929, the United States stock market crashed, bringing the Roaring Twenties to a shuddering halt. By the end of November investors had lost more than $100 billion in assets, instigating a worldwide economic slump which would later become known as the Great Depression. Braddock's fighting career mirrored the dispiriting economic landscape as he lost sixteen of his next twenty-six fights. On September 25, 1933, he suffered the misfortune of breaking his right hand again, this time on the jaw of twenty-year-old heavyweight Abe Feldman. Braddock duly announced his retirement to an indifferent public and started working on the docks of Hoboken and Weehawken to help feed his family. In 1934 he got an unexpected opportunity to fight John "Corn" Griffin, also known as "The Ozark Cyclone," in a contest designed to further the latter's career progression. Griffin, a soldier based in Fort Benning, Georgia, was viewed by some of the boxing cognoscenti as the next Jack Dempsey and had established a fearsome reputation for his punching power. By the time Braddock was offered the fight he was in difficult financial circumstances and later explained that he would have fought a gorilla to help support his family.[6] In advance of the fight he told journalists that the manual labor he had been forced to engage in had toughened him up and made him hard as nails.[7] When writer Jack Kofoed saw Braddock enter the ring he was inclined to agree with the fighter's own assessment of his condition, as his muscles looked like iron from his dockwork.[8] At the start of the second round Braddock was knocked to the ground for only the second time in his boxing career but managed to recover. Later he spoke of the desperate motivation that spurred him to get up and continue. He needed to win the fight to put food on the family table.[9] To the surprise of nearly everyone, Braddock knocked Griffin out in the third round, scoring his first knockout in eighteen months and only his second in four years, before going on to cut a swathe through some of the heaviest hitters in the business. After defeating future light heavyweight champion John Henry Lewis he won a purse of $750, not even enough to pay the seven months of rent owed on the family apartment. Braddock was next pitted against Art Lasky. Lasky was the five-to-one favorite but Braddock was happy just to get the fight, as he badly needed the money to pay off debts and was by then living on government relief. On March 22, 1935, he broke Lasky's nose in a fifteen-round victory, earning $2000 for his troubles, of which he gave $300 to the relief funds of Union City to pay back the $240 he had previously been given. His victory over Lasky opened up a previously undreamed of opportunity to fight heavyweight champion Max Baer. At six foot two and a half inches and weighing 210 pounds, "The Livermore Larupper" was purpose built for heavyweight boxing. The self-deprecating Baer famously said he had "a million dollar body and a ten cent brain." While he was not stupid, Baer went through life with a light heart; Ron Fimrite described him well in a 1958 edition of *Sports Illustrated* as a lover and not a fighter. That such a man should have become a heavyweight champion of the world and might have killed two men in the ring was one of the most remarkable paradoxes in the history of sport, Fimrite wrote.[10] Braddock was seen as an easy payday by Baer's backers, and when the fighter was informed that the soon-to-be-named "Cinderella Man" was challenging him for the title he reportedly said it was the biggest laugh he had had in months.[11] In advance of the fight, sports journalists created a rags-to-riches narrative around Braddock, and it was Damon Runyon who came up with the sobriquet Cinderella Man, a name the fighter grew to detest. Braddock prepared assiduously for the contest at a training camp in the Catskills and was quietly confident of his chances, telling one journalist that there was no chance Baer would get ahead of him in the early rounds, as he would soon be the boss of proceedings.[12] It was, he said, the most important fight of his life and he would have to be carried out of the ring feet first. The press was fascinated by the fact that Braddock had gone from relative riches in his early fighting career to poverty, and when it became known that he had been on government relief the journalists were agog. When asked about it his reply was succinct: "Sure I was. I'm not ashamed of it either. I didn't mind for myself but I couldn't let the kids starve."[13]

When he hurt several ribs during a sparring session, Braddock had one of his trainers construct a padded corset so that he could continue the practice bouts. Baer was confident that Braddock would pose little problem and the majority of the press agreed. Allen Gould of the Associated Press contended that the champion had the speed and the power to achieve his objective and predicted an early knockout. Damon Runyon did not think it so clear-cut and believed that a fast clever boxer could always make Braddock look futile, but Baer was neither. Braddock was more difficult to hit than many observers thought and had a style all of his own which could prove deceptive, Runyon noted.[14] The venue, Long Island Bowl, had become known as the Graveyard of Champions; no reigning champion had held a successful defense there. Others pointed to aspects of the encounter which related to the number thirteen. James Braddock had thirteen letters in his name when his middle initial was omitted. The fight was to take place on the thirteenth of the month, while some journalists, erroneously, noted that Baer was the thirteenth heavyweight champion since John L. Sullivan (he was the fourteenth).

On June 13, 1935, Braddock entered the ring as a ten-to-one outsider with nothing to lose and he knew it. After what he had been through in the previous two years, a Bengal Tiger or a Max Baer looked like a house pet, he said.[15] Here was a man who had experienced the same trauma as millions of other Americans and his individual story was that of much of the population writ large. As Red Smith famously said of Braddock, "His time was the Great Depression and he was a man of his time."[16] Only a boxer could have reflected the story of the nation in as broad a mirror in that benighted era. The sport's popularity was remarkable. At a time when the New York Yankees attracted an average crowd of 9,000 to home games, a nontitle fight between Joe Louis and Max Baer attracted 100,000 to Yankee Stadium, while in June 60,000 came to see the nontitle fight between Louis and Primo Carnera at the same venue. Even the lightweight title fight between Barney Ross and Jimmy McLarnin attracted 40,000 to the Polo Grounds. The popularity of boxing was also reflected in financial terms. Lou Gehrig was the highest paid baseball player in 1935 with a salary of $40,000, while Max Baer earned $215,000 for his bout with Joe Louis, over five times the annual income of "the Iron Horse."

Baer, who had barely trained for the fight with Braddock, had dreamed that he had killed his opponent in the contest, but when it started he was shocked by Braddock's ability to absorb punch after punch. Braddock eventually won on points after fifteen draining rounds. Baer took his defeat graciously and went over to congratulate Braddock on taking the title, telling him that he hoped he would make a lot of money from it.[17] When Braddock eventually managed to make his way back to the dressing room he was interviewed by NBC's Graham McNamee, who asked him what thoughts had been going through his mind during the fight; once again Braddock spoke of the needs of his family. In 1936 Braddock was due to defend his title against German Max Schmeling but the fight was canceled in suspicious and convoluted circumstances. Braddock claimed that he could not fulfill the obligation because of his arthritic hands, but most likely he was holding out for a fight with Joe Louis, the new heavyweight on the block. The Boxing Commission insisted Braddock was obliged to defend his title against the German, and when he did not turn up for the weigh-in on June 3 the commission fined him $1000. It resulted in a farcical scenario with Schmeling turning up for a physical examination on his own. Braddock was unrepentant, calling the fine "a mosquito bite," and pointed out the financial incentive to take on Louis. He had not been ducking Schmeling but poverty, he said. On February 19, 1937, at Chicago's LaSalle Hotel, Braddock signed a contract to fight Joe Louis on the following June 22. Louis had come to the attention of the wider public when he defeated the six foot six inch, 265-pounder former heavyweight champion Primo Carnera. Since Dempsey had lost the title in 1929, heavyweight boxing had descended into a morass of limited fighters, fixed contests, thrown matches, and organized crime.

On his last day in training camp Braddock expressed his confidence to a group of journalists and described some of the physical hardships he had endured during his boxing career. He had fought with cracked hands for a purse of $150 and had broken his nose and a number of his ribs for a couple of hundred dollars. He even once had his nose broken, an eardrum busted, and his eyebrows laid open in a fight that paid him a mere $8, he told them.[18] When asked how he would manage to repel the formidable Louis, Braddock cited his Irishness.[19]

If Joe Louis won he would be the first black heavyweight champion since Jack Johnson. On the eve of the fight the *Chicago Daily News* polled thirty-eight sportswriters and boxing experts, with twenty-seven predicting a Louis win. The *New York Enquirer* was critical of the venue, pointing out that Comiskey Park was right in the depths of the worst cesspool of vice and crime in America, an area known as "Little Hell" where the toughest elements of the region plotted their nefarious crimes. It noted that thousands of outside blacks had come from Detroit, Memphis, St. Louis, Birmingham, and New York: "Numbers racketeers, *agents provocateurs,* scallywags, street walkers, nymphs, panderers, demimondaines and cadets were operating openly," while "the remnants of the Detroit Purple Mob and the still-strong Capone combination, coupled with Egan's notorious St Louis 'Rats,' were having a Roman holiday."[20]

Civic leaders expressed fears of race riots. At the previous mixed title bout held at Comiskey Park two spectators had been killed and scores wounded, and there was wide concern that there would be a repeat. Ten thousand policemen patrolled the area around the park, while 4,000 special deputies were assigned to monitor areas of black population. Braddock, unlike some of his predecessors, had never expressed any racist views and ate and showered with his black sparring partners. Louis had lost to Schmeling the previous year and Hype Igoe of the *New York Evening Journal* thought it would affect him.[21] In what may have been gamesmanship, Louis received a parcel at his hotel on the morning of the fight and when he opened it found a record of the song "You Can't Take That Away From Me" signed by Braddock.

The great and the good among the 60,000 crowd at Comiskey Park included

Al Jolson, James Cagney, Jack Benny, George Burns, Gracie Allen, Cab Calloway, Bing Crosby, Clark Gable, George Raft, Bill "Bojangles" Robinson, Edward G. Robinson, and Mae West, while former boxing greats Jack Dempsey, Jess Willard, and Gene Tunney were introduced to the enthusiastic spectators. The announcer asked the crowd to respect the highest ideals of sportsmanship regardless of race, religion, or creed, after which Braddock entered the ring first, a large white shamrock on the back of his green robe.

The cognoscenti were shocked when Braddock dropped Louis to the canvas in the first round with an uppercut to the chin, but the challenger immediately got back on his feet. Louis was relentless over the next few rounds, and Braddock could be heard moaning softly whenever he was hit by a powerful punch. He had never felt pain like it previously, he later told journalists. By the start of the eighth round Braddock had taken punishment that seemed beyond human endurance, but even as the crowd gasped in pity, he shook his head and advanced on the jabbing challenger. Occasionally a left or right would crash through Louis's guard but Louis would counter, set Braddock back on his heels, and follow through with another heavy blow.[22] Henry McLemore could only assume that all Braddock saw through the red mist was a "weaving brown figure, full of fury, whose fists jolted with power to stop

James J. Braddock (left), former heavyweight champion of the world, and his manager, Joseph Gould, practicing rifle calisthenics under instruction from Sergeant John A. Bender at the Atlantic Coast Transportation Corps Officers Training School, Fort Slocum, New York, in 1942 (Prints and Photographs Division, Library of Congress).

the heart of an ordinary fighter."[23] Then the inevitable happened. Louis caught Braddock with a short right, a blow American writer Grantland Rice described as one of the most terrific single punches he had ever seen delivered in the ring.[24] Braddock had to be carried to his corner, blood pouring from multiple cuts with his head hanging to one side. A posse of policemen immediately surrounded Louis in case of a ring invasion. When Braddock eventually recovered he was taken back to his dressing room, where he told reporters he would come back and defeat Louis after a few more fights to get him into better shape. However, his manager, Joe Gould, was more sanguine, recognizing that Louis was one of the fastest and hardest punchers ever seen.[25] The following day Braddock told a group of journalists that he had not seen the punch coming and that it was the persistent left jabbing of Louis which had caused him the most problems. He had found it hard to lift his hands up from the start of the fifth round and went on to memorably describe the power of Louis's punches. His left jab felt like someone was jamming an electric light bulb in his face and screwing it in, while Louis's right was like being hit by a crowbar. In later years he would describe the punch by telling the questioner that if he had electric bulbs on his toes during the fight they would have lit up. On other occasions he used a sailing metaphor to describe the blow, comparing it to a boat hit by a bolt of lightning in a storm.[26]

Braddock had now achieved the financial stability he had craved but was intent on continuing his boxing career. On January 21, 1938, he entered the ring against the tough Welshman Tommy Farr in front of a full house of 17,000 people at Madison Square Garden. In an exciting ten-round contest, Braddock took the victory on a contentious split decision. Ten days later Braddock announced his retirement to a group of journalists, explaining that he had spent fifteen years in the ring and that it was only fair to his wife and children that he finished boxing for good.[27] Nat Fleischer was effusive in his praise of the retired fighter, describing him as one of the most likable boxers in the history of the sport, a game where men of his character were few and far between.[28] Braddock had fought eighty-six bouts with fifty-one wins, twenty-six of those by knockout. He enlisted in 1942, serving in Saipan, where he trained soldiers in hand-to-hand combat. In the 1960s, Braddock, having seen a few business ventures go south, was forced to seek employment and worked as a crane driver on the construction of the Verrazzano-Narrows Bridge connecting Staten Island and Brooklyn. When interviewed by Gay Talese, Braddock was typically direct, saying that he had no problem working in construction because he had always liked hard work.[29] When he did achieve a degree of economic stability, Braddock showed his integrity by repaying the government relief money he had been given during the Depression years as well as supporting the Catholic Worker Movement, which had given him a helping hand earlier in his life. He was glad that none of his children had followed in his footsteps, telling one journalist that boxing looked more glamorous than the reality.[30]

Braddock died peacefully in his sleep on November 29, 1974, at the age of sixty-nine. On the day of his burial his passing was marked at Madison Square Garden by a ceremonial ten-count on the ring bell. In its obituary the *New York Times* noted that Braddock's soft voice, twisted smile, and diffident demeanor made him seem more like an old-time friendly Irish cop on the beat than a prize fighter. His patient manner, it believed, was better described by the nickname "Plain Jim," given to him by John Kieran, than the better known Cinderella Man, although, it conceded, there was a pertinence in Damon Runyon's observation that his career was a remarkable crystallization of a boxing narrative, embracing as it did a promising start, a skid to oblivion and retirement, a desperate return to fighting from the relief rolls of the Depression era, and, as a fairy-tale climax, the winning of the heavyweight boxing championship of the world, the richest individual prize in the realm of sports.[31] The inimitable Jimmy Cannon wrote in the *New York Post* that Braddock was serene and unafraid and that there was about him an "inspiring calmness that transcended his ability."[32] Braddock was inducted into the International Boxing Hall of Fame in 2001, while 2005 saw the release of *Cinderella Man,* a biopic of his life directed by Ron Howard with Australian actor Russell Crowe in the title role.

Thirteen

Great White Irish Hopes

"I coulda had class. I coulda been a contender. I coulda been somebody, instead of a bum, which is what I am, let's face it."
—*On the Waterfront*[1]

WHILE SULLIVAN, CORBETT, AND BRADDOCK MANAGED to fight their way to the very top of the heavyweight tree, there were other Irishmen and those of Irish American ancestry who went very close. John Mahan, born on January 26, 1851, in the village of Kells, County Meath, embodied the possibilities America could offer an Irish emigrant in the nineteenth century. As well as finding success in boxing, he became involved with Tammany Hall politics and later worked as the coroner of Jersey City. Going against type, Mahan fought under the more British-sounding name Steve Taylor. One of his first major fights was a seventeen-round loss against Billy Edwards at the Brooklyn Rink in New York on June 5, 1876, before going on to achieve an eighteen-round victory over Charles McDonald later that year.[2] On November 17, as was frequently the case at the time, his bout against Brooklyn champion John J. Dwyer at the Lyceum Theatre was interrupted by the New York City Police Department and the referee had no other option but to declare the contest a draw. On March 23, 1877, Mahan lost a rematch with Dwyer, this time in a gloved contest. A regular customer in Harry Hill's bar, he worked as a sparring partner for Paddy Ryan in advance of the latter's successful world title fight against Jem Mace in 1880 and was also a training partner for Joe Goss, who was beaten for the title by John L. Sullivan in the same year.[3] On March 31, 1881, at a testimonial benefit in Harry Hill's famous establishment, John L. Sullivan offered $50 to any man who could last four rounds with him under the Marquis of Queensberry rules and Mahan bravely took up the challenge. The contest was refereed by Matt Grace, a well-known collar and elbow wrestler, while Dick Hollywood and Billy Madden were the corner men for Mahan and Sullivan, respectively. Mahan was knocked out in the second round by Sullivan, who sportingly offered half the prize to his opponent.[4] Notwithstanding his quick loss, Mahan went on an exhibition tour with Sullivan, Herbert Slade, Pete McCoy, and Mike Gillespie later in the year. On October 19 Mahan and Gillespie put on an exhibition at the local opera house in McKeesport, Pennsylvania, where the former outweighed the latter by forty pounds; a wag in the audience shouted at Gillespie that he should "either stand on a chair or put his glove on a broomstick."[5] On the morning after holding a two-day exhibition bout at the People's Theater in St. Louis, Missouri, on November 5 and 6, Mahan and Sullivan were arrested and charged with violating a state law prohibiting public sparring and boxing exhibitions. Subsequent to posting bail, they were forced to forfeit their bonds and ordered not to make a scheduled tour of California. On October 6, 1884, Mahan fought exhibition bouts against Mike Cleary and Jack Burke at Turn Hall in New York City and went on to join Sullivan on another national tour organized by manager Pat Sheedy which included fighters Joe Lannon, George LaBlanche, Jimmy Carroll, and Patsy Kerrigan. As part of the venture, Mahan fought Jimmy Carroll to a three-round victory at the Masonic Hall in Portland, Oregon, on December 10, while on another occasion he took part in a "wrestler against boxer" match with Charles Bixamos in Saint Charles Theatre in California, having just fought a four-round bout against local lightweight Pat Kendrick.[6] On March 28, 1887, Mahan and Joe Lannon sparred with Sullivan in Hoboken, New Jersey, and he would continue to face Sullivan for several months.[7] Three months before Sullivan embarked on a tour of Europe they sparred for the last time in Boston on August 8, 1887. Mahan's last recorded fight was reportedly in Sligo, Ireland, against Peter Maher, to whom he lost in a three-round knockout in 1891. According to Harry Hill, while testifying before the Lexow Committee, he claimed that Mahan was working as a bartender in Boston when questioned by lawyer John Goff.

There was one Irish heavyweight boxer who claimed the world title but his coronation was extremely dubious and has not stood the test of time. The aforementioned Peter Maher, born on March 16, 1869, in Kilbannon, a small village near Tuam, County Galway, immigrated to America in 1891, having captured the middleweight championship of Ireland in 1888 and the heavyweight championship in 1890. He settled in Pittsburgh, where he immediately began to ply his sporting trade, scoring first-round demolitions over Jack Smith and "Sailor" Brown in New York during December 1891. After winning seven fights—six by knockout—Maher took on and defeated the talented Joe Godfrey in Philadelphia, earning him a tilt at former middleweight champion Bob Fitzsimmons, widely viewed as the most legitimate opponent for James Corbett after Peter Jackson. On March 2, 1892, Maher was well beaten by the wily Australian in New Orleans and was forced to retire at the end of the twelfth round. He had been unable to deal with the "red-hot fighting" skills of his opponent and, according to the *New York Herald,* ended up bruised, battered, and bloody.[8] However, the Irish fighter dusted himself down and, after defeating Mike Monahan, challenged Australian heavyweight champion Joe Goddard, an uncompromising fighter who had twice defeated Joe Choynski and drawn a bout with Peter Jackson. Maher appeared to have the upper hand in the early exchanges with his relentlessly aggressive style but was stunned by a knockout punch in the third. The *Standard Union* was less than impressed with the contest, caustically noting that any claim Maher might have as a champion of any category was buried so deep in the earth that no miner could resurrect it.[9] Nor was it impressed by Goddard, and predicted that either of the two would be nothing more than a "play-toy" in the hands of a boxer the caliber of Corbett or Choynski. After an impressive 4–0–1 record over the course of 1893, Maher took on the colored heavyweight champion George Godfrey on May 28, 1894, in Boston. It was Godfrey's hometown but the 3,000 in the crowd, including the great John L. Sullivan, were largely Irish American and firmly on Maher's side. In the sixth round Maher floored Godfrey, to the delight of the audience. In the typical casually racist tone of the time, the *Boston Globe* noted that "the Darky lay motionless in the center of the ring, his eyes and nose cut and blood pouring from his mouth."[10] After defeating Godfrey, Maher had a succession of eight knockout victories, albeit over inferior opponents.

After James Corbett retired, Bob Fitzsimmons, Joe Choynski, and Peter Jackson were considered the top three contenders for his title. However, Corbett disliked Fitzsimmons intensely and, favoring Maher's stronger Irish heritage, decided that a fight between his former sparring partner and Australian Steve O'Donnell would be for his vacant world title. The date of the encounter was set for November 11, 1895, at the Empire Athletic Club, Long Island, New York, and Corbett proclaimed that he would personally announce the winner despite having absolutely no authority to do so, albeit in an era when there was no proper controlling body. The fight was scheduled to last twenty-five rounds but the fans ended up with a mere sixty-three seconds of action before Maher knocked O'Donnell to the canvas. Jim Corbett immediately entered the ring and hugged his fellow Irishman and intoned, "On this spot, I give you the championship; because I know you can protect it. I shall never fight again." When asked by a journalist from the *Police Gazette* why he had chosen Maher, he replied that he would prefer to have the title in the hands of an Irishman and not under the custody of an Australian or an Englishman.[11]

The press had little time for Maher. The *Los Angeles Herald* noted that "scarcely a ripple of excitement" had resulted after his victory and predicted he would not be the champion for long, as it had been the easiest ever earned.[12] The caustic journalist wrote that Maher was no "talking machine" and, even if he did have something to say for himself, no one would listen to him. Maher belonged to the John L. Sullivan school of fighters, the paper ventured, and against a boxer as adept as Fitzsimmons stood little chance of winning. On February 21, 1896, after clamorous appeal from the boxing public, a crowd of 200 paid $20 each to see Maher take on Bob Fitzsimmons in Coahuila de Zaragoza, a small township just over the Mexican border.[13] The fight had been due to take place in El Paso, Texas, but the legislators passed a law banning prize-fighting in the state just prior to the encounter. This presented a dilemma for the organizer and promoter Dan Stuart. Legend has it that the famed Judge Roy Bean (he was actually a justice of the peace and not a judge) heard about the situation and sent a cable to Stuart informing him that his town of Langtry would be happy to stage the fight and that he would be able to circumvent any legal issues. His solution was a masterstroke. Bean, who also occupied his time as the town tax collector and coroner and was known as the "Law, West of the Pecos," proposed to stage the fight on a sandbar in the Rio Grande where spectators could view it from the river bank in front of his saloon.[14] As the location was technically in Mexico the Texas Rangers had no jurisdiction there. Among those who came to see the fight was Bat Masterson—also known as "Black Bat"—the famous lawman who had cleaned up Dodge City in Kansas and who had been hired by Bean as head of security for the occasion. (Masterson's mother was Irish and he would later become the sports editor of the *New York Evening Telegram*.[15]) A couple of days before the fight a group of Irish laborers working on a nearby railway project came to Langtry to support their fellow countryman. When a Chinese worker was killed in a barroom brawl, Roy Bean was called upon to open his informal court. Knowing that it would be unwise to impose a stiff sanction on the Irish navvies he consulted his law book and noted that there were many prohibitions against homicide but no specific law mentioning Chinese. On the day of the fight the boxers were protected by a thirty-man Texas military unit while 200 Mexican troops guarded their border. Maher weighed 180 pounds, and Fitzsimmons 165. The boxers wore five-ounce gloves and fought under the Marquis of Queensberry Rules, while Bean proposed to host the winner in a fight against Corbett in Langtry at a date to be arranged. It took Fitzsimmons all of ninety-six seconds to dethrone the Irish man with a vicious left hand to the chin, but there was scant time for Fitzsimmons to bask in his new-found glory as there were immediate shouts of warning that the pontoon bridge was in danger of being washed away by the strong current of the Rio Grande. All involved had to quickly gather their possessions and rush for the US border. Perhaps the biggest winner of all was the inimitable Judge Roy Bean. His name appeared in newspapers all over the world and he was always happy to tell his story to journalists, never afraid to add embellishments. Bean frequently recounted how he had named Langtry after the actress Lily Langtry, who he claimed was the great love of his life despite the fact that he had never met her. The town had actually been named by a railway engineer. He also named his saloon-cum-courthouse The Jersey Lilly [sic] in her honor. Fitzsimmons had such scant regard for the fight that he never claimed it as a championship encounter. There had been plans to film the encounter but it was over before the cameras were rolling, so the combatants faced each other in Madison Square Garden eight days later when they boxed to a no-decision over three rounds for the sake of leaving a visual record. On November 16 of the same year Maher took on the ferocious Joe Choynski at the Broadway Athletic Club in New York in front of a crowd of 5,000. A natural light heavyweight, Choynski was possessed of a relentless jabbing style, and earlier in the year he had hit Jim Jeffries so hard that he had to have a tooth removed with a pocketknife after it became embedded in his lip. In 1910, Jack Johnson and James Jeffries publicly acknowledged that the hardest punch they had received in their professional careers was the "ambush" right punch by Choynski.[16] Inevitably, the encounter between Maher and Choynski was fierce from the very start, and after five vicious toe-to-toe rounds, during which the Jewish fighter was largely in the ascendant, Maher finally dropped his opponent in the sixth in what was, for most of the boxing cognoscenti, an unforeseen result. Maher had fought a clever battle according to the *New York Journal* and displayed the "purest kind of grit at the critical moment."[17] It was to prove Maher's finest hour and the much-anticipated championship contest between Choynski and Fitzsimmons would never take place. Maher would go on to fight again and had victories over George "Old Chocolate" Godfrey, a one-time holder of the world colored heavyweight championship, Frank "The Harlem Coffee Cooler" Craig, another world colored middleweight champion, Charles A.C. "The Black Thunderbolt" Smith, and Joe "The Black Pearl" Butler, yet another former colored world middleweight champion. In May 1898 he took on Australian Joe "The Wild Man" Goddard in a contest he was expected to win. Goddard, forty years old by then, had announced that it would be his last fight and all indicators were that the Irishman, younger by eleven years, would easily account for him, but it was not to be, as Maher was floored after two minutes. The *San Francisco Examiner* predicted it would be the end of the Irishman's career.[18] Maher's final official bout took place on August 1, 1911, against Jim Dougherty in New York, where the forty-two-year-old veteran pugilist was victorious via a first-round knockout, and he made his last ring appearance in April 1913 when he fought Fred McCay in a three-round no-decision bout at the Arena Athletic Club in Philadelphia.[19] Despite not being overly appreciated by the boxing cognoscenti, Maher was an immensely popular character and numbered Teddy Roosevelt, William McKinley, and Wyatt Earp among his powerful friends. Like other champions of his time, he parlayed his fame into theater shows where he performed with a ragtag bunch of singers, actors, musicians, and freak-show accompanists, after which he would provide a demonstration of his fighting prowess in a sparring match. He was particularly well known for his presentations with Sam Lockhart's Performing Elephants. He died on July 22, 1940, at the age of seventy-one in Baltimore, Maryland, never having returned to his native Ireland.

Tommy Gibbons, born on March 22, 1891, in Saint Paul, Minnesota, to Thomas Gibbons and Mary Burke, was a versatile boxer who started his career in the middleweight division in 1911 before subsequently gravitating to the light heavyweight and heavyweight ranks. The Gibbonses hailed from County Mayo and brought their four small children—Mary, John, Patrick, and Bridget—to the United States, where Mary gave birth to three more children—Michael, Thomas, and Alice. For a number of years Gibbons fought in the shadow of his older brother Michael, a wrestler and boxer of some renown. Many of his earlier fights took place in the Wisconsin, New York, and Philadelphia areas, as boxing was outlawed in Minnesota until 1915.

On July 4, 1923, Gibbons fought Jack Dempsey in Shelby, Montana, in what was to prove a singular and much storied event in boxing history.[20] In early spring of that year a group of local men came up with the idea of staging a world title fight to promote the town based on the fact that they believed they were sitting on an oil field and that the newly opened railway connection would bring great riches the town's way. They decided that Tommy Gibbons was the most realistic contender for the great Dempsey. Jack Kearns, Dempsey's manager, wanted a purse of $300,000 and training expenses of $150,000 but subsequently agreed to a $300,000 purse and $10,000 expenses, with Gibbons's manager, Eddie Kane, settling for 50 percent of the gate receipts after Dempsey had been paid his $300,000. The promoters believed the gate would be at least a half a million, which would give Gibbons around $100,000 plus a crack at the title. Before his departure from Saint Paul, Gibbons was presented with a good luck rabbit's foot along with a large floral horseshoe from his legion of admirers. The mayor of Saint Paul had an intriguing story of origin for the rabbit foot, claiming it was the left hind foot of a buck rabbit killed at midnight in an Alabama cemetery under a full moon. On June 28 Gibbons was made an honorary member of the Blackfoot tribe and given the name "Thunder Chief." The promoters of the fight had relied on advance ticket sales to provide Dempsey's final $100,000 payment, but by the day of the fight they had only taken in $60,000 while the specially built Shelby Shell with 50,000 seats had a hugely disappointing 7,202 paying customers in what was shaping up as a financial disaster for the local boosters.[21] The gate was only $201,485, all of which went to Dempsey before the fight started. Gibbons knew he was fighting for nothing but a chance to win the heavyweight championship. The fight was scheduled for fifteen rounds but was to prove a disappointment for the spectators. The expected all-action style of Dempsey, with the ever-present possibility of a knockout punch, was replaced by a cat-and-mouse contest which went the full distance. Gibbons left Shelby with only his expenses money for his troubles, while the fight itself was a financial disaster for Shelby, with four of the main banks going out of business over the following months.[22] On August 9, Gibbons traveled across the Atlantic Ocean and took on Jake Bloomfield in London. He had been promised $50,000 but when he got to England the promoters told him that they would only be able to pay $25,000. This did not deter him, and when he returned to America journalists were curious as to why he settled for the lesser amount. He told them that a refusal would have given Americans a bad name for greed.[23]

On June 5, 1925, Gibbons fought Gene Tunney at the Polo Grounds in New York but at thirty-four years of age he was past his best, although he held his own in many of the early rounds before fading as the fight progressed. In the twelfth, Tunney put him down with a right but Gibbons managed to get up before he was hit with another right and counted out. Adding to his woes, his wife had recently been hospitalized for a nervous breakdown. Between his defeat, his wife's breakdown, and the fact that his brother Michael had lost the sight in his right eye in a fight, Gibbons decided the time had come to hang up his gloves. During his career he had recorded wins over George Chip, Willie Meehan, Billy Miske, Chuck Wiggins, Jack Bloomfield, and "Kid" Norfolk and had no-decision matches with George "K.O." Brown, Billy Miske, Harry Greb, Battling Levinsky, Bob Roper, Chuck Wiggins, and Georges Carpentier, among others. Only Greb, Miske, Dempsey, and Gene Tunney were able to score wins over Gibbons. After his retirement from boxing, Gibbons became a successful businessman and went on to spend four terms as the sheriff of Ramsey County, Minnesota. Gibbons was a fervent Catholic and donated $50,000 to build the Immaculate Conception Church in Osakis, Minnesota, from his purse from the Tunney fight and was knighted twice by the Catholic Church for his work, once as a Knight of St. Gregory and once as a Knight of St. George. Gibbons became a member of *Ring* magazine's Boxing Hall of Fame in 1963, the International Boxing Hall of Fame in 1993, and the Minnesota Boxing Hall of Fame in 2010.[24]

Tom "The Sailor" Sharkey, a man whose motto was "Don't Give up the Ship," was a singular individual and another one-time contender for the heavyweight title. Born in 1873 in the town of Dundalk, County Louth, on the east coast of Ireland, the adventurous Sharkey, if we are to believe his story, took it into his head to run away from home at the age of twelve and found work as a cabin boy on a ship, eventually making his way across the Atlantic to the United States, having spent time in China and Australia. Drama seemed to follow the young Irishman wherever he went, and he was later to claim that he had been shipwrecked four times. After sailing from New Orleans to New York, Sharkey took it in his head to join the U.S. Navy, and it was there that he first became acquainted with the pugilistic arts. When his training period was complete Sharkey was assigned to the USS *Philadelphia*, which

Tommy Gibbons (left) in his unsuccessful heavyweight title fight versus Jack Dempsey on July 4, 1923, in Shelby, Montana. The infamous bout bankrupted the town (Prints and Photographs Division, Library of Congress).

was deployed to Honolulu at the start of 1893 to protect American interests during an uprising against the ruling dynasty. While in Hawaii he got his first proper ring experience, although he found little opposition of note among his colleagues. Part of the British Navy was also based in Hawaii and a strong rivalry grew between the two forces, so much so that the British brought over their champion Jim Gardner to take on Sharkey. However, the Englishman was no match for him and was knocked out in four rounds on St. Patrick's Day of 1893, in what some boxing historians consider the Irishman's first professional fight.[25] Over the course of his eighteen months spent in Honolulu, Sharkey fought fourteen times, with all of his bouts ending in knockouts. The Sailor was renowned as a standup brawler with a ferocious punch and, with his unusually broad shoulders, square jaw, bull-like neck, and a star and battleship tattoo emblazoned on his chest, cut a singular dash. The *New York Times* noted that Sharkey, although not particularly tall, had a massive chest which stood out like a gigantic pair of bellows and looked almost twice that of an ordinary man.[26] His left ear had the appearance of a cauliflower, an indication of how rough some of the fights he had been through were.

When Sharkey later retired he placed an advertisement in a Californian newspaper offering $5,000 to anyone who could restore his ear to its former glory, but when a famous specialist took on the chore he got more than he bargained for. Complications developed in the course of the operation and the Irishman decided to call a halt to proceedings, reportedly turning to the medic and saying, "I guess you shouldn't interfere with nature so the ear stays put."[27] In addition to his build, Sharkey was blessed with extraordinarily strong hands and could reputedly bend silver dollars in his vise-like grip.

Not a fighter known for ability to control his temper or adopt a subtle approach to the sport, Sharkey frequently pushed referees and was known to head butt and hit on breaks and after the bell. Despite his uncompromising approach he was soon beating the best among the Californian

Tom "Sailor" Sharkey, born in Dundalk, County Louth, Ireland, in 1873, was widely regarded as one of the toughest and most uncompromising of fighters of his era and took on James J. Jeffries for the title in November 1899, a contest the Irishman lost on a twenty-five-round decision. He took his name from the fact that he claimed to have sailed around the world several times over (Bain News Service, George Grantham Bain Collection, Prints and Photographs Division, Library of Congress).

heavyweights, all of them inside nine rounds, but remained in relative obscurity until July 25, 1895, when he defeated the tough Australian heavyweight Billy Smith in the seventh round at the Colme Athletic Club, California. Sharkey's recipe for keeping in top physical shape included a twelve-mile run every day, some hours on the punch bag, skipping, sparring, sea bathing, and a strict diet.[28] He fought Alex Greggains to an eight-round draw in March 1896 at the Bush Street Theater in San Francisco, but it was the presence of leading heavyweight contender Joe Choynski on the night which was to prove most significant. As Sharkey was leaving the ring Choynski approached him and challenged him to fight, telling the Irishman that he would get the decision if he was still on his feet at the end of eight rounds. The pair met in the People's Palace in San Francisco in April 1896 in a contest

Tom Sharkey without shirt (Bain News Service, George Grantham Bain Collection, Prints and Photographs Division, Library of Congress).

where Sharkey took some savage treatment but still managed to hold on until the end to claim the victory. Jim Corbett was in attendance and was deeply impressed by his fellow Irishman. After the fight concluded he climbed into the ring to offer Sharkey a fight. They met in June, but the bout was deemed an exhibition and declared a draw after four rounds. Sharkey was convinced that he should have been declared the winner over the out-of-shape Corbett, who later cast aspersions on some of his opponent's tactics and claimed that he needed a longer fight to show off his scientific style. Corbett was prepared to come out of retirement to defend his title, which was in abeyance at the time, but Sharkey would have to fight Bob Fitzsimmons first. Meanwhile, Sharkey was in Jimmy Wakely's saloon in New York one evening where he happened to meet his great hero John L. Sullivan, who, by that stage of his life, had found himself down on his luck and awaiting the proceeds of a benefit night at Madison Square Garden. Sharkey had no hesitation in offering his services, and the two men fought a three-round exhibition which formed the main attraction on the night, with a grateful Sullivan taking away $100,000 for his efforts.[29]

On December 2 Sharkey fought Bob Fitzsimmons, then middleweight world champion, in a chaotic bout refereed by gunslinger Wyatt Earp at the Mechanics' Institute in San Francisco in front of a capacity crowd of 20,000. The fight was billed as one for the heavyweight title, as it was believed Corbett had retired. There was confusion before the fight when Earp had to be disarmed in the ring but he later claimed that he had just forgotten that he was wearing his gun. The early action was dominated by Fitzsimmons with long left-handed jabs and stiff right uppercuts; in the eighth Sharkey was caught by a vicious uppercut under the heart—Fitzsimmons's famed "solar plexus" punch. Sharkey went down but, in the confusion, Earp stopped the fight, ruling that Fitzsimmons had hit the Irishman below the belt.[30] He disqualified the Englishman and awarded the $10,000 purse to Sharkey, who had to be carried out of the ring as "limp as a rag."[31] In June 1897 Sharkey had another contentious encounter when he fought fellow Irishman Peter Maher at the Palace Athletic Club, New York, in a drawn contest where the fighters were surrounded by police officers at the conclusion. On March 5, 1898, Sharkey came up against his old foe Joe Choynski at the Woodward's Pavilion, San Francisco, in what proved to be yet another vicious brawl. The *Kansas City Star* reported that Sharkey repeatedly used his elbows and head and was lucky not to be disqualified in the early rounds.[32] At the start of the eighth Sharkey rushed Choynski and put him through the ropes, where he landed on the floor four feet below and in front of the local chief of police, who ordered him back into the ring, commanding the referee to declare a draw. Sharkey did not take the decision well and was warned by the referee that he would be arrested if he did not desist from his vehement remonstrations. The *Kansas City Star* thought the fight one of the most disgraceful exhibitions ever witnessed and termed Sharkey "a discordant element in pugilism" who had brought the sport into disrepute across the country.[33]

On May 6 of the same year Sharkey fought the up and coming James J. Jeffries at the Mechanic's Pavilion in San Francisco. Before the fight a couple of hastily built sets of bleachers collapsed, but luckily, no one was injured. In a titanic twenty-round battle Jeffries was given the victory on points. After knocking out Gus Rushlin in just over two minutes in June, Sharkey earned a tilt at Corbett, who had lost his title to Fitzsimmons by then. Held on November 22 at the Lennox Club in Brooklyn, it was to prove a typically contentious and barbaric encounter. Sharkey threw Corbett to the ground in the opening round and proceeded to hit him with a number of savage punches to the body and head. It seemed like Sharkey was on the cusp of victory but Jim McVey, one of Corbett's seconds, jumped into the ring in the ninth round to complain about Sharkey's behavior, and under the rules, the referee had no option but to disqualify Gentleman Jim. The crowd loudly disagreed with the result, but to no avail. The *Brooklyn Daily Eagle* was in agreement and wondered if the result was a fix, a question which was never answered.[34] In January 1899 Sharkey knocked out top-ranking heavyweight Kid McCoy—originator of the controversial "corkscrew punch"—in the tenth round, thus paving the way for a title tilt against the formidable Jim Jeffries, who had beaten Fitzsimmons in June. On November 3 the pair met in Coney Island Sporting Club in a scheduled twenty-five-round bout to decide the world heavyweight crown. Sharkey was conceding twenty-five pounds to his opponent and, at five foot eight, was the second shortest fighter ever to fight for the world title. The bout was the first ever title fight to be committed to film and the required light radiated a temperature of 100 degrees Fahrenheit, burning the tops of both fighters' heads despite them being covered by umbrellas at the break between rounds. Sharkey knew he had to carry the fight to Jeffries if he was to have any chance.[35] With a purse of $25,000 for the winner, it turned out to be one of the most punishing fights in ring history. During the course of the vicious bout Sharkey had his nose and two ribs broken but managed to go the full distance, with Jeffries declared the winner. Unknown to the boxers the cameras broke down while filming the last round, and when asked to reenact proceedings, Sharkey, in typical fashion, wanted to fight instead of mimicking the action. In the course of the contest Sharkey demonstrated his crude approach when he pinned Jeffries's left arm under his own, causing his opponent's glove to come off, and when the referee stepped in to allow Jeffries to put it back on, the Sailor took a ferocious swipe at his opponent. In his autobiography Jeffries wrote that Sharkey was the "roughest, gamest, and most willing fighter in the world."[36] Sharkey continued to fight and had a two-round victory over Joe Choynski in May 1900, but, when he lost to Bob Fitzsimmons three months later, it was evident that he was on the slide, a fact confirmed when he lost a series of fights to mediocre opposition, finally hanging up his gloves after a final defeat at the hands of Jack Monroe in February 1904. Sharkey possessed fearsome punching power and had a final record of thirty-seven knockouts in fifty-four fights. One commentator noted that he was a veritable nightmare to heavyweights and would sail in like a whirlwind, let go with both arms, and keep on slugging, terming him a "rugged, sawed-off Pier-Sixer with a brassbound sea chest of a torso and a rawhide constitution, who gave Jeffries his hardest fights."[37] The general consensus was that Sharkey was unlucky to come along at a time when there were so many other good heavyweights on the scene. Perhaps the greatest compliment paid to him was the assumption of the name Jack Sharkey by future world heavyweight champion Lithuanian American Joseph Paul Zukauskas, a fighter who gained the sobriquet "The Boston Gob" and is often associated with the phrase "we wuz robbed," words actually uttered by Max Schmeling's manager Joe Jacobs when the second meeting between Sharkey and his fighter was unexpectedly called for the Boston native.[38] At the end of his boxing career Tom Sharkey had amassed a fortune of $500,000 but squandered it all within a decade. After moving back to California he managed to get a few small acting roles but died virtually penniless on April 17, 1953, seven months short of his eightieth birthday. Before his death he had heard that James J. Jeffries had passed away and supposedly commented that it had taken a long time but he had beaten the bugger in the end.[39] An effort was made to organize the removal of his remains from the United States to the family plot in Ireland, but it never materialized.[40]

When Jack Johnson became the first black man to become heavyweight champion by defeating Tommy Burns on December 26, 1908, a formidable new king of the ring had come to the fore. Johnson was a force of nature and went on to demolish Al Kaufman, Stanley Ketchel, James Jeffries, "Fireman" Jim Flynn, and "Battling" Jim Johnson before a very brave Irishman stepped into the ring with him. Frank "The Fighting Dentist" Moran, born on March 18, 1887, in Cleveland, Ohio, was a talented all-around athlete and a singular character.[41] His father, Matthew J. Moran, came from Islandtaggart, Carrowholly, Westport, an island in picturesque Clew Bay off the west coast of Ireland.[42]

As well as being a boxer, Moran played professional football with the Pittsburgh Lyceums and Akron Pros and had the distinction of sparring with President Theodore Roosevelt while serving on the U.S.S. *Mayflower*. His sense of humor was evident when he gave his right hand the memorable sobriquet "Mary Ann" because she was such a knockout. On June 27, 1914, Moran entered the ring against Jack Johnson at the Vélodrome d'Hiver in Paris. The "Galveston Giant" was at that point thirty-five years old and had been living an infamously dissolute lifestyle for many years. The *Washington Post* estimated the fight would be worth a million dollars to Moran if he managed to knock Johnson out and would lift the white man's burden, causing as big a stir as the blows Admiral Dewey delivered in Manila Bay, which had won Uncle Sam the Philippine Islands.[43] While some among the American press gave Moran a fighting chance, the London *Times* was more circumspect, warning religious Americans that they would need to pray very hard if Moran was to have any hope against his fearsome opponent.[44]

The velodrome, designed for cycling, made for a remarkably unusual location for a fight. The sixteen-foot ring was roofed with a canopy of vivid purple in an effort to disguise the electrical tube lighting to provide suitable conditions for the filming of the bout. The result, the *Times* thought, was less than impressive as it threw a greenish tint over proceedings and made everything and everyone look ghastly.[45] It was certainly eclectic and matched those who had come to see the spectacle. As British boxing writer Fred Dartnell noted, the event had become something more than a sport or entertainment. Sitting near him were an "Eastern prince, a coffee coloured elegant with wonderful pearls and a radiant white woman with her hair dyed a kind of emerald gold."[46] The *Times* also commented on the diverse makeup of the crowd, noting that it seemed more like the first night of a new play than a boxing match, with scores of women wearing evening dresses in "many vivid hues and much bejeweled."[47] Among the women, it noted, were such great names in French society as the Baroness Henri de Rothschild, the younger Duchess d'Uzès, the Comtesse Mathieu de Noailles, the Princess de Lucinge, the Duchess de Rohan, and the Princess Morouzieff, while the prominent men present numbered the Duke of Westminster, the Earl of Sefton, the Marquis de Lafayette, the Duc d'Uzès, the Marquis de Breteuil, Baron James de Rothschild, the Comte de Clary, Mr. Spencer Eddy—a former American Ambassador to Argentina—Mr. Alfred Vanderbilt, Mr. Mortimer Schiff of New York, Senator Watson of West Virginia, and Mr. Richard Croker Jr. of New York, leader of Tammany Hall, while Mr. Georges Carpentier, the French champion, acted as referee.[48] Johnson was far from his physical best but managed to frustrate Moran by persistently holding him in clinches. He also goaded the Irishman by telling him that he did not know anything about fighting, despite the fact that the contest went the full ten-round distance. Afterward the press was divided in its opinion, with the *New York Times* terming it the poorest bout ever staged as a championship contest. On the other hand, Gus Rhodes of the *Defender* thought it the finest fistic encounter since gloved fighting was inaugurated in 1892.[49] Referee Georges Carpentier had warned Johnson for low punches on a number of occasions and many observers believed Moran should have been given the final decision. The Galveston Giant was complimentary to his opponent after the fight, praising Moran's ability to strike hard with either hand, and ventured the opinion that if

Frank Moran (left) and Jess Willard before their encounter on March 25, 1916, at Madison Square Garden in New York City. Moran, born of Irish parents, was known as "The Fighting Dentist" because of his professional training and once said that he earned more money knocking teeth out than he did fixing them (Bain News Service, Prints and Photographs Division, Library of Congress).

his punches had always landed there was no other boxer who could stand against him. Johnson was also willing to admit that he had not been as assiduous in his preparation as he could have been, having done little but "ride fast" for the previous two years.[50] Moran did not agree with the final decision and believed, at worst, that it should have been a draw because he had been the aggressor all of the time and had not been hurt. The cut he had suffered during the fight was only the reopening of one he had sustained in training and he believed he had the best of every round.[51] To add insult to Moran's injuries, his $25,000 purse was withheld, possibly due to the assassination of Austro-Hungarian heir apparent Archduke Franz Ferdinand in Sarajevo the following day or, more likely, because a Chicago brewer had secured a creditor's attachment on Johnson's purse over an unpaid debt. In addition, the French government had placed a moratorium on all civil debts after hostilities broke out and the canny promoter may have taken advantage of the situation.

Moran went on to twice defeat another Irish boxer in the shape of Jim "The Roscommon Giant" Coffey. Born on January 27, 1890, in the small village of Tully, Coffey only took up boxing on his arrival to the United States in 1910 at the age of twenty. Working as a trolley motorman on Third Avenue, Coffey had a chance meeting with New York Police Department officer Tom Shaw, a man known for his boxing and wrestling skills, sparking Coffey's interest in the sport. Shaw, the story goes,

Moran blocks left to the ribs. Frank Moran (left) lost to world champion Jack Johnson on June 29, 1914, at the Vélodrome d'Hiver, Paris (*New York World-Telegram* and the *Sun* Newspaper Photograph Collection, Library of Congress).

challenged Coffey to a wrestling match and promptly found himself on his back in a New York minute. Recognizing Coffey's potential, Shaw invited the Roscommon Giant to the police gymnasium to try his hand at boxing. Coffey took to the sport with alacrity and was soon invited to become a fulltime sparring partner for Carl Morris, an aspiring white hope, but the Irishman harbored ambitions of his own, a wish that was realized on January 26, 1912, when he was called in as a last-minute replacement and beat Nick Mueler over six rounds at the Polo Grounds, New York. Watching from the crowd that night was Billy Gibson, the boxing promoter and largest shareholder in Madison Square Garden, who would later go on to manage Gene Tunney. Gibson was impressed with Coffey's display and subsequently signed him up. Gibson, a master of public relations, introduced Coffey to the press, claiming he had just got to the United States and had only been boxing for three weeks. In an obvious attempt to further endear the Roscommon Giant to the public, Gibson announced that his broth of an Irish boy had been born on July 4, American Independence Day. Standing at six feet three inches tall and weighing 210 pounds, Coffey gained immense popularity among the Irish American community and was once introduced by the world-famous Irish tenor John McCormack as the next heavyweight champion, inspiring the audience to give a rendition of "When Irish Eyes Are Smiling."

On February 18, 1915, Coffey easily accounted for Jack "Twin" Sullivan at Fairmount Athletic Club New York City. The New York State Athletic Commission then

English boxer Bombardier Billy Wells (left) sparring with Jim Coffey in Rye, New York, to prepare for a fight with Al Panzer. Although the Irishman never won the heavyweight title, Coffey fought at the highest echelons of the sport (*New York Times*, June 26, 1912, Bain News Service, Prints and Photographs Division, Library of Congress).

decided that Moran and Coffey should fight to see who would take on Jess Willard for the title. The combatants met in Madison Square Garden on October 19 of the same year in a contest where Coffey was favorite and had by far the bigger support, many members of which had to be turned away. *Boxing News* described Coffey as "cool and confident" while Moran was his "usual dour self."[52] In the early rounds it was, according to the journalist, like a "carthorse versus a thoroughbred," with Coffey showing considerably more refinement than his opponent, but it was not to be for the Roscommon Giant. After Coffey had taken significant punishment from Moran's infamous Mary Ann, the referee stepped in to end the fight in the third round. Moran's boast that that one kiss on the chin from his famous punch would end a fight had come to pass. Coffey, the *Boxing News* noted, could only look out with lusterless eyes at the sea of faces while Frank Moran and his team did a war dance in the ring.[53] Billy Gibson sought a rematch, and on January 16, 1916, the pair took to the ring once again in Madison Square Garden. As was his wont, Moran pushed the boundaries during the early rounds and received a warning for roughing. Coffey looked to be on top but once again fell afoul of Mary Ann, this time in the seventh round.

Perhaps Coffey's most interesting fights of his later career were those against Bartley Madden, born in the neighboring county of Galway (Ireland) in the village of Caltra on September 3, 1917. Madden picked up his boxing skills when working with the British navy before immigrating to the United States. In their first encounter Coffey easily accounted for Madden, but when the pair met for a second time on November 23, 2017, the accolades were reversed. As it transpired, Coffey's clashes with Moran were the closest he came to a title fight. The Roscommon Giant returned to live in Ireland in 1923 and died on December 20, 1959. Bartley Madden went on to fight over three hundred times. Famous for his ability to keep standing, he was only ever put down by Gene Tunney in 1925. When Madden fought New Zealander Tom Heeny at Croke Park, Dublin, in August 1926, he was eleven years older than his opponent, but he made Heeney go all the way for the verdict. Heeny's share of the purse provided the New Zealander with the money to travel to America, where he eventually lost to Gene Tunney in a title fight.[54] Madden died nearly penniless at a Washington, D.C., hospital from injuries received in a twenty-foot fall from a landing at the Treasury Building. Tragically, his wife had died only three weeks earlier and they were survived by a young son.[55]

Frank Moran went on to earn a second tilt at the world title against Jess "The Pottawatomie Giant" Willard, who had finally accounted for Jack Johnson in a dubious fight in Havana in 1915. Willard immediately declared that he would never fight a negro again, and Grantland Rice, in keeping with the vast majority of white Americans, concluded that the big shadow over the fight game had finally lifted; when Jess Willard "wrestled the chaplet of apple blossoms from the sable brow of Jack Johnson, he had done something more than restore the heavyweight championship to the Caucasian caravanserai. He had swept away the big barrier which has clogged the game's popularity for five years."[56]

Moran fought the new champion at Madison Square Garden on March 25, 1916, in what was Willard's first defense of his crown. The fight, organized on a ten-round no-decision basis, meant Moran had to knock Willard out to claim the title. Willard was a monster of a man, six foot six inches tall and over 250 pounds weight. Among the huge crowd there to witness proceedings were former heavyweight champions John L. Sullivan, Jim Corbett, and Tommy Burns, but it was not to be for the brave Irishman; the bout went the full distance and Willard retained his title. Moran had to be content with his $23,750 payday, a lot more than he got for his troubles when he fought Jack Johnson. He fought unsuccessfully for the heavyweight championship of France against Marcel Nilles on December 22, 1922, after which he declared his retirement from the ring. After winning a role in a Broadway stage adaptation of Theodore Dreiser's novel *An American Tragedy* Moran got the acting bug and went on to have a successful career in film, starting with small roles in two silent films, *The Chinatown Mystery* and *Ships of the Night,* while in 1933 he appeared as himself in *The Prizefighter and the Lady* as well as in the Mae West vehicle *She Done Him Wrong*, in which he played a convict. During the 1940s Moran was one of the Preston Sturges company of character actors, appearing in all except one of his films where his only leading role was a shared credit with George Zucco in the 1944 *Return of the Ape Man*. Frank Moran died on December 14, 1967, at the age of eighty and, despite his many celluloid outings, is often best remembered for the line, "It pays me better to knock out teeth than put them in."

Fourteen

"The Pittsburgh Kid"
Billy Conn

"What's the point in being Irish if you can't be thick."
—Billy Conn

WHEN HOWARD SACKLER'S 1967 PLAY *The Great White Hope* debuted, the playwright was taken aback by the reaction of some critics who read the text as solely a treatise on racism. For him it was about the destiny of a man pitted against society, a metaphor of struggle between man and the outside world. While some people spoke of the play as if it were a cliché of white liberalism, Sackler insisted that it was not a case of blacks being good and whites being bad.[1] The play, based on the true story of Jack Johnson and his first wife Etta Terry Duryea, who died by suicide in 1912, won many awards, including a Pulitzer Prize, the New York Drama Critics Award, the Drama Critics Prize, and the Antoinette Perry Award as the best drama of the 1968–1969 season. It was also the first play to transfer to Broadway after premiering at a resident not-for-profit theater. The production was a massive logistical exercise with a cast of sixty-three actors playing 247 roles over twenty scenes in two acts and lasted three and a half hours. It ran for 546 performances on Broadway. Muhammad Ali was so impressed with James Earl Jones's performance in the lead role that he reportedly told him that he should take out the "interracial love stuff" because the play was really about him.[2] Given that Ali was fighting the draft for the Vietnam War, it was, arguably, an understandable reaction. The play was subsequently adapted for film by Sackler and released under the same title in 1970 with the role of Jack Johnson played by the six foot nine inch boxer James J. Beattie, the tenth ranking contender for the heavyweight title at the time. Critic Vincent Canby of the *New York Times* had not rated the play and thought the film similarly dramatized the protagonist's initial triumph, his subsequent persecution, and his humiliations, as if they were the "Stations of the Cross," and thought it one of those "liberal, well-meaning, fervently uncontroversial works that pretend to tackle contemporary problems by finding analogies at a safe remove in history."[3] (In an interesting footnote to the theatrical production on Broadway, an actor called Thomas Barbour was tasked with playing four different minor parts and was a nephew of William Warren Barbour, winner of the American and Canadian Amateur Heavyweight Championship in 1910 and 1911. Barbour had been touted by "Gentleman Jim" James Corbett as a man who could lower Jack Johnson's sails but he refused to assume the mantle, and in 1940, then representing New Jersey in the U.S. Senate, worked successfully to repeal the 1912 law prohibiting interstate transportation of boxing film footage.)

Born on October 8, 1917, in East Liberty, Pennsylvania, the oldest of five children of William David Conn, a steamfitter of Scots Irish extraction who worked for Westinghouse Electric Company, and Margaret McFarland, who had emigrated to the United States from County Cork when still a young child, Billy "The Pittsburgh Kid" Conn grew up in a staunchly Irish American neighborhood where by the age of thirteen he was well known as an accomplished street fighter. East Liberty was a hardscrabble area in a tough town. H.L. Mencken, the most famous journalist of the era, wrote of Pittsburgh in the 1930s that it was "so dreadfully hideous, so intolerably bleak and forlorn that it reduced the whole aspiration of a man to a macabre and depressing joke."[4]

Not one for education, Conn began working in an East Pittsburgh gym owned by Johnny Ray, a former professional boxer whom Conn always credited for developing his famous left jab. Ray was born Harry Pitler but changed his name because, by his own telling, there were far more Irish boxing enthusiasts than Jewish ones in Pittsburgh in that era.[5] Conn frequently told a story that the then heavyweight champion Max Baer was passing through Pittsburgh and came to Ray's gym looking for a workout. Ray suggested that he spar with Conn. The champion must have been surprised when he noticed that his opponent was four inches shorter and a good seventy-five pounds lighter. Conn later claimed that he brought blood to Baer's nose and came off better with his hard and fast style. At the conclusion of the session Baer smiled at his young opponent and told him that he hoped Conn would not grow up until he had retired.[6]

At the age of seventeen, having never fought as an amateur, Conn launched his professional career as a welterweight and, after winning nine out of his eighteen fights in 1935 and going undefeated in nineteen bouts during 1936, including a hard-fought decision over the welterweight contender Fritzie Zivic, Conn moved up to the middleweight division and defeated four ex-champions in 1937 alone: Babe Risko, Vince Dundee, Teddy Yarosz, and Young Corbett III. After Conn defeated the middleweight champion Fred Apostoli in a nontitle fight on January 6, 1939, in Madison Square Garden, Bill Corum of the *New York Journal-American* punningly described the encounter as "a story of Conn-fidence and Conn-quest."[7] To further bolster his confidence, Conn defeated Apostoli for a second time a month later over fifteen rounds.

Conn got his chance to fight for the light heavyweight title on July 13, 1939, against Melio Bettina, an all-action New Yorker who had won the vacant title four months earlier after the retirement of John Henry Lewis due to eye problems. The 19,295 crowd in Madison Square Garden saw Conn take the fight on a unanimous decision, and he went on to defend the title by beating Bettina on September 25 at Forbes field in Pittsburgh. He also successfully defended it against Gus Lesnevich in November 1939 and June 1940. Tall at six feet one inch, Conn had a good solid punch but his main talents were his fine boxing skills and excellent footwork. When Warner Brothers were shooting *Gentleman Jim* they used Conn's footwork for the closeup shots. While Errol Flynn was well able to dramatize the role of Corbett, Jack

Joe Louis (left) and Billy Conn on the canvas with referee Eddie Josephs observing, at the World Heavyweight Championship, Polo Grounds, New York, New York (Photo by Wm. C. Greene, *New York World-Telegram* and the *Sun* Newspaper Photograph Collection, Library of Congress).

Warner was adamant that Conn was the only boxer he would consider for the finer details.[8]

Wearing his trademark green shorts with shamrock decal, Conn developed a huge following among the Irish American community, including a raucous female fan base. The *New York Daily News* once described him as a "beauteous boxer who could probably collect coinage by joining the ballet league if he chose to flee the egg-eared and flattened nose fraternity."[9] Conn went on to knock out the heavyweight contender Bob Pastor in the thirteenth round in September 1940, with further victories over Al McCoy in ten rounds and Lee Savold in twelve rounds in the same year. In May 1941 he relinquished the light heavyweight crown to become a full-time heavyweight. On June 18 of the same year Conn nearly won the title from the legendary Joe Louis in what was widely considered a mismatch. Conn was attempting to become the first light heavyweight champion in boxing history to take the top gong without going up in weight. Louis, unbeaten in sixteen title fights, was eleven-to-five to win by knockout, but Conn was undaunted and described his opponent as "a big, slow-moving Negro" who was only a "mechanical fighter," unable to think his way through things when he came under pressure in the ring.[10] Louis had a pithy and uncompromising reply: "I never heard of him getting no college degrees. He talks too much and I'm going to push some of his gab down his throat." Louis versus Conn was the classic match-up: the power puncher against the clever slickster, bull against matador.[11] Almost 60,000 gathered to see the contest, the largest crowd in the Polo Grounds since the famous Dempsey–Firpo brawl in 1923. Many gave Conn a good chance of taking the title from Louis, who was making his eighteenth defense, despite a weight difference of over thirty pounds. If he could manage it he would reverse the trend of failure; four previous light-heavyweights had attempted to take the heavyweight title but none had succeeded. Louis had no problems with Conn in the early rounds, but in the seventh the Irish American went on the attack and took command of the fight. Louis later admitted that Conn was just too fast for him and that he got tired as the fight went on, particularly struggling with some of his opponent's left hooks. Going into the thirteenth round Conn led on all scorecards. Having staggered Louis with a left hook in the twelfth, the Irish American believed his time had come. For the first two minutes of the thirteenth Louis looked vulnerable, but as Conn tried to end the fight by knockout, Louis struck his jaw with a powerful right, then hurt him with a left, and dropped him for the count with a jolting right. Louis later said it was the toughest of all his fights, while Conn woefully said that he lost his "head and a million bucks." When asked by a reporter why he went for the knockout, Conn famously replied, "What's the use of being Irish if you can't be thick [i.e., stupid]?" Always one for the one-liners, Conn later told Frank Deford of *Sports Illustrated* that he had asked Joe Louis why he could not have let him hang on to the title for six months, to which Louis supposedly replied, "I let you have it for twelve rounds, and you couldn't keep it. How could I let you have it for six months?"[12]

Despite his loss to Louis, Conn achieved celebrity status and starred in the title role in *The Pittsburgh Kid*, a semi-autobiographical movie produced in 1941 by Republic Pictures and based on the novel by Octavus Roy Cohen, centering on the dilemma faced by a young boxer with divided loyalties between a pretty girl and an unscrupulous manager. Shortly after the Louis fight, on July 1, 1941, Conn married Mary Louise Smith, a union which produced three sons and a daughter. He won a bruising slugfest with middleweight champion Tony Zale on February 14, 1942, while in the same year he enlisted in the U.S. Army and fought exhibition fights with divisional champions in the European theater. A Louis–Conn rematch was planned for June 25, 1942, but when the Irish American broke his left hand in a scuffle with his father-in-law the contest was delayed. Billy did not get along with Mary's father, Jimmy Smith, a former major league baseball player for the Cincinnati Reds known as "Greenfield Jimmie." The contest was postponed, but world affairs intervened on December 7, 1941, when hundreds of low-flying Japanese war planes bombed Pearl Harbor, killing 2,335 US servicemen and sixty-eight civilians.[13] Secretary of War Henry L. Stimson announced that Louis, who was still in the army, would not be making any more title defenses for the duration of the war and a return match with Conn conflicted with the standards and interests of the Army. Boxing promoter Mike Jacobs finally signed both fighters for a rematch to take place in June 1946. When Louis was asked by reporters if Conn might win by decision, the champion famously replied, "He can run, but he can't hide." The fight was at Yankee Stadium in front of a disappointing crowd of 45,295 (largely because it was the first ever televised world heavyweight championship, attracting 100,000 viewers, setting a record for the most seen world heavyweight bout in history to that point). If it had not been televised, it was most likely that the stadium would have been full, although some boxing writers also pointed to the high cost of seats. Ringside seats went for $100, the highest in the history of the sport, while the "ringside" area itself had expanded much further than previously. Total income from the fight came to $1,925,564, falling just short of that for the return contest between Jack Dempsey and Gene Tunney in 1927 and remaining the second highest grossing contest until it was finally surpassed by the Muhammad Ali–Ken Norton fight in September 1973. The contest, however, did not do justice to the figures. Conn was heavier and slower by then, while Louis no longer had the awesome power of old in his fists. The first seven rounds were cat and mouse, but in the eighth the Brown Bomber launched a meaty right uppercut through Conn's defense and followed it up with a short left hook to the chin, causing the Irish American's head to snap back before he fell to the canvas. Conn was duly counted out and the indomitable Louis had made the twenty-second successful defense of his title. Wilfred Smith of the *Chicago Daily Tribune* was definitive in his summation of the encounter: "Tonight, Louis settled for all time this question of the puncher and the boxer. Conn is a great lightweight—he once held this title—but tonight it was all too clear he was a boy on a man's errand."[14]

Conn won his final two fights in 1948 with ninth-round knockouts and boxed with Louis in a six-round exhibition in his final appearance as a professional on December 10, 1948. In the course of his thirteen-year career Billy Conn won sixty-three fights (fourteen by knockout), lost eleven, and fought one draw. A third of his professional fights were against world champions, all of whom he defeated with the exception of Louis. After his retirement from the ring, Conn invested money in oil wells and a highly profitable car dealership, as well as managed the Stardust Club in Las Vegas, refereed boxing, carried out public relations work, and made personal appearances at boxing-related events. He was elected to the Boxing Hall of Fame in 1965 and the International Boxing Hall of Fame in the inaugural class of 1990. In 1981 the editors of *Ring* magazine rated his first bout with Louis as the greatest fight of all time and selected Conn at number twenty-five in their list of the top fifty boxers pound-for-pound of all time. Conn maintained his boxing skills into his later years, and in 1990, at the age of seventy-three, stepped into the middle of a robbery at a Pittsburgh convenience store after the thief punched the store manager. Conn took a swing at the robber and ended up on the floor of the store, scuffling with him. "You always go with your best punch—straight left," Conn told television station WTAE afterward. The robber managed to escape but not before Conn pulled off his coat which contained his name and address. His wife said jumping into the fray was typical of her husband. "My instinct was to get help," she said at the time. "Billy's instinct was always to fight." In the last two years of his life, Conn suffered from pugilistic dementia and died of pneumonia at a Veterans Affairs hospital in Pittsburgh and is buried in Calvary Cemetery.[15] A portion of North Craig Street in the Oakland neighborhood of Pittsburgh is named Billy Conn Boulevard, while he is famously mentioned in the classic movie *On the Waterfront*. In the timeless "I could have been a contender" scene, Rod Steiger (playing Marlon Brando's brother) reflects on Brando's character Terry's early promise as a boxer with the words, "You could have been another Billy Conn."

Fifteen

"There's no quit in a Quarry"

The Tragedy of Jerry Quarry

> "Well, he fell kinda awkward."
> —Jerry Quarry's reply when asked if he had found Jack Bodell an awkward opponent. (Quarry won their fight in sixty-four seconds in November 1971.)

As time passed there were fewer and fewer fighters of Irish extraction in the heavier weight divisions. "Irish" Jerry Quarry, also known as "The Bellflower Bomber," has the distinction of being the only boxer to have fought Muhammad Ali and Joe Frazier twice and, during the peak of his career between 1968 and 1971, was rated the most popular fighter in the sport by *Ring* magazine. There was no doubting the hard-earned basis of his popularity. Quarry came from an uncompromising background. His father Jack bragged of being a cotton picker and a boxer in New Mexico before migrating to Bakersfield, California, where Jerry was born. Quarry Senior had his knuckles tattooed, "Hard" on his left hand and "Luck" on his right, while his unforgiving credo was "There's no quit in a Quarry," a motto that would prove fatal later in his sons' lives.[1] Jerry Quarry once recounted a story where his father made him wear a diaper and suck a bottle in front of his sisters because he refused to retaliate when hit by a playmate.[2] Quarry first came to prominence in the boxing world in 1965 when he won the National Golden Gloves Championship at the age of nineteen and, weighing only 183 pounds, captured the public imagination by knocking out all of his five opponents in the course of the tournament in Kansas City, a feat never matched before or subsequently. In 1965 between May and December he had fourteen professional matches, the majority of which took place at the Olympic Auditorium in Los Angeles, where he became an established draw. Despite competing in the professional ranks, Quarry's earnings were meager and he supplemented his boxing paydays by working as a tire changer at a Greyhound bus terminal. He had three draws on his record by the time of his first loss, which came in his twenty-first bout in July 1966 against Eddie Machen, a fighter best known for breaking Sonny Liston's run of knockouts. Quarry bounced back to win his next ten fights. Although he was a Californian he became most popular in Madison Square Garden, where he was a hero to the Irish American community.

After Muhammad Ali was stripped of the World Boxing Association crown, a heavyweight tournament was held in his absence to come up with the best opponent.

Jerry Quarry's first fight in the competition was against Floyd Patterson, which he won on a split-decision victory before going on to knock out the highly regarded Thad Spencer in his second bout, qualifying him to take on ex-middleweight Jimmy Ellis in the final. Prior to the bout Quarry sustained a broken back from an injury on the diving board at a pool that later developed into gangrene. This time Quarry lost on a split decision but went on to win a sequence of fights, including a facile victory over U.S. Olympic champion Buster Mathis, which set him up for a title bout with Joe Frazier. On June 23, 1969, the men met at Madison Square Garden in what *Ring* magazine later voted its "Fight of the Year." Quarry was now, inevitably, being touted as a Great White Hope. Unfortunately for the Irish American, the bout was stopped in the seventh round with Quarry bleeding heavily from a cut under his eye. As was his style, he had absorbed a number of punishing punches from Frazer but had kept coming forward. In December Quarry fought Canadian George Chuvalo in a controversial encounter. In the seventh round, Chuvalo knocked Quarry down. Quarry rose at the count of four, and then took a knee, but on rising exactly at the count of ten, he found referee Zach Clayton ruled a knockout.

Quarry boxed in Britain twice, knocking out the British heavyweight champion Jack Bodell in sixty-four seconds at Wembley in November 1971, and the following year outpointing his fellow American Larry Middleton. When he fought Bodell, the notoriously unorthodox Derbyshire southpaw, prefight speculation hinged on how long it would take Quarry to solve the style of a man who had just trounced Joe Bugner over fifteen rounds. "Did you find him awkward?" said an eager journalist in the dressing room inquest. "Well," said Quarry. "He sure fell awkward...." He also twice defeated the British heavyweight Brian London in California, in 1967 and 1969.[3]

When Muhammad Ali successfully sued to win a right to return to fight professionally, he approached all of the top ten ranked heavyweights for a match: Quarry was the only man to accept the challenge. Promoter Harold Conrad had unsuccessfully sought a venue in twenty-two states including California, where the then Governor Ronald Reagan said he would not allow a fight in which a draft dodger was competing. Because there was no state athletic commission in Georgia, it only required the imprimatur of the mayor of Atlanta for the fight to take place. Ironically, Mayor Sam Massell, a former critic of black civil rights, responded to pressure exerted by a black state senator named Leroy Johnson and, much to the chagrin of Georgia governor and segregationist Lester Maddox, a date was fixed for the showdown. Maddox went as far as calling for a boycott and proclaimed a day of mourning on the eve of the match. On October 26, 1970, the combatants met at the City Auditorium in front of an enraptured crowd Thomas Hauser described as the "greatest collection of black power and black money ever assembled."[4] Among the celebrities present were Diana Ross, Jesse Jackson, Sidney Poitier, Curtis Mayfield, Mary Wilson, Arthur Ashe, Bill Cosby, Julian Bond, and Whitney Young, with music provided by the Temptations and the Supremes. George Plimpton later memorably recalled men with "felt hatbands and feathered capes ... stilted shoes, the heels like polished ebony, many smoking stuff in odd meerschaum pipes."[5] Nothing like it had been seen before, he concluded. The fact that Quarry was white inevitably added to the mix of symbolism and politics on display. For Quarry, it meant a $338,000 purse, the biggest single payday of his fighting career.[6] However, it was to prove a disappointing night for him as he was badly cut over his left eye by an accidental head butt in the third round and was not allowed to continue in the fourth, despite his vehement protestations.

On June 27, 1972, Quarry met Ali for a second time at the Las Vegas Convention Center on a night dubbed "The Soul Brothers Versus the Quarry Brothers."[7] Jerry Quarry's younger brother Mike fought Bob Foster for the light heavyweight title on the undercard, but it was to prove a disappointing night for the siblings. Mike Quarry was knocked unconscious for ten minutes and there were initial worries that he had suffered serious injury.

After landing a half a dozen blows on Quarry at the start of the seventh round, Ali waved the referee in to stop the fight. As well as the physical beating they received, the Quarry family was subjected to racial insults by some of Ali's supporters. In retrospect, it would have been wiser for Jerry Quarry to hang up his gloves earlier than he did. He went on to stop Ron Lyle in twelve rounds in February 1973 and scored a first-round knockout of Ernie Shavers ten months later. In June he was at the receiving end of a torrid beating by Joe Frazier in what was the last fight ever refereed by Joe Louis, and on March 24, 1974, he was stopped by Ken Norton in the fifth round of another punishing encounter. After retiring twice, Quarry went on to make two comebacks, the second in the newly created cruiserweight division in 1983, by which time he was thirty-eight years of age. Ultimately he was to pay a high price for his bravery in the ring, and in some respects he was the architect of his own downfall, as he sparred without headgear and always concentrated on attacking his opponent in the ring, paying scant regard to defensive duties. Already showing signs of brain damage, Quarry, having been denied a license to fight in a number of states, was finally granted one in Colorado, allowing him to take on Ron Cranmer, sixteen years his junior, on October 30, 1992, for a meager payday of $1,050. Inevitably, Quarry, now forty-seven, was demolished, losing two of his front teeth in the process. There had been signs as early as 1982 of his having dementia pugilistica but he had gone on to fight three more times. He fought more than 200 times as an amateur and finished his professional career with fifty-three wins, nine draws, and three losses. For better or ill, Quarry also played a small role in bringing Don King to the world of boxing promotion. King was managing Earnie Shavers at the time he was knocked out by Quarry in the first round. Believing he might find more succession promoting fights than managing boxers, King changed direction, and the rest is history.[8] The general consensus on Jerry Quarry's fighting career was that he was born too late to compete with heavyweight champions of similar size, such as Patterson and Rocky Marciano. Instead, he fought and lost to bigger men—twice to Ali and Frazier and once each to Ken Norton and Jimmy Ellis. However, in Buster Mathis, Mac Foster, Thad Spencer, and Ernie Shavers, he beat four of the bigger heavyweights of his era. After his first retirement Quarry had a brief career as a television boxing analyst and an even briefer one as a lounge singer, even appearing once on the *Ed Sullivan Show*.

Yet even when he had finally hung his gloves up for the final time, Jerry couldn't resist throwing punches. Describing one of his fights with Frazier to a reporter one day, Quarry wanted to show the reporter his left hook. The reporter said it wasn't necessary. Quarry insisted. The reporter relented. Quarry threw what he thought was a friendly punch and broke one of the reporter's ribs.[9]

Jerry Quarry had never been an easy man to deal with. Don Chargin, a sometimes promoter for Quarry, noted that he was articulate and could be very charming, but he could also be very mean: "He didn't make a lot of friends. He took any criticism as a conspiracy against him."[10] Chargin said that he and corner men pleaded with Quarry not to beat up sparring partners and to avoid getting hit so much in training, but their pleas fell on deaf ears.

Near the end of his life Quarry summed up his feelings on his boxing career in a pithy poem: "I've been in the ring with the best of all men / Some say the best of all time / I gave my all, round after round / And the world knows I tried / I fought with heart / But needed much more / A bridesmaid but never a bride."[11]

Jerry Quarry died on January 3, 1999, at the age of fifty-three in Templeton, California. A neurologist who examined his brain noted that it was similar to that of an eighty-year-old man. In 1994 his older brother Jimmy established the Jerry Quarry Foundation for Dementia Pugilistica with the aim of helping other victims of the condition. Mike and Bobby, two of Jerry's siblings who also took up boxing, suffered brain damage in what must be one of the most tragic of all boxing family stories. Ultimately, the Quarry brothers paid a high price for their never-say-die attitude and their relentless ability to take punches. As one journalist noted, Jerry Quarry's name was sadly appropriate because at the end of his life his brain was a quarry emptied of its bedrock capacity to think and to remember.[12] His personal life and finances were a quarry mined as ruinously as his mind and body. Three wives, $2.1 million in boxing purses, and $500,000 in savings were lost in a swirling decline fueled by alcohol and drugs.[13]

Sixteen

Gerry Cooney
The Last Great Irish White Hope

> All of the sports have a safety net, but boxing is the only sport that has none. So when the fighter is through, he is through. While he was fighting his management was very excited for him, but now that he is done, that management team is moving on.
>
> —Gerry Cooney

> Growing up training, I use to get up so early I would wave to the garbage men going by. So, I had this relationship with Blue Collar America and I really liked it. I felt that lots of those people looked forward to me winning.
>
> —Gerry Cooney

Irish American Gerald Arthur Cooney, better known as Gerry Cooney, was born on August 4, 1956, and challenged unsuccessfully for the world heavyweight championship title in 1982 and 1987, but has had much better luck outside the ring than Jerry Quarry. His father Tony, an ironworker who lived in Brooklyn with his wife Eileen, moved the family to Huntington, Long Island, after she expressed a desire to get away from the urban maelstrom of New York City. Cooney Senior pushed his sons to try their hand at boxing, getting them up to run at five in the morning as well as constructing a homemade gym and boxing ring in the family garage. Sadly, Tony Cooney died from lung cancer at the age of fifty-five, shortly before Gerry became the New York Golden Gloves Heavyweight Champion. By his own admission Cooney had a tough upbringing. He once told journalist Eamon Carr that he learned five things during his childhood: He was no good. He was a failure. He was not going to amount to anything. Never trust anybody. Do not tell anybody your business. These were all things he had to later unlearn, he said. After a stellar amateur career consisting of fifty-five wins and three losses, Cooney made his professional debut on February 15, 1977, when he knocked out Billy Jackson in the first round. Within four years he had stopped twenty-two opponents in twenty-five fights, and by 1980 Cooney was ranked as the number-one contender by the World Boxing Council (WBC) and was spoiling for a fight with champion Larry Holmes. The following year he knocked out former champion Ken Norton in fifty-four seconds, breaking the Madison Square Garden record for a main event, a gong held by Lee Savold since 1948. Holding out for a big payday, Cooney and his management opted not to fight for thirteen months in order to get a tilt at Holmes. The buildup to the fight was remarkable. Cooney made the front cover of *Time* and *Sports Illustrated,* sharing the former with Sylvester Stallone and the latter with Holmes. Some commented on the fact that *Sports Illustrated* had Cooney on the main cover and the champion on the pullout section.[1] The magazine predicted a win for Cooney in five rounds. Should he defeat Holmes, he would be the first Caucasian heavyweight champion since the Swedish fighter Ingemar Johansson had conquered Floyd Patterson twenty-three years previously. Holmes came into the fight with thirty-nine straight victories, twenty-nine of which were by knockout, while Cooney entered the fray with twenty-five straight victories, twenty-two of them knockouts. Cooney was, in the widely touted words of Don King, "The Great White Hope."[2] Others did not rate his chances so highly; to some he was "The Great White Hype" or, even more unkindly, "The Great White Dope." Some suggested he was rushed through the ranks because he was white while, there was also criticism that Cooney was going in against Holmes with less than six rounds of boxing under his belt in slightly over two years. Accusations of greed were leveled at his managers Mike Jones and Dennis Rappaport because they insisted on an even split of the purse instead of the customary arrangement whereby the champion got the larger share. The "Gold Dust Twins," as they were termed by some in the media, were also accused of having handpicked easy opponents for their man on the way to the title fight.

There did appear to be some genuine ill will between the two fighters. Cooney referred to his future opponent as a "jerk," and the postponement of the fight from its original scheduled date of March 15 to June 11 because of injury to the Irishman irked Holmes. Cooney told UPI before the contest that Holmes acted like a five-year-old and was "a low-class kind of guy."[3] He believed Holmes was playing the race card when it was just a fight between two heavyweights. There was ultimate irony in the racist dimension to the Holmes–Cooney fight when the Irishman subsequently discovered that his grandmother's mother was African American through a DNA test. Cooney stated that he believed that Don King controlled Holmes's head and mouth and that the fighter's biggest problem was that he did not command the same adulation as Muhammad Ali had during his boxing career.[4] There had also been previous ill will between Cooney and Holmes. After Holmes crushed Leon Spinks inside three rounds in June 1981, Cooney came over to where the victor was being interviewed by ABC's Howard Cosell. Holmes did not take kindly to the intrusion and lashed out, managing to cut Cosell's mouth with his elbow.

All of this served to ratchet up the sense of palpable tension before the fight. Rappaport bullishly predicted that Cooney could become the first billion-dollar athlete and that his marketability could be limitless. Cooney had everything except the heavyweight title and he was going to have that on the night of June 11, Rappaport pronounced. His charge had the good looks of an Irish baritone and was as understated in his humility as a Victorian maiden. He could become the living true-to-life version of "the Greatest American Hero" with a telephone number worth, including the direct dialing prefix. There was controversy on the night when Holmes's name was announced first, as some considered it standard to name the challenger before the title holder. In fact, Holmes's name had also been first announced when he was the challenger against Ken Norton for the title. Holmes, a former car wash attendant and truck driver, had staged eleven successful defenses of the title since his defeat of Ken Norton on a split decision over fifteen brutal rounds four years earlier. The fact that it had only taken Cooney just short of a minute to achieve the same feat was grist to the mill of the indefatigable Don King. One paper had run with the headline "Four Punches From Death" to describe the helpless state of Norton before the referee intervened, and the shameless King was quick to remind the press of that time.[5]

There were inevitable racist dimensions in the buildup to the fight. White supremacist groups announced that they would have agents ready to shoot Holmes when he entered the ring, while black groups countered with threats to have assassins of their own on duty. As a precaution, police snipers were placed on the roofs of nearby hotels. It was only years later that the media learned that Holmes had to move his wife Diane and their children out of the family home in Easton, Pennsylvania, after a group of white supremacists—what Holmes termed "a carload of rednecks"—shot at his mailbox on the front lawn.[6]

Holmes asserted that his challenger would not be getting equal pay if he wasn't white. Cooney tried to calm the issue by encouraging members of his team to wear shirts with this slogan: "Not The White Man, The Right Man."[7]

The fight was broadcast in over 150 countries, while 9,214 attendees paid $6,239,050 for the privilege of attending. Over 450 closed-circuit theaters showed the bout in the United States and Canada, while almost a thousand media correspondents from all corners of the world gathered at ringside. President Ronald Reagan called to wish Cooney good luck on a line which had been set up in the boxer's dressing room for that specific purpose but Holmes did not receive a similar call, adding fuel to the fire of those who saw a racist dimension to the encounter. The temperature at ringside was 120 degrees when Cooney, lathered in sweat, entered the ring to huge roars of approval from his vocal support. By comparison, Holmes was greeted with muted applause and boos. Cooney was brave from the start but suffered a knockdown in the second round and was deducted three points in the tenth for repeated low blows. Holmes gradually wore down his plucky opponent and halfway through the thirteenth landed a cross flush on Cooney's left cheek, causing the Irishman's legs to buckle. When Cooney landed against the ropes beside his own corner Holmes moved in for the kill, but the Irishman's trainer, Victor Valle, had seen enough and stepped into the ring to prevent further damage to his fighter, who had, by then, shipped a bad cut over his left eye. For his troubles Gerry Cooney pocketed ten million dollars. While the Irishman was well beaten, two of the judges had Holmes only two points ahead before the fight was stopped. If the three points he had been deducted for low blows had been taken out of the equation, Cooney would have been ahead in their estimation. Cooney, distraught after his loss, apologized to the crowd on the microphone.

In 1987 Cooney challenged former world heavyweight and light heavyweight champion Michael Spinks in a title bout but was knocked out in the fifth round, while in 1990 he suffered another knockout at the hands of the former world champion George Foreman in a contest Bert Sugar cleverly tagged as "Two Geezers at Caesars," as it took place in the eponymous venue in Atlantic City with neither participant in the first flush of youth.[8]

Cooney ultimately compiled a professional record of twenty-eight wins and three losses, with twenty-four knockouts, while none of his twelve- or fifteen-round matches went the full distance. The general consensus among the boxing fraternity was that Cooney had a powerful left jab and hook but lacked stamina. Gerry Cooney would later be critical of his managers and would partially blame them for his poor showing against Holmes. They had only been interested in the big payday and had not developed his talent or given him the experience that would have brought to a level where he could have competed with boxers like Holmes, he believed.[9] Larry Holmes went on to defend his title twenty-three times before losing a close decision to Michael Spinks in 1985.

When Mike Tyson was released from prison his much-trumpeted return to the ring took place against Irish American Peter "The Hurricane Man" McNeeley, a boxer with an impressive record on paper. He had fought thirty-eight times with thirty-seven victories, twenty of them by knockout in the first round. On closer inspection there were significant question marks over the figures. Fifteen of his opponents had never won a fight, while between them all they had a record of 168 wins, 366 defeats, and fifteen draws, a combined success rate of thirty percent. At the prefight press conference McNeeley informed Tyson that he was going to wrap him in a cocoon of horror. As has always been his wont, Don King did not hold back on the stereotypes: "People all over the world from Ireland's Belfast to New York and Chicago will be decked out in green. The leprechauns will be dancing from glen to glen, and the shamrocks will be shining."[10] The fight lasted a mere eighty-nine seconds. When Tyson caught his opponent with a shuddering right uppercut, the "Medfield Mauler" pitched against the ropes and then tumbled to the canvas like he had reached home after "a long night on the Guinness."[11]

McNeeley was not the last Irish fighter to do battle with "Iron Mike." After suffering a knockout loss to Danny Williams in 2004, Tyson stayed out of the ring for a year. With his continuing financial woes his handlers were looking for a marketable and beatable opponent and came up with Kevin "the Clones Colossus" McBride. Born on May 10, 1973, in Ireland's Monaghan, McBride represented the Smithboro club, the same nursery which brought Barry McGuigan to wider attention, and had a successful early career, having won three All Ireland boxing titles by the age of eighteen and representing Ireland at the 1992 Olympic Games in Barcelona. If nothing else, McBride was a giant. At six foot six inches he was a full seven inches taller than his opponent and at 271 pounds, thirty-eight pounds heavier than Tyson when the fight took place on June 11, 2005, at the MCI Center in Washington, D.C. With the sound of bagpipes blaring, the nine-to-one outsider climbed into the ring to take on the "Baddest Man on the Planet." In a foul-ridden encounter it was clear to all present that age had caught up with Tyson. It was an ignominious night for "Iron Mike," who head-butted McBride at the start of the final round, for which he was deducted two points. At the end of the sixth round Tyson went to ground after being pushed by McBride, but it was ruled a slip. The "Baddest Man on the Planet" had nothing left in the tank and quit on his stool. Tyson, just three weeks short of his thirty-ninth birthday, had succumbed to a fourth successive loss and later announced his retirement from boxing. In his autobiography he wrote that while he could still train, he didn't have the guts for fighting anymore.[12] His heart was no longer in the game and he was not going to disrespect the sport anymore by losing to the caliber of McBride. For his troubles Tyson banked $5 million, with McBride taking home $150,000. In advance of the fight Tyson had said he would gut McBride like a fish, but it was he who looked gutted at the end. People wondered if Ireland had at last brought another heavyweight boxer who could dine at the top table, but it was not to be. McBride lost six of his next eight fights and retired after being knocked out by Poland's Mariusz "the Viking" Wach in April 2011 in a bout to decide the World Boxing Council international heavyweight title, a bauble of dubious merit in the eyes of American boxing aficionados. In what would be a remarkable development in other sports, but all too familiar in the world of boxing, McBride, at the grand old age of forty-seven, announced he would take on Tyson if the opportunity arose. Working as a laborer for Hoarty Brendan Tree and Landscaping in Brighton, Massachusetts, he told TMZ Sports that he would love to get in the ring with Tyson again and that he could use the money to help put his kids through college.[13] In the same year, Mike Tyson, at the age of fifty-four, was back in the ring against fifty-one-year-old Roy Jones Junior in an exhibition bout in which a knockout was precluded and no winner could be declared.

Part 2

Non-Heavyweight Boxers

Seventeen

He Ain't Heavy, He's My Irish Brother

Irish and Irish American boxers were not confined to the heavyweight division, and many achieved remarkable and enduring success in lower divisions. The light-heavyweight division, for example, was created in 1903 by Lou Houseman, a Chicago-based journalist, boxing manager, and promoter. Houseman matched his own fighter Jack Root with Kid McCoy because the former could no longer make the weight for the middleweight division and promoted the fight as being for the light heavyweight championship of the world. The boxing press accepted the new weight division and Root was deemed the inaugural world champion but was defeated in his first title defense by Irishman George Gardner. Born on March 17, 1877, in Ballinalacken near Lisdoonvarna, County Clare, on the southwest coast of Ireland, Gardner was part of a talented sporting family, with his brothers Billy and Jimmy and father Patrick also achieving boxing success. His family immigrated to Lowell, Massachusetts, in his early childhood and he fought his first of sixty-five professional bouts in 1897. Of these he won forty-one (nineteen inside the distance), drew ten, lost eleven, and fought three without decision. His chief offensive weapon was an accurate left jab that opponents found difficult to counteract. Gardner traveled to England to fight in 1900, where he defeated Frank Craig in four rounds; by the end of 1901 he had lost only one of his first thirty-five fights, a single reversal against the then world welterweight champion Jersey Joe Walcott on points over twenty rounds. He gained his revenge over Walcott the following year before fighting the best year of his career in 1903, after which he moved up to the heavyweight division and stopped Peter Maher in the first round before defeating Marvin Hart on points.

On July 4, 1903, Gardner took on Root at Fort Erie, Canada, where the Irishman knocked out his opponent in the twelfth round in what the latter later remembered as the most vicious fight of his career. Gardner lived in Chicago and moved to San Francisco two weeks before his November 1903 title defense in the Yosemite Athletic Club against Cornwall native Bob Fitzsimmons to train with Alex Greggains. Chosen because of his age, forty-one-year-old Fitzsimmons was handicapped by a low weight limit of 168 pounds and the fact that his last fight had been a knockout defeat sixteen months earlier. Despite these impediments, Fitzsimmons knocked Gardner down four times and, even though he suffered heavily toward the end, held on to defeat the champion on points after twenty rounds. Gardner's career declined afterward with only one win from his final nine fights before his retirement in 1908.

He was one of the minority of white boxers who would fight black opponents and was defeated on points by future heavyweight champion Jack Johnson in October 1904, remarking afterward that he felt as if he had fought a buzz saw.[1] After his retirement Gardner opened a saloon in Chicago, and married Margaret Smith of South Bend, Indiana. His son Morgan, born in 1905, also became a professional boxer in the light-heavyweight division, while his brother Jimmy claimed the world welterweight title in 1908, making the Gardner brothers the first Irish American siblings to hold world titles. Gardner died at age seventy-seven on July 8, 1954, in Chicago.

Jack McAuliffe, born on March 24, 1866, in Cork city to Cornelius McAuliffe and Jane Bailey, emigrated with his family in 1871 to the United States, where he spent his early years in Bangor, Maine. He made his first appearance as an amateur boxer in 1883 and turned professional soon after, fighting Jem Carney over seventy-eight rounds to a draw at Revere Beach, Massachusetts. In 1886, he captured the American lightweight title by knocking out Billy Frazier in the seventeenth round and went on to take the world title by stopping Canadian Harry Gilmore in 1887. He fought Billy Dacey for the lightweight championship and a $5,000 purse in 1888 knocking him out in eleven rounds. He beat Young Griffo in 1894, retired shortly afterward, made a comeback in 1896, and retired for good after his 1897 battle against Philadelphia Tommy Ryan.

Nicknamed "Napoleon of the Ring" because of his unique stance, McAuliffe was the star of the division during the transition period between bare-knuckle and gloved fighting. He is one of only fifteen world boxing champions to retire without a loss and was the first to hold the world lightweight title, a bauble he held between 1886 to 1893. McAuliffe was one of only nine men to retire unbeaten over his entire career; the others were Young Mitchell, Jimmy Barry, Rocky Marciano, Laszlo Papp, Terry Marsh, Ji Won Kim, Ricardo López, and Sven Ottkeack. In 1897 McAuliffe successfully defended his title against Billy Myer in a highly publicized match at the Olympic Club, New Orleans. According to the International Boxing Hall of Fame he had thirty-six professional fights with thirty wins, of which twenty-two were by knockout, and had five draws and one no-decision. He successfully defended his world lightweight title against six different boxers. He was also the first European boxer to retire as an undefeated world champion and was inducted into *Ring* magazine's Boxing Hall of Fame in 1954 and the International Boxing Hall of Fame in 1995. Jack McAuliffe died on November 5, 1937, in Forest Hills, New York.

The first title fight with gloves in the bantamweight category was between Chappie Moran and Ray Lewis in 1889. At that time, the limit for this weight class was 110 pounds, but in 1910 the British settled on a limit of 118.[2] James "The Little Tiger" Curran Barry was born on March 7, 1870, in Chicago to Irish parents and held the world bantamweight championship from 1894 to 1899 and retired undefeated with a record of fifty wins, no defeats, and ten no-decisions. Barry fought out of Chicago as a bantamweight and a flyweight, retiring with a record of 59–0. Along with Rocky Marciano, Ricardo López, Ji-Won Kim, and Joe Calzaghe, Barry is one of only five boxing champions to retire undefeated. Barry won the Bantamweight Championship of the World match five times. On December 6, 1897, in London, England, Barry knocked out Walter Croot in the sixteenth round to claim the World Bantamweight title for the fifth time. Croot struck his head on the floor and died of a brain injury. Barry was exonerated, but he never knocked a fighter out again. He was inducted into the International Boxing Hall of Fame in 2000.

"Terrible" Terry McGovern, born on March 9, 1880, in Johnstown, Pennsylvania, began boxing at Brooklyn's Greenwood Athletic Club at the tender age of sixteen and claimed later in life that he had never gone to school.[3] His lack of formal education did not hold back his boxing career, and he went on to hold the world bantamweight and featherweight titles during his storied career. In his first thirty-six bouts McGovern won an astounding thirty, losing only to Johnny Snee and Tim Calahan. On September 12, 1899, at Tuckahoe, New York, he took the vacant world bantamweight championship in a first-round knockout of British boxer Thomas "Pedlar" Palmer at the age of nineteen in a fight billed as the 116-pound championship, the first ever first-round knockout under the newly introduced Queensberry Rules.[4] It was a hugely significant victory as Palmer, also known as "Box O' Tricks" because of his flamboyant fighting style, had held the title for the previous four years. For his troubles the young Irish American, clad in his trademark lucky green shorts, pocketed $7,500.[5] Having never defended the title, McGovern relinquished it the following year. On January 9, 1900, he defeated the hugely impressive George Dixon to take the world featherweight championship by scoring a technical knockout in the eighth round although the ruling was disputed by many of those in attendance.[6] He first defended his title against Eddie Santry on February 1 of the same year in Chicago with a fifth-round technical knockout. On March 9, he knocked out Oscar Gardner in the third round in what proved a controversial fight because he had been knocked down in the first round but held on to Gardner's leg. The referee did not start to count until after six seconds had elapsed.[7] On June 12, 1900, McGovern defended his title against Tommy White at the Seaside Sporting Club in Brooklyn. White was no match for McGovern; he was knocked down once in the opening round, twice in the second, and three in the deciding round.[8] On November 2 of the same year McGovern went on to defend his title against New York Jewish featherweight Joe Bernstein in Louisville, Kentucky, a bout which ended in a seventh-round knockout in favor of the Irishman.[9] On December 13, McGovern knocked Joe Gans out in the second round but the future lightweight champion subsequently claimed he took a dive.[10] On April 30, 1901, before a crowd of 8,000, McGovern once again defeated Oscar Gardner at the Mechanics Pavilion in San Francisco in a fourth-round knockout. This time Gardner was knocked down three times before losing to a ten count after a blow to the stomach.[11] There were initial concerns that Gardner had been badly hurt but he soon recovered from his thumping. McGovern stayed on in San Francisco to defend his featherweight title on May 29 against Aurelio Herrera in a contest the Irishman won in the fifth round, but his opponent was later to bizarrely complain that he was doped by his own seconds.[12] On November 28, 1901, McGovern came face to face with the formidable Young Corbett II in Hartford, Connecticut. Born William H. Rothwell—he had taken the name in honor of his hero James J. Corbett—the young American easily accounted for McGovern and assumed the mantle of world bantamweight champion, going on to defend it against the Irishman on March 21, 1903, in San Francisco.[13] Over the next six years McGovern did not enter any title fights but defeated "Harlem" Tommy Murphy by knockout in the first round in 1905, lost a newspaper decision to Battling Nelson in 1906, and had fight decision draws with Jimmy Brett and Young Corbett II in the same year. His last fight was against Frank "Spike" Robson on May 26, 1908, which ended in another newspaper draw. McGovern finished his career with a record of sixty-five wins of which forty-two were knockouts, five losses, and five draws. In 2003, McGovern was named in *Ring* magazine's list of 100 greatest punchers of all time, while boxing historian Nat Fleischer ranked McGovern as the greatest featherweight ever. McGovern's later life was marred by mental illness, and he died of pneumonia and Bright's disease in the charity ward of Kings County Hospital, Brooklyn, New York, on February 22, 1918, at the age of thirty-eight.[14]

Eighteen

"Bold" Mike McTigue

"I just ran out of money in a thirteen-horse race. I was the youngest."[1]
—Mike McTigue on his humble family background

"BOLD" MIKE MCTIGUE, BORN ON NOVEMBER 26, 1892, the son of Patrick McTigue and Ellen Nealon, in Lickaun, Kilnamona, County Clare, was one of thirteen children and, as the line quoted indicates, had a good line in self-deprecating humor.[2] By his own account he got into a dispute with a British soldier while still a young teenager in Clarer and left Ireland for Sheffield, England. After briefly returning home he set sail for America on board the S.S. *Baltic* from Cobh, County Cork, with just $25 in his pocket.

The tale of his initiation into the prizefight game is an interesting and oft-told one in his native place. While working as a beef handler in New York he reputedly defended his foreman from two assailants and was encouraged by his employer to go into boxing.[3] McTigue was taken on by respected trainer George "Elbows" McFadden and began boxing in 1914. McFadden, an old lightweight, got his name because he was never afraid to use his elbows if his fists failed to make contact with his opponent. Famed New York journalist and cartoonist Tad A. Dorgan of the *New York Journal* contended that McFadden should have worn four

"Bold" McTigue, born in 1892 in Lickaun, Kilnamona, County Clare, was the light heavyweight champion of the world from 1923 to 1925 (Wikipedia).

gloves, two on his hands and two on his elbows.[4] On McFadden's recommendation McTigue later went on to be coached by Dan Hickey at the New York Athletic Club and finally began boxing at professional level in 1909 as a welterweight, when he quickly became known for his ability to outwit opponents. McTigue befriended Jack Britton, a former welterweight world champion who had him spar with his right hand tied down so that he could learn how to use his left better. In his later career McTigue's left jab improved greatly.

As Jersey Jones noted in *Ring* magazine, McTigue's style was not particularly flashy or spectacular, his physical presence not particularly impressive, but he was rangy and wiry, a boxer who was a lot stronger than he looked.[5] He was a "cutey," avoiding aggressive tactics and fighting along cautious and conservative lines. However, he was smart and knew how to get the maximum result with the minimum effort and was a master at feinting, drawing his opponent into leads, and countering with powerful left hooks and right crosses. State law in New York at the time meant that many of his fights were technically ten-round "no decision" exhibitions (unless one of the participants was knocked out), although these usually had "popular" or "press" decisions to make rankings and illegal gambling easier. McTigue was initially a middleweight and established a reputation as a clever and skillful boxer with good defense but limited firepower. In an era when heavy hitters were the main draw, McTigue's conservative tactics meant it was difficult for promoters to find good matches for him and he was he was left fighting journeymen in small venues in the New York area. Fans came to see so-called "blood bucket" fights, not the sweet science of boxing.[6] McTigue fought forty times from 1915 through 1916, or less than three weeks between fights on average. Despite his lack of firepower, his excellent defense made him a much-sought-after sparring partner, which helped supplement his income. He often sparred with legendary future heavyweight champion Jack Dempsey and prominent middleweight Mike Gibbons.

In 1918 McTigue joined up with the storied Fighting 69th Division of the American Army and saw action at the Battle of the Argonne in France, a bloody encounter which lasted seven weeks and brought the First World War to a close. For his efforts on the field of battle McTigue was awarded the Distinguished Service Cross for exceptional bravery. In 1920 he married Cecelia Cuniff, a New Yorker whose parents were from Cahersiveen, County Kerry, and the couple went on to have three daughters. McTigue decided to try his luck in Canada, where he caused a significant upset by knocking out the undefeated Canadian middleweight title holder Eugene Brosseau in April 1920, going on to establish himself as a box-office draw in Montreal with a series of knockout victories over the next eighteen months. After defeating "Panama" Joe Gans in Jersey City by a newspaper decision in September 1921, he was rewarded with a fight against Jeff Smith in Madison Square Garden in December. Unfortunately, McTigue reverted to type and the match proved a dull affair, with a dismissive *New York Times* reporting that neither fighter exhibited any qualifications which would warrant serious consideration for a championship contest.[7] Although he won, the Irishman entered a long period of mediocre opposition, and after eleven lackluster fights, it looked like McTigue's career was nearing an end when he had a brainwave. Crossing the Atlantic Ocean in 1922 he fought three mediocre fighters in England, knocking Johnny Bashham and Harry Reeve out in three, and accounting for Harry Knight in four. McTigue sought fights against more talented opposition like Ted "Kid" Lewis and Joe Beckett to no avail, but then he had the good fortune to meet Irish boxing promoter and racehorse owner Tom Singleton, who told him he might be able to get him a fight in Dublin. McTigue told Singleton that he was intending to return to America but took his contact details anyway. Things evolved rapidly. The luck of the Irish had come to rest on the brow of Mike McTigue.

When the Senegalese "Battling" Siki defeated the French world light heavyweight champion Georges Carpentier in six rounds in September of 1922 there was a moral outcry. Siki's real name was Louis Mbarick Fall and he was sometimes billed as the "West African Jungle Child." After his defeat of the Frenchman he was promptly banned from any further fights in France, Britain, or America, with the English authorities prohibiting him from entering the country. Battling Siki had left Senegal thanks to a French woman who, having failed in an attempted adoption, abandoned him in Marseilles. Forced to make his own way in the world, he decided to do so as a fighter. An unremarkable early career was interrupted by his enlisting in the French army, where he was decorated for bravery, and he afterward resumed his boxing career with far greater success. As a black African, however, Siki was subject to appalling racism in France, with frequent comparisons to baboons in the press. After his defeat of Carpentier, Siki became the first African world champion and was happy to flaunt his new status, not doing himself any favors in the process. He had a penchant for heavy drinking, flashy clothes, and white women, and enraged the citizenry of Paris by marching through the streets with a lioness on a leash. If that was not enough to draw attention to himself, he was also in the habit of firing pistols in the air to make his Great Danes perform party tricks.

Racism in boxing was nothing new to the American press or public of course. The race riots that had ensued after Jack Johnson beat James J. Jeffries for the world heavyweight championship in 1910 had provided a more than salutary warning. *The Springfield Rifle* wrote that victories like that of Siki could make colonial subjects lose their attitudes of respectful admiration for white men.[8] Sportswriters frequently referred to Siki as a jungle beast, while one journalist claimed he was only one generation removed from a "prominent family of Senegalese baboons."[9] The British Home Office decided that a fight between a white man and a black man was not a good idea when you control an empire where a very large number of blacks are ruled by a very small number of whites and refused to allow Siki a tilt at British champion Joe Beckett.

Mike McTigue was unaware that any of this might affect him as 1922 was closing. He was planning his family's return to the United States after trying and failing to get a match with Joe Beckett. He fought Harry Reeve, who had defeated Battling Siki in Liverpool in January. Reeve was heavily favored, but McTigue knocked him out in the third round. His plan was then to visit Ireland with his family before heading home, but Irish racehorse owner Tom Singleton watched him beat Reeves that night, and offered him a chance to fight in Ireland. Mike was looking for any payday he could find, and agreed to the bout, with no idea who the opponent might be. Singleton saw his chance and invited Siki to Dublin to take on McTigue on St.

Patrick's Day, 1923, at the La Scala Theatre, Dublin, an echo of the controversial days of Jack Johnson in the United States. Singleton had been at the Siki–Carpentier fight and had tentatively made an agreement with Siki's manager, Charles Brouillet, to host a fight in Dublin. Siki was a less than enthusiastic participant as he now had his eyes firmly set on the United States and the big money to be earned there. The Senegalese native was not short of offers and had no interest in the fight in Ireland, where the £2,000 would be split seventy-five to the winner and twenty-five to the loser.[10] Singleton and Brouillet hatched a plan, telling Siki they were sailing from Cherbourg to New York, but were actually heading to Dublin via Cobh in the south of Ireland. They made Siki so inebriated that before he knew it he was walking down the gangplank in Cobh and onward by train to Dublin. The men had come to Ireland at a particularly fraught time with an ongoing vicious civil war, often pitting brother against brother. After five Free State soldiers were killed by a mine in County Kerry on March 6, nine Republican prisoners were tied to a mine and blown up in retaliation. After six more Republican prisoners were executed on March 13 the Republicans issued a statement declaring a mourning period where all "amusements" were banned for an indefinite period. It was clearly directed at the fight.[11]

Republican guerrillas issued death threats against both boxers in an effort to discredit the government, which hoped to show the world that it was capable of organizing a major sporting occasion and was bringing the country back to normality after years of upheaval. The sense of tension was heightened when three Republican soldiers were murdered in the week before the fight. A reporter from the *Sporting Chronicle* wrote on the eve of the fight that "if the McTigue–Siki fight takes place tomorrow night, it will be literally at the point of a bayonet."[12] On the morning of the fight, McTigue got a letter, supposedly from Republicans, telling him that he would be hanged if he turned up for the fight. The boxers were transported to the venue under armed escort, with Siki's party forced to thwart an ambush. When he heard gunfire Siki thought it was fireworks. However, it would have been unlikely that Republicans would have injured him, as it would have had severe ramifications for their ongoing military campaign. The Free State Government was taking no chances and sent 500 troops and several armored cars to the venue. Shortly before the fight began a landmine exploded near the venue, while a gun battle raged in the streets outside afterward. The bomb exploded fifty yards away in Henry Place next to the Pillar Picture House, blowing two large exit doors inward and causing large parts of the plaster to fall to the floor. Remarkably, the only injury was to a nearby boy who was cut by flying glass while tending to his mother's fruit stall. Despite the all too apparent dangers, the fighters had been received rapturously during their pre-bout public appearances and a huge crowd gathered outside La Scala on the night of the fight. The encounter had garnered considerable interest in the international press; among the papers represented were four from Paris, four New York dailies, and a large contingent of British and Irish outlets. Jack Farrell of the *New York Times* described the scene eloquently: "Machine guns to the right of 'em, steel jacketed bullets to the left of 'em. Milling mobs of belligerent Irishmen. Bombs bursting amid the ear-splitting din."[13] The 15,000 capacity crowd was introduced to Georges Carpentier—who announced that he was challenging the winner—and to American heavyweight Frank Moran and British champion Joe Beckett. From the start McTigue used his evasive tactics, cautious of being caught by one of Siki's heavy blows. McTigue fought defensively for the first ten rounds against his much larger opponent but attacked more as Siki tired, although the Irishman was somewhat hampered when he hurt his thumb in the tenth round. In what was the last world title bout fought over twenty rounds, McTigue won a points victory, although the general consensus was that Siki had done at least enough to merit a draw.[14] The Senegalese fighter was incensed at the outcome and swore that he would never fight in Ireland again. Georges Carpentier called the result "incomprehensible and indefensible," while the Parisian newspaper *Le Journal* termed it "iniquitous."[15] Afterward, McTigue returned to a skeptical America as the world champion. He agreed to defend his title against William Lawrence "Young" Stribling in Columbus, Georgia, in October 1923 but, appearing to have fractured the little finger on his left hand, McTigue voiced his objection to going ahead with the fight. The story goes that he had to be brought to the ring under armed guard, aided by the encouragement of local members of the Ku Klux Klan. The referee ruled the fight a draw but his decision incited a riot and he had the good sense to quickly reverse his decision. The following day, when he was safely away from the threats of the Klansmen, the referee contacted newspapers to tell them that McTigue had retained his title. The Irishman held on to his title for two years through a combination of injury claims and no-decision fights, neither of which endeared him to some in the boxing fraternity and which limited his paydays. Eventually he secured a $50,000 purse against former Olympic wrestling champion Paul "The Astoria Assassin" Berlenbach, who put up a decent fight against the Irishman before losing on a points decision after fifteen rounds on front of a crowd of 45,000 in New York on May 30, 1925, a contest that was to lead to a renaissance in McTigue's boxing fortunes. Just before Christmas of that year, McTigue was given the sad news that his former foe Siki had been shot dead in Hell's Kitchen at the age of twenty-eight in murky circumstances. After an operation on his right hand, and developing a more aggressive boxing style under new manager Jimmy Johnson, McTigue became a genuine contender and gained the sobriquet "the Methuselah" of boxing. His return bout with Berlenbach in January 1927 may have been his greatest display, when, despite being nine years older, McTigue had his opponent on the floor four times before having him counted out in just the fourth round. This win set him up for a contest with Jack Sharkey on March 3, the winner of which would meet Jack Dempsey in a final eliminator for a shot at Gene Tunney's world heavyweight title. Despite conceding ten years, two stone (twenty-eight pounds) in weight, and four inches in height, McTigue outboxed Sharkey and was leading on points in the twelfth round when he suffered a chipped tooth which burst an artery, stopping the fight and heralding the future use of mouth guards. On October 10, 1927, he fought Tommy Loughran for the vacant light-heavyweight title, this time conceding ten years and fifteen pounds to his opponent, and was unlucky to lose on a split decision in a highly regarded contest. It was to prove the peak of Mike McTigue's boxing career. Knocked out in the first round of his next fight, he went nine fights and eighteen months without winning but continued to box regularly until his retirement in 1930. In 174 professional fights, McTigue won seventy-seven (fifty-two inside the distance), drew nine, and lost twenty-six, while two were declared no-contests and the rest were officially no-decision bouts. In the late 1920s he was sitting pretty with a palatial home in Jackson Heights, Queens, along with some $250,000 worth of investments, but fell victim to the financial crash and an avaricious business agent. In his latter years McTigue worked variously as a laborer, as a floor manager in a ballroom, and as a physical instructor on a naval base. Unfortunately, he also drank heavily and became estranged from his wife and daughters. McTigue's final years were marked by mental illness, leaving him unable to recall much about his boxing career. According to his nephew Joe, Mike still reminisced about those days of his career that he could remember. His favorite concerned his famous St. Patrick's Day victory in Dublin and how one of the Free State soldiers had come near the corner, prodded him with his bayonet, and said, "I got three pounds' bet on you. God help you if you lose."[16] Mike McTigue died on August 12, 1966, in Queens General Hospital, New York.[17] Among those in attendance at his funeral were former boxing greats Jack Dempsey, Gene Tunney, and Tommy Loughran. In 2001 the Kilnamona Community Centre in County Clare was named after McTigue.

Nineteen

"The Phantom of Philly"
Tommy Loughran

> I wouldn't say he was dirty so much as he was expedient. He was so eager to get the damage done that his head and shoulders went with a punch. He was a fast and furious man.
> —Tommy Loughran on Harry Greb[1]

It was typical of Tommy Loughran to be as circumspect as he was when asked about the ferocious Harry Greb, a man some boxing historians suggest may have been the dirtiest boxer in the history of the gloved era. Certainly the gory details of Greb's encounters with Gene Tunney would lend significant credence to the atavistic instincts of Greb in the ring. Loughran is retrospectively regarded as one of the sport's great gentlemen, an accolade rarely bandied about in the toughest trade of all.

Tommy Loughran, later to become known as "The Phantom of Philly," was the son of Patrick Loughran, who left the town land of Crosscavanagh near the village of Galbally in County Tyrone around 1895 for the United States. Patrick found work as a milkman and later married Anne Haley, a Philadelphia-born daughter of Irish emigrants who had fled Ireland during the Famine.[2] They went on to have seven children, of which Tommy was the third. At the tender age of fourteen, Tommy took it into his head to run away from home to join the U.S. Army and managed to convince a recruiting office in Georgia that he was

Tommy Loughran photographed training at Wright Field in West Palm Beach, Florida, while preparing for his encounter with Primo Carnera on March 1, 1934, at Madison Square Garden. The Irish American lasted fifteen rounds, but his Italian opponent's sheer size—Loughran was a full eighty-six pounds lighter—carried the day and Carnera won by unanimous decision (Wikipedia).

twenty-three, but luckily, his parents were able to track him down and have him sent back to Philadelphia. Loughran had his first professional fight in 1919 at the age of seventeen, in which he knocked out Eddie Carter, making the grand sum of 11 cents. In 1923 Loughran was matched against world light heavyweight champion Mike McTigue for the first time but the contest was deemed a challenge fight, and he had to wait four years before he finally got a crack at the title. By all accounts Loughran was not a devastating puncher and was more in the mold of his great friend Jim Corbett: a technician, innovator, and master of the jab and move technique. He had a weak right hand but compensated by developing swift strong legs and one of the most effective and precise left hands in boxing. Ahead of his time, Loughran built a gym in the basement of the family home complete with wall mirrors, where he practiced for hours on end. The young Irishman put much emphasis on training and perfecting his skills and instincts, and because of his uncanny ability to dodge punches and sneak up on opponents he acquired the well-suited moniker the Phantom of Philly.[3] Loughran had ambitions to take the heavyweight title but Gene Tunney refused to give him a shot; instead, he turned his attention to the light-heavyweight championship. After his victory over McTigue in 1927 he returned triumphant to Philadelphia on a special train and was greeted by 40,000 adoring fans in the boxing-mad and heavily Irish and Irish American city.[4] Over the following two years he took on Jimmy Slattery, Leo Lomski, and Peter Latzo, before coming up against the formidable James Braddock.

One commentator wrote of the encounter: "Riding to victory on the greatest exhibition of super-boxing in his entire career, Tommy Loughran fought his last fight as king of the world light-heavyweights here at Yankee stadium when he conquered James J. Braddock. In magnificent triumph the gallant proved again that the great boxer is the ruler of them all. Like old Alexander, the Macedonian, there are none left for him to conquer. Braddock was the last of them."[5]

By then Loughran was finding it increasingly difficult to make the light-heavyweight limit and decided to step up to the heavyweight division, where he challenged Joseph Paul Zukauskas, otherwise known as Jack "The Boston Gob" Sharkey, in a fight he was expected to win but, it was not to be. After the heavyweight title changed hands between Sharkey, Max Schmeling, Primo Carnera, and Max Baer, Braddock went on to write his name in the history books when he dethroned Baer in 1935. He had hoped to get another shot at the title but "The Cinderella Man" refused to grant him a chance, a fact that engendered bad feelings between the two Irishmen afterward. However, Loughran had not given up his dreams of taking the heavyweight title and, after a rematch win over Sharkey in 1933, challenged holder Primo Carnera. Variously known as "The Ambling Alp" and "The Vast Venetian," Carnera was a huge man who outweighed Loughran by six stone (84 pounds). Loughran went into the fight knowing he needed a knockout to win the title, but the contest went the distance and it was not to be for the Irishman.

In the first round, Primo Carnera lumbered out of his corner and shuffled his huge feet while Tommy Loughran dabbed his lantern jaw with a left jab. In the second and third rounds the champion tried to rush the challenger against the ropes but failed; Loughran, fast on his feet, landed one solid right-hand punch. The fourth round was Loughran's, but by now Carnera had learned how to crowd his opponent into the corners. In the fifth, he caught Loughran against the ropes and began to smash his face with wide clublike blows. A blonde woman near the ringside let out a piercing scream. Alarmed, Carnera turned his head to see what was the matter. When he looked back, Loughran had danced out of reach.

Weeks of intensive sneers in the press had led them to believe that the bout between a 270-lb. champion from Italy and a challenger who was five years older and 86 lb. lighter was as unfair as it sounded. Now, on a windy evening with rain pattering on rows and rows of empty $20 seats, they became aware that the spectacle under the warm cone of light at the center of Madison Square Garden was an exciting contest between a clever, courageous boxer and a nervous, clumsy monster, embarrassed by his own size and the hostility of the crowd. When Loughran ended the fifth round with a smashing right to Carnera's chin it looked for a moment as if the little man might win after all. After the fifth round Carnera did better. Loughran's tactics of running in and clinching made it impossible to land a knockout punch but Carnera wrestled away from the challenger as best he could. He rushed out of his corner in the eighth and caught Loughran against the ropes for a second. In the tenth, he made the mistake of courteously touching gloves, as if it were the last round. At the end of the fourteenth, Loughran was dazed enough to start for the wrong corner of the ring. During the next round, Loughran managed to cling groggily to his huge adversary until the bell ended the fight. Three judges gave Carnera a unanimous decision. Loughran retired in 1935 at the age of thirty-four after beating Sonny Boy Walker in front of a raucous home crowd in Philadelphia. Loughran is credited with 170 professional matches, ninety of which were wins, only suffering three knockouts. He defeated ten champions in all classes from welterweight to heavyweight.[6] Loughran enlisted in the Marine Corps at the start of World War II and subsequently moved to New York, where he became a sugar broker on Wall Street. He also became a successful boxing referee, respected television presenter, and popular after-dinner speaker. Known for his philanthropy, he kept a box at Yankee Stadium where he brought disadvantaged kids to see baseball games. Loughran, who never married, moved into a U.S. Army veterans' home in 1974 and spent his time walking and reminiscing with former foes like Dempsey about their days in the ring. Tommy Loughran passed away on July 7, 1984. The *Philadelphia Inquirer* noted in its obituary that he had sometimes been called the "altar boy" during his boxing career and had actually become one when he hung up his gloves, serving at mass at noon every day at Our Lady of Victory Church.[7] The journalist interviewed Jack Sharkey on his memories of Loughran, and Sharkey recalled that while Loughran could not break eggs with his punches, he threw so many that it seemed like they were making them in a factory and throwing them out the window.[8] Sharkey acknowledged they had their battles but that Loughran was a gentleman and a truly scientific boxer. Seven years later he was inducted into the International Boxing Hall of Fame, and in July 2006 the Pennsylvania Historical and Museum Commission installed and dedicated a Pennsylvania Historical Marker to him at Philadelphia's St. Monica Roman Catholic Church, where he was an active member. In 2017 "The Phantom of Philly" was inducted into the U.S. Marine Corps Sporting Hall of Fame.[9]

Twenty

The Other Dempsey
Jack "Nonpareil" Dempsey

> Oh! Fame, why sleeps thy favored son
> In wilds, woods and weeds?
> And shall he ever thus sleep on
> Interred his valiant deeds?
> 'Tis strange New York should thus forget
> Its "Bravest of the Brave"
> And in the wilds of Oregon
> Unmarked, leave Dempsey's grave.

A Kildare Champion

"NONPAREIL" JACK DEMPSEY, BORN JOHN EDWARD Kelly on December 15, 1862, in Athgarvan Curran, County Kildare, may have been the first holder of the world middleweight championship, an honor he may have won on July 30, 1884, by defeating George Fulljames in Great Kills, Staten Island, by knockout in the twenty-second round.[1] It is likely that he took the name "Nonpareil" from the English boxer Jack Randall. Pierce Egan noted that Randall also had Irish parentage and was sometimes referred to as "Prime Irish Lad."[2] Whatever the exact nature of his achievements, Dempsey was a hugely popular character of the 1890s sporting world and was second only to John L. Sullivan in the volume of press attention he garnered during his boxing career. In 1867, at the age of four, he immigrated with his family to Brooklyn, New York, where his father died while he was still a child. His mother remarried, to Patrick Dempsey, and he acquired a new surname. On leaving school he worked as a cooper and earned money on the side as a professional wrestler, performing as a double act with his half-brother under the name "The Wrestling Dempseys." Nonpareil fought his first professional boxing match in a dilapidated hall on Staten Island, on April 7, 1883, against the Irish-born Ed McDonald, whom he knocked out in twenty-one rounds.[3] He was described by an Irish paper of the era as "one hundred and fifty-eight pounds of strength, strategy, grace and chivalry" and a man of "sterling honesty and gentlemanly bearing in that raw pioneer period, when good qualities were at a premium."[4] Dempsey's uncanny skill and unquestionable pluck could only be appreciated when the gray-eyed wizard with the light brown, wavy hair was pitted against some fierce cave man battling with desperate ferocity, the journalist continued poetically, noting that he was a master of strategy who opened a new chapter in ring-craft with his powerful arms and restless, slender legs. The *Brooklyn Eagle* believed he had three things in his favor as a boxer: the legs of a champion elbow and collar wrestler; the arms of a Donnelly—long in the reach; and the head of a lawyer.[5] He was able to stop blows aimed at him by his adversaries with much skill, and hit his antagonists with such terrific force and comparative ease that he astonished and terrified his opponents beyond measure, according to the inimitable Fox. Although he was only five feet eight inches and a few pounds over ten stone (140 pounds), Dempsey was never afraid to take on bigger adversaries. The famed heavyweight later took his name from Nonpareil and once told Roger Kahn that when he was a child living near the Colorado mining camps it was the ambition of all the boys who liked to fight to be like Dempsey. During his career Nonpareil fought under both London and Queensberry rules, both bare-fisted and in buckskin gloves. Dempsey scored knockouts in eight of his first fourteen bouts and decisively defeated Billy Dacey for the lightweight championship of New York in March 1884 but soon abandoned the class to his friend and protégé, the Cork-born Jack McAuliffe, to compete in the middleweight division. Accepting the challenge of Canadian champion George Fulljames, who offered to fight any claimant for the vacant world title, Dempsey scored a knockout victory in the twenty-second round in Great Kills, New York, on July 30, 1884. Though some boxing historians date his world middleweight championship from this victory, his claim was disputed until 1886, when he successively vanquished two highly regarded rival claimants in Jack Fogarty and George LaBlanche, thereby securing universal recognition.

Through his four prime years of 1884 through 1887, Dempsey was unbeaten in fifty-two fights while none of his non-title contests lasted longer than ten rounds. The period culminated in his most famous fight, a titanic struggle against Johnny Reagan at two separate outdoor seaside locations on Long Island on December 13, 1887. The start of the storied contest took place in an improvised ring aboard an old barge which had been securely moored to two stakes in the water, but after it became partly submerged it had to be cut loose and towed out into Long Island Sound. Both the principals were about to resume when a squall struck the barge and a heavy snow shower covered the slippery deck. A truce was called after eight rounds and the party went ashore. Someone remembered an old boathouse about twenty miles away which might provide a suitable venue for the fight to continue. After a laborious journey, when another sixteen rounds and almost an hour of furious fighting had been completed, word filtered through that two policemen were in the vicinity. Then, disdaining heavier clothing, the fighters plunged into the woods, where their followers found a clearing amid the snow; here Dempsey and Reagan finally fought to a finish. After the resumption Dempsey took command, but Reagan repeatedly attempted to save himself by intentionally going to ground. It was not the only underhand tactic used by Reagan. Early in the fight, Reagan's sharply spiked shoes had opened a four-inch gash in Dempsey's shin. Reagan had been observed paring the spikes before the fight. With another interruption looming amid a blinding snowstorm, Dempsey concluded proceedings with a knockout blow to his opponent's jaw in the forty-fifth round in a contest that had lasted over four hours with almost anything allowed except biting and kicking. It was the very definition of a titanic struggle.

Twenty. The Other Dempsey

After Dempsey soundly beat Dominick McCaffrey on January 21, 1888, *The Brooklyn Daily Eagle* noted that he danced, walked, ran, and skipped about the Pittsburgh man till the latter got the idea that there were a dozen Dempseys surrounding him. In probably one of the most worthy compliments, after Dempsey beating three men in one night, *The New York Times* wrote, "The old sports admitted that if he were a little bigger he would prove a dangerous opponent for the invincible Sullivan."[6]

A rematch against George LaBlanche on August 27, 1889, was declared a non-title fight when the challenger weighed in over the limit. In the thirty-second round, LaBlanche, struggling desperately and nearing defeat, suddenly knocked Dempsey unconscious by pivoting on his heel and sweeping his stiffened right arm in an arc to land a backhand blow with the knuckles on the champion's jaw. Though the "pivot blow"—also called the "LaBlanche swing"—was widely decried as unethical, and soon officially outlawed, the referee refused to call a foul, and Dempsey, while retaining his title, lost his unbeaten record.[7] Nonpareil defeated Australian Billy McCarthy over twenty-eight rounds in San Francisco in the first world middleweight title fight contested under Marquis of Queensberry Rules with padded gloves and three-minute rounds on February 18, 1890. Competing for a record purse of $12,000, he lost his title to the Cornish-born, New Zealand-reared Bob Fitzsimmons in New Orleans on January 14, 1889. Though a two-to-one favorite, Dempsey was comprehensively beaten, unable to fathom Fitzsimmons's unorthodox style. Knocked out in the thirteenth round, he lamented that he would have been less troubled if he had lost the title to an Irishman or an American, "but to an Englishman, that's what kills me."[8] To that point it had been the biggest purse in prizefight history.

Dempsey's fitness rapidly declined and, suffering the early stages of tuberculosis, he only fought three more times. In his last fight he was beaten in three rounds by Tommy Ryan for the world welterweight title on January 18, 1895. Over a twelve-year professional career, Dempsey suffered three defeats in sixty-eight contests, with his forty-eight victories including twenty-five knockouts. Sadly, his health began to decline quickly after that and his friends arranged for the poverty-stricken boxer to move to the Portland home of his wife's parents, where he died at the tragically young age of thirty-two on November 1, 1895, due to a recurrence of the disease. He was initially buried in an unmarked grave at Mount Calvary Cemetery because his father-in-law refused to permit former world champion John L. Sullivan to raise funds to erect a monument over his grave.[9] In its 1895 obituary to "Nonpareil" the Portland *Oregonian* noted: "Dempsey was cool under fire and never got rattled.... He changed his tactics in almost every battle, and his adversary never knew just how to size him up. If a man made a rushing fight, Jack would give him a whirlwind scrap. If, on the other hand, his adversary made a defensive fight, Jack would take more time and whip him at leisure."[10]

Bridging the transition between the London and Queensberry rules, Dempsey is listed as the first modern world middleweight champion and was elected to *Ring* magazine's hall of fame in 1954 and the International Boxing Hall of Fame in 1992.

In 1899, M.J. McMahon of Portland, Dempsey's attorney and friend, had a poem epitaph inscribed on his gravestone.

A Kildare Champion

Far out in the wilds of Oregon
On a lonely mountain side
Where Columbia's mighty waters
Fell down to the ocean's tide,
Where the giant fir and cedar
Are imaged in the wave
O'ergrown with weeds and lichens,
I found Jack Dempsey's grave.

*

I found no marble monolith
No broken shaft or stone
To tell of the great triumphs
This vanished hero won;
No rose, no shamrock I could find,
No mortals here to tell,
How sleeps in this forsaken spot
The immortal Nonpareil.

*

A winding rock-strewn canyon road,
That mortals seldom tread,
Leads up this lonely mountain
To the bivouac of the dead.
And the western sun was sinking
In the Pacific's golden waves
And solemn pines kept watching
O'er poor Jack Dempsey's grave.

*

Forgotten by ten thousand throats
That thundered his acclaim;
Forgotten by his friends and foes
Who cheered his very name
Oblivion wraps his faded form
But ages hence shall save
The memory of that Irish lad
That sleeps in Dempsey's grave.

*

Oh! Fame, why sleeps thy favored son
In wilds, woods and weeds?
And shall he ever thus sleep on
Interred his valiant deeds?
'Tis strange New York should thus forget
Its "Bravest of the Brave"
And in the wilds of Oregon
Unmarked, leave Dempsey's grave.

Twenty-One

"The Toy Bulldog"
Mickey Walker

"Sober or stiff, I belted the guts out of the best of them."[1]
—Mickey Walker

IRISH AND IRISH AMERICAN FIGHTERS WERE once a significant force in the welterweight division. The first known instance of the term "welterweight" may be from 1831, meaning "heavyweight horseman," while some venture to suggest that the first known use of it in boxing dates back to 1896. However, as with the nature of these things, others posit the theory that the word may date to the fifteenth century when "welt" meant to beat severely. Whatever the origin of the term, Irish American Paddy Duffy, born in Boston on November 12, 1864, is considered the first world welterweight champion of boxing's gloved era. Duffy was to have a tragically short life but found considerable success in the ring while alive. On February 1, 1884, at the age of nineteen, Duffy won his inaugural professional fight by knockout against "Skin" Doherty and went on to fight three bouts with Paddy Sullivan in Massachusetts the following year; the first two ended in draws, and the third, on June 28, 1884, ended in a hotly contested six-round win by points decision.[2,3] On December 19 of the same year he lost to fellow Bostonian Jack McGee by a second-round knockout, one of only two losses in his career.[4] On July 28, 1886, Duffy defeated Walter "The Kentucky Rosebud" Edgerton, a boxer described by one journalist as a "plucky colored pugilist," on a points decision in Philadelphia.[5] Duffy went on to fight Billy Frazier—a future boxing instructor at Harvard University—to a four-round draw on January 14, 1887, at the Adelphi Ring in New Bedford, Massachusetts. In a fiercely fought contest, he drew with Bill Dunn on March 1, 1887, at the Theatre Comique in Philadelphia.[6] Duffy then contested a four-fight series with Jack McGinty in Boston in 1887: a seven-round win on April 19, two seven-round draws in May and October, and an eight-round draw in November. Duffy defeated McGinty on February 9, 1888, by a technical knockout after the latter had been forced to retire with a broken thumb in the ninth round.[7] The *Boston Globe*, recognizing the skill of both boxers, considered the contest the decider for the American welterweight title.[8] On May 10 of the same year Duffy beat Tom Murphy when he put him to ground five times in the fourth round, while on October 30 of the same year Duffy fought an important bout against William McMillan in Fort Foote, Virginia.[9] McMillan had taken the championship of England against Tom Keenan and that of Scotland against Tom

Kelly, both in 1887.[10] In a contest which lasted one hour and eight minutes, where both competitors wore thin skin-tight gloves and competed for a purse of $350, Duffy was eventually declared the winner after McMillan was disqualified for head butting at the start of the seventeenth round.[11] Duffy secured the world welterweight title against British-born Australian champion Tom Meadows on March 2, 1889, in a forty-five-round bout at San Francisco's California Athletic Club for a $1,000 purse. Meadows went down four times in the forty-third round and three in the next before resorting to head butting, resulting in his disqualification. Just over a year after his win over Meadows, and still the reigning champion, Duffy died of tuberculosis on July 10 at the tragically young age of twenty-five. He ended his career with 51 wins, eleven draws and three losses and he was inducted into the International Boxing Hall of Fame in 2008.[12]

Mike "Twin" Sullivan, born in Cambridge, Massachusetts, on September 23, 1878, began his boxing career on March 25, 1901, by defeating Jack Dwyer at the Business Man's Athletic Club, Boston, in ten rounds and had a similar victory over Belfield Walcott a month later.[13] Sullivan went on to fight the renowned world lightweight champion Joe Gans three times in 1905 and 1906. The men fought to a draw in Maryland in September 1905, while Sullivan had victories over his opponent in January and March of 1906. One journalist noted the wonderful form of Gans at the San Francisco encounter and acknowledged that he was "easily the master of his white antagonist at all times," although the first three rounds were relatively even.[14] Sullivan next had a three-fight series with Rube Smith, a highly regarded welterweight of the era. After defeating Smith by an eighteenth-round knockout in April, Sullivan fought to draws with him in July and August, with all three fights taking place in Colorado. On February 21, 1907, he lost to future welterweight Harry Lewis in a ten-round points decision in Denver. (Lewis would use this victory and his subsequent knockout of Honey Mellody one year later on April 20, 1908, to establish what most boxing historians consider a legitimate claim to the world welterweight title. However, many boxing sanctioning organizations today simply fail to list world welterweight champions prior to 1910, as most of these organizations did not exist during that period and there was less widespread recognition of world champions.) Sullivan fought Honey Mellody on April 23, 1907, in a welterweight world championship match in Naud Junction Pavilion in Los Angeles, a fight the Irishman won over twenty rounds and in which he was in the ascendant from the very start according to newspaper reports.[15] Sullivan relinquished the title in October 1908 as he was above the welterweight limit.[16] While he went on to fight other high-profile opponents including Jimmy Gardner, Jimmy Slaby, Stanley Ketchel, and Paddy Lavin, he never won another title and died on October 31, 1937.[17]

Jimmy Gardner, born on Christmas Day, 1885, in Lisdoonvarna, County Clare, Ireland, fought in America from 1901 to 1917. Jimmy was the brother of one-time light heavyweight champion George Gardner and was known as a clever fighter rather than a power hitter, only losing four fights in his first eight years. Gardner recorded sixty-one wins, thirty-six by knockout, and eight losses.

However, of all the Irish and Irish Americans who fought at welterweight, it was Mickey Walker who lived longest in the public imagination. Known as "The

Toy Bulldog" because of his stocky stature and aggressiveness, Mickey Walker was a larger-than-life character and an immensely popular boxer of the Gilded Age. If Jack Dempsey had not dominated the public consciousness to the extent that he did, there is little doubt that Walker would have been the man to occupy the imagination of the boxing public. He was the absolute essence of the fighting Irishman: intemperate, feisty, indomitable, and, according to many of the boxing cognoscenti, courageous to the point of near insanity. Born Edward Patrick Walker in Elizabeth, New Jersey, on July 13, 1901, Mickey was expelled from school at the age of fourteen, and after his father had "whaled the daylights" out of him for his early exit from formal education, the young Irish American went through various jobs before going to work as a riveter in a local shipyard.[18] The story goes that one day at work he got into a fight with a professional boxer called Eddie McGill who reputedly told the Irish teenager to go and look for a bottle of radium.[19] On finding this an inevitably impossible task, and taking offense at the nature of the prank, Walker challenged Gill to a fight. The men supposedly fought for twenty-five minutes in front of an audience of 5,000 workers, after which Walker was given the unanimous decision—and his notice from the company. At seventeen he decided to become a professional boxer and had his first fight against Dominic Orsini, resulting in a four-round no-decision. Walker later told a story about how his mother observed the fight from a window in the roof because women were not allowed inside the venue. According to Walker's account his mother was shadow boxing when her hand went through the window, causing shards to drop onto the participants below. It was the type of tale Walker loved telling throughout his life, and it may be that many of them should best be taken with a grain or two of salt.[20] Walker only stood five feet six inches tall and weighed around 120 pounds but had a natural desire to take on anyone from a young age. He joined up with former amateur athlete and distance runner Johnny Anthes, who tended to his training and ring education and rapidly developed his punching, complete with a strong right hand and a terrific left hook. The strength on his left side, he always maintained, resulted from a childhood collision with a motorcycle that broke his collarbone and, fearing that the injury might derail his chance to become a baseball player, he started to work overtime with the left hand, becoming ambidextrous. On April 29, 1919, he was defeated for the first time by Phil Delmont with a knockout in the first round but subsequently went on to defeat Benny Cohen, a fighter tipped for the big time who went by the cognomen of "Irish Cohen." In 1920 Walker fought twelve times with two victories and ten no-decisions. All his bouts were held in his native New Jersey, one of the few jurisdictions where scoring systems had not been instituted in boxing. If a fight lasted the scheduled distance it was automatically declared a no-decision, regardless of who the better boxer had been. On July 18, 1921, he took on world welterweight champion Jack Britton in a twelve-round bout with no change of title if the match went the distance. Britton, who had won the title from Kid Lewis four years earlier, was widely considered one of the shrewdest boxers in the game. The encounter did go the distance, but Walker earned significant kudos. On November 1, 1922, he fought Britton for a second time, on this occasion for the world welterweight title at Madison Square Garden. By then Britton was thirty-seven while Walker was a fresh-faced twenty-one. Britton was floored several times and took a torrid beating in the tenth but refused to concede, despite the referee advising him to do so. The Irishman eventually outpointed Britton over the fifteen rounds to take the title. The Toy Bulldog went on to fight thirteen times in 1923, winning eleven, with one no-decision and one no-contest. He defended the title twice each against Pete Latzo and Jimmy Jones. After successfully defending his title against Latzo in 1923, Walker was given his nickname by publicist Francis Albertanti, in an obvious reference to the Irishman's tenacity and persistence in the ring combined with his size.[21] In 1924 Walker won six of his nine bouts, including three title defenses. In June he defended his title against Lew Tendle in front of 18,000 fans in Philadelphia in a fight where the referee awarded him eight of the ten rounds. One journalist reporting on the fight described the Irishman as "a fast, game, and explosive hitter" who reveled in a bristling contest. When punched he was raised to fury which was the mark of a thoroughbred fighter, the writer concluded.[22] In 1925, Walker went up a division to middleweight and fought champion Harry Greb on July 2 at the Polo Grounds in front of 65,000 fans. In what almost amounted to a street brawl, Greb took the victory on points. An often recounted story goes that they engaged in an actual street brawl following the fight on the same night.[23] Walker then went back to the welterweight division, defending his title against Dave Shade on September 21, 1925, a year when he won three bouts, lost one, and had three no-decisions. On May 20, 1926, Walker defended his world welterweight title in a rematch with Pete Latzo in Scranton, Pennsylvania, in a disappointing encounter in which he lost at the end of ten rounds, a result that many attributed to his high-octane lifestyle. Five weeks later he lost to Johnny Dundee after the referee drew things to a premature conclusion in the eighth round. By then it was clear to most that he was no longer a welterweight and would need to move up a division to further his career. He was at this point managed by Jack Demsey's former handler Jack Kearns, a man so loathed by the New York State Athletic Commission that he had been barred from attending the middleweight championship bout between Walker and Harry Greb in 1925. This unofficial blacklist meant Walker—and by extension, Kearns—had an artificial cap on his earnings. Under Kearns's tutelage Walker set about a strenuous work program, including a period in Nova Scotia where he spent ten hours a day working as a lumberjack. In October he stopped a hard-punching hometown Chicago prospect named "Shuffles" Callahan and, after two further wins, and thanks to Kearn's dealing ability, he received a shot at middleweight king Theodore "Tiger" Flowers in Chicago.

Flowers had defeated Harry Greb to become the first African American champion after Jack Johnson to hold a world boxing title. Known for his spirituality, he was sometimes referred to as "Deacon" Flowers, often carrying a Bible up the ring steps. The fight, which took place in front of 11,000 spectators on December 3 at the Coliseum in Chicago, proved a contentious encounter. Flowers was given the nod after ten rounds but there were serious question marks over the decision. The Illinois Commission investigated proceedings but could find no evidence of dishonesty by the referee and confirmed Walker's status as the new middleweight champion. A rematch was precluded when Flowers, seeking to remove scar tissue from around his eyes, died on the operating table little more than a year after Harry Greb had passed away in very similar circumstances. Walker's first defense of the title was in London against British champion Tommy Milligan, who fought bravely in front of his home crowd but was outclassed by the Irishman. Down twice in the seventh, Milligan fought back, but in the ninth he was just saved by the bell. In the tenth he fell again and rose to his feet with nothing left. Walker hesitated, giving referee Eugene Corri a chance to call it. When Corri refused to act, the champion sent Milligan to the blood-spattered canvas for the count. On November 1, Walker destroyed former light-heavyweight champion Mike McTigue in one round, leaving his fellow Irishman unconscious for several minutes afterward. Later in the same month he beat Paul Berlenbach, another one-time champion of the division. In March of 1928 he nearly won the light-heavyweight title in ten brutal rounds with Tommy Loughran, but it ended with a split verdict for Loughran even though Walker had gained the edge on the referee's scorecard. By then his home life was suffering through his womanizing, as eloquently noted by one journalist some years later: "Mickey will not go down in history as one of the world's leading family men. Cupid has speared him a hundred times and each time the arrow hurt."[24] His pregnant wife Maude finally tired of his escapades and filed for divorce. Walker then began concentrating on winning the world middleweight championship, and on November 22 of the same year, he finally defeated Jock Malone. On December 3, he reclaimed the world middleweight title with a controversial ten-round decision over Tiger Flowers. Perhaps the most bizarre ring outing ever occurred in 1930 when Walker received word that his fight with heavyweight Paul Swiderski was canceled.[25] He went drinking, but there had been a mix-up in communication and he had a fight to get ready for after all. Walker reportedly stumbled into the ring and was knocked to the canvas at least five times inside the opening round. The story goes that his manager Jack "Doc" Kearns managed to save his drunken charge from a knockout by banging a water bottle off the timekeeper's bell to bring the round to an early conclusion. When Walker was dropped again in the second, Kearns pulled a fuse to send the arena into darkness. Once the chaos had come to an end, Walker had sobered up enough during the blackout to turn things around, sending Swiderski to the floor sixteen times before an eventual decision triumph.[26] On June 19, 1931, Walker decided to vacate his world middleweight title and move up to the heavyweight division. Walker made his debut on July 22 at Ebbets Field, Brooklyn, New York, against former world heavyweight champion Jack Sharkey in what the vast majority of the boxing cognoscenti of the time considered a foolish move. Sharkey was almost six inches taller than his tenacious opponent, as well as having a seven inch advantage in reach, and was roughly thirty-five pounds heavier. A crowd of more than 30,000 paid a remarkable $233,356 to watch a contest in which it was later alleged there was Mafia involvement.[27] At the end of a ferocious contest, where neither man gave an inch, the two ringside judges had it one for Sharkey and the other even. Referee Arthur Donovan had it eleven to four to Walker, and the three-way split on the vote meant the fight was a draw. In 1932 he won five fights, including a ten-round decision in front of 20,000 yelling fans at the Chicago Stadium over light-heavyweight contender Harris Kracòw, otherwise known as "Kingfish" Levinsky, a colorful character, managed by his tough-talking sister, who had grown up on the West Side of the city in a family of local fish peddlers. He then turned his attention to former world heavyweight champion Max Schmeling. Walker's preparations got off to a terrible start when he suffered a cut during some horseplay with Kearns, which resulted in the fight being postponed for two weeks. During the enforced layoff he gained weight and entered the ring at a bloated 172 pounds, although that was probably of little consequence. In what may have been the worst beating that Walker would ever take, Kearns stepped in to take his man ashore in the eighth round. In 1933 he went down to the light-heavyweight division, where he lost a fifteen-round decision to Maxie Rosenbloom for the world title. The next year, Walker fought Rosenbloom again and was awarded a ten-round decision in a non-title encounter. Afterward, Kearns saw the writing on the wall and the pair parted company. Undaunted, Walker kept campaigning in that division until 1935, when he finally retired after losing to Eric Seelig by a seven-round technical knockout. In his retirement Walker opened a bar across the road from Madison Square Garden, appropriately named the Toy Bulldog. He subsequently opened a bar in his hometown of Elizabeth with the even more appropriate title of The First Round. Walker was frequently his own best customer, but despite his heavy drinking, he found the time to work as a goodwill ambassador for President Roosevelt during World War II. He also developed an interest in art and frequently recounted how he first became interested in it. One evening Walker and his wife Eleanor were at the local theater watching *The Moon and Sixpence*, a film based on Somerset Maugham's story of the French painter Gauguin. A couple of days later, sitting alone half-way through his third viewing of the film, he jumped up and went to an art store in Elizabeth to get supplies to try his hand at painting. He sought guidance from Maxwell Simpson, with whom he had trained at the YMCA gym while in his teens. Simpson had ventured to Paris in later years where he studied painting, and by then was one of America's premier artists. Walker also became an accomplished painter with many of his works exhibited at New York and London art galleries, including a one-man show at the Associated American Artists Galleries on Fifth Avenue in April of 1955.[28] Of his art, he once said: "There's not much difference between prizefighting and painting. It's just a matter of time. As a youth I could express myself with my fists. Physical expression belongs to youth. Then the years go by. I found art and expression in colors."[29] Walker was married six times, twice to Clara Helmers and twice to Maude Kelly, but sadly, ended up in poor circumstances. He was found lying on a street in Freehold, New Jersey, by police in 1974 and taken to a nearby hospital, where he was initially thought to be just drunk but tests revealed he was suffering from Parkinson's syndrome, arteriosclerosis, and anemia. At the time he had been living in a boardinghouse in Elizabeth, surviving on Social Security payments and handouts from friends. Walker was subsequently admitted to Marlboro Psychiatric Hospital for a period of time and died on April 28, 1981, in Freehold.[30] During his storied sixteen-year career Walker defeated five Hall of Fame boxers and got the better of ten rivals who outweighed him by twenty pounds or more. Of his 165 documented fights he scored sixty knockouts, many with his powerful left hook, and won thirty-three by decision, with four draws. He lost eleven by decision, three on fouls, and five by knockouts. Forty-five more bouts were no-decisions, and one was ruled no contest.[31] Walker is widely considered one of the greatest fighters ever, with ESPN ranking him seventeenth on its list of the fifty greatest boxers of all time, while boxing historian Bert Sugar placed him eleventh in his Top 100 Fighters catalog and described him as the ultimate "Happy Warrior" with his happy-go-lucky attitude and penchant for attempting seemingly impossible odds.[32] Statistical website *BoxRec* rates Walker as the sixth best middleweight ever, with *Ring* magazine founder Nat Fleischer placing him at number four. The International Boxing Research Organization ranked Walker as the number-four middleweight and the number-sixteen pound-for-pound fighter of all time. Walker was inducted into *Ring* magazine's Hall of Fame in 1957 and the International Boxing Hall of Fame as a first-class member in 1990. It was estimated he earned more than $3 million in the ring but frittered it all away. Walker was a man who loved to fight, who never knew when to quit, and who famously replied to Jack Kearns after the manager had halted the Schmeling fight and said, "I guess this was one we couldn't win," with the retort, "Speak for yourself."[33] A worthy epitaph might be the words that close his own published remembrances: "Live today," he advised his reader, "forget yesterday, and have hope for tomorrow."[34]

Twenty-Two

"The Baby-Faced Assassin"
Jimmy McLarnin

"I never met a fighter I didn't like. Thing is, they were always trying to knock my ears off."

—Jimmy McLarnin[1]

JAMES "JIMMY" ARCHIBALD MCLARNIN, BORN ON December 19, 1907, in Hillsborough, County Down, in what is now Northern Ireland, had that most unusual of things for a boxer—a long, happy, and healthy life.[2] His early life was also atypical for that of an Irish emigrant. McLarnin's father Sam was a Dublin-born Methodist and trained butcher who traveled throughout Ireland and England for work before heading to Alberta to try his hand on cattle ranches. McLarnin senior subsequently returned home and married Belfast woman Mary Ferris, and there he set up his own shop. He must have liked Canada, however. When Jimmy McLarnin was three years old the family emigrated to Saskatchewan, where they began work as wheat farmers near the village of Mortlach but, after one harsh winter too many, moved to Vancouver, where they opened a secondhand furniture store in the east end of the city.[3] As a youngster McLarnin demonstrated an aptitude for football, baseball, and boxing, but it was the latter he was to be drawn to, encouraged by former professional wrestler and boxer Charles "Pop" Foster, a lifelong mentor who would later leave McLarnin his estate.[4] Foster was to prove an astute manager who only selected fights he thought were important to his fighter's career and also saw the advantages in highlighting McLarnin's Irishness, so McLarnin never entered the ring without his trademark bright green robe with his name in gold lettering on the back. When Foster first saw Jimmy in the gym his father had constructed in the basement of the family home he was convinced that the young Irish boy had the makings of a good fighter and told Samuel that his son's boxing style was reminiscent of Jim "The Welsh Wizard" Driscoll. McLarnin proved a precocious talent, and before reaching his sixteenth birthday he had compiled a record of twenty wins and no defeats and held the amateur flyweight title of British Columbia.[5] His first recorded victory was against "Young Fry" on December 19, 1923.[6] After realizing the paltry purses available in Vancouver, Foster and his young charge moved south to San Francisco, then known as the "Cradle of Fistic Stars," but his youthful appearance made it difficult for McLarnin to find fights and he was forced to lie about his age.[7] Additionally, there had been a recent fatality in the ring in San Francisco and the authorities had clamped down on boxing, with the result that Foster and his young protégé decamped to Oakland, where McLarnin made his winning American debut against Frankie Sands on February 23, 1924, after which "The Baby-Faced Assassin" scored fifteen victories and two draws—one to Olympic flyweight champion Fidel La Barba and once to future hall of fame member "Memphis" Pal Moore—before losing to future bantamweight champion Bud Taylor over four rounds on June 2, 1925. Despite the loss, McLarnin got a significant break when he was offered a non-title match against reigning world flyweight champion Pancho Villa on Independence Day. In the match held in Emeryville, California, the Irishman took the decision over an out-of-sorts Villa, who going into the fight had a serious tooth infection,

James Archibald McLarnin (December 19, 1907–October 28, 2004) was a two-time welterweight world champion and is considered by some to be the greatest Irish boxer of all time (*Los Angeles Times* Photographic Collection at the UCLA Library, Creative Commons 4.0).

which tragically killed him ten days later, two days shy of his twenty-fourth birthday.[8] McLarnin went on to defeat another Olympic champion—Jackie Fields, the 1924 featherweight gold medalist. On October 18, 1927, McLarnin won an eighth-round knockout against Louis "Kid" Kaplin, a rough-and-tumble Russian fighter from Connecticut and former world bantamweight champion. It was a hard-earned victory as McLarnin suffered two knockdowns and when he visited his dentist later discovered he had broken his jaw. After making a full recovery, McLarnin was pitted against New Yorker Sid "The Galloping Ghost of the Ghetto" Terris at Madison Square Garden in February 1928. It was virtually over before it began, as McLarnin knocked his opponent out in one minute and forty-seven seconds and took home a purse of $19,645, as well as $1,000 for movie rights, the biggest payday of the young Irishman's career.[9] From then on McLarnin was an enormously popular fighter and a hero to the huge Irish American community in New York.

After his victory over Terris, *Ring* magazine, with McLarnin pictured on the cover against a green background and the strap line "Jimmy McLarnin Next Lightweight Champion," reported that many Irish Americans celebrated for two days and noted that it was the first time in sixteen years that "the Celts had a real, honest-to-goodness chance to root for one of their own."[10] Stanley Weston of *Boxing and Wrestling* magazine believed that the 18,000 present at the fight left the venue believing they had seen the best lightweight puncher since "Terrible" Terry McGovern fifty years previously. Although he lost his first title shot on May 21, 1928, in a fifteen-round decision against world lightweight champion Sammy Mandell at the Polo Grounds, New York, McLarnin went on to beat the same opponent twice in the following two years in non-title bouts. It would be five more years before he would next get a title shot, during which time he knocked out gifted Jewish fighters Al Singer and Ruby Goldstein, as well as having a high-profile win over an aging Benny "The Ghetto Wizard" Leonard in 1932, an encounter which sent the revered fighter into retirement and gave little pleasure to McLarnin, as he had defeated one of his idols. On May 29, 1933, 20,000 people gathered at Wrigley Field baseball stadium in Los Angeles to watch the then twenty-five-year-old McLarnin take on the world welterweight champion Young Corbett III, an Italian American whose real name was the rather poetic Raffaele Capabianca Giordana. McLarnin was considered the underdog, but Corbett had one crucial flaw. He tended to lean in just before he threw his right arm forward. As McLarnin recalled, his plan was always to lull the reigning champ into a false sense of security before taking advantage of this weakness. "He did it a couple of times and I didn't react," McLarnin told the *Los Angeles Times* years later. "He kept doing it. It was the third time, and bing!"[11] The fight took little longer than it took to say his name when McLarnin put his opponent through the ropes after two minutes and thirty-seven seconds. He told one journalist that the fact that his seventy-one-year-old father was there to see his victory was the most satisfactory aspect of the proceedings.[12] Following his title success, McLarnin took a long deserved break from the ring, although not all were happy that he spent much of his time golfing and mixing with the great and the good in Hollywood. Eddie Borden of *Ring* magazine said he should either put his title on the line or retire, as there were plenty of other good contenders knocking around. Pop Foster's retort was simple: Come up with $40,000 and they would take on the challenge immediately.[13] McLarnin, whose other nicknames included the "Jew Beater," the "Hebrew Scourge," the "Murderous Mick," and the "Belfast Spider," had his biggest and most lucrative fights against Jewish boxers. McLarnin fought a famed three-fight series with Jewish boxer Barney Ross. On May 28, 1934, the pair met at Long Island Bowl in front of a crowd of 45,000 where McLarnin was offered $50,000 or forty percent of the gate, whichever was the greater, and ended up with $58,936—such was the interest in the fight. Ross—born Barnet David Rasofsky as the son of Russian emigrants who had fled the pogroms—had taken the world lightweight title the previous year and was now vying to become the first boxer to hold it and the welterweight title. In a terrific contest that went the full fifteen rounds, Ross won on a split decision, after which there was an immediate clamor for a rematch. Four months later the pair met again, this time at the Polo Grounds in New York, in front of a crowd of 23,777, in what proved another close and hard-fought contest. Paul Gallico of the *New York Daily News* pithily contextualized the role of race in his ringside dispatch: "The Jews said it was Ross, the Irish said it was McLarnin and the Italians said they didn't know."[14] When McLarnin was declared the victor by announcer Joe Humphries the decision was roundly booed; twenty-two of the twenty-eight ringside journalists believed Ross should have got the nod. After the dust settled Pop Foster thought it better that McLarnin hang up his gloves, but the Irishman had other ideas and a third encounter was penciled in for May 28, 1935, exactly a year after their first fight. At the end of another hotly contested encounter, refereed by the great Jack Dempsey, Ross was awarded the crown by unanimous decision. McLarnin had lost his title for the final time in a narrow decision that, by all accounts, he never quite came to terms with afterward. The Irishman retired in November 1936 at the age of thirty-one, having won his last two fights against Tony Canzoneri and Lou Ambers, leaving the arena with a record of sixty-two wins, three draws, and one no-decision in seventy-seven professional fights. Despite frequent lucrative offers he never returned to the ring. In 1966 McLarnin was named Canada's "Boxer of the Half-Century" and inducted into the Canadian Sports Hall of Fame, while in 1996 *Ring* magazine voted McLarnin the fifth-greatest welterweight of all time.[15] *BoxRec* still ranks McLarnin as the greatest Canadian boxer of all time and the second greatest welterweight ever. In his book *The 100 Greatest Boxers of All Time* Bert Sugar rated McLarnin twenty-second greatest boxer of all time and the second-best welterweight behind Sugar Ray Robinson.[16] After his retirement McLarnin opened an electrical goods store in Glendale, California, and also did some acting, golfing, and lecturing. In 1937 he appeared with boxers Maxie Rosenbloom, James J. Jeffries, Jack Dempsey, and Jackie Fields in MGM's *Big City*, a film involving underhand practices between two rival taxi companies. In 1938 he appeared in a gymnasium scene in the successful MGM boxing movie *The Crowd Roars* with fellow sluggers Abe Hollandersky, Joe Glick, Maxie Rosenbloom, Jack Roper, and Tommy Herman, while in 1946 he appeared in Monogram Pictures' boxing movie, *Joe Palooka, Champ*, a vehicle which included cameos by boxing luminaries Joe Louis, Henry Armstrong, Ceferino Garcia, and Manuel Ortiz.[17] Looking back on his boxing career, McLarnin told Earl Gustkey of the *Los Angeles Times* that he got a dollar for his first fight and $25,000 for his last and had never met anyone who didn't turn out to be at least a halfway decent human being. McLarnin died on October 28, 2004, at the age of ninety-six in Richland, Washington, and is interred in the Forest Lawn Memorial Park Cemetery in Glendale, California.

Twenty-Three

The Pride of Achill Island
Johnny Kilbane

> A man can have two arms of steel, a punch of dynamite
> But if he lacks a fighting heart he'll miss the greatest height
> He may possess an iron fist and strength beyond his need
> Then too he may be quick of mind and blessed with extra speed
> He may have great ability or be a fancy Dan
> But without faith and fighting heart he's just an also-ran
> This need of heart is not just for the pugilist who fights
> But it holds true for all of us who battle for our rights
> For when the chips of life are down and troubled waters mount
> A fighting heart will see us through however long the count.[1]
> —Johnny Kilbane, "Fighting Heart"

JOHN PATRICK KILBANE, BORN ON APRIL 9, 1889, on West 28th Street, near old River Avenue, Cleveland, Ohio, to John Kilbane and Mary Gallagher of Achill Island, County Mayo, holds the singular distinction of being the longest holder of the world featherweight title, an honor he retained for a remarkable eleven years. Kilbane did not have it easy growing up: His mother died when he was three years old and his father went blind when he was ten. He was an only child and, in his own words, ran wild "like Topsy."[2] During his time at St. Malachy's School on Washington Avenue he was the victim of frequent taunts about the thinness of his legs and

Johnny Kilbane was born in Cleveland, Ohio, of Irish parents from Achill Island, County Mayo. He held the world featherweight title from 1912 to 1923, the longest period in the division's history, having defended the title against four contenders during the reign (Bain News Service, George Grantham Bain Collection, Library of Congress).

arms. It was only when Jimmy Dunn put him to work shoveling sand that he began to develop his chest and stomach muscles, and by his own account, it was probably his puniness that resulted in his "fondness for buck and wing dancing."[3] At school Kilbane gained a particular love for gymnastics and developed a strong ability in the horizontal bars, which he hoped to incorporate into a future stage act in which he also aspired to sing, play the violin, and act. However, when he went to see a boxing exhibition match between Tom Sharkey and Otto Craig at the nearby La Salle Club in the winter of 1906, the scales dropped from his eyes and he began to envision a completely different sporting future. While the bout was not particularly dramatic, Kilbane, by his own admission, was entranced by the fact that he was seeing a fighter who had taken on Corbett, Jeffries, and Fitzsimmons, and combined with the lights and the crowd, the prominent Clevelanders present, the heavy cigar smoke, and the general atmosphere of romance, the event made a deep impression on him. He decided then and there against the "horizontal bars, the buck and wing, voice and the violin." Kilbane confided his dreams to his childhood friend Perk Gibbons, who referred him on to Jimmy Dunn of Crystal Beach, a talented lightweight boxer who would quickly tell him whether he had the talent to make it as a boxer or not. However, Kilbane did not have the thirty-cent fare to visit Dunn even though he was working for the Pennsylvania railroad as a switch boy at the time, having spent his previous pay on dance tickets and the entrance fee for the Sharkey fight. His difficult job was another reason he decided to take up boxing as, given his frail physique, he was unable to move the switches by hand and was forced to throw his whole body weight behind them. At the time, the only fights held in Cleveland were in private clubs and it was in the La Salle Club that Kilbane encountered his first opponent in the shape of a local tough guy called "Kid" Campbell. The men were polar opposites in body type: Kilbane was tall and thin, Campbell short and stocky. Kilbane relied largely on his jab and run; Campbell was used to knocking out his foes with roundhouse swings. Despite the fact that his opponent was twenty-five pounds heavier and the purse a miserly $8, Kilbane was happy to take on the fight and duly knocked out his opponent in the sixth round, much to the surprise of those present. In an interesting coincidence a boxer called Tommy Kilbane lived in the next street over from Johnny, but the families were not related. A contest between the two had long been mooted and they eventually met in the ring in a three-round draw at the Eagles Club for which Johnny received $5.[4] A month later they met again, this time in a four-rounder in Cleveland, with another drawn contest the result. The series demanded a resolution and the combatants met in the fall of the following year on Watson's Farm in a twenty-five-round contest, the venue chosen because laws did not permit competitive fighting within the city limits. (Mayor Herman Baehr would rescind the ban in December with the first fight between Paddy Kilbane and Charley White. The ban was reinstated in December of the following year by Mayor Newton D. Baker.) For the next five years Kilbane worked assiduously on his trade, losing only twice, once to Joe Rivers and once to the great Abe Attell in 1910. The first big year for Johnny was in 1909 when ring work became plentiful again and he started mixing with quality fighters such as Jack White, Johnny Whittaker, Biz Mackey, and Happy Davis. On September 4, 1911, Kilbane fought Rivers for a second time at Vernon, California, this time knocking him out in the sixteenth round, a victory that put him firmly on the boxing map. All that stood in his way now was Fred Conley, whom he easily accounted for on September 30. On February 22, 1912, at the Vernon Arena, California, Kilbane was pitted against Abe Attell for the second time for the featherweight title, against a fighter who was widely believed to be virtually unbeatable. Attell had dominated the featherweight class since 1901, holding the world featherweight title between 1901 and 1905, and again from 1906 until 1912, and, as noted, had defeated Kilbane less than two years earlier, on October 24, 1910, in a title match held in Kansas City.

Almost 10,000 people crowded into the 8,400 venue, the largest fight crowd in the history of the Los Angeles arena, while a further 5,000 disappointed punters were turned away.[5] The total gate receipts were around $25,000, a formidable total at that time, while the combatants fought for a $10,000 purse, of which it was agreed that Attell would receive $6,500, irrespective of the result. To further sweeten the deal, the fight was filmed, with the men agreeing on an even split of the motion picture privilege. Kilbane wrote that he did not mind the half-hearted cheers he received, or the roof-smashing cheers that went to his opponent, but rather kept his mind focused on victory from the very start.[6] Throughout the contest Attell did not fight cleanly. He locked Kilbane's arms in the clinches, heeled him on one occasion, and tried to bend his left arm back on another. In the sixteenth round he surged into a clinch and butted Kilbane so severely that the Irishman sustained a deep gash over his left eye. The Jewish fighter was consistently booed by the spectators as his behavior deteriorated, but the Irishman decided not to rush Attell and aimed to have, in his own words, a "reception committee consisting of a couple of rights and a few lefts there to greet him."[7] Despite some slating by his opponent, Kilbane stayed the course and won by decision. Kilbane had fought forty-three times in three and a half years prior to his title fight with Attell. Boxing writer J.P. Garvey described him as "Irish as Paddy's pig, a 22-year-old boy with sparkling eyes, ready wit, whose every action is peppery, effervescent, indicative of a lightning brain and panther body," and a worthy successor to Abe Attell.[8] While Kilbane did not have an Irish accent, Garvey noted, his general air of uncontrollable activity and flashing eyes were redolent of "shamrocks in full bloom, the bogs, the turf, the clay pipes and the black tea."[9]

When Kilbane returned to Cleveland on St. Patrick's Day more than 100,000 people turned up to celebrate his victory. Mayor Newton D. Baker, the former Secretary of War under President Wilson, was a personal friend of Kilbane and coordinated the reception for the new champion. Throughout his career Kilbane achieved huge popularity, so much so that his name was once used as a verb. On May 16, 1912, the *New York Times* described an incident in a baseball match between the Detroit Tigers and the New York Yankees where Ty Cobb of the Tigers chased after a heckler and "'Johnny Kilbaned' him right where he stood," putting an end to his profane and intolerable language.[10]

After winning the title, Kilbane spent some time on the vaudeville circuit before turning his eyes toward the ring again. He was now a highly sought-after opponent, but Jimmy Dunn, ever the shrewd manager, decided Kilbane would only fight in New York City, where the best money was to be had. On May 14, 1912, he was pitted against Frankie Burns at St. Nicholas Arena in a twelve-round contest where he was guaranteed $5500. Once again he proved a major draw and several thousand fight fans were unable to gain admission to a fight in which he pulverized his unfortunate opponent. Despite the three-year ban on boxing in Cleveland between 1914 and 1917, Kilbane managed to fight thirty-seven times. Arguably, only three were of any consequence, with defeats over bantamweight champion Kid Williams and two future champions in Johnny Dundee and Benny Leonard. On April 29, 1913, he met Dundee for a second time in Los Angeles in a drawn encounter. Jack London was at the match and contended that Kilbane had won seventeen of the twenty rounds.[11] On March 17, 1914, Kilbane challenged Kid Williams for his bantamweight title, but the incumbent held on to his crown after six closely fought rounds. Given that the Irishman had to make the 118 pounds limit, it was an impressive feat. It could be argued that the only real mistake of Kilbane's career was his decision to step up to the lightweight division to take on Benny Leonard for the title on July 25, 1917. The bigger and stronger Ghetto Wizard knocked Kilbane out in three rounds, and such was the beating the Irishman received that Dunn vowed it would be his charge's last fight. Four times Kilbane had stepped into the ring against another champion and three times he had come out on the right side, but it was not to be against Leonard. Soon after their encounter both Leonard and Kilbane were called to military service, accepting appointments as army boxing instructors, Kilbane at Camp Sherman, Ohio.[12]

Kilbane retained his featherweight title until losing to Frenchman Eugene Criqui on June 2, 1923, in the Polo Grounds, New York. Perhaps it was a fitting coronation, as Criqui had his jaw reconstructed from wire, silver, and goat leg after it was shattered while doing guard duty in Verdun during World War I.[13]

Unlike so many others, Kilbane got out of the game while the going was good and once turned down an offer by Tex Rickard to fight any boxer of his choice for $30,000. There were many disappointed fans, including journalist Bob Edgren, who remembered a time when Kilbane would have taken on any fight just for the fun of it. In his day, according to Edgren, Kilbane could fight "anything from a Mexican wildcat to a grizzly bear" and had "a poke like a lightning bolt and a sidestep that made his opponents miss more swings than there are on all the gates in the county."[14] When he felt like dancing he could hop, skip, and jump around a ring in a way that would make Johnny Dundee look like a loaded truck trying to go up Fort Lee Hill on an icy morning. No boxer could hit him with a "bucket of birdshot" because when they arrived he was no longer there. After finishing his fighting career, Kilbane worked as a referee, operated a gym, sold real estate, and taught physical education on a part-time basis in some local schools. Though unsuccessful in his campaigns for Cleveland City Council in 1921 and sheriff in 1928 and 1948, he was elected state senator from 1941 to 1942 and state representative in 1951. He left the State House in 1952 when he was elected clerk of courts, a post he would hold until his death in 1957. Kilbane was often photographed with his family. His wife Irene, to whom he was married forty-seven years, was always on hand to cook his meals in training camp, but she refused to watch him fight. Looking back on his boxing career and personal life, Johnny always credited his wife for her support, claiming, in 1951, "My life has been a very happy one. Ninety-nine percent of this is because of my wife, and the other one percent is the Luck of the Irish."[15] However, Kilbane was a realist when it

John "Johnny" Patrick Kilbane (1889–1957) with his wife and daughter on board the steamship *Aquitania* **for a trip to England on March 21, 1922 (George Grantham Bain Collection, Library of Congress).**

came to boxing and once said to a group of reporters, "Show me a business where I can make more money than I can in the ring and I'll never fight again. I don't fight because I like it. I fight because it means a living for my family and myself."[16]

He died on May 31, 1957, in Cleveland, Ohio.[17] In 1995 Kilbane was inducted into the International Boxing Hall of Fame, and in 2012, Herman Avenue, the street on which he grew up, was renamed Kilbane Town. In 2012 a statue was unveiled in his honor on Achill Island, County Mayo, with a similar honor bestowed upon him in Cleveland's Battery Park in 2014.[18]

Epilogue

THE LANDSCAPE OF BOXING IN THE United States is now at a vast remove from the golden era when there was one heavyweight champion. The alphabet soup into which the sport descended has long been a matter of derision in many quarters. The very future of the sport is questioned by many, including eminent neurologists. Only time will tell on that one.

There have been few Ireland-based boxers of note operating in the United States. In terms of those based in America, Sean Mannion from Rosmuc, County Galway, is the most notable. Based in Boston, he fought Mike McCallum for the vacant WBA title on October 19, 1984, a bout he lost in a unanimous fifteen-round decision in front of a hugely partisan crowd of 20,000 in Madison Square Garden. It was the first of Mannion's fights to be televised by RTE, Ireland's national television station. Thousands of people had flown over from Ireland for the fight. Mannion later said that he should not have gone ahead with the fight as he had received stitches to a cut above his eye beforehand which limited him to only two days of sparring in preparation for the fight. When he returned to Ireland for a visit after the encounter he was given a huge welcome at Shannon airport. He later said that he felt he had not deserved such a welcome as he had let the country down.

Irish Micky Ward competed between 1985 and 1993, challenging for the IBF light welterweight title in 1997 and briefly holding the WBU light welterweight title in 2000. However, despite his name, Ward's connection to the old sod were far distant: His maternal great-grandmother Annie Greenhalge (Carroll) was born there, the daughter of Michael and Mary (Flood) Carroll, while his maternal great-great-great grandparents Peter McMahon and Ann Quinn were from County Tyrone. There are still Irish boxers fighting in America, but none have achieved anything notable as boxing slips further toward the sporting margins.

There is still an element of bare-knuckle fighting in Ireland. Between 1997 and 2009 Irish documentarist followed the story of bare-knuckle fighting between groups of Irish Travellers, which culminated in the theatrical release of *Knuckles* in 2011. The contests, which often involved heavy betting and substantial prize money, took place in a netherworld of secret locations in Great Britain and Ireland, redolent of long past eras. It was readily apparent that these fights were part of a long-running tradition and were extremely well organized, for the most part. When Michael Quinn McDonagh, one of the principal participants, was interviewed by Corey Kilgannon of the *New York Times* he explained how such encounters sorted out interfamily issues and stopped larger violence in the Traveller community. While other people used guns and knives to sort out problems, they used fists, McDonagh said.[1] The feud highlighted in the film was supposedly started by a torched Traveller's cart at a horse fair, and renewed in 1992 by a deadly fight outside a London pub, for which McDonagh's brother Paddy served prison time for manslaughter. During the course of one fight between McDonagh and Paddy "The Lurcher" Joyce in the documentary, a bemused spectator is heard to say, "At least wars are about something." Part of the documentary explains how the feuding families regularly send each other videos issuing challenges and demonstrating their fighting prowess.

On August 30, 2012, Jacqueline McDonagh, wife of Michael McDonagh and mother of his three children, was found dead in her home at College Manor, Hoey's Lane, Dundalk, County Louth. She had been beaten to death. Her husband was convicted of her murder in 2015. During the course of his trial it became evident that the fifteen-year marriage had been violent and troubled, and it was noted that the only time she had peace was when McDonagh was training for his bare-knuckle boxing fights.[2] The boxing tradition among Travellers also extends to traditional amateur and professional boxing. Irish Traveller Francie Barrett represented Ireland at the 1996 Olympics, while Andy Lee fought for Ireland at the 2004 Olympics and later became the first Traveller to win a professional boxing world championship when he won the World Boxing Organization (WBO) middleweight title in 2014. Tyson Fury is of Irish Traveller heritage and defeated long-reigning Wladimir Klitschko in 2015 to become the unified heavyweight world champion. Other names that have echoed down the halls of fame of Irish Traveller bare-knuckle fighting include Gypsy Jack Cooper, Bartley Gorman, Uriah Burton, Joe "The Hulk" Joyce, and Paddy "Jaws" Ward, to name just a few.

Bare-knuckle fighting has recently made an unlikely official comeback in the United States in the form of the Bare Knuckle Fighting Championship (BKFC) based in Philadelphia. BKFC, it claims, is the first promotion to hold an official state-sanctioned and commissioned bare-knuckle boxing event in the United States since 1889. Its first event was held in 2018, and there have been forty-nine "numbered" events held as of August 2023. Each fight takes place in a specialized circular four-rope ring, referred to as the "Squared Circle." The ring incorporates elements of historical bare-knuckle fighting by containing two scratch lines, three feet apart and in the middle of the ring, as per the Broughton Rules. Each fighter must start each round with their front foot on their scratch line. This is referred to as "Toe the Line," and it is an instruction given to the fighters at the beginning of each round, followed by "Knuckle Up," which signals the beginning of the round. BKFC 1, which took place on June 2, 2018, featured the first American sanctioned women's bare-knuckle fight in modern history. The Bare Knuckle Boxing Hall of Fame recognized this milestone and awarded the victor of this contest, Bec Rawlings, the National Police Gazette World Diamond Belt. Richard K. Fox would have been happy. However, controversy has never been far away from the sport's reincarnation. On August 20, 2021, BKFC was involved in controversy after the death of boxer Justin Thornton at BKFC 20. Thornton died as a result of spinal injury suffered during his BKFC debut.

He had a five-fight losing streak ahead of the fight, and the matchmaking and regulations were widely criticized following the news of his demise. Boxing has largely become the preserve of other ethnic groups in the United States in recent decades, with Hispanic fighters very much to the fore. As a sport there is no doubt that there are question marks over its very existence in the future. There have been too many Muhammad Alis and Jerry Quarrys over the years.

Appendix
The Rules of Boxing

Mr. Broughton's Seven Boxing Rules of 1743

1. That a square of a yard be chalked in the middle of the stage; and every fresh set-to after a fall, or being parted from the rails, each second is to bring his man to the square and place him opposite to the other; and till they are fairly set-to at the lines, it shall not be lawful for one to strike the other.

2. That in order to prevent any disputes as to the time a man lies after a fall, if the second does not bring his man to the side of the square within the space of half a minute he shall be deemed a beaten man.

3. That, in every main battle, no person whatever shall be upon the stage, except the principals and their seconds; the same rule to be observed in the bye-battles, except that in the latter Mr. Broughton is allowed to be upon the stage to keep decorum, and to assist gentlemen in getting to their places; provided always he does not interfere in the battle; and whoever presumes to infringe these rules to be turned immediately out of the house. Everybody is to quit the stage as soon as the champions are stripped, before they set-to.

4. That no champion be deemed beaten, unless he falls coming up to the line in the limited time; or that his own second declares him beaten. No second is to be allowed to ask his man's adversary any questions or advise him to give out.

5. That in the bye-battles, the winning man to have two-thirds of the money given, which shall be publicly divided upon the stage, notwithstanding any private agreement to the contrary.

6. That to prevent disputes, in every main battle, the principals shall, on the coming on the stage, choose from among the gentlemen present two umpires, who shall absolutely decided all disputes that may arise about the battle; and if the two umpires cannot agree, the said umpires to choose a third, who is to determine it.

7. That no person is to hit his adversary when he is down, or seize him by the ham, the breeches, or any part below the waist; a man on his knees to be reckoned down.

London Prize-Fight Rules 1853 (gradually revised from 1838)

1. That the ring shall be made on turf, and shall be four-and-twenty feet square, formed of eight stakes and ropes, the latter extending in double lines, the uppermost line being four feet from the ground, and the lower two feet from the ground. That in the center of the ring a mark be formed, to be termed a scratch; and that at two opposite corners, as may be selected, spaces be enclosed by other marks sufficiently large for the reception of the seconds and bottle-holders, to be entitled "the corners."

2. That each man shall be attended to the ring by a second and a bottle-holder, the former provided with a sponge and the latter with a bottle of water. That the combatants, on shaking hands, shall retire until the seconds of each have tossed for choice of position, which adjusted, the winner shall choose his corner according to the state of the wind or sun, and conduct his man thereto, the loser taking the opposite corner.

3. That each man shall be provided with a handkerchief of a color suitable to his own fancy, and that the seconds proceed to entwine these handkerchiefs at the upper end of one of the center stakes. That these handkerchiefs shall be called "the colors"; and that the winner of the battle at its conclusion shall be entitled to their possession, as the trophy of victory.

4. That two umpires shall be chosen by the seconds or backers to watch the progress of the battle, and take exception to any breach of the rules hereafter stated. That a referee shall be chosen by the umpires, unless otherwise agreed on, to whom all disputes shall be referred; and that the decision of this referee, whatever it may be, shall be final and strictly binding on all parties, whether as to the matter in dispute or the issue of the battle. That the umpires shall be provided with a watch, for the purpose of calling time; and that they mutually agree upon which this duty shall devolve, the call of that umpire only to be attended to, and no other person whatever to interfere in calling time. That the referee shall withhold all opinion till appealed to by the umpires, and that the umpires strictly abide by his decision without dispute.

5. That on the men being stripped, it shall be the duty of the seconds to examine their drawers, and if any objection arise as to insertion of improper substances therein, they shall appeal to their umpires, who, with the concurrence of the referee, shall direct what alterations shall be made.

6. That in future no spikes be used in fighting boots except those authorized by the Pugilistic Benevolent Association, which shall not exceed three-eighths of an inch from the sole of the boot, and shall not be less than one-eighth of an inch broad at the point; and, it shall be in the power of the referee to alter, or file in any way he pleases, spikes which shall not accord with the above dimensions, even to filing them away altogether.

7. That both men being ready, each man shall be conducted to that side of the scratch next his corner previously chosen; and the seconds on the one side and the men on the other, having shaken hands, the former shall immediately return to their corners, and there remain within the prescribed marks till the round be finished, on no pretense whatever approaching their principals during the round, under penalty of 5s. for each offense, at the option of the referee. The penalty, which will be strictly enforced, to go to the funds of the Association. The principal to be responsible for every fine inflicted on his second.

8. That at the conclusion of the round, when one or both of the men shall be down, the seconds and bottle-holders shall step forward and carry or conduct their principal to his corner, there affording him the necessary assistance, and no person whatever be permitted to interfere with this duty.

9. That at the expiration of thirty seconds (unless otherwise agreed upon) the umpire appointed shall cry "Time," upon which each man shall rise from the knee of his bottle-holder and walk to his own side of the scratch unaided, the seconds and the bottle-holders remaining at their corner; and that either man failing so to be at the scratch within eight seconds, shall be deemed to have lost the battle.

10. That on no consideration whatever shall any person be permitted to enter the ring during the battle, nor till it shall have been concluded; and that in the event of such unfair practice, or the ropes and stakes being disturbed or removed, it shall be in the power of the referee to award the victory to that man who in his honest opinion shall have the best of the contest.

11. That the seconds and bottle-holders shall not interfere, advise, or direct the adversary of their principal, and shall refrain from all offensive and irritating expressions, in all respects conducting themselves with order and decorum, and confine themselves to the diligent and careful discharge of their duties to their principals.

12. That in picking up their men, should the seconds or bottle-holders willfully injure the antagonist of their principal, the latter shall be deemed to have forfeited the battle on the decision of the referee.

13. That it shall be "a fair stand-up fight," and if either man shall willfully throw himself down without receiving a blow, whether blows shall have previously been exchanged or not, he shall be deemed to have lost the battle; but that this rule shall not apply to a man who in a close slips down from the grasp of his opponent to avoid punishment, or from obvious accident or weakness.

14. That butting with the head shall be deemed foul, and the party resorting to this practice shall be deemed to have lost the battle.

15. That a blow struck when a man is thrown or down, shall be deemed foul. That a man with one knee and one hand on the ground, or with both knees on the ground, shall be deemed down; and a blow given in either of those positions shall be considered foul, providing always, that when in such position, the man so down shall not himself strike or attempt to strike.

16. That a blow struck below the waistband shall be deemed foul, and that, in a close, seizing an antagonist below the waist, by the thigh, or otherwise, shall be deemed foul.

17. That all attempts to inflict injury by gouging, or tearing the flesh with the fingers or nails, and biting, shall be deemed foul.

18. That kicking, or deliberately falling on an antagonist, with the knees or otherwise when down, shall be deemed a foul.

19. That all bets shall be paid as the battle-money, after a fight, is awarded.

20. That no person, on any pretense whatever, shall be permitted to approach nearer the ring than ten feet, with the exception of the umpires and referee, and the persons appointed to take charge of the water or other refreshment for the combatants, who shall take their seats close to the corners selected by the seconds.

21. That due notice shall be given by the stakeholder of the day and place where the battle-money is to be given up, and that he be exonerated from all responsibility upon obeying the direction of the referee; and that all parties be strictly bound by these rules; and that in future all articles of agreement for a contest be entered into with a strict and willing adherence to the letter and spirit of these rules.

22. That in the event of magisterial or other interference, or in case of darkness coming on, the referee shall have the power to name the time and place for the next meeting, if possible, on the same day, or as soon after as may be.

23. That should the fight not be decided on the day, all bets, instead of being drawn, shall be put together and divided, unless the fight shall be resumed the same week, between Sunday and Sunday, in which case the bets shall stand and be decided by the event. That where the day named in the articles for a fight to come off is altered to another day in the same week, the bets shall stand. The battle-money shall remain in the hands of the stakeholder until fairly won or lost by a fight, unless a draw be mutually agreed upon.

24. That any pugilist voluntarily quitting the ring previous to the deliberate judgment of the referee being obtained, shall be deemed to have lost the fight.

25. That on an objection being made by the seconds or umpire, the men shall retire to their corners, and there remain until the decision of the appointed authorities shall be obtained; that if pronounced "foul," the battle shall be at an end, but if "fair," "time" shall be called by the party appointed, and the man absent from the scratch in eight seconds after shall be deemed to have lost the fight. The decision in all cases to be given promptly and irrevocably, for which purpose the umpires and the referee should be invariably close together.

26. That if in a rally at the ropes a man steps outside the ring, to avoid his antagonist or escape punishment, he shall forfeit the battle.

27. That the use of hard substances, such as stones, or sticks, or of resin, in the hand during the battle shall be deemed foul, and that on the requisition of the seconds, of either man, the accused shall open his hands for the examination of the referee.

28. That where a man shall have his antagonist across the ropes in such a position as to be helpless, and to endanger his life by strangulation or apoplexy, it shall be in the power of the referee to direct the seconds to take their man away, and thus conclude the round, and that the man or his seconds refusing to obey the direction of the referee, shall be deemed the loser.

29. That all stage fights be as nearly as possible in conformity with the fApporegoing rules.

The Marquess of Queensberry Rules

1. To be a fair stand-up boxing match in a 24-foot ring, or as near that size as practicable.
2. No wrestling or hugging allowed.
3. The rounds to be of three minutes' duration, and one minute's time between rounds.
4. If either man falls through weakness or otherwise, he must get up unassisted, 10 seconds to be allowed him to do so, the other man meanwhile to return to his corner, and when the fallen man is on his legs the round is to be resumed and continued until the three minutes have expired. If one man fails to come to the scratch in the 10 seconds allowed, it shall be in the power of the referee to give his award in favour of the other man.
5. A man hanging on the ropes in a helpless state, with his toes off the ground, shall be considered down.
6. No seconds or any other person to be allowed in the ring during the rounds.
7. Should the contest be stopped by any unavoidable interference, the referee to name the time and place as soon as possible for finishing the contest; so that the match must be won and lost, unless the backers of both men agree to draw the stakes.
8. The gloves to be fair-sized boxing gloves of the best quality and new.
9. Should a glove burst, or come off, it must be replaced to the referee's satisfaction.
10. A man on one knee is considered down and if struck is entitled to the stakes.
11. No shoes or boots with springs allowed.
12. The contest in all other respects to be governed by revised rules of the London Prize Ring.

Chapter Notes

Preface

1. "Boxers of Many Races," *National Police Gazette*, August 22, 1903, 3.
2. He took his ring name from his two idols, Irish heavyweight contender Tom Sharkey and heavyweight champion Jack Dempsey, to gain acceptance in the Irish-dominated boxing world of Boston.
3. Theodore Dreiser, *A Book About Myself* (New York: Boni and Liveright, 1922); Elliott J. Gorn, *The Manly Art, Bare Knuckle Prize Fighting in America* (Ithaca, N.Y.: Cornell University Press, 1986), 1.

Introduction

1. "How Notre Dame became the Fighting Irish," University of Notre Dame, accessed July 15, 2023, https://www.nd.edu/stories/whats-in-a-name.
2. Dave Hannigan, "America at Large, Fenway Park Steeped in Ireland's Own Troubled Past," *The Irish Times*, September 16, 2015.
3. Daniel Taylor, "Notre Dame, Nativism and the "Fighting Irish," Ancient Order of Hibernians, October 13, 2020, https://aoh.com/2020/10/13/notre-dame-nativism-and-the-fighting-irish.
4. Dave Hannigan, "Notre Dame's Fighting Irish Leprechaun Needs Its Ass Kicked," *The Irish Times*, July 9, 2010.
5. *Ibid*.
6. *Ibid*.
7. Jack Beresford, "Notre Dame University Defends Use of 'Fighting Irish' Nickname and leprechaun mascot," *The Irish Post*, July 19, 2020.
8. Taylor, "Notre Dame, Nativism and the "Fighting Irish."
9. *Ibid*.
10. *Ibid*.
11. "How Notre Dame Became the Fighting Irish," University of Notre Dame.
12. Neil Cosgrave, "Claims of Notre Dame Leprechaun Offensiveness is Media Malarkey," Ancient Order of Hibernians, August 26, 2021. https://aoh.com/2021/08/26/claims-of-notre-dame-leprechaun-offensiveness-is-media-malarkey.
13. "How Notre Dame became the Fighting Irish." University of Notre Dame.
14. Neil Cosgrave, Ancient Order of Hibernians.
15. Josh Slagter, "Lou Holtz Upset over Calls to Change Notre Dame's 'Fighting Irish' Nickname," July 14, 2020. https://www.mlive.com/sports/2020/07/lou-holtz-upset-over-calls-to-change-notre-dames-fighting-irish-nickname.html.
16. "How Notre Dame became the Fighting Irish," University of Notre Dame.
17. Meghan A. Conley and Billy Hawkins, *"From Apes and Thick Micks to the Fighting Irish: Cultural Misappropriation at the University of Notre Dame"* (Athens: University of Georgia Press, 2012), 12. https://getd.libs.uga.edu/pdfs/conley_meghan_a_201608_phd.pdf.

Chapter One

1. Patrick Timony, "The Great Prize Fight Between Tom Hyer and Yankee Sullivan for $10,000," in *The American Fistiana, Containing a History of Prize Fighting in the United States, with All the Principal Battles for the Last Forty Years, and a Full and Precise Account of All the Particulars of the Great $10,000 Match Between Sullivan and Hyer, with Their Method of Training for the Fight* (New York: H. Johnson, 1846), 3–4.
2. Robert Snell, "Yankee Sullivan v Hammer Lane," *BoxRec*, August 25, 2007. https://boxrec.com/forum/viewtopic.php?t=68442.
3. "The Prize Fight," *New York Daily Herald*, February 9, 1849.
4. Timony, *The American Fistiana*, 1.
5. Timony, *The American Fistiana*, 3.
6. Horace Greeley, "The Slaughter of McCoy," *New York Tribune*, September 19, 1842.
7. Claudia Thomas, *Hyer and Allied Families: Historical & Personal Accounts—Notable & Notorious* (Independently published, 2022), 128–168.
8. Ed Hughes, "Remember Tom Hyer," *Austin American*, February 21,1925. The Broughton Rules are attached as an appendix.
9. "Hyer and Sullivan Old Time Fighters," *The Indianapolis Star*, February 29, 1910.
10. George Siler, *Inside Facts on Pugilism* (Chicago: Laird & Lee Publishers, 1907), 144.
11. *The National Police Gazette*, June 12, 1880.

12. Timony, *The American Fistiana*, 2.
13. Timony, *The American Fistiana*, 3 (advertisement—sometimes referred to as a card in the literature—appeared on June 1 in the *New York Herald* answered in the following day's edition)
14. *Ibid.*
15. *Ibid.*, 10.
16. *Ibid.*
17. Full account of this fight at *Fistiana*.
18. *Ibid.*,11.
19. *Ibid.*, 12.
20. *Ibid.*
21. *Ibid.*
22. *Ibid.*,13.
23. *New York Herald* cited in Elliott J. Gorn, "The First American Championship Prizefight," *OAH Magazine of History* 7 (Summer 1992), *Fistiana*, 25.
24. A. Winch, *Life and Battles of Yankee Sullivan, Embracing Full and Accurate Reports of the Fights with Hammer Lane, Tom Sector, Harry Bell, Bob Caunt, Tom Hyer, and John Morrissey* (Philadelphia: A. Winch, 1854), 29.
25. *St. Louis Globe-Democrat*, August 23, 1880.
26. *National Police Gazette*. July 3, 1880, 14.
27. Timony, *The American Fistiana*, 25.
28. *Ibid.*
29. A hat made of beaver or rabbit fur.
30. *Ibid.*, 26.
31. "The Fight Between Hyers and Sullivan," *Milwaukee Sentinel*, February 9, 1849.
32. Elliott J. Gorn, *The Manly Art: Bare-Knuckle Prize Fighting in America* (Ithaca, N.Y.: Cornell University Press, 2010), 36.
33. *Ibid.*
34. *Ibid.*
35. *Ibid.*
36. *Ibid..*
37. *Milwaukee Sentinel and Gazette*, March 14, 1849.
38. *American Celt*, September 24, 1856.
39. Kasia Boddy, *Boxing, A Cultural History* (London: Reaktion Books. 2009), 28.
40. Gorn, *The Manly Art: Bare-Knuckle Prize Fighting in America*, 37.
41. Gerald R. Gems, *Boxing: A Concise History of the Sweet Science* (Lanham, Md.: Rowman & Littlefield Publishers, 2014), 19.
42. "Death and Vigilante Committee in Suicide of Yankee Sullivan," *The Placer Herald*, June 7, 1856.
43. "Yankee Sullivan No More," *New York Times*, June 30, 1856.
44. Kenneth Bridgham, *International Boxing Research Organization Journal*, December 2022.

Chapter Two

1. "Old Smoke Was a Fiery Character," *The Irish Voice*, March 26, 2021. https://www.theirishvoice.com/feature/old-smoke-was-a-fiery-character.
2. James C. Nicholson, *The Notorious John Morrissey: How a Bare-Knuckle Brawler Became a Congressman and Founded Saratoga Race Course* (Lexington: University Press of Kentucky, 2016).
3. Rodney P. Carlisle, "Morrissey, John (1831–1878), Gambler, Prizefighter, and U.S. Congressman," *American National Biography Online* (Oxford University Press). https://www.anb.org/display/10.1093/anb/9780198606697.001.0001/anb-9780198606697-e-0500547;jsessionid=7AB1850ED11144EF9E08B88E7969182D.
4. *Chicago Daily Tribune*, May 3, 1878.
5. *San Francisco Call*, May 8, 1910.
6. "Rambler Follows Story of Morrissey to West Coast Scenes," *Evening Star*, October 3, 1926.
7. *Ibid.*
8. *Ibid.*
9. *New York Clipper*, October 15, 1853.
10. They are included as appendices.
11. *San Francisco Call*, May 8, 1910.
12. "Prize Fight between Sullivan and Morrissey," *Daily Evening Star*, October 14, 1853.
13. "The Prize Fight between Morrissey and Sullivan," *The Jackson Standard*, October 27, 1853.
14. "Morrissey's Trial," *New York Clipper*, July 22, 1854.
15. "Prize Fight in New York," *The Lancaster Ledger*, August 9, 1854.
16. *Daily Evening Star*, July 28, 1854.
17. Joseph Williams, "The Real Bill the Butcher from 'Gangs of New York' Was a Xenophobic Pugilist With a Short Temper," allthatsinteresting, accessed October 3, 2019, https://allthatsinteresting.com/bill-the-butcher.
18. *The New York Herald*, February 26, 1855.
19. Eric Stanway, *Bill the Butcher: The Life and Death of William Poole* (San Bernardino, Calif.: EUM Books, 2019), 155.
20. "The Championship of America," *New York Clipper*, October 30, 1858.
21. "Burial of John C. Heenan," *New York Clipper*, November 8, 1873.
22. Fred J. Henning, *Fights for the Championship: The Men and Their Times* (London: Licensed Victuallers' Gazette, 1896), 367.
23. *Ibid.*
24. "The Championship of America," *New York Clipper*, October 30, 1858.
25. "The Great Prize Fight," *Wheeling Daily Intelligencer*, October 25, 1858.
26. *Ibid.*
27. "The Championship," *Bell's Life in London and Sporting Chronicle*, April 17, 1860.
28. Fred Dowling, *The Championship of England. Being a Continuation of "Fights for the Championship. To which is Added a Brief History of Tom Sayers and (J. C. Heenan) the Benicia Boy, and an Account of Their Chief Prize Battles* (London: "Bell's Life" Office, 1860), 74–80.
29. Patrick R. Redmond, *The Irish and the Making of American Sport 1835–1920* (McFarland, 2015), 23.
30. *New York Herald*, October 21, 1858.
31. *Ibid.*

32. *Springfield Weekly Republican,* October 23, 1858.
33. "The Championship of America," *New York Clipper,* October 30, 1858.
34. *Springfield Weekly Republican,* October 23, 1858.
35. *Ibid.*
36. Lambert A. Wilmer. *Our Press Gang; or, a Complete Exposition of the Corruptions and Crimes of the American Newspapers* (J.T. Lloyd, 1860), 168.
37. "The Fight of the Century," *The New York Herald,* October 22, 1858.
38. "John Morrissey vs John Heenan," *The New York Herald,* October 22, 1858:
39. A quarterstaff (plural quarterstaffs or quarterstaves) is a traditional European pole weapon, which was especially prominent in England during the period. The term is generally accepted to refer to a shaft of hardwood from 6 to 9 feet (1.8 to 2.7 m) long, sometimes with a metal tip, ferrule, or spike at one or both ends.
40. Redmond, *The Irish and the Making of American Sport 1835–1920.*
41. *Springfield Weekly Republican,* October 3, 1858. The Kilkenny cats are a fabled pair of cats from County Kilkenny (or Kilkenny city in particular) in Ireland, who fought each other so ferociously that only their tails remained at the end of the battle.
42. "Morrissey, The American Pugilist," *Cork Examiner,* April 30, 1860.
43. "Arrival of John Morrissey," *Bell's Life in London and Sporting Chronicle,* April 1, 1860.
44. "John Morrissey as a Sporting Man," *New Orleans Daily Crescent,* August 31, 1860.
45. "Losses of Gambling—A Caution," *Chicago Daily Tribune,* January 22, 1862.
46. Edward Hotaling, *They're Off!: Horse Racing at Saratoga* (Syracuse, N.Y.: Syracuse University Press, 1995), 41–50.
47. "The Funeral of John Morrissey," *The Toledo Chronicle,* May 9, 1878.
48. *Ibid.*
49. *Ibid.*

Chapter Three

1. *Wilkes' Spirit of the Times,* April 7, 1860.
2. Peter Duffy, "America's First Sports Superstar How the Bare-Knuckle Fighter John C. Heenan United the Country before the Civil War," *Slate,* May 5, 2010. https://slate.com/culture/2010/05/john-c-heenan-america-s-first-sports-superstar.html.
3. Duffy, "America's First Sports Superstar.".
4. *Harper's Weekly,* April 5, 1860; *The Manchester Guardian,* April 16, 1860.
5. Gorn, *The Manly Art: Bare-Knuckle Prize Fighting in America,* 156.
6. *Ibid.,* 157.
7. *Philadelphia Press,* May 2, 1860.
8. *New York Times,* March 17, 1860.
9. "Chivalry of the Prize Ring," *People's Magazine: An Illustrated Miscellany for All Classes,* February 9, 1867.
10. Boddy, *Boxing: A Cultural History,* 79.
11. George Mifflin Dallas, *A Series of Letters from London during the Years 1856, '57, '58, '59 and '60, Vol. 1* (Philadelphia: J. B. Lippincott & Co, 1869), 211.
12. Boddy, *Boxing: A Cultural History,* 80.
13. Henry Miles Downes, *Pugilistica: The History of British Boxing Containing Lives of the Most Celebrated Pugilists,* Volume 3 (1906), 34. Bittock is a word most commonly used in Scotland to mean a little bit or a short distance.
14. *Ibid.,* 35.
15. Frank Keating, "Heenan v Sayers: The Fight That Changed Boxing Forever," *The Guardian,* April 14, 2010.
16. *Ibid.*
17. *Ibid.*
18. *Burke's Peerage* was established by John Burke in London in 1826 during the reign of King George IV. Since then, it has become the definitive guide to the genealogy and heraldry of historical families worldwide.

Debrett's Peerage, in full *Debrett's Peerage and Baronetage,* guide to the British peerage (titled aristocracy), was first published in London in 1802 by John Debrett as *Peerage of England, Scotland, and Ireland. Debrett's Peerage* contains information about the royal family, the peerage, Privy Counsellors, Scottish Lords of Session, baronets, and chiefs of clans in Scotland.

19. Miles Downes, *Pugilistica: The History of British Boxing Containing Lives of the Most Celebrated Pugilists,* 38.
20. Mitchell Rawson, "The Bare-Knuckle Legacy of Boxing," *Sports Illustrated,* February 20, 1961.
21. *New York Herald,* April 18, 1870.
22. Duffy, "America's First Sports Superstar How the Bare-Knuckle Fighter John C. Heenan United the Country before the Civil War," *Slate,* May 5, 2010, https://slate.com/culture/2010/05/john-c-heenan-america-s-first-sports-superstar.html.
23. Frank McNally, "Fury Brothers—Frank McNally on the History of Boxing, James Joyce, and the Curse of Cold Guinness," *The Irish Times,* February 25, 2020.
24. James Joyce, *Ulysses* (Paris: Shakespeare and Company, 1922), 831.
25. "Departure of John C. Heenan," *Bell's Life in London and Sporting Chronicle,* July 8, 1860.
26. *Ibid.*
27. Henning, *Fights for the Championship: The Men and Their Times,* 470.
28. "The Great Fight, This Day," *London Evening Standard,* December 10, 1863.
29. "Train Accident," *London Evening Standard,* June 29, 1864.
30. Adah Isaacs Menken, *Infelicia* (Philadelphia:

J.B. Lippincott & Co, 1868), 12. https://quod.lib.umich.edu/a/amverse/BAD8997.0001.001?view=toc.

31. "Tammany," *The New York Herald*, February 18, 1870.

32. *South London Chronicle*, November 15, 1873.

Chapter Four

1. "The Cowardly Englishman." The National Library of Scotland, English Ballads. New song called The cowardly Englishman—Ireland—English ballads—National Library of Scotland

2. "Joe Coburn Dies," *The Sun*, New York, December 7, 1890.

3. "Joe Coburn," *The San Francisco Call*, December 7, 1890.

4. *New York Clipper*, November 28, 1857.

5. *New York Clipper*, May 25, 1862.

6. Jamey Casey, "Joe Coburn: 125 Years," *Irish Post*, December 6, 2015.

7. *New York Clipper*, May 10, 1856.

8. Jamey Casey, "Joe Coburn: 125 Years," *Irish Post*, December 6, 2015.

9. According to the *Clipper*, Coburn–Price was the longest fight conducted in America to date, lasting three hours and twenty-five minutes. *New York Clipper*, May 10, 1856

10. *New York Clipper*, May 24, 1856.

11. *New York Clipper*, November 28, 1857.

12. Ernest A. McKay, *Civil War and New York City* (Syracuse, N.Y.: Syracuse University Press, 1991), 116.

13. *New York Herald*, December 13,1858.

14. *New York Times*, December 30, 1858, and *New York Herald*, December 30, 1858.

15. *Ibid.*, both.

16. *New York Times*, May 9, 1859.

17. *New York Herald*, January 31, 1863.

18. *New York Herald*, May 6, 1853.

19. *New York Clipper*, May 16, 1853.

20. Nat Fleischer, *The Heavyweight Championship: An Informal History of Heavyweight Boxing from 1719 to the Present Day* (New York: G.P. Putnam's Sons, 1949), 58.

21. *New York Clipper*, July 18, 1863.

22. *New York Clipper*, March 26, 1864.

23. *New York Clipper*, April 23, 1864; *Hartford Daily Courant*, March 16, 1864.

24. *New York Clipper*, May 21, 1864.

25. *New York Clipper*, March 5, 1864.

26. *New York Clipper*, May 21, 1864.

27. Casey, "Joe Coburn: 125 Years."

28. *Ibid.*

29. Downes Miles, *Pugilista*, accessed October 4, 2023, https://www.gutenberg.org/cache/epub/59465/pg59465-images.html (no page numbers provided).

30. *Ibid.*

31. *New York Clipper*, October 22, 1864. See also *New York Clipper*, November 5, 1864.

32. James M. Healy, *The Mercier Book of Old Irish Street Ballads*, Volume 3. (Dublin: Mercier Press, 1968)

33. Henning, *Fights for the Championship: The Men and Their Times, Volume 2*, 49.

34. Casey, "Joe Coburn: 125 Years."

35. "Sullivan vs. Coburn Tonight," *Buffalo Evening News*, January 20, 1883; "Sullivan and Coburn," *The San Francisco Examiner*, January 31, 1883; "But No Real Harm Resulted," *The Boston Globe*, March 20, 1883; "Mace Stock on the Decline, " *The Boston Globe*, April 19, 1883;"Slade and Coburn," *The Times*, Philadelphia, April 24, 1883.

36. "Joe Coburn Arrested and Discharged," *The Republic*, May 18, 1885.

37. "Clarke Beats Coburn," *Times Union*, Brooklyn, New York, December 15, 1888.

Chapter Five

1. Sean Kearns, "James Elliot," *Dictionary of Irish Biography* (Dublin: Royal Irish Academy, 2015). https://www.dib.ie/biography/elliott-james-a2906.

2. Pauline Murphy, "Athlone Born Jimmy Elliot—The Heavyweight Champion of the World," *Athlone Advertiser* April 19, 2018.

3. *Ibid.*

4. *New York Clipper*, January 18, 1862.

5. *Ibid.*

6. *New York Clipper*, May 23, 1863.

7. *Ibid.*

8. *Ibid.*

9. *Trenton State Gazette*, May 15, 1863.

10. *New York Clipper*, January 9, 1864.

11. *New York Clipper*, May 14, 1864.

12. *New York Clipper*, June 4, 1864; *New York Clipper*, June 11, 1864.

13. Sean Kearns, "James Elliot," *Dictionary of Irish Biography* (Dublin:Royal Irish Academy, 2015). https://www.dib.ie/biography/elliott-james-a2906, accessed on January 20, 2023.

14. *Ibid.*

15. *Ibid.*

16. J.B. McCormack, *The Square: Stories of the Prize Ring* (1897), cited in
Sean Kearns, "James Elliot," *Dictionary of Irish Biography* (Dublin: Royal Irish Academy, 2015). https://www.dib.ie/biography/elliott-james-a2906)

17. Pauline Murphy, "Athlone Born Jimmy Elliot—The Heavyweight Champion of the World," *Athlone Advertiser*, April 19, 2018.

Chapter Six

1. "Mike McCoole," *The Evening Telegraph*, Philadelphia, August 31, 1867.

2. "Mike McCoole," *The Times Picayune*, New Orleans, October 18, 1886.

3. *The New York Times*, September 1, 1867.

4. *Ibid.*

5. "Mike McCoole vs Tom Allen," *New York Herald*, June 16, 1869.
6. *Ibid.*
7. "Pugilism," *New York Daily Herald*, June 16, 1869
8. "Spoiling for a Fight," *Ottawa Daily Citizen*, September 23, 1873.
9. *The New York Times*, September 24, 1873.
10. *Daily Commonwealth*, September 24, 1873; *The Brooklyn Daily*, September 24, 1873.
11. "A Man Murdered," *The Fort Wayne Journal Gazette*, October 31, 1873.
12. "A Prizefighter Named Manley," *The Perry County Democrat*, Bloomfield, Pennsylvania, November 5, 1873.
13. "Death of Pugilist McCoole," *The Baltimore Sun*, October 19, 1886.
14. *"The New Orleans Daily,"* November 19, 1878.
15. "Latest News," *La Plata Home Press*, Missouri, October 2, 1880.
16. "Mike McCoole Drowned," *The Daily Gazette*, Wilmington, Del., September 30, 1880.
17. "Mike McCoole," *The Times Picayune*, New Orleans, October 18, 1886.

Chapter Seven

1. Dave Hannigan, "America at Large: How Trojan Giant Paddy Ryan Helped Change the Face of Boxing, Tipperary-Born Boxer to Take His Place in the International Boxing Hall of Fame," *The Irish Times*, March 25, 2020, https://www.irishtimes.com/sport/other-sports/america-at-large-how-trojan-giant-paddy-ryan-helped-change-the-face-of-boxing-1.4210981.
2. "Crimes and Casualties," *The Salem Monitor*, November 29, 1873.
3. "Fight for the Championship of the World," *New York Daily News*, September 8, 1876.
4. Walter Kelly, "The Wide World of Sport," *The Buffalo Courier*, December 13, 1900.
5. Harold William Thompson, *Body, Boots and Britches*, cited in Dave Hannigan, *The Irish Times*, March 25, 2020, https://www.irishtimes.com/sport/other-sports/america-at-large-how-trojan-giant-paddy-ryan-helped-change-the-face-of-boxing-1.4210981.
6. "The Goss–Ryan Fight," *Pittsburgh Daily Post*, June 1, 1880.
7. "Joe Goss and Paddy Ryan," *The St. Paul Globe*, May 30, 1880.
8. C. Robert Barnett, "Goss–Ryan Heavyweight Fight," in *e-WV: The West Virginia Encyclopedia*, July 14, 2011, https://www.wvencyclopedia.org/articles/2135.
9. *New York Sun*, May 9, 1880.
10. *New York Times*, May 19, 1880; *New York Sun*, May 19, 1880.
11. *New York Tribune*, May 25, 1880.
12. *Wheeling Daily Intelligencer*, June 2, 1880.
13. *Ibid.*
14. "Great Prize Fight in America," *Glasgow Herald*, June 3, 1880.
15. "Hunting the Pugs," *Wheeling Daily Intelligencer*, June 5, 1880.
16. Guy Reel, *The National Police Gazette and the Making of the Modern American Man, 1879–1906* (New York: Palgrave Macmillan, 2006).
17. The term "yellow journalism" came from a popular *New York World* comic called "Hogan's Alley," which featured a yellow-dressed character named the "the yellow kid." Determined to compete with Pulitzer's *World* in every way, rival *New York Journal* owner William Randolph Hearst copied Pulitzer's sensationalist style and even hired "Hogan's Alley" artist R.F. Outcault away from the *World*. In response, Pulitzer commissioned another cartoonist to create a second yellow kid. Soon, the sensationalist press of the 1890s became a competition between the "yellow kids," and the journalistic style was coined "yellow journalism."
18. Tom Hunt, "John L Sullivan: The Son of Kerry Who Became America's First Sporting Icon," *Irish Examiner*, February 5, 2021.
19. *Ibid.*
20. *Police Gazette Sporting Annual* (New York: Richard K. Fox Publishing Co., 1896–1912).
21. *Ibid.*
22. Tom Wolfe, Foreword, *The Police Gazette*, ed. Gene Smith and Jayne Barry (New York: Simon and Schuster 1972),10.
23. Fred Henning, *Fights for the Championship: The Men and Their Times* (London: Licensed Victuallers' Gazette Office, 1902).
24. *Ibid.*
25. Robert Green Ingersoll and Herman E Kittredge, *The Works of Robert G. Ingersoll, Vol. 8* (New York: Dresden Publishing, 1900), 580.
26. *New York Times*, September 2, 1893.
27. *St. Paul Daily News*, February 15, 1890.
28. *Overland Monthly and Out West Magazine*, no. 201, September 1899.
29. Elliott J. Gorn, "John L. Sullivan: The Champion of All Champions," *VQR: A National Journal of Literature and Discussion*, Autumn 1986, https://www.vqronline.org/essay/john-l-sullivan-champion-all-champions.
30. *The Fort Worth Daily Gazette*, February 19, 1887.
31. *Milwaukee Daily Sentinel*, June 2, 1880.
32. *Daily Picayune*, September 18, 1890.
33. *Boston Daily Advertiser*, May 27, 1891.
34. *San Francisco Morning Call*, October 23, 1892.
35. Gorn, *The Manly Art*, 164.
36. T.S. Andrews, *Ring Battles of the Centuries* (Tom Andrews Record Book Co, 1924), 51.
37. *Chicago Tribune*, March 19, 1897.
38. *New York Times*, March 13, 1897.
39. *Chicago Tribune*, July 16, 1910.
40. Walt Whitman, *The New York Atlas*, October 10, 1858.
41. Walt Whitman, *Leaves of Grass* (London: Oxford University Press, 1990)

42. John Boyle O'Reilly, *Ethics of Boxing and Manly Sport* (Boston: Ticknor and Company, 1888).
43. *Ibid.*; Jeffrey T. Sammons *Beyond the Ring: The Role of Boxing in American Society* (Champagne: University of Illinois Press, 1990).
44. *Ibid.*
45. *Ibid.*
46. Dave Roos, "How Teddy Roosevelt Crafted an Image of American Manliness," www.history.com, 2009, accessed October 4, 2023; https://www.history.com/news/teddy-roosevelt-american-manliness-rough-riders.
47. Roosevelt, *The Strenuous Life*, 319.
48. *Ibid.*, 42.
49. G. Stanley Hall, *Life and Confessions of a Psychologist* (New York: D. Appleton and Company, 1923), 578–579.
50. Oliver Wendell Holmes, "The Autocrat of the Breakfast Table," *Atlantic Monthly*, May 1958, 1881.
51. *Ibid.*
52. Charles Eliot Norton, "Harvard University in 1890," *Harper's New Monthly Magazine*, 81, no. 484 (September 1890).
53. Leroy Ashby, *With Amusement for All: A History of American Popular Culture since 1830* (Lexington: University of Kentucky Press, 2006).
54. Theodore Roosevelt, *An Autobiography* (New York: The Macmillan Company, 1913), 44.
55. Theodore Roosevelt, *Professionalism in Sports*, 191.
56. Boyle O'Reilly, *Ethics of Boxing and Manly Sport*, 166.
57. Richard J. Sullivan, "On This Day: Irish Poet, Writer, and Nationalist John Boyle O'Reilly Died in 1890," Irishcentral.com, August 10, 2022, https://www.irishcentral.com/roots/history/irish-american-john-boyle-oreilly.
58. Boyle O'Reilly, *Ethics of Boxing and Manly Sport*, 166.
59. *Ibid.*
60. *Ibid.*, 167.
61. *Ibid.*, 76.
62. James Jeffrey Roche and Mary Murphy O'Reilly, *Life of John Boyle O'Reilly: Together with His Complete Poems and Speeches* (New York: Cassell Publishing Company, 1891), 379.
63. *St. Paul Daily Globe*, July 21, 1891. Also see James Moynihan, *The Life of Archbishop John Ireland* (New York: Harper, 1976), 256.
64. *New York Times*, July 20, 1891.
65. *New York Times*, October 13, 1893.
66. *Chicago Tribune*, September 11, 1892.
67. *Daily Nevada State Journal*, February 4, 1897; *San Francisco Call*, March 15, 1897.
68. "The Reverend John Tallmadge Bergen to the Editor," *New York Times*, October 6, 1893.
69. *St. Paul Daily Globe*, July 21, 1891.
70. *New York Times*, September 25, 1893.
71. *Boston Investigator*, August 19, 1891.
72. *New York Times*, October 2, 1893.
73. *Milwaukee Sentinel*, September 5, 1892.

Chapter Eight

1. *New York Times*, July 21, 1989, http://www.nytimes.com/1989/07/21/sports/sports-of-the-times-tyson-ali-armstrong-and-john-l.html
2. Christopher Klein, *Strong Boy: The Life and Times of John L. Sullivan, America's First Sports Hero* (Lanham, Md.: Lyons Press, 2015), 4.
3. Klein, *Strong Boy*, 5; A term used to describe the social aristocracy of the Massachusetts families enriched from the trade in codfish.
4. Klein, *Strong Boy*, 16.
5. Klein, *Strong Boy*, 11.
6. Geoffrey. C. Ward, *Unforgivable Blackness: The Rise and Fall of Jack Johnson* (New York: Alfred A. Knopf, 2004), 16.
7. Ward, *Unforgivable Blackness*, 16.
8. Klein, *Strong Boy*, 11.
9. Michael T. Isenberg, *John L. Sullivan and His America* (Champaign: University of Illinois Press, 1994), 33.
10. Klein, *Strong Boy*, 13.
11. David L Hudson, *Boxing in America: An Autopsy* (New York: Praeger, 2012).
12. Hudson, *Boxing in America: An Autopsy*.
13. There is an account of Mahan's life and career at a later point in this book.
14. Klein, *Strong Boy*, 30.
15. *Ibid.*
16. Patrick Connor, "Sullivan vs Ryan 1882," *Boxiana*, February 7, 2020.
17. Klein, *Strong Boy*, 41.
18. Hudson, *Boxing in America: An Autopsy*, 5
19. *Ibid.*
20. *Ibid.*
21. *Ibid.*
22. Mark Duncan, "John L. Sullivan & the Making of an Irish-American Sporting Legend," *Century Ireland*, March, 2018, accessed October 5, 2023, https://www.rte.ie/centuryireland/images/uploads/further-reading/John_L_Sullivan__the_Making_of_an_Irish-American_Sporting_Legend_by_Mark_Duncan.pdf.
23. Hudson, *op. cit.*
24. John Boyle O'Reilly, "The Prize Fight,"*Boston Pilot*, February 18, 1882.
25. Hudson, *op. cit.*
26. Patrick Connor, "Sullivan vs Mitchell," *Fight City.com*, May 14, 2022, https://www.thefightcity.com/may-14-1883-sullivan-vs-mitchell-johnl-sullivan-the-boston-strong-boy-charlie-mitchell-pugilism-boxing-boston-queensbury-rules.
27. *The Enquirer*, April 1, 1883.
28. Connor, "Sullivan vs Mitchell." The schottische is a partnered country dance of German origin, and was one of the many popular dances of the Victorian era. It is most often composed in 2/4 time, and is known for including a hop at the end of the main melodic phrase.
29. Connor, "Sullivan vs Mitchell."
30. *Ibid.*
31. Christopher Klein, "John L. Sullivan Fights America," April 30, 2014, *The Public*

Domain Review, accessed October 5, 2023, https://publicdomainreview.org/essay/john-l-sullivan-fights-america.
32. *Ibid.*
33. *Ibid.*
34. *Ibid.*
35. *Ibid.*
36. Hudson, *Boxing in America: An Autopsy,* 6.
37. *Ibid.,* 7.
38. *Ibid.*
39. Klein, *Strong Boy,* 92.
40. *Ibid.*
41. *Ibid.,* 98.
42. *New York Times,* April 30, 1905.
43. Beston, *The Boxing Kings: When American Heavyweights Ruled the Ring,* 10.
44. Hudson, *Boxing in America: An Autopsy,* 7.
45. "John L. Sullivan: The First Irish American Boxing Champion and 'The Hand That Shook the World," *IrishIdentity.com,* accessed October 5, 2023, http://www.irishidentity.com/geese/stories/sullivan.htm.
46. The stone was put into a tower of the Blarney Castle in 1446 and has become one of Ireland's most successful tourist attractions. As the legend goes, if one kisses the stone, one is said to be bestowed with the gift of eloquence and the skill of flattery.
47. *Ibid.*
48. *Ibid.*
49. Sullivan, "The Life and Reminiscences of a 19th Century Gladiator."
50. "The Charles Mitchell v. John L. Sullivan draw belt," *thehistoryblog,* July 31, 2015, http://www.thehistoryblog.com/archives/37553.
51. *Ibid.*
52. *Ibid.*
53. Beston, *The Boxing Kings: When American Heavyweights Ruled the Ring,* 11.
54. Klein, *Strong Boy,* 55.
55. Beston, *Ibid.,* 8.
56. *Ibid.*
57. *Ibid.*
58. Isenberg, *John L. Sullivan and His America,* 55.
59. Klein, *Strong Boy,* 54.
60. *Ibid.*
61. *Ibid.*
62. *Ibid.,* 118.
63. Frank Butler, *A History of Boxing in Britain* (London: Littlehampton Book Services, 1972), 5.
64. Beston, *The Boxing Kings: When American Heavyweights Ruled the Ring,* 1.
65. *Ibid.,* 8.
66. *Ibid.*
67. *Ibid.*
68. *Ibid.*
69. *Ibid.*
70. *New York Times,* July 9, 1889.
71. Vachel Lindsay, "John L. Sullivan, The Strong Boy of Boston," in *Collected Poems* (New York: Macmillan, 1925).
72. Hudson, *Boxing in America: An Autopsy,* 9.
73. *Ibid.*
74. Isenberg, *John L. Sullivan and His America,* 13.
75. *Ibid.*
76. *Ibid.*

Chapter Nine

1. Patrick Myler, *Gentleman: Jim Corbett, the Truth behind a Boxing Legend* (London: Robson, 1998), 46.
2. James Rogers, "How Irish American Athletes Slugged Their Way to Respectability What it Means to be an American," *A National Conversation Hosted by the Smithsonian and Arizona State University,* May 18, 2017, https://www.whatitmeanstobeamerican.org/identities/how-irish-american-athletes-slugged-their-way-to-respectability.
3. Myler, *Gentleman: Jim Corbett,* 46.
4. Mark Twain, *Selected Letters,* ed. Charles Neider (New York: Book Sales, 1982), 224 cited in Boddy, *Boxing: A Cultural History,* 113.
5. Myler, *Gentleman: Jim Corbett,* 46.
6. Patrick Myler, "Gentleman Jim Won over the Irish," *Irish Independent,* July 7, 2012.
7. James Silas Rogers, *Irish-American Autobiography: The Divided Hearts of Athletes, Priests, Pilgrims, and More* (Washington, D.C.: Catholic University of America Press, 2010), accessed on October 5, 2023, https://books.google.ie/books?id=ldSOnQAACAAJ&pg=PT5&source=gbs_selected_pages&cad=1#v=onepage&q&f=false, no page numbers given.
8. Greg L. Hamon, "A Lesson in Grit From the Greatest Heavyweight Champion You've Never Heard Of," October 26, 2014, https://greglhamon.com/ Https://greglhamon.com/a-lesson-in-grit-from-the-greatest-heavyweight-champion-youve-never-heard-of.
9. Beston, *The Boxing Kings: When American Heavyweights Ruled the Ring,* 19.
10. *New York Times,* September 2, 1892.
11. Hudson, *Boxing in America: An Autopsy,* 10.
12. *Ibid.*
13. *Ibid.*
14. Gorn, *The Manly Art: Bare-Knuckle Prize Fighting in America.*
15. Jeffrey T Sammons, *Beyond the Ring: The Role of Boxing in American Society* (Champaign: University of Illinois Press, reprint edition, 1990), 17.
16. *Ibid.*
17. "'Gentleman Jim' Corbett Knocks Out John L. Sullivan, 1892," *EyeWitness to History,* accessed on January 22, 2023, http://www.eyewitnesstohistory.com/corbett.htm.
18. James John Corbett, *The Roar of the Crowd: The True Tale of the Rise and Fall of a Champion* (New York: Grosset & Dunlap, 1926), cited in Betson, *The Boxing Kings: When American Heavyweights Ruled the Ring,* 261.

19. Isenberg, *John L. Sullivan and His America,* 318.
20. *Overland Monthly and Out West Magazine,* October 1892, 447.
21. Isenberg, *John L. Sullivan and His America,* 318.
22. *Ibid.,* 318.
23. Hudson, *Boxing in America: An Autopsy,* 11.
24. *Ibid.,* 21.
25. *Boston Investigator,* September 18, 1889.
26. *New Jersey Morning Call,* May 1906.
27. Corbett, *The Roar of the Crowd,* 166.
28. Gorn, *The Manly Art: Bare-Knuckle Prize Fighting in America.*
29. *Ibid.*
30. Mark Duncan, "John L. Sullivan & the making of an Irish-American sporting legend," Century Ireland," https://www.rte.ie/centuryireland/articles/john-l-sullivan-the-making-of-an-irish-american-sporting-legend.
31. Peter Duffy, "Lords of the Ring," *New Republic,* August 17, 2010, https://newrepublic.com/article/76398/lords-the-ring, accessed on January 4, 2023.
32. *Ibid.*
33. Geoffrey C. Ward, *Unforgivable Blackness: The Rise and Fall of Jack Johnson* (New York: Vintage, 2006), 15.
34. Ward, *Unforgivable Blackness,* 17.
35. *Ibid.*
36. *Ibid.*
37. *Ibid.*
38. Gorn, *The Manly Art: Bare-Knuckle Prize Fighting in America,* 227.
39. James Silas Rogers, "How Irish American Athletes Slugged Their Way to Respectability," *What It Means to Be an American: A National Conversation Hosted by the Smithsonian and Arizona State University,* May 18, 2017, https://www.whatitmeanstobeamerican.org/identities/how-irish-american-athletes-slugged-their-way-to-respectability.
40. Rogers, *Irish-American Autobiography.*
41. Beston, *The Boxing Kings: When American Heavyweights Ruled the Ring,* 22.
42. Hudson, *Boxing in America: An Autopsy,* 2.
43. "Griswold's Description of Corbett vs. Mitchell," *Nebraska History,* accessed on October 30, 2023, https://history.nebraska.gov/griswolds-description-of-corbett-vs-mitchell.
44. *Daily Huronite,* January 26, 1894.
45. Alan Woods, "James J. Corbett: Theatrical Star," *Journal of Sport History,* vol. 3, no. 2 (1976), 164–175.
46. *Weekly Irish Times,* July 14, 1894.
47. Hudson, *Boxing in America: An Autopsy,* 2.
48. Dennis Condon, "Irish Audiences Watch Their First U.S. Feature: The Corbett-Fitzsimmons Fight (1897)," in *Screening Irish-America: A Reader* ed. Ruth Barton (Dublin: Irish Academic Press, 2009), 135–147.
49. *San Francisco Call,* March 6, 1897.
50. *Denver Evening Post,* February 13, 1897.
51. *San Francisco Call,* February 22, 1897.
52. *The Toledo Commercial,* March 18, 1897.
53. James Slater, "Bob Fitzsimmons vs. James J. Corbett and the Solar Plexus Punch Source," *BoxingRec,* April 30, 2021, https://www.boxing247.com/boxing-news/bob-fitzsimmons-vs-james-j-corbett-and-the-solar-plexus-punch/177201.
54. Boddy, *Boxing, A Cultural History,* 408.
55. "Ave, Fitzsimmons!," *Evening Herald,* March 18, 1897.
56. *Irish Independent,* March 18, 1887.
57. Gilbert Odd, *The Fighting Blacksmith: A Biography of Bob Fitzsimmons* (London: Pelham, 1976), 8.
58. Arne K. Lang, "Prizefighting," cited in Patrick Sauer, *The Boilermaker vs. the Gentleman: A Look Back at the Last Heavyweight Title Fight in Brooklyn,* https://www.vice.com/en/article/pgnyk9/the-boilermaker-vs-the-gentleman-a-look-back-at-the-last-heavyweight-title-fight-in-brooklyn.
59. *Brooklyn Daily Eagle,* May 11, 1900.
60. Lang, "Prizefighting," *Ibid.*
61. *Brooklyn Daily Eagle,* May 11, 1900.
62. Lang, "Prizefighting," *Ibid.*
63. *Brooklyn Daily Eagle,* May 12, 1900; *New York Times,* May 12, 1900.
64. *Los Angeles Herald,* May 13, 1900.
65. *Sacramento Union,* May 11, 1913.
66. *Brooklyn Daily Eagle,* May 12, 1900.
67. Patrick Myler, "Gentleman Jim Won Over the Irish," *Irish Independent.* July 7, 2012.
68. Beston, *The Boxing Kings,* 22.
69. *Times Union,* 1931 https://fultonhistory.com/Fulton.html Albany NY Times Union 1931–1788.pdf.
70. Tony Thomas, Rudy Behlmer and Clifford McCarty, *The Films of Errol Flynn* (New York: Citadel Press, 1969), 116–117.
71. Alden Chodash, "Fight City Legends: Gentleman Jim," Fight City, November 19, 2024.
72. Monte Cox, "James J. Corbett: Turning Point in Pugilism," coxscorner, accessed on October 5, 2023, https://coxscorner.tripod.com/corbett.html.
73. "Death of Jim Corbett," *Leominster Daily Enterprise,* February 20, 1933.
74. *Ibid.*
75. "Three Champions Mourn Gentleman Jim's Death," *United Press,* Los Angeles, February 18, 1933.
76. *Buffalo Evening News,* February 18, 1933.

Chapter Ten

1. Reel, *The National Police Gazette and the Making of the Modern American Man, 1879–1906,* 1.
2. James R. Barrett, *The Irish Way: Becoming American in the Multiethnic City* (New York: Penguin, 2013), 52.
3. *Ibid.*

4. Tyler Anbinder, *Five Points: The 19th-Century New York City Neighborhood That Invented Tap Dance, Stole Elections, and Became the World's Most Notorious Slum* (New York: Free Press, 2010).
5. *Ibid.*
6. *Ibid.*
7. *Ibid.*
8. Barrett, *The Irish Way*, 21.
9. *Ibid.*
10. *Ibid.*
11. *Ibid.*
12. *Ibid.*, 22.
13. *Ibid.*
14. *Ibid.*, 27.
15. Rolano Vitale, *The Real Rockys: A History of the Golden Age of Italian Americans in Boxing 1900–1955* (York, United Kingdom: York Publishing, 2014).
16. Barrett, *The Irish Way*, 1.
17. Mike Silver, *Stars In The Ring: Jewish Champions in the Golden Age of Boxing*, cited in Gerald Eskenazi, "When Jewish Boxers Were Lords of the Ring," *Haaretz*, accessed on January 7, 2023, https://www.haaretz.com/life/books/.premium.MAGAZINE-when-jewish-boxers-were-lords-of-the-ring-1.5384078.
18. *Ibid.*
19. "The Long Last Night in the Ring for Benny Leonard," *New York Times*, October 4 1983.

Chapter Eleven

1. Rick Hogan, "Fighter and Thinker Both—Remembering Overlooked Boxing Great Gene Tunney," *Chicago Tribune*, August 19, 2016.
2. "Michael Carbert, "Fight City Legends: The Fighting Marine," *The Fight City*, December 14, 2022; "Tunney was Lumberjack for Ottawa Company," *The Globe*, September 28, 1926.
3. James R. Fairs, "Blood, Sweat, Toil but No Tears from Tunney," *Sports Illustrated*, March 27, 1967.
4. *Ibid.*
5. Monte D. Cox, "*Harry Greb, The Human Windmill ..."A Perpetual Motion Machine*," coxscorner, accessed on October 30, 2023, https://coxscorner.tripod.com/greb.html.
6. Fairs, "Blood, Sweat, Toil but No Tears from Tunney."
7. Gene Tunney, *Arms for Living* (Literary Licensing, LLC, 2011).
8. Bruce, J. Evensen, *When Dempsey Fought Tunney Heroes, Hokum and Storytelling in the Jazz Age* (Knoxville: University of Tennessee Press, 1996).
9. *The Franklin Evening Star*, September 21, 1927.
10. James P. Dawson, "Tunney Always Master," *New York Times*, September 24, 1926.
11. Pat Murphy, "How Gene Tunney brought down a boxing legend and an era," *Troy Media*, July 10, 2019.
12. William Nack, "The Long Count: Seventy Years Ago, in a Heavyweight Title Bout in Chicago, Jack Dempsey Knocked Gene Tunney to the Canvas. What Happened Next Made This the Most Famous Fight in the Golden Age of Sports," *Sports Illustrated*, October 7, 2019.
13. "Tunney Becomes Suddenly Poetic Considers Himself 'Man of Destiny,'" *Greenfield Recorder MA*, September 22, 1926.
14. Clarke H. Kelsey, " Kelsey Tells What Manner of Man Gene Tunney Really Is," *eugenecarsey.com*, accessed October 4, 2023, www.eugenecarsey.com/boxingnewspapers/news/dempsey_tunney1927/dempsey_tunney1927.html.
15. *Chicago Daily Tribune*, September 23, 1927.
16. William Nack, *Sports Illustrated*, October 7, 2019.
17. *Ibid.*
18. *Ibid.*
19. *Ibid.*
20. "Gene Tunney, Who Beat Dempsey Twice for Ring Title, Is Dead at 80," *The New York Times*, November 9, 1978.
21. Shirley Povich, *Washington Post*, November 10, 1978.
22. James Bone, "The Dempsey vs Tunney Boxing Match Controversy," *The Guardian*, October 7, 2020.
23. George Kimball, "Unlikely Tale of the Playwright and the Pugilist," *The Irish Times*, September 23, 2010.
24. Norman Klein, "Talk of the Town," *New Yorker*, August 4, 1928.
25. *Ibid.*
26. *Ibid.*
27. Gene Tunney, "The Communist Menace and How We Can Safeguard Ourselves," *Public Service Announcement, WNYC*, date unknown, NYC Municipal Archives WNYC Collection, NYC archives ID: 150492 Municipal archives ID: LT4163.
28. Eoin O'Callaghan, "Long Friendship with Gene Tunney Was One That George Bernard Shaw Could Count On," *Irish Examiner*, October 6, 2017.
29. George Bernard Shaw, "Note on Modern Prizefighting" (1901), appended to *Cashel Byron's Profession* (London, 1925), 341.
30. Kasia Boddy, *Boxing: A Cultural History* (London: Reaktion, 2008), 120.
31. *Ibid.*
32. Kimball, "Unlikely Tale of the Playwright and the Pugilist."
33. O'Callaghan, "Long Friendship with Gene Tunney."
34. *Ibid.*
35. *Ibid.*
36. *Ibid.*
37. *Ibid.*
38. Michael Holroyd, *Bernard Shaw* (London: Harmondsworth, 1990), 341.
39. *Ibid.*
40. *Ibid.*
41. "Tunney's Daughter Accused of Slaying Husband," *New York Times,* March 30, 1970.

42. Tom Murphy, *A Whistle in the Dark* (Dublin: Methuen Drama,1989), Act 1, 31.
43. John Hutchinson, "GENE-IUS Navy Hero, Lumberjack and Boxing Legend Gene Tunney Still Holds Record for Heavyweight Undefeated Streak in a Life More Colorful than Even Fury or Wilder," *The Irish Sun*, September 19, 2019.
44. *Ibid.*
45. "Gene Tunney, Who Beat Dempsey Twice for Ring Title, Is Dead at 80," *The New York Times*, November 9, 1978.
46. Ajay Bhai Amrit, "Extraordinary life of Gene Tunney—Born on May 25, 1898—Died on November 7, 1978," *The Fiji Times*, January 14, 2023.
47. "Gene Tunney, Who Beat Dempsey Twice for Ring Title, Is Dead at 80," *The New York Times*, November 9, 1978.

Chapter Twelve

1. Charles Perrault, "Cendrillon, ou la petite pantoufle de verre," *Histoires ou contes du temps passé, avec des moralités: Contes de ma mère l'Oye* (Paris, 1697); Andrew Lang, *The Blue Fairy Book* (London: Longmans, Green, and Co., ca. 1889), 64–67.
2. Jessica Traynor, *The Irish Times*, December 5, 2018.
3. Michael C. DeLisa, *Cinderella Man: The James J. Braddock Story* (Preston, UK: Milo Books, 2000), 31.
4. *Ibid.*, 50.
5. *Ibid.*, 55.
6. *Ibid.*, 138.
7. *Ibid.*
8. *Ibid.*, 139.
9. *Ibid.*
10. Jeremy Schaap, *Cinderella Man: James J. Braddock, Max Baer, and the Greatest Upset in Boxing History* (Boston: Houghton Mifflin, 2005).
11. *Ibid.*, 158.
12. *Ibid.*
13. *Ibid.*, 165.
14. *Ibid.*, 168.
15. Jessica Traynor, "'Cinderella Man' James Braddock, the Irish-American Boxer Who Became World Champion," *The Irish Times*, December 5, 2018.
16. Schaap, *Cinderella Man*.
17. *Ibid.*
18. Donald McRae, *Dark Trade: Lost in Boxing* (Mainstream Publishing, 2005), 196.
19. *Ibid.*, 201.
20. *Ibid.*
21. *Ibid.*, 197.
22. *Ibid.*, 212.
23. *Ibid.*
24. *Ibid.*, 214.
25. *Ibid.*, 214.
26. *Ibid.*
27. *Ibid.*, 225.
28. *Ibid.*, 226.
29. *Ibid.*, 233.
30. *Ibid.*
31. "Braddock Who Beat Baer for Title Dies," *New York Times*, November 30, 1974.
32. Schaap, *Cinderella Man*, 22.

Chapter Thirteen

1. *On the Waterfront* directed by Elia Kazan, Horizon Pictures, 1954.
2. Adam J. Pollack, *John L. Sullivan: The Career of the First Gloved Heavyweight Champion* (Jefferson, N.C.: McFarland, 2006), 25–27.
3. John L. Sullivan and Dudley A. Sargent, *Life and Reminiscences of a 19th Century Gladiator* (Boston: J.A. Hearn, & Co., 1892), 44.
4. *Ibid.*, 44.
5. *Ibid.*, 122.
6. *Ibid.*, 142.
7. *Ibid.*, 173.
8. *New York Herald*, March 3,1892.
9. *The Standard Union*, August 13, 1892.
10. *New York Herald*, March 3,1892.
11. *National Police Gazette*, December 14, 1895.
12. *The Los Angeles Herald*, September 8, 1895.
13. C.L. Sonnichsen, *Pass of the North: Four Centuries on the Rio Grande* (El Paso: Texas Western Press, 1968).
14. Thomas Myler, *Ringside With the Celtic Warriors: Tales of Ireland's Boxing Legends* (Dublin: Currach Press, 2012), 104.
15. *Ibid.*, 105.
16. Mike Goodpaster, "Peter Maher: An Irish Tribute," *The Grueling Truth*, February 2, 2021, https://thegruelingtruth.com/boxing/peter-maher-a-irish-tribute.
17. *New York Journal*, November 17, 1896.
18. *San Francisco Examiner*, May 15,1898.
19. Myler, *Ringside With the Celtic Warriors*, 107.
20. "Dempsey versus Gibbons," *Great Falls Tribune*, July 4, 1923.
21. Jack Dempsey vs. Tommy Gibbons at Shelby, Montana," *Springfield Republican*, July 5, 1923.
22. For a full account see Jason Kelly, *Shelby's Folly: Jack Dempsey, Doc Kearns, and the Shakedown of a Montana Boomtown* (Lincoln: University of Nebraska Press, 2010).
23. George D. Blair, "Tommy Gibbons," *Tom and Mike Gibbons Society Page*, http://www.tmgps.com/Tommy%20Gibbons%20Biography%20By%20George%20Blair.htm.
24. "Tommy Gibbons, Boxer, 69, Died," *New York Times*, November 20, 1960.
25. Not to be confused with the Irish boxer of the same name.
26. Myler, *Ringside With the Celtic Warriors*, 90.
27. Myler, *Ringside With the Celtic Warriors*, 91.
28. "Sailor Tom to Be Added," *Irish Independent*, January 31, 2003.
29. *Ibid.*92.

30. Alan Barra, "Backtalk; When Referee Wyatt Earp Laid Down the Law," *New York Times*, November 26, 1995.
31. *Ibid.*
32. Myler, *Ringside with the Celtic Warriors*, 95.
33. *Sacramento Daily Union*, March 12, 1898.
34. Myler, *Ringside With the Celtic Warriors*, 98.
35. Tom Sharkey, "I Fought the Best of Them," *Liberty Magazine*, February 1939, 29.
36. Hugh S. Fullerton, *Two-Fisted Jeff* (Chicago: Consolidated Book Publishers, 1929).
37. John McCallum, *The World Heavyweight Boxing Championship* (Radnor, Pa.: Chilton Book Company. 1974).
38. Thomas Calvert McClary, "We Wuz Robbed," *Esquire*, November 1937.
39. Myler, *Ringside With the Celtic Warriors*, 101.
40. "Sailor Tom to Be Added," *Irish Independent*, January 31, 2003.
41. Edwin McGreal, "Mayo's 'Great White Hope' Is Part of Fighting Irishmen Exhibition," *The Mayo News*, May 17, 2010.
42. *Ibid.*
43. Ward, *Unforgivable Blackness*, 358.
44. *Ibid.*
45. *Ibid.*
46. *Ibid.*
47. *Ibid.*
48. "U.S. Boxer Jack Johnson Beats Frank Moran in Paris," *The Guardian*, June 29, 1914.
49. Ward, *Unforgivable Blackness*, 360.
50. *Ibid.*,358.
51. *Ibid.*
52. *Boxing News*, July 8, 1918.
53. *Ibid.*
54. "Famous Western Boxer Knocked Out Only by Gene Tunney," *Connacht Tribune*, March 15, 1930.
55. *Ibid.*
56. McRae, *Dark Trade*, 23.

Chapter Fourteen

1. Clive Barnes, "Theater: Howard Sackler's 'Great White Hope," *The New York Times*, October 4, 1968.
2. Pete Hamill, "Muhammad Ali: "This Is about Me,'" *Life*, October 25, 1968.
3. Vincent Canby, "'Great White Hope' Brought to Screen," *The New York Times*, October 12, 1970, https://www.nytimes.com/1970/10/12/archives/great-white-hope-brought-to-screen.html.
4. Richard Nordquist, " H.L. Mencken's 'The Libido for the Ugly,' " *thoughtco.com*, updated on April 22, 2019, https://www.thoughtco.com/libido-for-the-ugly-by-mencken-1690254.
5. Myler, *Close Encounters With the Gloves Off*, 195.
6. *Ibid.*
7. Myler, *Close Encounters With the Gloves Off*, 195.
8. *Ibid.*
9. Steve Neal, "William David, Jr. ("Billy")," *encyclopedia.com*, accessed on November 6, 2023, https://www.encyclopedia.com/humanities/encyclopedias-almanacs-transcripts-and-maps/conn-william-david-jr-billy-0.
10. *Ibid.*
11. Robert Portis, "June 18, 1941: Louis vs Conn 1," *thefightcity.com*, accessed on November 6, 2023, https://www.thefightcity.com/joe-louis-vs-billy-conn.
12. Frank Deford, "The Boxer and the Blonde: Billy Conn Won the Girl but Lost the Fight," *Sports Illustrated*, June 17, 1985, https://www.si.com/boxing/2015/02/13/si-60-billy-conn-joe-louis-boxer-blonde.
13. Myler, *Close Encounters With the Gloves Off*, 195.
14. *Chicago Daily Tribune*, June 20, 1946.
15. "Billy Conn, 75, an Ex-Champion Famed for His Fights With Louis," *The New York Times*, May 30, 1993.

Chapter Fifteen

1. Chris Dufresne, "Quarry Provides Living Proof of Boxing's Side Effects: Aftermath: Brother Blames Father for Retired Fighter's Deteriorated Mental Condition," *Los Angeles Times*, October 31, 1995.
2. *Ibid.*
3. Bob Mee, "Obituary: Jerry Quarry," *The Independent,* January 5, 1999.
4. Michael Carbert, "Ali vs Quarry I," *fightcity.com*, October 26, 1970, https://www.thefightcity.com/muhammad-ali-vs-jerry-quarry.
5. Dufresne, "Quarry Provides Living Proof of Boxing's Side Effects."
6. Steve Springer, "Boxer Quarry Is Dead," *Los Angeles Times,* January 4, 1999.
7. *Ibid.*
8. *Ibid.*
9. *Ibid.*
10. *Ibid.*
11. Rick Assad, "Remembering Jerry Quarry: The 'Bridesmaid' in a Golden Era of Heavyweights," *The Sweet Science,* May 14, 2018.
12. Michael Hirsley, "Punches Took Deadly Toll on Quarry," *Chicago Tribune*, January 5, 1999.
13. *Ibid.*

Chapter Sixteen

1. "Larry Holmes vs Gerry Cooney," *Sports Illustrated*. June 7, 1982.
2. Joe Carnicelli,"Gerry Cooney: Is He Great White Hope Or Great White Hype?," UPI, accessed on November 6, 2023, https://www.upi.com/Archives/1982/05/27/Gerry-Cooney-Is-He-Great-White-Hope-Or-Great-White-Hype/21623913200000

3. *Ibid.*
4. *Ibid.*
5. Jeff Powell, "The Gerry Cooney and Larry Holmes Show That Divided a Nation," *The Daily Mail*, June 7, 2022.
6. Colin Hart, "Holmes Horror: Larry Holmes Reveals 40-Year Secret That Almost Overshadowed Gerry Cooney Fight after Racist Rednecks Shot at his Home," *The Irish Sun*, May 19, 2022.
7. Powell, "The Gerry Cooney and Larry Holmes Show That Divided a Nation."
8. James Slater, "On This Day: George Foreman flattens Gerry Cooney," January 15, 2020, *boxingnewsonline.net*, https://www.boxingnewsonline.net/on-this-day-george-foreman-flattens-gerry-cooney.
9. Thom Loverro, *Washington Times*, Sunday June 11, 2017.
10. McRae, *Dark Trade*, 275.
11. McRae, *Dark Trade*, 276.
12. McRae, *Dark Trade*, 275.
13. Robert Hynes, "Irishman Kevin McBride Who Forced Mike Tyson into Retirement Wants Rematch," *Irish Mirror*, November 28, 2020.

Chapter Seventeen

1. Nicholas Alllen, "George Gardner," *Dictionary of Irish Biography*, October 2009. https://www.dib.ie/biography/gardner-george-a3426.
2. Harry Mullan, *The Ultimate Encyclopedia of Boxing* (London: Carlton Books, 1996), 178.
3. John Grasso, *Historical Dictionary of Boxing* (Scarecrow Press), 275.
4. *Ibid.*
5. "Lucky Punch That Switches Titles," *The Day*, February 6, 1917.
6. "McGovern–Dixon Fight," *Washington Evening Star*, January 9,1900.
7. Grasso, *Historical Dictionary of Boxing*, 276.
8. "Another Win for Terry," *Evening Star*, Washington, June 13, 1900.
9. "Out in the Seventh," *Topeka State Journal*, November 3, 1900.
10. Grasso, *Historical Dictionary of Boxing*,276.
11. "McGovern in Four Rounds," *Akron Daily Democrat*, May 1, 1901.
12. Grasso, *Historical Dictionary of Boxing*, 276.
13. "Corbett the Winner," *Bismarck Daily Tribune*, April 1, 1903.
14. "The Terry McGovern We All Knew and Loved," *The Pittsburgh Post*, February 25, 1918.

Chapter Eighteen

1. Myler, *Ringside with the Celtic Warriors*, 59.
2. According to his boxing biographies, the date was November 26, 1892, but in Andrew Gallimore's biography of McTigue, he says Mike was actually 28 when he started training in 1914 but said that he was 22.
3. Jim Shanahan, "Mike McTigue," *Dictionary of Irish Biography*. October 2009, https://doi.org/10.3318/dib.005764.v1.
4. Myler, *Ringside with the Celtic Warriors*, 59.
5. Myler, *Ringside with the Celtic Warriors*, 175.
6. Joe Gannon, "The St. Patrick's Day Champ: Clare's 'Bold Mike' McTigue," *thewildgeese.irish*, accessed on November 6, 2023, https://thewildgeese.irish/profiles/blogs/bold-mike-mctigue-the-st-patrick-s-day-champion.
7. *Ibid.*
8. *Ibid.*
9. *Ibid.*
10. *Ibid.*
11. *Ibid.*
12. *Ibid.*
13. *Ibid.*
14. *Ibid.*
15. *Ibid.*
16. *Ibid.*
17. *Irish Independent*, August 15, 1966.

Chapter Nineteen

1. Douglas Cavanaugh, "Bad Rap?,"*Boxiana*, December 28, 2022.
2. Andy Watters, "Tommy Loughran 'The Phantom of Philly' and Tyrone's Light-Heavyweight World Champion," *The Irish News*, September 7, 2019.
3. Karen Galle, "Tommy Loughran, Boxing's "Philly Phantom," *Pennsylvania Heritage*, Fall 2020, http://paheritage.wpengine.com/article/tommy-loughran-boxings-philly-phantom.
4. *Ibid.*
5. *Ibid.*
6. *Ibid.*
7. *Philadelphia Inquirer*, July 11, 1982.
8. *Ibid.*
9. Galle, "Tommy Loughran, Boxing's "Philly Phantom."

Chapter Twenty

1. *Leinster Leader*, June 12, 1926.
2. Lester Bromberg, *Boxing's Unforgettable Fights* (New York: Ronald Press Company, 1962), 7; David Snowdon, *Writing the Prizefight: Pierce Egan's Boxiana World* (New York: Peter Lang, 2013) (*Boxiana*, vol. II, 1818).
3. Lawrence White and William Rouse, "John Jack Dempsey ('The Nonpareil')," *Dictionary of Irish Biography*, 2012.
4. *Leinster Leader*, June 12, 1926.
5. Joseph S. Page, *Nonpareil Jack Dempsey: Boxing's First World Middleweight Champion* (Jefferson, N.C.: McFarland, 2019): The legendary Irish boxer Dan Donnelly.
6. *The Brooklyn Daily Eagle*, January 22, 1888.
7. Any backward stroke that uses the knuckles to hit the target. This punch is now deemed a foul.

8. Myler, *The Fighting Irish*.
9. *Tacoma Daily Times*, Washington, March 13, 1909.
10. Earl Gutskey, "This Jack Dempsey Was 'Nonpareil' =: The 1880s Fighter Was World Middleweight Champion in John L. Sullivan's Era," *The Los Angeles Times*, April 23, 1992.

Chapter Twenty-One

1. Mathieu Brousseau, "Fight City Legends: The Toy Bulldog," *Fight City*, accessed on May 9, 2022, https://www.thefightcity.com/fight-city-legends-the-toy-bulldog-mickey-walker-harry-greb-jack-kearns-max-schmeling-jack-sharkey-tiger-flowers; from *Mickey Walker—The Toy Bulldog and His Times* (New York: Random House, 1961).
2. "Death of a Pugilist," *The San Francisco Examiner*, July 11, 1890.
3. "Hotly Contested Bout in Gloucester," *Boston Daily Globe*, June 29, 1884.
4. "Pugilistic," *The Evening Telegraph*, December 20, 1884.
5. "A Plucky Colored Pugilist," *The Times*, Philadelphia, July 29, 1886.
6. "Duffy and Dunn," *The Times*, Philadelphia. March 2, 1887.
7. "Jack McGinty Breaks His Thumb," *Chicago Tribune*, February 10, 1888.
8. "Duffy-McGinty Fight," *The Boston Globe*, February 8, 1888.
9. "Good All-Round Battles," *The Boston Globe*, May 11, 1888.
10. "Paddy Duffy," *Cyber Boxing Zone*, accessed on February 15, 2023, http://www.cyberboxingzone.com/boxing/duffy-p.htm.
11. "Duffy Defeats McMillan," *The Inter-Ocean*, November 1, 1888.
12. "Paddy Duffy Is Dying," *The Evening World*, New York, January 4, 1890.
13. "After Bouts for Brothers," *Bismarck Daily Tribune*, February 17, 1910.
14. "Joe Gans Proves the Better Man," *Rock Island Argus*, January 20,1906.
15. "'Twin' Sullivan Wins," *The Caucasian*, Shreveport, Louisiana, April 25, 1907; "Sullivan Bested Honey Mellody," *Washington Evening Star*, April 24, 1907.
16. Nat Fleischer and Sam Andre, *An Illustrated History of Boxing* (New York: Kensington Publishing, 1997), 264; "Sullivan and Clabby Draw," *Calumet News*, Michigan, 5 February 1910.
17. "Mike Twin Sullivan and Lavin Have Ten Rounds," *Los Angeles Herald*, September 3, 1910.
18. Ronnie D. Lankford Jr., "Walker, Edward Patrick ('Mickey')," *Scribner Encyclopedia of American Lives, Thematic Series: Sports Figures*, accessed on May 9, 2022, .https://www.encyclopedia.com/humanities/encyclopedias-almanacs-transcripts-and-maps/walker-edward-patrick-mickey
19. Kelly Nicholson, "The Great Mickey Walker," International Boxing Research Organization, accessed on May 2, 2022, https://www.ibroresearch.com/the-great-mickey-walker.
20. Patrick Connor, "Victoria aut Mors—Mickey Walker," *Beloved Onslaught*, March 2, 2012, https://www.belovedonslaught.com/2012/03/victoria-aut-mors-mickey-walker.html.
21. Ronnie D. Lankford, Jr., *Scribner Encyclopedia of American Lives, Thematic Series: Sports Figures*.
22. *Beloit Daily News*, October 20, 1924.
23. There are a number of accounts of this supposed happening, including a detailed one in Walker's autobiography.
24. *Beloit Daily News*, April 24, 1932.
25. "Toy Bulldog: The Unique Life of Mickey Walker," *Box Raw*, accessed on May 22, 2022, https://boxraw.com/blogs/blog/the-unique-life-of-mickey-walker.
26. *Ibid.*
27. There are a number of detailed accounts of this.
28. Deane McGowen, "Mickey Walker, Who Captured 2 World Titles, Dies at 79," *New York Times*, April 9, 1961.
29. *Ibid.*
30. "Mickey Walker Still Fighting," *Asbury Park Press*, February 6, 1976.
31. McGowen, "Mickey Walker, Who Captured 2 World Titles, Dies at 79."
32. Lankford Jr., "Walker, Edward Patrick ('Mickey')."
33. Brousseau, "Fight City Legends: The Toy Bulldog,"
34. *The Will to Conquer*, 1953.

Chapter Twenty-Two

1. Tom Hawthorn, "Jimmy (Baby Face) McLarnin, World Welterweight Champion Boxer (1907–2004)," November 29, 2004, http://tomhawthorn.blogspot.com/2009/12/jimmy-baby-face-mclarnin-world.html
2. There was often confusion over McLarnin's exact place of birth and his date of birth. McLarnin himself was unsure as to the exact location and at various times claimed to be born in Inchicore, Dublin, or the Lisburn Road in Belfast, Adding to the confusion, he went by nicknames the Dublin Destroyer and Belfast Spider. It was Irish boxing historian Patrick Myler who later unearthed McLarnin's birth certificate, which showed that McLarnin was born in Hillsborough, County Down, Ireland, in 1907.
3. "Obituaries: Jimmy McLarnin," *The Observer*, December 11, 2015.
4. *Ibid.*
5. Michael Carbert, "Fight City Legends: The Irish Lullaby," *The Fight City*, December 18, 2022, https://www.thefightcity.com/the-belfast-spider-jimmy-mclarnin.
6. Grasso, *Historical Dictionary of Boxing*, 279.

7. Myler, *Ringside With the Celtic Warriors,* 2012, 153.
8. *Ibid.,* 154.
9. *Ibid.,* 2012, 157.
10. *Ibid.,* 157.
11. "Jimmy McLarnin, The Groundbreaking Irish-Canadian Boxer," The Irish Emigration Museum, accessed on March 8, 2023, https://epicchq.com/story/jimmy-mclarnin-the-groundbreaking-irish-canadian-boxer.
12. *Ibid.*
13. Myler, *Ringside With the Celtic Warriors* 2012, 161.
14. Myler, *Ringside With the Celtic Warriors* 2012, 163.
15. Mike Lewis, "Jimmy McLarnin," *The Guardian,* November 11, 2004.
16. Jack Cavanaugh, "Jimmy McLarnin, Top Boxer Called Baby Face, Dies at 96," *The New York Times,* November 10, 2004.
17. *Ibid.*

Chapter Twenty-Three

1. Johnny Kilbane, "In His Own Words," *Johnny Kilbane,* accessed on June 12, 2023, http://www.johnnykilbane.com/in-his-own-words.html.
2. *Ibid.*
3. *Ibid.* Buck-and-wing dancing refers to a fast and flashy dance usually done in wooden-soled shoes and combining Irish clogging styles, high kicks, and complex African rhythms and steps such as the shuffle and slide; it is considered the forerunner of rhythm tap/tap dancing. It was frequently part of vaudeville acts.
4. Mike Casey, "The Irish Jewel of Cleveland: The Great Johnny Kilbane," *Cyber Boxing Zone,* accessed on June 12, 2023, http://www.cyberboxingzone.com/boxing/casey/MC_McLarnin.htm.

5. *Ibid.*
6. Johnny Kilbane, "In His Own Words."
7. *Ibid.*
8. Casey, "The Irish Jewel of Cleveland."
9. *Ibid.*
10. "Johnny Kilbane, Boxer, 68, Dead. Featherweight Champion of World, 1912–23, Went Into Politics in Cleveland Gave Fans a Show," *The New York Times,* June 1, 1957.
11. Jim Dubelko, "Kilbane Town," Cleveland Historical, accessed on June 12, 2023, https://clevelandhistorical.org/items/show/288?tour=6&index=6
12. *Los Angeles Herald,* February 7, 1921.
13. Don Stradley, "Marcel Thil & Eugène Criqui: Two Forgotten Frenchmen Immortalized at Last," *The Ring,* June 2005, 84 (5): 74–75.
14. *Los Angeles Herald,* February 7, 1921.
15. "Johnny Kilbane: The Making of a Boxer," Irish Archives, Accessed on February 26, 2023, http://www.irisharchives.org/pdf/JohnnyKilbane.pdf.
16. *Ibid.*
17. "Johnny Kilbane, Boxer, 68, Dead. Featherweight Champion of World, 1912–23, Went Into Politics in Cleveland, Gave Fans a Show," *The New York Times,* June 1, 1957.
18. Anton McNulty, "Statue of Former Boxing Champion Unveiled," *The Mayo News,* June 13, 2016.

Epilogue

1. Corey Kilgannon, "Capturing a Tradition, Blow by Blow," *The New York Times,* November 25, 2011.
2. "Jacqueline Beaten to Death in Her Own Home," *Irish Independent,* February 14, 2015.

Bibliography

Adelman, Melvin L. *A Sporting Time: New York City and the Rise of Modern Athletics, 1820–1870*. Urbana: University of Illinois Press, 1990.
Akenson, Donald H. *The Irish Diaspora*. Belfast: Queen's University of Belfast, 1993.
Anbinder, Tyler. *Five Points: The 19th-Century New York City Neighborhood That Invented Tap Dance, Stole Elections, and Became the World's Most Notorious Slum*. New York: Free Press, 2010.
Anbinder, Tyler. *Nativism and Slavery: The Northern Know Nothings and the Politics of the 1850s*. Oxford: Oxford University Press, 1992.
Andrews, Thomas S. *Ring Battles of Centuries: Only and Most Complete Record of the Roped Arena from Figg, 1719 to the Present Day*. Milwaukee: T.S. Andrews, 1914.
Asbury, H.A. *The Gangs of New York, An Informal History of the Underworld*. London: Arrow Books, 2002.
Ashby, Leroy. *With Amusement for All: A History of American Popular Culture since 1830*. Lexington: University of Kentucky Press, 2006.
Aycock, Colleen, and Mark Scott. *Joe Gans: A Biography of the First Black American World Boxing Champion*. Jefferson, N.C.: McFarland, 2008.
Aycock, Colleen, and Mark Scott (editors). *The First Black Boxing Champions: Essays on Fighters of the 1800s to the 1920s*. Jefferson, N.C.: McFarland, 2022.
Barrett, James R. *The Irish Way: Becoming American in the Multiethnic City*. New York: Penguin, 2012.
Basso, Mathew, Laura McCall, and Dee Garceau-Hagen. *Across the Great Divide: Cultures of Manhood in the American West*. New York: Routledge, 2001.
Bederman, Gail. *Manliness and Civilization: A Cultural History of Gender and Race in the United States, 1880–1917*. Chicago: University of Chicago Press, 1995.
Beston, Paul. *The Boxing Kings: When American Heavyweights Ruled the Ring*. Lanham, Md.: Rowman & Littlefield, 2017.
Beynon, John. *Masculinities and Culture*. Philadelphia: Open University Press, 2002.
Birley, Derek. *Sport and the Making of Britain*. Manchester: Manchester University Press, 1993.
Blewett, B. *The A–Z of World Boxing: An Authoritative and Entertaining Compendium of the Fight Game From Its Origins to the Present Day*. London: Robson Books, 1999.
Boddy, Kasia. *Boxing, A Cultural History*. London: Reaktion Books, 2009.
Bodnar, John. *The Transplanted: A History of Immigrants in Urban America*. Bloomington: Indiana University Press, 1985.
Bodner, Allen. *When Boxing Was a Jewish Sport*. New York: Praeger, 1997.
Boyle O'Reilly, John. *Ethics of Boxing and Manly Sport*. Boston: Ticknor and Company, 1888.
Brady, William A. *A Fighting Man*. Indianapolis: Bobbs-Merrill Company, 1916.
Brailsford, Dennis. *Bareknuckles: A Social History of Prize Fighting*. Cambridge: Lutterworth, 1988.
Bromberg, Lester. *Boxing's Unforgettable Fights*. New York: Ronald Press Company, 1962.
Brooke-Ball, P. *The Boxing Album: An Illustrated History*. London: Hermes House, 2001.
Broughton, Jack. *Rules to be Observed in all Battles on the Stage*. London, 1743.
Burrows, Edwin G., and Mike Wallace. *Gotham: A History of New York City to 1898*. Oxford: Oxford University Press, 1999.
Burstyn, Varda. *The Rites of Men: Manhood, Politics, and the Culture of Sport*. Toronto: University of Toronto Press, 1999.
Byron, Reginald. *Irish America*. Oxford: Oxford University Press, 1999.
Callis, Tracy, and Chuck Johnston. *Boxing in the Los Angeles Area, 1880–2005*. Victoria, B.C.: Trafford Publishing, 2009.
Carroll, Bret E. *American Masculinities: A Historical Encyclopedia*. Thousand Oaks, Calif.: Sage Publications, 2003.
Cavanaugh, Jack. *Tunney: Boxing's Brainiest Champ and His Upset of the Great Jack Dempsey*. New York: Ballantine Books, 2007.

Chandler, David, John Gill, and Tania Guha (editors). *Boxer: An Anthology of Writings on Boxing and Visual Culture*. London: Institute of International Visual Arts (INIVA), 1999.
Chill, Adam. *Bare-Knuckle Britons and Fighting Irish: Boxing, Race, Religion and Nationality in the 18th and 19th Centuries*. Jefferson, N.C.: McFarland, 2017.
Conley, Meghan A., and Billy Hawkins. *From Apes and Thick Micks to the Fighting Irish: Cultural Misappropriation at the University of Notre Dame*. Athens: University of Georgia Press, 2012.
Cooney, Gerry. *Gentleman Gerry: A Contender in the Ring, a Champion in Recovery*. Lanham, Md.: Rowman & Littlefield, 2019.
Corbett, James J. *Scientific Boxing: The Deluxe Edition*. Toronto: Promethean Press, 2008.
Corbett, James John. *Jabs*. Cleveland: Buckeye Publishing Co., 1907.
Corbett, James John. *The Roar of the Crowd: The True Tale of the Rise and Fall of a Champion*. New York: Arno Press, 1975.
Curl, James. *Jack Sharkey: A Heavyweight Champion's Untold Story*. Iowa City: KO Publishing, 2015.
Dallas, George Mifflin. *A Series of Letters from London during the Years 1856, '57, '58, '59 and '60*, Vol. 1. Philadelphia: J.B. Lippincott & Co., 1869.
Dalton, Kathleen. *Theodore Roosevelt: A Strenuous Life*. New York: Random House, 2004.
Daniels, Roger. *Coming to America: A History of Immigration and Ethnicity in American Life*. New York: HarperCollins, 1990.
DeLisa, Michael C. *Cinderella Man: The James J. Braddock Story*. Preston, England: Milo Books, 2005.
Dinan, John, *Sports in the Pulp Magazines*. Jefferson, N.C.: McFarland, 1998.
Dizikes, John. *Sportsmen and Gamesmen*. Boston: Houghton Mifflin, 1981.
Dolan, Jay P. *The American Catholic Experience: A History from Colonial Times to the Present*. Garden City, N.Y.: Doubleday, 1985.
Donovan, Mike. *Roosevelt That I Know: Ten Years of Boxing with the President and Other Memories of Famous Fighting Men*. New York: B.W. Dodge & Co., 1909.
Dowling, Vincent George. *Fistiana; or, the Oracle of the Ring*. London: Wm. Clement, 1841.
Downes Miles, Henry. *Pugilistica Being One Hundred and Forty-Four Years of the History of British Boxing*. London: Weldon & Co., 1880.
Downes Miles, Henry. *Pugilistica: The History of British Boxing containing lives of the most celebrated pugilists; full reports of their battles from contemporary newspapers, with authentic portraits, personal anecdotes, and sketches of the principal patrons of the prize ring, forming a complete history of the ring from Fig and Broughton, 1719–40, to the last championship battle between King and Heenan, in December 1863*, vols. 1–3. Edinburgh: J. Grant, 1906.
Dribble, R.F. *John L. Sullivan: An Intimate Narrative*. Boston: Little, Brown, 1925.
Drieser, Theodore. *A Book about Myself*. New York: Boni and Liveright, 1922.
Early, Gerald. *The Culture of Bruising: Essays on Prizefighting, Literature and Modern American Culture*. New York: W. Norton & Co., 1994.
Egan, Pierce. *Boxiana; or, Sketches of Ancient and Modern Pugilism from the Championship of Gribb to the Present Time*, Vol. 1. 1818. Reprint, London: George Virtue, Ivy Lane, 1830.
Egan, Pierce. *Boxiana; or, Sketches of Ancient and Modern Pugilism from the Championship of Gribb to the Present Time*, Vol. 2. 1818. Reprint, London: Sherwood, Jones, and Co., 1824.
Ernst, Robert. *Immigrant Life in New York City, 1825–1863*. Syracuse: Syracuse University Press, 1994.
Evensen, Bruce J. *When Dempsey Fought Tunney: Heroes, Hokum and Storytelling in the Jazz Age*. Knoxville: University of Tennessee Press, 1996.
Fanning, Charles. *New Perspectives on the Irish Diaspora*. Carbondale: Southern Illinois University Press, 2000.
Fleischer, Nat. *The Boston Strong Boy: The Story of John L. Sullivan*. New York: O'Brien, 1941.
Fleischer, Nat. *The Heavyweight Championship: An Informal History of Heavyweight Boxing from 1719 to the Present Day*. New York: G.P. Putnam and Sons, 1949.
Fleischer, Nat, and Sam Andre. *An Illustrated History of Boxing*. New York: Kensington, 1997.
Flynn, Barry. *The Little Book of Irish Boxing*. Dublin: The History Press, 2015.
Ford, John. *Prizefighting: The Age of Regency Boximania*. Newton Abbot, England: David and Charles, 1971.
Fox, Richard K. *The Life and Battles of Jack Johnson, Champion Pugilist of the World*. New York: Richard K. Fox, 1912.
Fox, Richard K. *The New Book of Rules: Official and Standard; together with the Rules of the Amateur Athletic Union*. New York: Richard K. Fox, 1913.
Gallimore, Andrew. *Babyface Goes to Hollywood—Fighters, Mobsters and Film Stars: The Jimmy McLarnin Story*. Dublin: O'Brien Press, 2009.
Gee, Tony. *Up to Scratch: Bare Knuckle Fighting and Heroes of the Prize-ring*. London: Queen Anne Press, 1998.
Gems, Gerald R. *Boxing: A Concise History of the Sweet Science*. Lanham, Md.: Rowman & Littlefield, 2014.
Gerstner, David A. *Manly Arts: Masculinity and Nation in Early American Cinema*. Durham: Duke University Press, 2006.

Gorn, Elliott, J. *The Manly Art: Bare-Knuckle Prize Fighting in America*. Ithaca: Cornell University Press, 1986.
Gorn, Elliott J., and Warren Jay Goldstein. *A Short History of American Sports*. Urbana: University of Illinois Press, 2004.
Grasso, John. *Historical Dictionary of Boxing*. Lanham, Md.: Scarecrow Press, 2013.
Hall, G. Stanley. *Adolescence: Its Psychology and Its Relations to Physiology, Anthropology, Sex, Crime, Religions, and Education*. 2 Volumes. New York: D. Appleton and Company, 1905.
Hall, G. Stanley. *Life and Confessions of a Psychologist*. New York: D. Appleton and Company, 1923.
Hall, G. Stanley. *Youth: Its Education, Regimen, and Hygiene*. New York: D. Appleton and Company, 1907.
Hauser, Thomas. *The Black Lights: Inside the World of Professional Boxing*. New York: Simon & Schuster, 1986.
Hawks, Robert Bryan. *Boxing Men: Ideas of Race, Masculinity, and Nationalism*. University of Mississippi, unpublished thesis, 2016.
Healy, James M. *The Mercier Book of Old Irish Street Ballads, Volume 3*. Dublin: Mercier Press, 1968.
Heiskanen, Benita. *The Urban Geography of Boxing: Race, Class, and Gender in the Ring*. London: Routledge, 2021.
Hendricks, King, and Irving Shepard (editors). *Jack London Reports: War Correspondence, Sports Articles, and Miscellaneous Writings*. Garden City, N.Y.: Doubleday, 1970.
Henning, Fred. J. *Fights for the Championship: The Men and Their Times*. London: Licensed Victuallers' Gazette, 1902.
Higginson, Thomas Wentworth. *Saints, and Their Bodies. Out-door Papers*. Boston: Ticknor and Fields, 1863.
Holroyd, Michael. *Bernard Shaw*. London: Harmondsworth, 1990.
Hotaling, Edward, *They're Off! Horse Racing at Saratoga*. Syracuse: Syracuse University Press, 1995.
Hudson, David L. *Boxing in America: An Autopsy*. New York: Praeger. 2012.
Hurley, John. *Self-Defense; or, Art of Boxing*. 1879. Reprint, West Long Beach: Caravat Press, 2004.
Ignatiev, Noel. *How the Irish Became White*. New York: Routledge, 1995.
Imhoff, Sarah. *Masculinity and the Making of American Judaism*. Bloomington: Indiana University Press, 2017.
Ingersoll, Robert Green, and Herman E Kittredge. T*he Works of Robert G. Ingersoll, Vol. 8*. New York: Dresden Publishing, 1900.
Isenberg, Michael T. *John L. Sullivan and His America*. Urbana: University of Illinois Press. 1988.
Jeonguk, Kim. *Boxing the Boundaries: Prize Fighting, Masculinities, and Shifting Social and Cultural Boundaries in the United State, 1882–1913*. University of Kansas, unpublished thesis, 2010.
Johnston, Alexander. *Ten and Out! The Complete Story of the Prize Ring in America*. New York: I. Washburn, 1947.
Kahn, Roger. *A Flame of Pure Fire: Jack Dempsey and the Roaring '20s*. New York: Harvest/Harcourt, 1999.
Kelly, Jason. *Shelby's Folly: Jack Dempsey, Doc Kearns, and the Shakedown of a Montana Boomtown*. Lincoln: University of Nebraska Press, 2010.
Kimball, George, and John Schulian (editors). *At the Fights: American Writers on Boxing*. New York: Library of America, 2011.
Kimmel, Michael. *Manhood in America: A Cultural History*. New York: Free Press, 1996.
Klein, Christopher. *Strong Boy: The Life and Times of John L. Sullivan, America's First Sports Hero*. Lanham, Md.: Lyons Press, 2013.
Kofoed, Jack. *Brandy for Heroes: A Biography of the Honorable John Morrissey, Champion Heavyweight of America and State Senator*. New York: E.P. Dutton and Co., 1938.
Lang, Arne K. *Clash of the Little Giants: George Dixon, Terry McGovern and the Culture of Boxing in America, 1890–1910*. Jefferson, N.C.: McFarland, 2022.
Lardner, Rex. *The Legendary Champions*. New York: American Heritage Press, 1972.
Lee, J.J., and Marion R. Casey (editors). *Making the Irish American: History and Heritage of the Irish in the United States*, New York: New York University Press, 2006.
Levine, Peter. *Ellis Island to Ebbets Field: Sport and the American Jewish Experience*. Oxford: Oxford University Press, 1993.
Lewis, Alfred Henry. *Richard Croker*. New York: Life Publishing Company, 1901.
Liebling, A.J. *The Sweet Science*. Viking Press, 1956. Reprint: New York: North Point Press, 2004.
Life and Battles of Yankee Sullivan, Embracing Full and Accurate Reports of the Fights with Hammer Lane, Tom Sector, Harry Bell, Bob Caunt, Tom Hyer, and John Morrissey. Philadelphia: A. Winch, 1854.
Lindsay, Vachel. *The Golden Whales of California and Other Rhythms in the American Language*. New York: Macmillan Company, 1920.
London, Jack. *Abysmal Brute*. New York: Century Co., 1913.
London, Jack. *The Game*. 1905. Reprint: London: Macmillan Company, 1910.
Lynch, J.G. Bohun. *Knuckles and Gloves*. London: W. Collins Sons, 1924.

Lynch, J.G. Bohun, and J.H.W. Knight-Bruce. *The Complete Boxer.* New York: Frederick A. Stokes Company, 1914.
Mace, Jem. *In Memoriam, Book 1: Fifty Years a Fighter: The Life Story of Jem Mace.* 1908. Reprint: n.p: Caestus Books, 1998.
McCallum, John D. *The World Heavyweight Boxing Championship: A History.* Radnor, Pa.: Chilton Book Co., 1974.
McIlvanney, Hugh. *McIlvanney on Boxing.* New York: Beaufort Books, 1983.
McKay, Ernest A. *Civil War and New York City.* Syracuse: Syracuse University Press, 1991.
McRae Donald. *Dark Trade: Lost in Boxing.* Edinburgh: Mainstream Publishing, 2005.
Menken, Adah Isaacs. *Infelicia.* Philadelphia: Lippincott, 1888.
Miller, Kerby. *Emigrants and Exiles: Ireland and the Irish Exodus to North America.* Oxford: Oxford University Press, 1985.
Miller, Patrick B., and David K. Wiggins (editors). *Sport and the Color Line: Black Athletes and Race Relations in Twentieth Century America.* New York: Taylor & Francis, 2003.
The Modern Gladiator: Being an Account of the Exploits and Experiences of the World's Greatest Fighter, John L. Sullivan. St. Louis: Athletic Pub. Co., 1889.
Mrozek, Donald J. *Sport and American Mentality 1880–1910.* Knoxville: University of Tennessee Press, 1983.
Mullan, Harry, and Bob Mee. *The Ultimate Encyclopedia of Boxing.* London: Carlton Books, 2013.
Murphy, Tom. *A Whistle in the Dark.* Dublin: Methuen Drama, 1989.
Myler, Patrick. *Close Encounters With the Gloves Off.* Chichester, United Kingdom: Pitch Press, 2016.
Myler, Patrick. *Gentleman Jim Corbett.* London: Robson Books, 1998.
Myler, Patrick. *Regency Rogue: Dan Donnelly, His Life and Legends.* Dublin: O'Brien, 1976.
Naughton, W.W. *Heavyweight Champions.* San Francisco: John Kitchen, Jr. Co., 1910.
Naughton, W.W. *Kings of the Queensberry Realm.* Chicago: Continental Publishing Co., 1902.
Nicholson, James C. *The Notorious John Morrissey: How a Bare-Knuckle Brawler Became a Congressman and Founded Saratoga Race Course.* Lexington: University Press of Kentucky, 2016.
Oates, Joyce Carol. *On Boxing.* New York: Harper Perennial, 2006.
Odd, Gilbert. *Encyclopedia of Boxing.* New York: Crescent Books, 1983.
O'Riordan, Turlough, and Terry Clavin. *Irish Sporting Lives.* Dublin: Royal Irish Academy, 2022.
Page, Joseph S. *Nonpareil Jack Dempsey: Boxing's First World Middleweight Champion.* Jefferson, N.C.: McFarland, 2019.
Parkinson, Nick. *Boxing on This Day: History, Facts & Figures from Every Day of the Year.* Edinburgh: Pitch Publishing, 2013.
Peterson, Bob. *Peter Jackson: A Biography of the Australian Heavyweight Champion, 1860–1901.* Jefferson, N.C.: McFarland, 2011.
Pettegrew, John. *Brute in Suits; Male Sensibility in America, 1890–1920.* Baltimore: Johns Hopkins University Press, 2007.
Pleck, Elizabeth H., and Joseph H. Pleck (editors). *The American Man.* Englewood Cliffs, N.J.: Prentice Hall, 1980.
Pollack, Adam J. *John L. Sullivan: The Career of the First Gloved Heavyweight Champion.* Jefferson, N.C.: McFarland, 2006.
Pollack, Adam J. *In the Ring with Bob Fitzsimmons.* Iowa City: Win by KO Publications, 2007.
Pollack, Adam J. *In the Ring with James J. Corbett.* Iowa City: Win by KO Publications, 2012.
Pollack, Adam J. *In the Ring with John L. Sullivan.* Jefferson, N.C.: McFarland, 2006.
Polley, Martin. *Moving the Goalpost: A History of Sports and Society since 1945.* New York: Routledge, 1998.
Pope, S.W. *Patriotic Games: Sporting Traditions in the American Imagination, 1876–1926.* New York: Oxford University Press, 1997.
Putney, Clifford. *Muscular Christianity: Manhood and Sports in Protestant America, 1880–1920.* Cambridge: Harvard University Press, 2003.
Rader, Benjamin G. *American Sports: From the Age of Folk Games to the Age of Televised Sports.* Upper Saddle River, N.J.: Prentice Hall, 2004.
Redmond, Patrick R. *The Irish and the Making of American Sport 1835–1920.* Jefferson, N.C.: McFarland, 2015.
Reel, Guy. *The National Police Gazette and the Making of the Modern American Man, 1879–1906.* New York: Palgrave Macmillan, 2006.
Remnick, David. *King of the World: Muhammad Ali and the Rise of an American Hero.* New York: Random House, 1999.
Riess, Steven A. *City Games: The Evolution of American Urban Society and the Rise of Sports.* Urbana: University of Illinois Press, 1989.
Riess, Steven A. *Major Problems in American Sport History.* Boston: Houghton Mifflin, 1997.
Riess, Steven A. *Sport in Industrial America, 1850–1920.* Malden, Mass.: John Wiley and Sons, 2013.
Ripley, George, and Charles A. Dana (editors). *American Cyclopaedia: A Popular Dictionary of General Knowledge,* Vol. 14. New York: D. Appleton and Company, 1875.

Roberts, Randy. *Joe Louis*. New Haven: Yale University Press, 2010.
Roche, James Jeffrey, and Mary Murphy O'Reilly. *Life of John Boyle O'Reilly: Together with His Complete Poems and Speeches*. New York: Cassell Publishing Company, 1891.
Rodriguez, Robert G. *The Regulation of Boxing: A History and Comparative Analysis of Policies Among American States*. Jefferson, N.C.: McFarland, 2009.
Roediger, David R. *Wages of Whiteness: Race and the Making of the American Working Class*. London: Verso Books, 1991.
Rogers, James Silas. *Irish-American Autobiography: The Divided Hearts of Athletes, Priests, Pilgrims, and More*. Washington, D.C.: Catholic University of America Press, 2010.
Roosevelt, Theodore. *An Autobiography*. New York: Macmillan Company, 1913.
_____. *Ranch Life and the Hunting-Trail*. New York: Century Co., 1888.
Ross, Greggory M. *Boxing in the Union Blue: A Social History of American Boxing in the Union States During the Late Antebellum and Civil War Years*. London, Ont.: University of Western Ontario, 2014.
Rotundo, E. Anthony. *American Manhood: Transformations in Masculinity from the Revolution to the Modern Era*. New York: Basic Books, 1993.
Ryan, Dennis P. *Beyond the Ballot Box: A Social History of the Boston Irish, 1845–1917*. Madison, N.J.: Fairleigh Dickinson University Press, 1983.
Sammons, Jeffrey T. *Beyond the Ring: The Role of Boxing in American Society*. Urbana: University of Illinois Press, 1988.
Saum, Lewis O. *The Popular Mood of America, 1860–1890*. Lincoln: University of Nebraska Press, 1990.
Saxon, A.H. *P.T. Barnum: The Legend and the Man*. New York: Columbia University Press, 1989.
Schaap, Jeremy. *Cinderella Man: James J. Braddock, Max Baer and the Greatest Upset in Boxing History*. New York: Houghton Mifflin, 2006.
Schulberg, Budd. *Ringside: A Treasury of Boxing Reportage*. Chicago: Ivan R. Dee, 2006.
Schulian, John. *Writers' Fighters and Other Sweet Scientists*. Fairway, Kans.: Andrews & McMeel, 1983.
Shannon, William V. *The American Irish: A Political and Social Portrait*. Amherst: University of Massachusetts Press, 1898.
Shaw, George Bernard. *Cashel Byron's Profession*. London, 1925.
Siler, George. *Inside Facts on Pugilism*. Chicago: Laird & Lee, Publishers, 1907.
Silver, Mike. *The Arc of Boxing: The Rise and Decline of the Sweet Science*. Jefferson, N.C.: McFarland, 2008.
Silverman, Jeff (editor). *Greatest Boxing Stories Ever Told: Thirty-six Incredible Tales from the Ring*. Guilford, Conn.: Lyons Press, 2004.
Smith, Gene, and Jayne Barry Smith (editors). *The Police Gazette*. New York: Simon & Schuster, 1972.
Smith, Kevin, *Boston's Boxing Heritage: Prizefighting from 1882 to 1955*. Mount Pleasant, S.C.: Arcadia Publishing, 2002.
Somers, Dale A. *Sports in New Orleans*. Baton Rouge: Louisiana State University Press, 1972.
Spears, Betty, and Richard A. Swanson. *History of Sport and Physical Activity in the United States*. Dubuque: William C. Brown Publishers, 1978.
Sperber, Murray. *Shake Down the Thunder: The Creation of Notre Dame Football*. Bloomington: Indiana University Press, 1993.
Spindel, C. *Dancing at Halftime: Sports and the Controversy over American Indian Mascots*. New York: New York University Press, 2000.
Stanway, Eric. *Bill the Butcher: The Life and Death of William Poole*. San Bernardino: EUM Books, 2019.
Stott, Richard. *Jolly Fellows: Male Milieus in Nineteenth-Century America*. Baltimore: Johns Hopkins University Press, 2009.
Streible, Dan. "Female Spectators and the Corbett–Fitzsimmons Fight Film." In Aaron Baker and Todd Boyd (editors), *Out of Bounds: Sport, Media, and the Politics of Identity*. Bloomington: Indiana University Press, 1997.
Streible, Dan. *Fight Picture: A History of Boxing and Early Cinema*. Berkeley: University of California Press, 2008.
Struna, Nancy. *People of Prowess: Sport, Leisure, and Labor in Early Anglo-America*. Urbana: University of Illinois Press, 1996.
Sugar, Bert Randolph. *Boxing's Greatest Fighters*. Guilford, Conn.: Lyons Press, 2006.
Sugden, John. *Boxing and Society: An International Analysis*. Manchester: Manchester University Press, 1996.
Sullivan, John L. *Reminiscences of a 19th Century Gladiator*. Reprint: Toronto: Promethean Press, 2008.
Takaki, Ronald. *Iron Cages: Race and Culture in Nineteenth Century America*. New York: Oxford University Press, 1990.
Thernstrom, Stephen, Ann Orlov, and Oscar Handlin. *Harvard Encyclopedia of American Ethnic Groups*. Cambridge: Belknap Press of Harvard University Press, 1980.
Thomas, Claudia, *Hyer and Allied Families: Historical & Personal Accounts—Notable & Notorious*. Independently published, 2022.
Thomas, Tony, Rudy Behlmer, and Clifford McCarty. *The Films of Errol Flynn*. New York: Citadel Press, 1969.

Timony, Patrick. *The American Fistiana*. New York: H. Johnson, 1846.
Van Loan, Charles E. *Taking the Count: Prize Ring Stories*. New York: George H. Doran Company, 1915.
Vincent, Ted. *The Rise and Fall of American Sport: Mudville's Revenge*. Lincoln: University of Nebraska Press, 1994.
Vitale, Rolano. *The Real Rockys: A History of the Golden Age of Italian Americans in Boxing 1900–1955*. York, United Kingdom: York Publishing, 2014.
Ward, Jeffrey C. *Unforgivable Blackness: The Rise and Fall of Jack Johnson*. New York: Alfred A. Knopf, 2004.
Whitman, Walt. *Leaves of Grass*. Reprint: Oxford: Oxford University Press, 1990.
Wiebe, Robert H. *The Search for Order, 1877–1920*. New York: Hill and Wang, 1967.
Wilcox, Ralph C. "Irish Americans in Sports: The Nineteenth Century." In J.J. Lee and Marion R. Casey (editors), *Making the Irish American: History and Heritage of the Irish in the United States*. New York: New York University Press, 2006.
Wilcox, Ralph C. "The Shamrock and the Eagle: Irish Americans and Sport in the Nineteenth Century." In George Eisen and David K. Wiggins (editors), *Ethnicity and Sport in North American History and Culture*. Westport, Conn.: Praeger, 1995.
Wilmer, Lambert A. *Our Press Gang; or, a Complete Exposition of the Corruptions and Crimes of the American Newspapers*. Philadelphia: J.T. Lloyd, 1859.
Zola, Gary Philip, and Marc Dollinger. *American Jewish History: A Primary Source Reader*. Waltham, Mass.: Brandeis University Press, 2014.

Journal Publications

Abbott, Lyman, and Hamilton W. Mabie. "Prize Fighting in New York." *Outlook* 99 (September 9, 1911): 56–57.
Abbott, Lyman, and Hamilton W. Mabie. "The San Francisco Prize-Fight." *Outlook* 95 (June 25, 1910): 360–361.
Anbinder, Tyler. "Moving beyond 'Rags to Riches': New York's Irish Famine Immigrants and Their Surprising Savings Accounts." *Journal of American History* 99 (2012): 741–770.
Austin, Alf. "The Old and the New Pugilism." *Outing* 37, no. 6 (March 1901): 682–687.
Austin, Alf. "A Plea for Style in Boxing." *Outing* 19, no. 2 (November 1891): 140–143.
Austin, Alf. "Theory and Practice of Boxing." *Outing* 15, no. 6 (March 1890): 413–419.
Bever, M. "Fuzzy Memories: College Mascots and the Struggle to Find Appropriate Legacies of the Civil War." *Journal of Sport History* 38 (3): 447–463.
Campbell, Malcolm. "The Other Immigrants: Comparing the Irish in Australia and the United States." *Journal of American Ethnic History* 14 (1995): 3.
Carey, K. "The Brave New World of College Branding." *The Chronicle of Higher Education*, March 25, 2013. http://www.chronicle.com.
Edgren, Robert. "The Modern Gladiator: Why the American Succeeds—Brute Strength Superseded by Scientific Cleverness." *Outing* 41, no. 6 (March 1903): 735–747.
Gorn, Elliott J. "John L. Sullivan: 'The Champion of All Champions.'" *VQR: A National Journal of Literature and Discussion*, Autumn 1986. https://www.vqronline.org/essay/john-l-sullivan-champion-all-champions.
Gorn, Elliott J. "'Gouge and Bite, Pull Hair and Scratch': The Social Significance of Fighting in the Southern Backcountry." *American Historical Review* 90, no. 1 (February 1985): 18–43.
Hill, David S. "An Experiment with Pugilism." *Pedagogical Seminary* 13, no. 1 (March 1906): 125–131.
Holmes, Oliver Wendell. "The Autocrat of the Breakfast Table." *Atlantic Monthly* 1 (May 1958): 881.
Ireland, John. "The Saloon." *Donahoe's Magazine* 19, no. 6 (June 1888): 519–527.
Jeffries, James. "The Need of an Athletic Awakening." *Physical Culture* 21, no. 6 (May 1909): 397–400.
London, Jack. "Intellectualism of New Pugilism." *Current Opinion* 54, no. 2 (February 1913): 130–131.
London, Jack. "Psychology of the Prize Fight." *Current Literature* 49, no. 1 (July 1910): 57–58.
McCorry, Peter. "The Ethics of Boxing and Manly Art." *Donahoe's Magazine* 20, no. 1 (July 1888): 24–31.
McCorry, Peter. "The Ethics of Boxing and Manly Art." *Donahoe's Magazine* 20, no. 2 (August 1888): 148–157.
Norton, Charles Eliot. "Harvard University in 1890." *Harper's New Monthly Magazine* 81, no. 484 (September 1890): 581–633.
Osborne, Duffield. "Defense of Pugilism." *North American Review* 146, no. 377 (April 1888): 430–435.
Parker, Anthony. "Physical Culture: Boxing for Health and Strength." *Health* 57, no. 4 (April 1907): 264.
Police Gazette Sporting Annual. New York: Richard K. Fox, 1896–1918.
Roosevelt, Theodore. "Professionalism in Sports." *North American Review* 151, no. 405 (August 1890): 187–191
Roosevelt, Theodore. "Recent Prize-Fight." *Outlook* 95 (July 16 1910): 550–551.

University of Glasgow. "Climate Change Is Affecting the Way Europe Floods, Experts Warn." October 25, 2019. https://www.gla.ac.uk/news/headline_681850_en.html.
Whitney, Caspar. "The Atlantic Development at West Point and Annapolis." *Harper's Weekly* 36 (May 21, 1892): 496.
Whitney, Caspar. "The Sportsman's Viewpoint." *Outing* 39, no. 6 (March 1902): 723–733.
Woods, Alan. "James J. Corbett: Theatrical Star." *Journal of Sport History* 3, no. 2 (1976): 164–175.

Newspapers, Periodicals, and Magazines

American Celt
Athlone Advertiser
Belfast Telegraph
Bell's Life in London Sporting Chronicle
Boston Daily Globe
Boston Investigator
Boxing News
Brooklyn Daily Eagle
Clare Champion
Connacht Telegraph
Connacht Tribune
Daily Nevada State Journal
Denver Evening Post
Esquire
The Evening Herald
The Evening Press
The Fort Wayne Journal Gazette
Fort Worth Daily Gazette
The Galway Advertiser
Great Falls Tribune
The Guardian
The Inter Ocean
The Inter-Ocean (Chicago)
Irish Examiner
Irish Independent
Irish Mirror
The Irish New
The Irish Post
The Irish Times
Jackson Standard
Kansas City Star
Kentucky Irish American
Kildare Nationalist
Leinster Leader
London Saturday Review
Los Angeles Herald
National Police Gazette
New Jersey Morning Call
New Republic
New York
New York Clipper
New York Evening Telegram
New York Express
New York Herald
New York Journal
New York Sun
New York Times
New York Tribune
New York Weekly Review
The Observer
The Ottawa Daily Citizen
People's Magazine: An Illustrated Miscellany for All Classes
Philadelphia Press
The Placer Herald
Ring magazine
The Sacramento Daily Union
Saint Paul Daily Globe
Saint Paul Daily News
The San Francisco Examiner
Sports Illustrated
Springfield Republican
The Standard Union
The Standard Union
The Sun (Baltimore)
Tacoma Daily Times
Tacoma Daily Times
The San Francisco Examiner
The Times (London)
Times-Picayune (New Orleans)
The Toledo Commercial
Trenton State Gazette
Troy Daily Whig
Tuam Herald
Vermont Patriot and State Gazette
Western People
The Wheeler Intelligencer
Wheeling Daily Intelligencer
Wilkes' Spirit of the Times
Zanesville Signal

Index

Achill Island, County Mayo, Republic of Ireland 194
Ali, Muhammad 108, 109, 150, 154, 156, 157, 161, 163
Allen, Gracie 131
Allen, Tom 56–58
American Youth Congress 120
Anti-Saloon League 94
Apostoli, Fred 151
Asbury, Herbert 28
Ashton, Jack 77, 79
Attell, Abe 109, 118, 195
Athlone, County Westmeath, Republic of Ireland 50

Baer, Max 127, 130, 177
Ballinrobe, County Mayo, Republic of Ireland 89, 98
Bandon, County Cork, Republic of Ireland 12
Barnum, Phineas T. 64
Barry, James Curran 167
Barrymore, Lionel 104
Bean, Judge Roy 136
Beasley, Tom 14
Beecher, Henry Ward 64
Belfast, Northern Ireland 61
Benny, Jack 130
Berlin, Irving 117
Bettini, Melio 151
Blake, William 55
Bloomfield, Jack 138
Booth, John Wilkes 36
Bowery Boys 14, 27
Boy Scouts of America 120
Braddock, James J. "The Cinderella Man" 125–132, 177
Brady, William A. 98, 101
Broughton, Jack 14
Broughton Rules 14
Burke, Jack 134
Burns, George 131
Burns, Tommy 94, 143, 149
Butler, Joe "The Black Pearl" 136

Cagney, James 130
Callaghan, "Mushy" 104, 111
Calloway, Cab 130
Capone, Al 108
Caponi, Tony 109
Cardiff, Paddy 81
Carnegie, Andrew 120
Carnera, Primo 130, 177, 178
Carpentier, Georges 122, 138, 144, 173, 174
Carroll, Jimmy 134
Casey, James P. 21
Catholic Church 67, 70, 99, 106, 138
Catholic Youth Club 120
Caunt, Robert 15
Chaplin, Charlie 117
Chiariglione, Andrew (also known as "Fireman" Jim Flynn) 109
Chip, George 138
Choynski, Joe "Chrysanthemum" 90, 134, 135, 136, 141, 142, 143
Chuvalo, George 157
Cinderella Man (film) 132
Civil War (American) 6, 64, 77
Clarke, Bill 45
Cleary, Mike 134
Cleveland, Pres. Grover 67, 92
Clew Bayo, County Mayo, Ireland 143
Cline, Maggie 82
Coburn, Joe 43–49, 56
Coffey, Jim "The Roscommon Giant" 146, 147
Cohan, George M. 117
Conley, Frankie 109
Conn, Billy "The Pittsburgh Kid" 150–155
Cooney, Gerry "The Easton Express" 160–163
Corbett, James, J. "Gentleman Jim" 63, 68, 87–108, 117, 134, 134, 141, 142, 149, 150, 151, 195
Corbett, Young III 151
Corby, Father William 6
Courtney, Peter 100
Craig, Frank "The Harlem Coffee Cooler" 136
Creckett, Davy 107

Creedon, Frank 79
Criqui, Eugene 197
Crosby, Bing 130
Crowe, Russell 132
Cullen, Archbishop Paul 47

Dana, Charles A. 96
Davis, Bill 53, 55
Dead Rabbits gang 27
Dementia pugilistica 158
Democratic Party 13, 37, 67
Dempsey, Jack 108, 115–130, 139, 154, 171, 175, 194
Dempsey, Jack "Nonpareil" 179
De Valera, Éamon 5, 6, 8
Dickens, Charles 38, 107
Dillon, Jim 90
Dixon, George "Little Chocolate" 92, 96
Dohagany, James 62
Donaldson, John 72
Donneybrook Fair 108
Donovan, Mike 84
Dougherty, Hughey 53
Dougherty, Jim 137
Dreiser, Theodore 95, 149
Dublin, Ireland 98, 103, 172, 173
Ducharme, George 62
Duffy, Paddy 183
Dugan, Jimmy 109
Dundalk, County Louth, Republic of Ireland 138
Dundee, Angelo 108
Dundee, Johnny 197
Dunn, James 50
Dwyer, "Big Bill" 53
Dwyer, JJ 53, 133

Earp, Wyatt 137, 141–142,
East End, London 12
Edwards, Billy 133
Elliot, James "Jimmy" 50–54
Ellis, Jimmy 158

Fairbanks, Douglas 117
Fall, Louis Mbarick "Battling Siki" 172
Farnborough, Hampshire, England 37

Farr, Tommy 131
Fenians Canadian invasion 54
Fenway Park, Boston 5, 6
Finnegan, "Irish" Eddie 109
Firpo, Luis 115
Fitzsimmons, Robert "Bob" ("The Freckled Wonder"; "Ruby Robert" 63, 67, 99–102, 104, 134, 135, 136, 141–142, 166, 181, 195
Fleischer, Nat 77, 97, 118, 131, 169, 189
Fleming, Will 76
Flood, John "The Bull's Head Terrier" 72
Flynn, Errol 104, 151
Flynn, Jim "Fireman" 109, 143
Ford, John 104
Foreman, George 161
Foster, Mac 158
Fox, Richard Kyle 60, 72, 73, 81, 95, 96
Frazier, Joe 156
Fulljames, George 179

Gable, Clark 130
Gallagher, Charles 53
Gans, "Panama" Joe 171, 184
Gardner, Billy 166
Gardner, George 166
Gardner, Jim 140, 166, 184
Gehrig, Lou 130
Gentleman Jack (play) 98
Gentleman Jim (film) 151
Gibbons, Mike 171
Gibbons, Tommy 115, 137, 139
Gibson, Billy 147
Gibson, Charles Dana 77
Gilded Age 61, 77
Gillespie, Mike 133
Gleason, Bobby 109
Goddard, Joe 134, 136
Godfrey, George 134, 136
Godfrey, Joe 134
Gorn, Elliot 63, 92, 96, 108
Goss, Joe 48, 58, 60, 62
Grant, Ulysses S. 77
Great Depression 128
The Great White Hope (play by Howard Sackler) 150, 157, 161
Greb, Harry 113–115, 137, 176
Greggains, Alex 141
Gribben, Harry 44
Griffin, John "Corn" 127

Hall, Jim 67
Hall, Stanley G. 64
Hammond, Vincent 13
Harkins, Kate 94
Harrison, Benjamin 92
Hart, Marvin 92
Heenan, John Camel the "Benicia Boy" 29, 65
Heeney, Tom 118, 148

Hefey, Maurice 75
Hemingway, Ernest 120
Hicks, Jack "The Elastic Potboy" 49
Higginson, Thomas Wentworth 64
Hill, Harry 46, 72, 133, 134
Hogan, Ben 58
Holmes, Larry 160–163
Holmes, Oliver Wendell 64
Honest Hearts and Willing Hands (John L. Sullivan play) 88
Houseman, Lou 166
Howard, Ron 132
Howells, William Dean 66
Hughes, Thomas 64
Hyer, Joseph 13
Hyer, Tom 12–15, 20

Igoe, Hype 126
Ireland, Archbishop John 67

Jackson, Peter "The Black Prince" 91, 96, 134, 135
James, Frank 74
James, Henry 120
James, Jesse 74
Jefferson, Thomas 20
Jeffries, James J. 94, 101, 136, 141, 143, 173, 193, 195
Jennings, Tom 55
Johansson, Ingemar 161
Johnson, "Battling" Jim 143
Johnson, Jack "The Galveston Giant" 136, 143, 144, 146, 148, 150, 173
Jolson, Al 117, 130
Jones, Aaron 55

Kaufman, Al 143
Kearns, Jack 137
Kendrick, Pat 134
Kerrigan, Patsy 134
Ketchel, Stanley 109, 143, 184
Kilbane, Johnny 194–198
Killoran, Jim 59
Kilraine, Jake (born John Joseph Killion) 81–86, 92, 97
Kiltimagh, County Mayo, Ireland 112
King, Don 161–163
King, Tom 40, 46
Know Nothing Party 18, 27, 70
Ku Klux Klan 8, 174

LaBlanche, George 134, 180
LaMotta, Jake 110
Lane, Hammer 13
Langham, Nat 48
Langtry, Lily 136
Lannon, Joe 134
Larkin, Tippie 109
Lasky, Art 127

Lauder, Polly 120
Lavin, Paddy 184
Lee, General Robert E. 6
Leonard, Benny 109, 192
Leonard, Sugar Ray 108
Lessing, Dr. Henry 66
Levinsky, "Battling" Barney 113, 137
Lewis, John Henry 127
Lewis, Ted "Kid" 110
Lewis Law 101
Lilly, Christopher 14
Lindsay, Vachel 86
Liston, Sonny 156
London Prize Ring Rules 26, 81
Loughran, Tommy 126, 174–178
Louis, Joe 130, 131, 151–154
Lyle, Ron 158

Mace, Jem 46–49, 56
Machen, Eddie 156
Madden, Bartley 148
Madden, Billy 71, 133
Madison Square Garden 74, 80, 131, 141, 147, 148, 156, 160, 188
Mahan, John (aka Steve Taylor) 72, 133
Maher, Peter 134–136, 142
Mandell, Sammy 192
Manley, Patsy 57
Mannion, Sean 199
Marciano, Rocky 109, 166
Marquis of Queensberry Rules 40, 42, 72, 75, 87, 133, 136, 168, 180–81, 206
Marx, Al 76
Masterson, Bat 135
Mathis, Buster 157
Mayo, County, Republic of Ireland 90
McAuliffe, Jack 92, 166
McBride, Kevin "The Clones Cyclone" 163
McCaffrey, Dominick 91, 180
McCann, Tom 24
McCay, Fred 137
McCheester, George 14
McCloskey, Country (aka George McCheester) 14
McCoole, Mike 45, 55–58
McCormack, John 147
Mc Coy, Al 153
McCoy, Charles "Kid" 100, 142, 166
McCoy, James 75
McCoy, Thomas 14
McDonald, Charles 133
McFadden "Elbows" George 170
McGovern, "Terrible" Terry 168–169, 192
McKinley, William 137

Index

McLarnin, James "Jimmy" Archibald ("Baby Faced Assassin") 130, 190–193
McNeeley, Peter "The Hurricane Man" 163
McTigue, "Bold" Mike 170–175, 177
Meehan, Willie 138
Mellody, Honey 14
Middleton, Larry 153
Miske, Billy 138
Mitchell, Charley 68, 74–75, 79, 95, 97
Monahan, Mike 134
Monroe, Jack 143
Moran, Frank "The Fighting Dentist" 143–149, 174
Morrissey, John "Old Smoke" 24–34, 46, 81
Muldoon, William "The Solid Man" 81, 95
Myer, Billy 92

Nary, Bill 55
Nast, Thomas 38
National Foundation for American Youth 120
Northwestern University 7
Norton, Charles Eliot 66
Norton, Ken 154, 160, 161

O'Brien, "Philadelphia Jack" 94, 109
O'Brien, T. C. 109
O'Donnell, Steve 135
On the Waterfront (movie) 155
O'Reilly, John Boyle 6, 66, 71, 74, 97

Partry, County Mayo, Republic of Ireland 98
Pastor, Bob 153
Patterson, Floyd 156, 161
Pep, Willie 109
Pickett, George 6
The Pittsburgh Kid (film) 153
Police Gazette 15, 16
Poole, William "Bill the Butcher" 27, 28
Protestant church 21, 106

Quarry, Jerry "The Bellflower Bomber" 156–159
Quarry, Mike 158
Quarry, Robert "Bobby" 159
Queensberry Rules 40, 42, 72, 75, 87, 133, 136, 168, 180–81, 206

Raft, George 130
Ray, Johnny 151
Reagan, Ronald 157, 161
Republican Party 101
Rickard, Tex 115, 120, 197
The Roar of the Crowd (autobiography of James Corbett) 88, 103
Roaring Twenties 126
Robinson, Bill "Bojangles" 130
Robinson, Edward G. 130
Robinson, Sugar Ray 193
Rockne, Knute 126
Roosevelt, Pres. Theodore 64, 66, 101, 137
Root, Jack 166
Roper, Bob 138
Rosenbloom, Maxie 188, 193
Ross, Barney 110, 130, 192
Runyon, Damon 126, 127, 128
Rushlin, Gus 142
Ruth, Babe 5
Ryan, Paddy 54, 58–60, 62, 72, 73
Rynders, Isaiah 15, 25

Saint John's University Redmen 6
Saint Patrick's Day 9, 99
Sargent, Dr. Dudley A. 92
Savold, Lee 153, 160
Sayers, Tom (The Brighton Titch) 33–39, 41
Scannell, Jack 71
Schmeling, Max 131, 177, 188
Sharkey, Jack (Joseph Paul Zukauskas) 143, 177, 178
Sharkey, Tom "Sailor" 138–143, 194
Shavers, Ernie 158
Shaw, George Bernard 120–121
Sheehan, Mike 75
Skelly, Jack 92–93
Slaby, Jimmy 184
Slade, Herbert 133
Smith, Billy 141
Smith, Charles A.C. "The Black Thunderbolt" 136
Smith, Jack 134
Smith, Jem 81, 82
Smith, Rube 184
Soldier's Field, Chicago 116
Sorin, Father Edward 9
Spanish American War 64
Spinks, Leon 161
Spinks, Michael 161
Sullivan, Jack "Twin" 147

Sullivan, James Ambrose "Yankee" (aka Frank Murray) 12, 16, 17, 20, 22, 25, 27, 28, 29, 32, 33
Sullivan, John L. 59, 61, 66, 67, 69, 94, 101, 108, 133, 141, 149, 181
Sullivan, Mike "Twin" 184
Sweeney, Thomas William 52

Tammany Hall 13, 19, 25
Templemore, County Tipperary, Republic of Ireland 24
Thackeray, William 38
Thompson, George 16
Thurles, County Tipperary, Republic of Ireland 34
Timony, Patrick 14, 16, 19
Tunney, Eugene "Gene" 112–124, 130, 138, 147, 148, 154, 175, 177
Tunney, Polly 124
Twain, Mark 64, 88, 104
Tweed, William Magear "Boss" 14, 27
Tyson, Mike 70, 109

Vietnam War 150
Villa, Pancho 191

Wach, Mariusz "The Viking" 164
Walcott, Jersey Joe 166
Walker, Mickey "The Toy Bulldog" 183–189
Ward, "Irish" Mickey 199
Wells, H.G. 120, 123
West, Mae 130, 149
Whitman, Walt 63
Wiggins, Chuck 138
Wilder, Thornton 120
Willard, Jess 116, 130, 144, 145, 147, 148
Wills, Harry 115, 118
Winkle, Hen 50
Wodehouse, P.G. 104
World Series 5
World War I 113

Young Corbett II 168–169
Young Corbett III 109, 151, 192

Zale, Tony 153

www.ingramcontent.com/pod-product-compliance
Lightning Source LLC
Chambersburg PA
CBHW060341010526
44117CB00017B/2919